Are Non-Christians Saved?

Are Non-Christians Saved?

Joseph Ratzinger's Thoughts on Religious Pluralism

AMBROSE MONG

ONEWORLD

A Oneworld Book

First published by Oneworld Publications, 2015

ISBN 978-1-78074-714-9
ISBN 978-1-78074-715-6 (eBook)

Typeset by Siliconchips Services Ltd, UK
Printed and bound in Great Britain by
TJ International Ltd, Padstow, Cornwall

Oneworld Publications
10 Bloomsbury Street
London WC1B 3SR
England

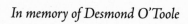

In memory of Desmond O'Toole

Contents

Preface and Acknowledgements

In 1965, near the end of the Second Vatican Council, the Roman Catholic Church published *Nostra Aetate*, a landmark document that seeks to draw humanity closer together through fostering interreligious understanding. In this declaration, the church re-examined its relationship with non-Christian religions in a more positive light than it had in recent history. It acknowledged that other religions also try to answer questions that affect our human existence at the deepest level – the meaning and aims of human life – admitting that ancient and venerable religions such as Hinduism and Buddhism have attempted to answer those questions with sophisticated concepts and languages.

Fifty years after the publication of *Nostra Aetate*, this declaration has lost none of its relevance and significance. In an age of globalization, secularization and continuing religious plurality, it is dialogue and not confrontation that can help us to resolve our problems. Since the Second Vatican Council, there have been hope-filled progress and promising developments in interreligious relations as well as periods of disillusionment, disappointment and anguish. There have been theologians who, taking *Nostra Aetate* seriously, enthusiastically embarked upon interreligious dialogue and imagined a positive role for religious pluralism in their writings and teachings but who were derailed by Joseph Ratzinger. In his speeches and writings, Ratzinger declared war on pluralist theology and its most dangerous correlate – relativism. He did not hesitate to rein in Catholic theologians whom he believed to have strayed from church teaching with the charge that they might adversely affect the faith of simple believers.

This work is a theological interpretation of Ratzinger's thoughts that involves looking into Ratzinger's educational, cultural and religious background to reveal his Eurocentric bias, particularly in his ecclesiology, ecumenical theology and attitude towards religious pluralism. Besides revisiting the cases of Tissa Balasuriya, Jacques Dupuis and Peter C. Phan, who were investigated and censured by the Congregation for the Doctrine of the Faith, this work also discusses the writings of Paul Knitter and Hans Küng. Through this analysis, it will be seen that Ratzinger's views attained hegemony over other positions in official Catholic circles not because they were inherently more compatible with the developing Catholic tradition, but because this singularly influential figure systematically used his authority to silence viewpoints that differed from his own.

I would like to thank Lai Pan Chiu and Peter C. Phan for their advice and guidance in writing this book. Thanks to Marie Whitcom for her superb and meticulous editorial assistance. Many friends have also helped me with their proofreading, support and friendship. They are as follow: Patrick Tierney FSC, Mary Gillis CND, Columba Cleary OP, Patrick Chia, Tommy Lam, Josephine Chan, Rosalind Wong, Scott Steinkerchner OP, David Seid OP, Beinidict Macionaoith OP, Javier González OP and Fausto Gómez OP. Some materials in this work are published with permission from: Wipf and Stock Publishers, *Ecumenical Trends*, *The Ecumenical Review*, *The Ecumenist*, *Asia Journal of Theology*, and *Dialogue and Alliance*. Last, but not least, special thanks to Novin Doostdar at Oneworld Publications for agreeing to publish this work. I would also like to thank Paul Nash, Laura McFarlane, James Magniac and Elizabeth Hinks for their help in the publication of this work. It is indeed a pleasure working with such an efficient and excellent publishing house. Whatever errors remain, they are my own.

Ambrose Mong OP

St Joseph House, Hong Kong

Introduction

Religious pluralism is thriving and becoming vitally important. This is not only the case in Asia with its myriad religious beliefs and practices, but also in Europe, which has seen the growth and development of many non-Christian religious traditions that compete with its Christian heritage. Joseph Ratzinger, former prefect of the Congregation for the Doctrine of the Faith (CDF) and now Pope-Emeritus Benedict XVI, is commonly regarded as a conservative theologian who sees religious pluralism as a challenge to the church's ability to proclaim the gospel with greater fidelity. This means that in the face of multiple religious beliefs, Christians must be convinced of the truth of their faith. In view of this, and as someone who grew up in Singapore, a multicultural and multireligious city-state, which has achieved great success in promoting harmony among different racial groups with their own religious beliefs, I hereby attempt to examine Ratzinger's thoughts on this issue of religious pluralism in order to evaluate how the official church has responded to the call of the Second Vatican Council to create a dialogue with non-Christian faiths.

As an accomplished scholar and a prominent member of the Roman Curia, Ratzinger wields authority and influence in his interpretation of Christian doctrine not only for the church, but for secular society as well. Consequently, his writings have great impact with many ramifications. By analysing Ratzinger's teachings, I hope to contribute to the ongoing discussion on the theology of religious pluralism, a subject that has become urgent in our postmodern society because of the need to understand 'the other'.

This study attempts to show that Joseph Ratzinger's teaching on the relationship of Christianity to other religions assumes the normative status of Western philosophical and theological thought. He sincerely believes that the Greek intellectual and cultural expression found in Christianity is part of

God's plan, and the relationship between faith and reason cast in Hellenistic philosophy is part of divine revelation and, hence, part of faith itself. This giving of precedence to Western thought makes him critical and suspicious of theologians operating from a different theological framework.

For example, in 1994, the CDF, the influential Vatican office Ratzinger had led for thirteen years, investigated and censured Tissa Balasuriya's book, *Mary and Human Liberation*, and, in 1997, a Notification of his excommunication was published. On 24 January 2001, the CDF released a Notification concerning Jacques Dupuis's book, *Towards a Christian Theology of Religious Pluralism*. In September 2007, the CDF investigated Peter C. Phan, a Vietnamese-born theologian, who had argued for a less Eurocentric church in his book, *Being Religious Interreligiously*. Ratzinger regards the reflections of these three theologians and others not as a theology, but as an ideology that arose from a particular philosophy of a certain period. If this is true, can we not say that Ratzinger's so-called official theology is also a product of history and of a particular mindset conditioned by his upbringing and education?

Ratzinger tends to see religious pluralism as an expression of relativism. Like John Henry Newman, Alasdair McIntyre and Gavin D'Costa, he is critical of Western theologians influenced by the Enlightenment because in granting equality to all religions, the Enlightenment denied all truth to any of them. This may be justifiable, but the problem is that Ratzinger tends to view theologians operating from a non-Western paradigm in the same light. He seems to regard them as products of post-Enlightenment thinking. The cases of Jacques Dupuis and Peter Phan highlight the fact that, while their theology falls within Catholic orthodoxy, they clashed with Ratzinger on a number of points regarding ecclesiology, praxis and Christology. Ratzinger's own theological position is not without justification within the Western context, but he fails to recognize the legitimacy of the positions of these 'dissident theologians' in the Asian context, which is distant from the post-Enlightenment, European context.

This work also proposes to show that Ratzinger's theology is distinctly normative in character. A number of documents from the CDF, signed by Cardinal Ratzinger as prefect, show an attempt to declare as normative his own theological viewpoints. Motivated by his perception of how the church should respond to the modern world, his theological writings are polemical and defensive. He takes a negative view of pluralism, which he equates with relativism, and believes it is important to protect the faith of ordinary believers by censoring dissident theologians. 'Pluralism' here is distinct from 'plurality' in that pluralism refers to a theory or system that justifies the coexistence of two or more groups. Plurality, on the other hand, simply means a large number of people or things. Thus plurality indicates a fact, while pluralism refers to a theory.

Ratzinger spelt out clearly what he saw as the greatest doctrinal threats of the day: the practical relativism of Europe and America and also Asia's theology in which Jesus Christ is viewed as no more than another sage comparable to Buddha or the Prophet Muhammad, and Christianity as one of several equally valid religious paths. He believes there is an unseemly closeness between Europe's post-metaphysical philosophy and Asia's theology, which can be observed in the phenomenon of religious relativism. If this were true, how might one explain the close affinity of early Christian theologians with Greek philosophy and the use of Hellenistic terms to express the mysteries of the Christian faith?

In many ways, Ratzinger's theological viewpoints are antagonistic to and insensitive of religious pluralism. His negative comment on the attraction of Buddhism as 'spiritual autoeroticism' has created indignation among its adherents. The uproar over the supposedly anti-Islamic quotation in his Regensburg lecture on 12 September 2006 remains fresh in most minds. Perhaps as an intellectual and academic, Ratzinger was not aware of the grass-root reaction of fervent believers of other faiths before this event had taken place.

Furthermore, Ratzinger takes a theoretical and dogmatic approach towards interreligious relations. Most of the church's declarations signed by him begin with an affirmation of the uniqueness and superiority of Catholicism and the necessity of the Catholic Church for the salvation of all humankind. They claim that the church holds the absolute truth on matters religious and that the Bible is the only inspired word of God. Only Christians have theological faith and enjoy the grace of God, whereas all others have, at best, a human religious belief. Interreligious dialogue is seen as part of the evangelizing mission of the church. Somewhat paradoxically, he strongly believes in dialogue with other religions, while stressing the church's evangelizing mission. This naturally raises the question of whether respect for Asian religions and their vitality demand a rethinking of the church's mission and an end to efforts to make converts.

Many Christians in Asia agree that Jesus Christ has to be proclaimed, but they believe that this proclamation has to be through deeds and the witness of life, rather than through words and doctrinal formulations. Asian theology has to do more with orthopraxis than orthodoxy, and the tension is between tradition and experience: Ratzinger stresses adherence to the tradition of the church, while Asian theology calls for adaptation to the lived experience of religious pluralism across the continent. These two approaches, although different, need not be confrontational; they can be harmonized. This means the tradition of the church should be interpreted according to the spirit rather than the letter. In many ways, Joseph Ratzinger challenges Asians to be authentic Christians without betraying their identities.

Related to this central theme is the Ratzinger–Kasper debate on the universal (catholic) church and local churches, a debate which has a large ecumenical dimension and interreligious relation. Ratzinger holds that the universal church is prior to the local church both historically and ontologically. He emphasizes the unity of the universal church. In this age of globalization and inculturation, is it more important than ever to have a centralized office that safeguards the unity of all the particular churches in the essentials of faith, morality and liturgy?

There is a difference in theological approach between the universal church as expressed by Ratzinger and local Asian churches. These differences inevitably spill over to the church's priorities and its understanding of the role that other religions play in the evangelizing mission. The tension between Rome and Asia has to do with how the church functions in Asia. While Rome is concerned with doctrinal orthodoxy, Asian theology is concerned with dialogue with Asia's cultures, religions and the poor.

While this study takes a critical view of Joseph Ratzinger's approach to religious pluralism from an Asian perspective, I also acknowledge the importance of his overall contribution to the church. In Ratzinger's interview with Peter Seewald, published in *Salt of the Earth: The Church at the End of the Millennium*, a wide range of topics was covered, including Ratzinger's biography, and in it many people found inspiration and encouragement because he was able to 'answer the deeper questions of the human spirit'. According to Vincent Twomey, most theologians attempt to interpret faith in the light of contemporary culture rather than interpret contemporary culture in the light of faith. Thus, today, Christian faith and morals tend to be diluted to suit our hedonistic generation. Ratzinger, in contrast, with his ability to shed new light on old truths in our postmodern world, holds firm to the truths of the faith, without compromise.[1]

As the guardian of orthodoxy, it is natural and appropriate for Ratzinger to take a cautious view of religious pluralism and interreligious dialogue. It was only after the Second Vatican Council that the church began to take steps towards understanding other religions. Therefore, interreligious dialogue is a topic that needs further clarification and guidance from the church. The CDF, under Ratzinger's direction, has provided an authoritative response, but it was not always well received as some theologians mistrust the magisterium. In his capacity as a private scholar, Ratzinger has continued to publish articles and books, offering for critical assessment his personal views on many important issues pertaining to the church and society.[2] In short, he is not against new ideas and changes, but rather he rises to the challenges they pose.

While Ratzinger holds fast to his conviction regarding the superiority of Catholic Christianity, he is not closed to appreciating other faiths. He believes that religions are not 'static' but 'dynamic' entities, and like the cultures they form and express, they are subject to change to the extent that they become 'open or closed to the universality of truth'.[3] Ratzinger believes that all the great world religions and traditions find their source in the great Christian vision of reality: 'The ethical vision of the Christian faith is not in fact something specific to Christianity but is the synthesis of the great ethical intuitions of mankind from a new center that holds them together.'[4] In other words, Christianity is a universal religion that can satisfy the spiritual longing of humankind.

Finally, Joseph Ratzinger's insights into the problem of truth, tolerance, religion and culture and the wisdom and hope he offers to Western culture may be relevant to Asian societies. Although he is against a religious pluralism that views all religions as equal, he supports a tolerance and freedom that have their basis in truth and are thus compatible with the reality of human nature. The religious landscape in Asia is vibrant and varied and Ratzinger's understanding of religion as a movement in history can enable different faiths to come together in their search for the truth. He supports a pluralist's view of religion that is not static but dynamic. It is a plurality that allows different religions to uphold their claims to truth and to their uniqueness. This kind of plurality is better than a pluralism that tries to eliminate all differences in order to reach a consensus on the nature of religious belief.

My methodology will be to present Ratzinger's theology and other alternative approaches, to highlight the contrasts and parallels in them and to indicate, where appropriate, the extent to which Ratzinger's theology has influenced the direction he has taken. This will help to bring out the polemical character of his theological viewpoints. I will also attempt to synthesize Ratzinger's writings in the different areas that are related to the topic of religious pluralism. 'Disputed questions' (*quaestiones disputatae*) such as pluralist theology, theological dissent, relativism and the Christian heritage of Europe that have occupied Ratzinger's mind will be studied, together with voices from Asia.

The standard typology in the Christian theology of religions – exclusivism, inclusivism and pluralism – will also be examined in relation to Ratzinger's writings on other religions and other Christian churches. Exclusivism has been the church's predominant attitude throughout its history. It regards other religious beliefs as false. In the Catholic Church we have often interpreted the axiom, *extra ecclesiam nulla salus* (outside the church there is no salvation) in an ahistorical manner. The expression *extra ecclesiam nulla salus* is believed to have come from St Cyprian of Carthage, a bishop in the third century. In this context, Cyprian was referring to Christian heretics who were not in union with the universal church. In 1442, the Council of Florence-Ferrara declared that the Holy Church of Rome firmly believes that no one – not just the heathens, but also Jews, heretics and schismatics – outside the Catholic Church can be saved unless they are received into the church before they die.[5]

Inclusivism regards the Christian faith as the fulfilment of other religions. This approach has been adopted by the Catholic Church since the Second Vatican Council. Traditional non-Christian religions are seen as genuine expressions of human beings' longing to answer the most fundamental question regarding their human existence. Religious pluralism holds all legitimate religions to be the same in that they can help us to reach God or find salvation.

The theology of religions is an important theological subject in view of the growing interest, in the academic world, in the issues of secularism and pluralism. My hope is that this study will provide important reflections regarding Joseph Ratzinger's understanding of the relationship of the Roman Catholic Church with other Christian churches, non-Christian religions, and the secular world as well. As a contribution to the academic community, this work will not only assist interested readers to have a better grasp of Catholic teachings, it will also help the church to appreciate the beauty of religious pluralism as a sign of God's abundant love for the world and all its peoples.

Through a critique of Joseph Ratzinger's theology, I hope to draw attention to the importance of other theological discourses originating from a non-European context. While I appreciate Ratzinger's penetrating insights and balanced point of view, my work will serve to highlight the gap between a dogmatic understanding of the faith and the pastoral realities of the Asian church, as well as the difficulties faced by Asian theologians who are trying to make their voices heard in a church still dominated by Western thinking. Regarding this point, I will mention the views of two scholars, Paul Hedges and Robert J. Schreiter.

Looking at the rise of European colonialism by the Spanish, Portuguese, British and Dutch, which resulted in Latin Christianity becoming dominant, Paul Hedges is of the opinion that our view of what is normative Christianity is conditioned by political power and not biblical truth.[6] Thus, Hedges contends that the Vincentian canon about the universality of the church is doubtful. Although we must not give up all traditions, he thinks that they are very much related to power struggles. Tradition, therefore, must not be taken as 'normative in the absolute sense'. In other words, Hedges stresses the fact that, like most systems, Christianity as a religion is tied to its cultural context and there is no such thing as universal truth coming down directly from God.[7] Consequently, Hedges believes that we must allow different expressions of Christianity to exist and this implies that the normative pattern of Western theology must be challenged.[8] In line with this, this work attempts, with the realities of Asia in mind, to evaluate Joseph Ratzinger's approach to religious pluralism, ecclesiology, ecumenism and other Western thinking that he regards as 'ideologies'.

The point made by Hedges, and particularly by Robert J. Schreiter, is that all theology is 'contextual'.[9] This means that contrary to Ratzinger's teaching, we cannot assume that Latin Christianity, as taught by the magisterium, is normative, while the Asian approach, for example, is contextual in relation to Rome. Schreiter, in fact, argues that plurality is normative: 'The universal theologies ... were in fact *universalizing* theologies; that is to say, they extended the results of their own reflections beyond their own contexts to other settings, usually without an awareness of the rootedness of their theologies within their own contexts'.[10] This point is also highlighted by the Document of the Office of Theological Concerns of the Federation of the Asian Bishops' Conference (FABC) which states: 'The impressive unity in the theological enterprise could only be achieved at the expense of theological pluralism. It is striking how Eurocentric, and even parochial, this theology now appears. The claim of being *the* universal way of doing theology is negated by the obvious limitation that it really is restricted to the particular context in which it originated'.[11]

In other words, we cannot favour one theological style such as so-called normative, orthodox Christianity over and above others. Schreiter insists that all theologies must be in relation to other cultural contexts so that we can attend to local needs while at the same time try to develop a theology that is ecumenical.[12] Joseph Ratzinger is very well acquainted with the rootedness of his own theology and champions it. As prefect of the CDF and head of the church, he regarded the Western theological discourse as normative and orthodox. This is not surprising and is to be expected, given his background and history, as we shall see in Chapter 1. However, in the religious pluralistic societies of Asia, where Christianity is a minority religion, there should be room for more adaptation and accommodation in its liturgy as well as theological formulations.

There is an urgent need to formulate an Asian theology in response to the challenges of poverty, nationalism, the conflict between tradition and modernity, and colonialism. Given the rich and diverse religions that are an integral part of the societies of Asia, some originating in Asia and some brought by colonizers, these issues are best addressed in the context of dialogue among other Christian churches and between Christian and non-Christian religions. This study concludes with the perspective of the FABC in relation to Joseph Ratzinger's theological stance on religious pluralism. Constructing an Asian theology, however, lies beyond the scope of this work, but I hope that this study will encourage more scholars to do research in this area.

Chapter 1

Foundations

We will begin with a biographical sketch of Joseph Ratzinger's life, paying particular attention to his experience of living under the shadow of the Third Reich and the lessons he drew from the horrors of the war. We will trace Ratzinger's roots in South Eastern Germany and show how his intellectual formation, which accounts for his early opposition to some modern philosophies, shapes his attitude towards the theology of religious pluralism and strengthens his conviction on the superiority of Christianity, Catholic Christianity in particular, over and above any other faith as a path to salvation.

In his 'Presentation of the Declaration *Dominus Iesus*', Joseph Ratzinger expresses his concern regarding the debate on the relationship of Christianity to other religions, believing that there is a widespread acceptance that all religions are of equal value in helping to gain salvation for their members.[1] He is particularly worried by the fact that this conviction is accepted not only in theology, but also among the Catholic faithful. Underlying this pluralist theology of religion are the following philosophical and theological presuppositions: the belief that divine truth is ineffable; a relativistic attitude towards truth exists; a deep opposition between Western and Eastern modes of thought exists; subjectivism as the only route to knowledge; an anti-metaphysical approach to theology; superficial eclecticism in theological research and disregard of church tradition in the study of scripture.[2]

Ratzinger believes that this kind of thinking eventually leads to seeing the person of Jesus as just another historical figure. It also leads to the denial of the absolute being of the Christian God as revealed in history. There are some 'moderate theologians' who, while recognizing Jesus Christ as true God and true man, think that this revelation of God must be seen in relation to other possible revelations, like the other great religious founders. This means that the church, its dogmas and sacraments have no absolute value.[3]

In view of the above beliefs, Ratzinger laments that the ideology of dialogue has taken the place of mission and the call to conversion, even in Catholic theological discourse. Dialogue is no longer perceived as a way to discover the truth, he complains, but is reduced to 'an exchange of opinions' with the purpose of achieving 'cooperation and integration' among the different religions.[4] Ratzinger thinks that the principle of tolerance promoted by the Second Vatican Council is 'being manipulated' to include the acceptance of other religious beliefs as of equal value to Christianity. This kind of tolerance avoids confronting questions of truth. He maintains that if the question of truth is not considered, then it is no longer possible to distinguish between true faith and superstition, and yet the positive value in any religion lies precisely in its truth.[5] Ratzinger asserts:

> The good that is present in the various religions offers paths toward salvation and does so as part of the activity of the Spirit in Christ, but the religions themselves do not … Goodness and truth, wherever they may be, come from the Father and are the work of the Holy Spirit. The seeds of the Logos are cast abroad everywhere. Yet we cannot shut our eyes to the errors and illusions that are present in these religions.[6]

Thus Ratzinger insists that respect and regard for other religious beliefs neither diminishes the 'unique status' of Jesus Christ nor restricts the missionary vocation of the church. This motive to evangelize is rooted in the 'mystery of Christ, who is true God and true man'.[7] Ratzinger believes Christianity is flourishing in parts of Asia due to the inherent deficiencies in the local belief systems. This perception of the truth in Christianity and his understanding of the role of the church as a means of salvation and a bastion against perverse ideologies was instilled in Joseph Ratzinger from the time of his early childhood in Bavaria.

BAVARIAN BACKGROUND

Joseph Aloysius Ratzinger was born on 16 April 1927, in the Bavarian village of Marktl am Inn, just two weeks before Adolph Hitler held the first Berlin rally of his National Socialist German Workers Party (Nazi). Ratzinger was the youngest of three children of a policeman and his wife. In his autobiography, *Milestones*, Ratzinger stresses the fact that he was born on Holy Saturday and baptized with the newly blessed Easter water. He looks back with fond memories on his family and the solid Catholicism of Bavaria, as evidenced in the liturgy and the faith of simple people. He recalls that 'The time the family spent in Marktl was not an easy one ... But there were many beautiful memories of friendship and neighbourly aid, memories of small family celebrations and of church life.'[8] Commenting on the beatification and canonization of Konrad of Parzham (1818–94), a Capuchin friar, he writes, 'In this humble and thoroughly kind man we saw what is best in our people embodied and led by faith to its most beautiful possibilities ... in this century of progress and faith in science, the Church should have found herself represented most clearly in very simple people ... who hardly seemed to be touched by the currents of the time.'[9]

Bavaria is one of the most traditional and conservative regions in Germany, and Aidan Nichols remarks that Ratzinger is very much a Bavarian theologian. It was in Bavaria, a region of wooded hills and small lakes, that the young Ratzinger realized his priestly vocation.[10] Ratzinger is also 'spiritually and culturally Bavarian' which means that he is most comfortable in a Catholic environment. Consequently, 'An appreciation for diversity was not something he [Ratzinger] imbibed growing up, and a preference for homogeneity remains part of his character.'[11] This reluctance to appreciate diversity, coupled with his belief in the superiority of the Roman Catholic faith and the Catholic Church as the sole path towards the fullness of salvation, won him many critics as well as supporters.

Ratzinger grew up in the shadow of Nazism: Hitler came to power in 1933 when Ratzinger was six and the war ended in 1945 when he was eighteen. Although Ratzinger's family opposed National Socialism, John Allen has observed that the rise of Nazism resulted in a revival of community values and authority, and a positive attitude towards faith and sacrifice: 'This wave of traditionalism carried Hitler to power, but it also produced yearning and hope within the church ... It was in some ways a romantic, optimistic time for German Catholicism, and that is the context in which Joseph Ratzinger's religious imagination took shape.'[12]

In 1939, Ratzinger entered the minor seminary in Traunstein, which is the name of the city as well as the county. Eventually, the seminary was transformed into a military hospital and Ratzinger returned to the *gymnasium* where he discovered the great literature of Goethe and Schiller. In his memoirs, he stressed the value of classical languages taught at the school: 'Latin, as the foundation of one's whole education, was then still taught with old-fashioned rigor and thoroughness, something I have remained grateful for all my life.' Ratzinger has also observed that a classical education in Latin and Greek antiquity 'created a mental attitude that resisted seduction by a totalitarian ideology'.[13] Thus we can see that Ratzinger is steeped in humanistic studies and classical languages that played an important part in the development of his theological beliefs.

LESSONS FROM THE WAR

Drafted into Hitler's army in September 1944 when he was seventeen, Joseph Ratzinger had to endure the 'fanatical ideologues who tyrannized us without respite'.[14] On 19 June 1945, he was released from the army and returned home. The horrors of the Third Reich made a great impact on his life and thinking. Ratzinger's view of the Catholic Church as a bulwark against totalitarian ideology is a direct result of the fact that Catholicism presented itself as a real challenge to the authority of National Socialism in Germany. He believes Catholicism can contribute to the cause of human dignity only by 'maintaining its own inner strength and discipline'. Only a unified church, firm in its core teachings, can resist the forces of military dictatorship.[15] Recalling his childhood, Ratzinger writes:

> I grew up in a family which really practiced its faith. The faith of my parents, of our Church, confirmed for me that Catholicism was a citadel of truth and righteousness against the realm of atheism and deceit which nazism represented. The collapse of the regime proved to me that the Church's premonitions were right.[16]

He has stressed the fact that his father was very critical of the Nazis to the extent of even voicing his anger against Hitler to the faces of the SS men who lodged in their home: 'My father ... was one who with unfailing clairvoyance saw that a victory of Hitler's would not be a victory for Germany but rather a victory of the Anti-Christ that would surely usher in apocalyptic times for all believers, and not only for them.'[17] Ratzinger is certain that it was his father's Bavarian patriotism and staunch Catholic faith that allowed him to see the evil of National Socialism.

Ratzinger is convinced of the Catholic Church's opposition to Nazism. At Dachau, more than 1,000 priests were killed, and about 12,000 religious persons, representing thirty-six percent of the clergy, were persecuted at that time.[18] He writes: 'No one doubted that the Church was the locus of all our hopes. Despite many human failings, the Church was the alternative to the destructive ideology of the brown rulers; in the inferno that had swallowed up the powerful, she had stood firm with a force coming to her from eternity'.[19] In the *Ratzinger Report*, Ratzinger characterizes the Catholic Church as 'a bastion against totalitarian derangement'.[20] John Allen says Ratzinger, today, believes that 'the best antidote to political totalitarianism is ecclesial totalitarianism'.[21] This means that the church must be authoritarian, clear in what it teaches and believes. In other words, only a pure church of unsullied belief and unity can effectively fight a political dictatorship.

John Allen also argues that Ratzinger's perception of the role of the Catholic Church during Hitler's time is based on a selective reading of the historical evidence. The truth is that during the Nazi era, the Catholic Church had, in some quarters, supported Hitler. Allen believes that Ratzinger's positive assessment of the church's moral courage is distorted and one-sided, writing: 'One gets the impression that the Third Reich has meaning for Ratzinger today primarily as an object lesson about church and culture, and only the details consistent with that argument have passed through the filter of his memory'.[22] Indeed, the church's war record revealed the temptation of the bishops to negotiate with the Nazis in order to preserve church institutions.

Allen's comment is not exactly fair because Ratzinger is actually very much aware of this problem with the bishops when he writes in his memoirs: 'Already then it dawned on me that, with their insistence on preserving institutions, these letters [pastoral] in part misread the reality. I mean that merely to guarantee institutions is useless if there are no people to support those institutions from inner conviction'.[23] There is enough historical evidence to show that the Catholic Church in Germany did compromise itself by negotiating with Hitler to protect its assets and Ratzinger does not deny it. He admits that 'while the Catholic Church can make tactical pacts, for the sake of lesser evil', by its nature, it cannot be tied to the state. The church is 'a bastion against totalitarian derangement'.[24]

An important lesson that Ratzinger learned from the war was the danger of preserving institutional ties. He believes the church would be better off if it did not depend too much on its universities, schools and hospitals, but relied more on its orthodox faith. He prefers a smaller but purer church. As such, he mistrusts national bishops' conferences, which he saw, during the war and later, as acting in self-interest and not sacrificing for the sake of the gospel. Ratzinger is suspicious of episcopal conferences when they try to act like autonomous national bodies. He understands the danger of institutionalism because of having witnessed the church's attempt to reach a compromise with Nazism in order to protect its own schools and hospitals.

Ratzinger claims that during the Nazi campaign, the state had attempted to transform Lutheran Christianity into a German Christianity in order to reinforce its absolute rule. This led Heinrich Schlier, a member of the Confessing Evangelical Church, to realize that 'theology either exists in the church and from the church, or it does not exist at all'. If theology is left on its own, without church support, Ratzinger argues, it becomes 'the plaything of the ruling powers'.[25] Thus he insists that theology must be tied to the church and that 'any other freedom is a betrayal both of itself and of the object entrusted to it'.[26] The office of teaching theology requires the guidance of the church magisterium without which it can be manipulated to serve totalitarianism, as Ratzinger had witnessed in the National Socialist State of Germany. Theology serves either the church or the powers that be. Ratzinger insists that theology must be rooted in the ecclesiastical life: 'a church without theology impoverishes and blinds, while a churchless theology melts away into caprice'.[27]

Anton Wessels also claims that Nazism was against the God of Abraham and Christianity. It sought 'to exterminate both the Jews and Christianity and replace them with a revival of Teutonic paganism'.[28] According to him, 'in the 1930s a Germanic theology came into being, represented by "German Christians". These Christians made a reprehensible concession to this reviving Germanic paganism by accepting the ideology and practice of National Socialism.'[29]

The Third Reich instilled in Ratzinger the importance of condemning evil in his lifetime which he prefers to do through the academic tradition of essays and books. David Gibson says that Ratzinger would avoid ugly confrontations: 'Maintaining a safe distance from the messiness of the temporal world, and pledging allegiance only to the pure ideal, would be a leitmotif for the rest of his life.'[30] Ratzinger's positive experience of the church during the war influenced his attitude towards political theology and the theology of religious pluralism that attempts to minimize the role of the church. It gives us an insight into the way, as prefect of the CDF, he treats the theology of liberation and theology of religions, which he perceives as deviating from magisterial teaching and confusing the simple faithful.

PRIESTLY STUDIES

Ratzinger entered the seminary at Freising in November 1945. He was grateful for the opportunity to make a new start, to serve the church and its people.
As well as enjoying the community life of the seminary, he was glad to be back
with his books: 'Together with this came a hunger for knowledge that had
grown in the years of famine, in the years when we had been delivered up to
the Moloch of power, so far from the realm of the spirit.'[31] Besides theology,
he read literary works and books on science so as to keep in touch with the
world. He was influenced by the work of Aloys Wenzel, a philosopher from
Munich, who tried to show that the deterministic worldview of science, which
denied God, had been dispelled by a new openness towards the unknown.[32]
As we shall see, all these readings came to influence his analysis of the crisis in
Europe at the present time.

In theology and philosophy, Ratzinger looked up to Romano Guardini,
Josef Pieper, Theodor Häcker and Peter Wust. The writings of John Henry
Newman were introduced to him by the prefect of studies, Alfred Läpple.
Ratzinger was also acquainted with the thought of Heidegger and Nietzsche.[33]
He had a solid intellectual training even at this stage, which included human-
istic and scientific studies on top of the usual priestly curriculum.

In his philosophical studies, Ratzinger was excited about the prospect
of returning to metaphysics 'which had been inaccessible since Kant'. Studying Martin Buber's philosophy of personalism was a spiritual experience for
him. Ratzinger associated personalism with the *Confessions* of St Augustine
with its powerful human passion. However, he had problems penetrating the
'crystal-clear logic' of St Thomas Aquinas which he found too rigid: 'neoscho-
lastic Thomism … was simply too far afield from my own questions … But
we, being young, were questioners above all.'[34] On the whole, he had a good
foundation in philosophy due to the efforts of a young professor, Jakob Fell-
ermeir, who gave him a comprehensive view of the 'intellectual struggle' in the
Western tradition, starting with Socrates.[35]

STUDIES IN MUNICH

On 1 September 1947, Ratzinger entered the Herzogliches Georgianum,
the theological institute attached to the University of Munich, which offered
a rigorous course of study for priests who wanted to pursue an academic

career in theology. Although the living quarters were crowded and the library inadequate, Ratzinger enjoyed walking through the beautiful park nearby, 'immersed in all sorts of thoughts'. This is the place where all his early decisions in life were made.[36]

Among the many distinguished professors, Ratzinger regarded Friedrich Wilhelm Maier, professor of New Testament exegesis, as the star of the new faculty at the Herzogliches Georgianum. Maier was the pioneer of the 'two-source theory' that is now generally accepted by most scholars.[37] According to this theory, the Gospel of Mark was written first before CE 70, followed by those of Matthew and Luke, which have nodding references to Mark. In addition, Matthew and Luke also depended on a collection of sayings of Jesus, the 'Q' source (from the German word *Quelle* or source). This contradicts the ancient tradition that regarded Matthew as the oldest gospel. Ratzinger says Maier's thesis 'was perceived to be a surrender to liberalism'. Persecuted by Rome, Maier was not allowed to teach. Although Maier 'harboured a certain bitterness against Rome', Ratzinger says that he was 'a man of deep faith and a priest who took great pains in the priestly formation of the young men entrusted to him'.[38] Years later, Ratzinger, as prefect of the CDF, was perceived by his critics as a persecutor of dissident theologians.

Ratzinger characterizes Maier's theological orientation as 'a liberalism restricted by dogma'. This implies that Maier looked upon dogma 'not as a shaping force, but only as a shackle, a negation, and a limit in the construction of theology'.[39] Ratzinger sees something positive in Maier's method in that it offers a direct approach to studying the scripture that in the past was restricted by dogmatic considerations. The Bible can now speak to us with newness and immediacy. However, Ratzinger believes that dogma is necessary to counteract those aspects of the liberal method that dilute the Bible and he calls for a 'balance between liberalism and dogma'.[40] At any rate, exegesis has remained the centre of Ratzinger's theological writings because of the interest that Maier had instilled in him.[41]

The Old Testament was taught by Friedrich Stummer who impressed Ratzinger with his 'scholarly carefulness'. From Stummer, Ratzinger learned that the New Testament is 'not a different book of a different religion' but 'an interpretation of "the Law, the Prophets and the Writings".' Ratzinger maintains that the Old Testament books had not been finalized at the time of Jesus. They were 'open-ended' and Judaism actually began during the first century after Christ with the 'end of the formation of the canons'.[42] He argues that 'the Christian faith described in the New Testament are two ways of appropriating Israel's Scriptures, two ways that, in the end, are both determined by the position one assumes with regard to the figure of Jesus of Nazareth. The Scripture we today call Old Testament is in itself open to both ways'.[43] Needless to say, this understanding of the scripture has important ramifications in interreligious dialogue, especially in relation with the Jewish religion.

JUDAISM AND CHRISTIANITY

In *Many Religions – One Covenant*, Ratzinger stresses the close bond between Judaism and Christianity based on Matthew's account of the Magi. The Epiphany shows that 'pagans can discover Jesus and worship him as Son of God and Saviour of the world only by turning toward the Jews and receiving from them the messianic promise as contained in the Old Testament'.[44] At the same time, Ratzinger insists that Christianity 'fulfils' Judaism, quoting St Augustine, 'The New Testament lies hidden in the Old; the Old is made explicit in the New.'[45] He has suggested that Jews could be fully true to their heritage by becoming Christians. Naturally, many Jewish leaders were upset by Ratzinger's comment.[46] His theological position on Judaism, Jewish history and scripture was perceived to be deeply offensive to some.

Ratzinger's understanding of Judaism in relation to Christianity seems to have shifted in his second volume of *Jesus of Nazareth*, published in 2011. He argues that the urgency of preaching the gospel in apostolic times was due not so much to the need for each person to know the message of Jesus Christ in order to gain salvation, but rather to this 'grand conception of history – if the world was to arrive at its destiny, the Gospel had to be brought to all nations'.[47] This understanding brings us to the question regarding the conversion of the Jews. Ratzinger admits that in the past, there were many misunderstandings, with grave consequences, regarding this issue. He quotes the advice given by Bernard of Clairvaux to Pope Eugene III on this matter: 'Granted, with regards to the Jews, time excuses you; for them a determined point in time has been fixed, which cannot be anticipated.'[48]

To reinforce this new reflection, Ratzinger also quotes from Hildegard Brem's comment on Clairvaux: 'In the light of Romans 11:25, the Church must not concern herself with the conversion of the Jews, since she must wait for the time fixed for this by God, "until the full number of the Gentiles come in" (Rom. 11:25). On the contrary, the Jews themselves are a living homily to which the Church must draw attention, since they call to mind the Lord's suffering (cf. *Ep* 363)…'[49] Consequently, while Ratzinger still believes that Christianity ultimately fulfils Judaism, thus overshadowing it, he also recognizes the complementarity of the Jewish and Christian faiths in our current age.

PROFESSOR, PREFECT AND POPE

After his ordination as a priest on 20 June 1951, Joseph Ratzinger worked as an assistant priest at a parish in the Archdiocese of Munich while pursuing postgraduate studies. He obtained a doctorate and later a *Habilitation* in theology from the University of Munich. Later, as a professor of theology, he taught at the Freising seminary (1958), the University of Bonn (1959–63) and the University of Münster (1964–6).[50]

Ratzinger participated in the Second Vatican Council, first as the adviser to Cardinal Josef Frings of Cologne, and later as an official *peritus*. He was one of the founding fathers of the international journal, *Concilium*, and became an important member of the International Theological Commission. From 1966–9, Ratzinger occupied the chair of dogmatic theology at Tübingen and wrote important works on the Christian faith and ecclesiology. These writings reveal his cautious approach to interpreting the Council. Ratzinger believes the Second Vatican Council's *aggiornamento* must not degenerate into liberalization of the faith and of the church itself.[51]

The student riots of 1968 shocked Ratzinger greatly with their anti-establishment attitude. Thus, in 1969, he decided to teach at the newly established University of Regensburg in his native Bavaria. At this time, Ratzinger began to question the success of modernity and his initial willingness to be open to the world disappeared. He believed the malaise in the church was the result of indiscriminate adaptation of the Christian faith to the world. Hence, he questioned the influence of *Gaudium et Spes*, a Second Vatican Council document with which he was ill at ease.[52]

In 1972, Ratzinger, together with Hans Urs von Balthasar, Karl Lehman, Henri de Lubac and other theologians, founded a new theological journal, *Communio*, to counteract the liberal influence of *Concilium*. This newly launched journal would become a forum for Ratzinger to express his theological ideas.[53]

On 24 March 1974, Ratzinger was made archbishop of Munich-Freising. Three months later, on 27 June, he was promoted to the Cardinalate by Pope Paul VI. Pope John Paul II appointed Cardinal Ratzinger as prefect of the CDF on 25 November 1981. A 'champion of orthodoxy', Ratzinger became very influential and helped to shape the Vatican's theological outlook and policy. As prefect of the CDF and as head of the International Theological

Commission (ITC), he tightened up discipline in matters of faith and morals and dealt decisively with instances of theological dissent.[54]

Besides being the prefect of the CDF, Ratzinger remained a theologian in his own personal capacity and published important works that include *Principles of Catholic Theology: Building Stones for a Fundamental Theology* (1987), *Church, Ecumenism and Politics: New Essays in Ecclesiology* (1988 and 2008), *The Nature and Mission of Theology: Essays to Orient Theology in Today's Debates* (1995), *The Spirit of the Liturgy* (2000) and *Value in a Time of Upheaval* (2006). Many of his works as a private theologian were meant to clarify and defend official church positions. Some of his favourite themes in ecclesiology include the primacy of the pope, relationship between church and politics, and the uniqueness of Christ and salvific necessity of the church in relation to interreligious dialogue.[55] His first papal encyclical was *Deus Caritas Est* (25 December 2005), followed by *Spes Salvi* (30 November 2007) and *Caritas in Veritate* (28 June 2009). He continues to publish in his own private capacity. In *Jesus of Nazareth* (2007), Ratzinger stresses the distinction between his official teaching position and his private opinion as a theologian.[56]

Ratzinger's theological viewpoints come from his reading of the church fathers, especially Augustine and Bonaventure. His doctoral dissertation, *The People and the House of God in Augustine's Doctrine of the Church* was defended in 1953 and his *Habilitationsschrift* (post-doctoral thesis) involved a study of Bonaventure's theology of history.

ST AUGUSTINE

Ratzinger describes himself as a 'decided Augustinian'. He follows the Augustinian *credo ut intelligam* maxim, according to which belief is a necessary prerequisite for understanding, 'just as creation comes from reason and is reasonable, faith is, so to speak, the fulfilment of creation and thus the door to understanding'.[57] As a student, he found scholasticism too dry and impersonal, but in the works of Augustine (354–430), he found 'the passionate, suffering, questioning man is always right there, and you can identify with him'.[58] Alfred Läpple, the prefect in Ratzinger's seminary in Freising, in an interview given soon after Ratzinger was elected pope, says, 'He's not interested in defining God by abstract concepts. An abstraction – he once told me – didn't need a mother.'[59]

As a writer, Ratzinger continues to draw inspiration from Augustinian thought as he says, 'Augustine has kept me company for more than twenty years. I have developed my theology in a dialogue with Augustine, though naturally I have tried to conduct this dialogue as a man of today.'[60] He acknowledges that Augustine's theology grew out of 'polemic against error', for without error, 'movement of a living, spiritual kind is hardly thinkable'.[61]

Augustine said, 'Seek not to understand that you may believe, but believe that you may understand.' This is what Ratzinger would have written, for he believes that faith is a gift from God and the dogmas of the church cannot be changed. His theology and intellectual gifts are not meant to create new things, but to preserve what God has revealed and to teach the faithful the truth of the gospel. He says, 'This is His Church and not a laboratory for theologians ...We are servants and don't ourselves determine what the Church is.'[62] In fact, Ratzinger believes that the crisis in the Catholic faith lies in the misunderstandings of the nature of the church. He writes:

> My impression is that the authentically Catholic meaning of the reality 'Church' is tacitly disappearing, without being expressly rejected. Many no longer believe that what is at issue is a reality willed by the Lord himself. Even with some theologians, the Church appears to be a human construction, an instrument created by us and one which we ourselves can freely reorganize according to the requirements of the moment.[63]

Ratzinger fears that without a spiritual view of the church, but with only a sociological understanding, Christology loses its divine substance. The church becomes just a human organization and the gospel becomes just a 'Jesus-project'.[64]

Ratzinger's interest in St Augustine led to writing his doctoral dissertation entitled *The People and the House of God in Augustine's Doctrine of the Church*. In this work, Ratzinger identifies two main points in Augustine's ecclesiology: his understanding of the church as the people of God and his concept of love in his presentation of the church as the 'house of God'. In his youth, Augustine's struggle with authority and scepticism led him eventually to the notion of faith, which included joining the universal church: 'Because of man's wounding through sin, the Church now becomes a necessary stage in the ascent of the soul to Wisdom.'[65]

In ancient times, it was believed that salvation could be attained only by a few enlightened people. Augustine was attracted to the Christian claim to be the 'royal highway' to salvation, universally accessible to all people, and the church which offered to mediate on behalf of both the learned and simple folk. He accepted communion with the church as 'a way of faith' rather than as a purely 'metaphysical search' current in his time. He had realized that truths come from faith.[66] In his *Confessions*, Augustine laments that the vision of God cannot be sustained in our memory due to our human weakness. He also realizes that a human being cannot take the 'divine "food" in its pure form', but needs the help of the church.[67]

Initially, Augustine's understanding of the church and the Christian faith was philosophical. His writings dealt with Platonist themes. However, he gradually moved towards the 'salvation-historical' approach to the scripture, which appeals to Ratzinger. Augustine started from a 'metaphysical theology' and moved towards 'a more historical understanding of Christianity'. The concrete historical form of Christianity is the church: 'The historical saving activity of God and its living presence in the Church ... belong entirely within the provisional and transient sphere of *mundus hic*.'[68]

At a later date, Augustine identified the church, the people of God, in the concrete world of reality. In the same way, as Ratzinger sees it, the human person is no longer just a sensuous being, but lives 'according to itself, serving its own purposes'. At the same time, the spiritual is not just the 'ideal', but lives according to God's will. Ratzinger affirms Augustine's transformation of the Neoplatonic dualism of the world into *historical* terms of accepting or rejecting God's grace, which is closer to the biblical view of human existence.[69] Needless to say, the necessity of the church for salvation, in Augustinian thought, remains ingrained in Ratzinger's theology and shaped his rather negative attitude towards religious pluralism.

In Augustine's theology, Ratzinger highlights charity in the ecclesiological context. This is called 'objective charity' and it means 'belonging to the Church, and more specifically to that Church which itself lives in charity ... in eucharistic love-relationship with (other Christians in) the whole world'.[70] The real meaning of charity in this context is grace and the Holy Spirit. The 'holy Church' is found within the Catholic Church, but is not identified with it. The Catholic Church consists of saints and sinners, growing together until the Kingdom comes. Ratzinger writes: 'Augustine can say: The Catholic Church is the true Church of the holy. Sinners are not really in her ... But on the other hand, he can stress that it is no part of the Church's business to discharge such sinners ... It is the Lord's task, who will awaken her (at the End) and give her the true form of her holiness.'[71] Augustine's philosophical understanding of salvation is now transformed into 'being in the Church' and 'being-in-love'. He has made the church a crucial aspect of our salvation in Christ and he uses the term 'people of God' on three levels: Israel, the spiritual church and the Catholic Church.[72]

Ratzinger, in his study of Augustine, also shows us how the sacrifice of Christ becomes the sacrifice of all humanity. This means that no one lives outside the 'true worship ... of the City of God'. We are all united with Christ by his spirit which is also his grace: charity is spread all over the world, in the hearts of men and women, by the Holy Spirit. This charity enables us to transcend the boundaries of individuals and to enter into communion with the church which is Christ's body, found in the sacrament of the Eucharist.[73]

In the *The Ratzinger Report*, Ratzinger says that he would like to write on original sin if he went back to academia: 'In fact, if it is no longer understood that man is in a state of alienation ... one no longer understands the necessity of Christ the Redeemer.' He believes the 'whole structure of the faith is threatened by this'.[74] This is another of Ratzinger's Augustinian traits. In *Confessions*, Augustine reveals his pessimism regarding human nature. He stresses the perdition of humankind and man's total dependence on God's grace to find salvation. The conversion of Augustine interests Ratzinger greatly because it deals with the saint's return to God, then to his church where the incarnate Logos, Jesus Christ, resides. Augustine's conversion, from a philosophical standpoint, leads one to the question of religion. The question of ontology and metaphysics is fundamental here. Ratzinger believes contemporary philosophy and theology must return to the ultimate principle that the pluralists and relativists of theology have abandoned.

In his interview with Peter Seewald, Ratzinger says, 'I have never tried to create a system of my own, an individual theology ... The point of departure is first of all the word. That we believe the word of God, that we try really to get to know and understand it, and then, as I said, to think it together with the great masters of the faith. This gives my theology a somewhat biblical character and also bears the stamp of the Fathers, especially Augustine.'[75] As a theologian, Ratzinger is praised for his scholarship rather than for his creativity. His critics consider this his weakness while his supporters think it is his forte. I am inclined to agree with Vincent Twomey who thinks that Ratzinger is an original and critical thinker.[76]

ST BONAVENTURE

In his introduction to the study of St Bonaventure (1221–74), Joseph Ratzinger claims that people are concerned with philosophical and theological issues in times of 'great crisis in the historical process itself'. He gives the example of Augustine's *City of God* which deals with the critical self-questioning concerning the fall of Rome as the first high point of reflection. At such times, people are more acutely aware of the transitory nature of life. The second high point of such self-questioning is found in Bonaventure's examination of the biblical story of creation in his *Collationes in Hexaemeron*.[77] Ratzinger's post-doctoral dissertation entitled *The Theology of History in St Bonaventure* was also very much in the Augustinian tradition. It is an analysis of this great Franciscan theologian's interpretation of the concept of history held by the twelfth century mystic and prophet, Joachim of Fiore (1135–1202).

The idea of salvation history was becoming popular in Catholic theology in the 1950s. It had given new understanding to the idea of revelation as not just simply 'a communication of truths to the intellect but as a historical action of God in which truth becomes gradually unveiled'.[78] Neoscholasticism had confined the idea of revelation to the intellectual realm. As a 'decided Augustinian', this new historical understanding of revelation excited Ratzinger. In time, his understanding of revelation as the act of God showing himself and not the object he reveals, manifests itself as the basis for the Second Vatican Council's document, *Dogmatic Constitution on Divine Revelation*, to which Ratzinger contributed a great deal. However, at the time of his *Habilitation*, it was still not accepted, especially by Professor Schmaus, one of the readers of his thesis.[79]

In his research on this topic, Ratzinger had found out that the concept of 'revelation' as we know it now was foreign to theologians in the thirteenth century. During the High Middle Ages, revelation was thought of as an act in which God shows himself, and 'not to the objectified result of this act'. This means that revelation is a dynamic process. The receiving subject is always part of revelation and, thus, if no one is there to receive it, revelation does not occur. It follows that 'revelation requires a someone who apprehends it'.[80] Ratzinger argues that if Bonaventure is right, then revelation comes before scripture. Revelation is not simply identical with scripture, but is greater than what is written. Ratzinger also claims that there can be no such thing as purely *sola scriptura* because 'an essential element of Scripture is the Church as understanding subject, and with this the fundamental sense of tradition is already given'.[81]

According to Augustine, history was *transitory* as shown by the rise and fall of empires. Only the 'citizenry of God' remains. Its 'sacramental expression is the Church', the people of God journeying towards the heavenly city of Jerusalem. This Augustinian concept of time has been replaced by Joachim's understanding of history, from which we can trace the origin of modernity.[82] In *Collationes in Hexaemeron*, Bonaventure reinterprets Joachim of Fiore's concept of history in the sense that he does not entirely reject the idea, as Thomas Aquinas did.

Joachim divided history into three epochs as divine progression: that of the Father (the Old Testament or period of the patriarchs), the Son (the Church since the New Testament or period of the priests) and, finally, the Holy Spirit (the period of the laity) 'which was about to break into history'.[83] In the third period, the age of the laity, Joachim believed the structures of the state and church would give way to a perfect society of free persons, led by the Holy Spirit from within. This exciting concept of history which Voegelin calls 'the immanentization of the eschaton' means that the end of history is 'the product of history's own inner movement toward ever greater perfection', in other words, 'the Kingdom of God on earth'. Our modern understanding of 'progress' has its roots in this philosophy from which diverse ideologies such as socialism and liberal capitalism sprang up. It affects our society profoundly and gives rise to aggressive secularism and even evolution.[84] In fact, according to Eric Voegelin, the origin of modernity can be traced to the ideas of Joachim of Fiore.[85]

Joachim's Gnostic speculations were being adopted by some Franciscans known as 'spirituals'. Their radical interpretation, of Franciscan poverty, combined with Joachim's apocalyptic interpretation, created a revolutionary movement. Joachim believed he had found a basis in scripture for his belief that a time would come when the Church of the Spirit would arise and the sons of St Francis of Assisi would initiate this new age. This interpretation created tension in the Franciscan Order and brought the spirituals out into open conflict with church authorities.[86] The spirituals threatened to split the Franciscan Order into two factions and create a schism. Bonaventure, the minister general, had to deal with this crisis by addressing Joachim's theories, which had been adopted by the spirituals.

Bonaventure acknowledged the possibility of a new age in human history exemplified in the person of St Francis of Assisi. His response to the Joachimite question consisted, 'not in a total rejection' but in a 'corrective interpretation'. Whereas the Joachimites went against tradition in following their leader, Bonaventure interpreted him within tradition. Aidan Nichols says that Ratzinger agreed with this 'ecclesial reinterpretation' of the radical theologians in preference to outright dismissal.[87] Gediminas T. Jankunas believes this shows that Ratzinger was not the absolutist depicted in the media. He 'never leaves out any traces of truth'. There are always some elements of truth in any important theory and those elements must be singled out so that they can help to create a common ground.[88] I think this is a misguided understanding of Ratzinger's theological position. Rather, Ratzinger is convinced that 'an error is all the more dangerous, the greater that grain of truth is, for then the temptation it exerts is all the greater'.[89]

Nonetheless, Ratzinger, in his thesis, approves Bonaventure's treatment of Joachim, but he goes further in claiming that Catholic doctrine teaches only one 'new age' – the second coming of Christ. Ratzinger also warns against Bonaventure's tolerance of Joachim: 'For, in a certain sense, a new, second "End" is set up next to Christ. Even though Christ is the centre, the one who supports and bears all things, still he is no longer simply that *telos* in whom all things flow together and in whom the world is ended and overcome.'[90]

The significance of this study is important for understanding Ratzinger's treatment of modern ideologies. His future dealings with philosophical and theological issues are likely to be deeply influenced by his study of Bonaventure's analysis of Joachim's concept of history. This is particularly true in his treatment of liberation theology based on a Marxist understanding of history, which has its roots in Joachim's theory. Ratzinger accused liberation theologians of trying to establish the Kingdom of God on earth, of doing away with the institutional church and replacing spirituality with politics. The conclusion that Nichols draws is this: 'Before the name "liberation theology" was ever heard of, Ratzinger had to arrive at some judgment about this uncanny thirteenth-century anticipation of liberationist eschatology.'[91]

ST BENEDICT

Joseph Ratzinger was elected pope on 19 April 2005, during the fourth ballot in the Sistine Chapel, and he chose the name Benedict XVI. He wanted to continue to be a pope of peace, overcoming theological division within the church and reaching out to the Eastern churches, as did Benedict XV. Ratzinger, as Pope Benedict XVI, in his first homily, hinted that he would promote dialogue within the church, to heal real divisions, and also dialogue with other Christian churches and non-Christian religions.

By taking the name of Benedict of Nursia (480–547), who was patron saint of Europe and considered one of the leading pioneers of Western monasticism and father of Western civilization, Ratzinger demonstrated his intention to focus on the church in Europe, which is going through a crisis of aggressive secularism. Although the Catholic Church in Latin America, Africa and Asia is flourishing, Europe needs to revive itself and to rediscover its Christian soul. The West not only exports technology, but also ideologies such as liberal capitalism and Marxism; both home grown in European soil. The philosophy of the 'hermeneutics of suspicion' promotes distrust of all traditions and authorities, which some believe is the cause of the crisis in Europe.[92] The churches in

Europe are sick and they must be healed before they do further damage and spread their disease to other parts of the world.[93]

Joseph Ratzinger thinks the recovery of the Christian roots of Europe is the only cure for the continent's spiritual malaise. These roots are found not only in scripture and church tradition, but also in Greek philosophy and the Roman legal system.[94] From this Western perspective, it does seem that Ratzinger's whole life has been a preparation for this papacy. His early life experience and education based on the study of the classics, literature, philosophy and theology in the best of European and Enlightenment traditions prepared him well for this enormous task of combating modern secular ideologies and preserving Catholic orthodoxy in the West. He is considered by some to be the most accomplished theologian to hold the papacy in a thousand years. However, in subsequent chapters, I will attempt to argue that in spite of his intellectual prowess, Joseph Ratzinger's theology lacks sensitivity towards the Asian traditions with their plurality of religions and cultures because of his Western presuppositions. Besides, there are some who question whether reviving European Christian roots is appropriate for contemporary pluralistic Western societies.

ONLY THE TRUTH WILL SET YOU FREE

Some critics believe that Joseph Ratzinger had been transformed from a liberal theologian, in his younger days, into a conservative one as the years progressed. It is not exactly fair to label people as either conservative or liberal, terms that often reflect unexamined prejudices to which most of us are prone. In fact, Ratzinger himself has argued that 'labeling a person conservative is practically synonymous with social excommunication, for it means, in today's language, that such a one is opposed to progress, closed to what is new and, consequently, a defender of the old, the obscure, the enslaving; that he is an enemy of the salvation that change is expected to bring about'.[95]

It is more correct, therefore, to say that there is continuity in Ratzinger's writings that are creative and original. His writings are characterized by his pastoral concern to protect the simple faithful against erroneous ideas and by his duty to clarify church teachings and to respond to the challenges posed to the church by religious pluralism. Having a critical and sharp mind, Ratzinger is an independent thinker, unmoved by any fad or fashion prevailing in the church or the world. While many theologians are still caught up in the liberal thinking of the late 1960s, Ratzinger, reading the signs of the times, has moved forward.[96] Thus, it is not correct to label his writings as conservative or liberal; they are characterized by his passion for the truth, to search for the truth and to safeguard the truth. It is this desire for the truth that helps him to be in dialogue with those who have disagreed with him. In other words, he is open to correction because he believes that truth will ultimately prevail.[97]

Ratzinger's theological position, therefore, can be summarized in one phrase: 'Only the truth will set you free' (John 8:23). To live a life of holiness is to live according to the truth, revealed by God, through Jesus Christ.[98] This means that a person must reject the human pride and 'absolute self-determination' that positivism, relativism and Marxism promote. It requires a true conversion, an opening up to God who is so much greater. Only then can we discover 'the truth as love, as a person'. For Ratzinger, 'Salvific truth was definitely revealed in Jesus Christ, the Son of God, as personal love beyond death and is articulated in the Christian tradition'.[99]

Ratzinger constantly stresses that this truth, the subject of faith, is entrusted to the Catholic Church. The human person can only receive faith from the church which, in turn, does not draw faith from itself, but from Jesus Christ. It is the church's prime duty to guard this truth so that it remains the truth and is not lost in history. It is in the 'sacramental structure of reality' that salvation and truth come to us.[100]

Modern secular society has problems in accepting an already given truth. There is a fundamental conflict between Christian faith and contemporary Western thinking, which also claims the 'prerogative of absolute self-determination'. In *Principles of Catholic Theology*, Ratzinger says that in the past, the problem of the relationship between 'being' and 'time' was solved in favour of 'being'. But after Hegel, 'being' becomes 'time'.[101] Ratzinger believes that the failure of scientific progress, Marxism, etc. to satisfy the deepest longing of human beings lies in their philosophical presuppositions:

> Truth becomes a function of time; the true is not that which simply *is* true, for truth is not simply that which *is*; it is true for a time because it is part of the becoming of truth, which *is* by becoming. This means that, of their very nature, the contours between true and untrue are less sharply defined; it means above all that man's basic attitude toward reality and toward himself must be altered. In such a view, fidelity to yesterday's truth consists precisely in abandoning it, in assimilating it into today's truth; assimilation becomes the form of preservation.[102]

This means that Christianity has meaning in its own specific way. It is true in its historical moment. It can still continue to be true while assimilating the current situation, 'the newly developing whole'.[103]

Regarding Marxism, Ratzinger says the notion of truth, in this ideology, is regarded 'as an expression of the vested interests of a particular historical moment'. Marxists deny the idea of enduring truth. They believe that what is true is what serves progress. However, Ratzinger insists that there must be 'a recognizable identity of man within himself' and that truth must remain true in every historical moment. This is why he is opposed to relativism and the pluralist theology of religion, which deny the notion of continuity of being in time: 'The question of hermeneutics is, in the last analysis, the ontological one, the question of the oneness of truth in the multiplicity of its historical manifestations.'[104]

There is a theme related to the notion of truth that recurs in Ratzinger's writings: the indictment of the 'liberal dogma of progress' and of the 'liberal worldview' in general which he records in his memoirs. Ratzinger claims that the destruction of men with modern technology during the First World War led people to turn to the church, its liturgy and sacraments.[105] It is clear that he places great value on church dogma, which he conceived 'not as an external shackle, but as the living source that made knowledge of the truth possible in the first place'.[106] Above all, for Ratzinger, the truth is found in the liturgy of the church and theological tradition. He is suspicious of theologies that come from the periphery, which we will discuss below.

'IRRUPTION' OF THE THIRD WORLD

For Ratzinger, the theology of liberation and the theology of religious pluralism share some common ground. Both theories resulted from the experience of life in the Third World: liberation theology arose from the poverty of Latin America and the theology of religious pluralism called attention to the fact that most Third World countries are non-Christian. They reflect the joys and hopes, the pains and anxieties that the Second Vatican Council speaks about.[107] Liberation theology seeks to establish the Kingdom of God on earth through political actions. The theology of religious pluralism affirms that elements of truth and grace can be found in non-Christian religions. Needless to say, Ratzinger regards liberation theology and religious pluralism as distorted versions of orthodox Christianity.[108] They share a distorted understanding of truth because they define truth as whatever serves progress, and emphasize praxis rather than orthodoxy.[109] In a speech given in Hong Kong in 1993, Ratzinger speaks of Christian universalism rather than religious pluralism:

The point of departure of Christian universalism was not the drive to power, but the certainty of having received the saving knowledge and redeeming love which all men had a claim to and were yearning for in the inmost recesses of their beings. Mission was not perceived as expansion for the wielding of power, but as the obligatory transmission of what was intended for everyone and which everyone needed.[110]

An important factor that reinforces Ratzinger's opposition to modern ideologies is his negative experience of the post-conciliar church: 'It is incontestable that the last ten years have been decidedly unfavourable for the Catholic Church ... Christians are once again a minority, more than they have ever been since the end of antiquity.'[111] He speaks of 'boredom and discouragement' in the church as a 'progressive process of decadence' setting in.[112] As we shall see in greater detail in Chapter 3, he likens the church of the post-conciliar period to a huge construction site where the blueprint has been lost. Everyone continues to build the church according to his fancies because a critical spirit has set in. Ratzinger blames 'the unleashing *within* the Church of latent polemical and centrifugal forces'.[113] We can conclude that, by this, he includes the theology of religious pluralism among other forces.

The cardinals who elected Joseph Ratzinger on 19 April 2005 understood that the greatest challenge for the church lies in Western Europe and the theologian from Bavaria, prefect of the CDF, is the person most qualified to deal with this crisis, as the successor of St Peter. By studying his early life and experience, his intellectual formation, his work as priest, professor and prefect, we can understand the choice of the conclave. However, when dealing with Asian realities, especially the growing churches in the East, perhaps Ratzinger falls short of incipient expectations in Asia.

After eight years, in a historic move on 28 February 2013, Joseph Ratzinger stepped down from the papacy, the first pontiff to resign in 598 years, 'After having repeatedly examined my conscience before God, I have come to the certainty that my strengths, due to an advanced age, are no longer suited to an adequate exercise of the Petrine ministry.'[114] His legacy and influence, however, will continue to be felt as he epitomizes a dominant viewpoint in the church.

Chapter 2

Religious Pluralism

In the previous chapter, we discussed the early upbringing of Joseph Ratzinger, his experience of the horrors of the Second World War and Nazism, his priestly studies in the seminary and his postgraduate work in the university. We also observed his early disdain for modern philosophies and his abiding faith in the superiority of Christianity as a path to salvation. In addition, we have seen that he is most comfortable in a Catholic environment and that an appreciation for other religious traditions was not something he imbibed in his early years. In this chapter we will examine Ratzinger's approach to religious pluralism.

Religious plurality and religious pluralism have at times been used interchangeably. Strictly speaking, the terms are not the same: religious plurality refers to the fact that there exist many different religious beliefs and traditions, while religious pluralism reflects the view that one's religion is not the exclusive source of truth. Pluralism, therefore, suggests that many different religions could be valid paths to the divine. Christian adherents of pluralism reject the premise that God reveals himself only through Jesus Christ.

In spite of his inclusivist position, which reflects the official teaching of the Catholic Church, this chapter seeks to show that Ratzinger's perception of non-Christian religions as valid paths to salvation is essentially pessimistic and negative. He believes that there may be revelation in these religious traditions but not salvation. In this sense, he is an exclusivist as he asserts the uniqueness of Jesus Christ as saviour of the world and the Church of Christ as subsisting in the Catholic Church. At the same time, Ratzinger, influenced by the early church fathers' teaching on the Logos, reveals an open inclusivism in which he acknowledges that truths found in non-Christian religions may be of significance for the church.

One thing is clear. Ratzinger's teaching on Christianity's relationship with other religions assumes the norm of Western philosophical and theological thought. He sincerely believes that the Greek intellectual and cultural expression found in Christianity is part of God's plan. For Ratzinger, the relation between faith and reason cast in Hellenistic philosophy is part of biblical inspiration and, thus, part of faith itself. This giving precedence to Western thought makes him rather critical and suspicious of theologians operating from a different theological framework and experience.

In *Theological Highlights of Vatican II*, published in 1966, Joseph Ratzinger writes that the more positive interpretation of world religions that has been suggested in recent times is not supported by scripture. In fact, he maintains that some ideas characteristic of modern theology lack biblical foundation. He also argues that an optimistic interpretation of other religions is foreign to the biblical worldview and even 'antipathetic to its spirit'. He maintains that the prevailing optimism about the salvific values of non-Christian religions is 'simply irreconcilable with the biblical assessment of these religions'.[1] Even as a young, progressive theologian, Ratzinger had great reservations about the positive values of non-Christian religions.

Ratzinger acknowledges that the establishment of Christianity in Asia has so far failed.[2] As a matter of fact, to be Christian means 'conversion to Europeanism' and thus few people in Asia become Christians. A Christian faith that should be the universal religion of humankind has not been able to move beyond its occidental roots. Ratzinger says that up till now, there has been no genuine, Asian version of Christianity, which reflects a profound grasp of the oriental culture and spirit.[3] This could be interpreted as openness to local theologies, but as prefect of the CDF, Ratzinger is cautious about using the term 'inculturation'.[4]

It is understandable that Joseph Ratzinger as prefect of the CDF takes a strong stand against those who would undermine Christian uniqueness, especially as it relates to that of salvation in Christ, which is a fundamental aspect of the faith. He also tends to give 'an exaggerated caricature' of religious pluralism and various aspects of it, such as Asian religions.[5]

Let us now take a brief look at the history of the church in connection with the issue of religious pluralism.

THE CHURCH AND RELIGIOUS PLURALISM

The church has not been unfamiliar with religious pluralism in the past. In fact, Christianity itself was born within the milieu of Judaism and mystery religions. As Christianity separated itself from Judaism, it encountered Greek philosophy which led it to attempt to interpret the gospel in Hellenistic philosophical terms.[6] Regarding Christianity's encounter with Greek philosophy, Ratzinger writes:

> The Christian faith opted ... against the gods of the various religions and in favor of the God of the philosophers, that is, against the myth of custom and in favor of the truth of Being itself and nothing else ... the early Church did indeed reject the whole world of the ancient religion, declaring none of it to be acceptable and sweeping the whole system aside as empty custom that was contrary to the truth.[7]

Later the threat of Gnosticism led to the formation of the biblical canon and the composition of the creeds. It was the challenge of the Gnostic heresy that also instigated the process of understanding Christianity in terms of exclusivity. Christological doctrine taught by the church upheld Christianity's claim to uniqueness and normativeness.[8]

This understanding of Christianity as a unique and true religion continued with the writings of church fathers such as Justin, Irenaeus, Tertullian, Clement and Origen, much influenced by the Greek notion of Logos. The theological dispute in the early church culminated in the long and crucial dispute between Arius and Athanasius over the nature of the relationship between God the Father and God the Son. Harold Coward claims that the significance of this dispute is that Arius' position of subordinating Jesus to God would have made Christianity more open to other religions.[9] However, Athanasius' view dominated the period, became orthodox teaching and resulted in a closed, exclusive Christianity that proclaimed Jesus as the 'only true incarnation' and the sole saviour of humanity.[10]

By 500, this version of Christianity based on exclusivity had destroyed the previous Greek and Roman religions and the Catholic Church began to identify itself with the Kingdom of God on earth. In the seventh century, Christianity had to compete with Islam as another missionary religion. In the sixteenth century, Western Christian missionaries encountered the ancient and venerable religions of Asia in the forms of Hinduism, Buddhism, Taoism and Confucianism. In spite of all these contacts, or perhaps because of them, the attitude of Western Christianity maintained its exclusive claim as the one, true religion.[11]

Thus it was not surprising that in 1442 the Council of Florence-Ferrara declared that the Holy Church of Rome firmly believed that no one – not just heathens, but also Jews, heretics and schismatics – outside the Catholic Church could be saved unless they were received into the church before they died. Edward Schillebeeckx says such thinking was acceptable at that time. For centuries, Catholics ardently proclaimed exclusivism and put their beliefs into action, even resorting to physical force.[12] However, at the Second Vatican Council, we heard a different message: those who through no fault of their own did not know the gospel, but nevertheless sought God with a sincere heart could also be saved.[13] As we can see, these two official church teachings appear to be diametrically opposed, but Second Vatican Council does not make clear what 'seeking God' really means, so it could be interpreted as explicitly searching for God or as doing charitable work.[14]

According to Schillebeeckx, the council fathers at Florence-Ferrara were right in proclaiming Jesus as the only way to God because they could not imagine any other means in which people could be saved. However, they were mistaken to think that God could not work outside Christianity for the salvation of humankind. At a deeper level, the mistake lies in confusing a personal conviction with a truth that can be known objectively. Schillebeeckx argues that although dogmas have become irrelevant with the passing of time, they still remain important for our understanding of faith. As Christians, we have to confess that Jesus Christ 'is the only way of life *for us*', though God leads others in different ways. We can remain sincere Christians without condemning others as heretics or infidels.[15] The multiplicity of religions is not just a historical fact but a matter of principle and there are genuine religious experiences in other faiths which are never realized in Christianity.[16]

It is against this historical background that the church now seeks to formulate an appropriate theological response to the reality of religious pluralism as the new context within which to witness the gospel. Christians now have to deal with this reality as a fact of contemporary life. In spite of Christian missionary efforts, religious diversity is here to stay. The Christian theology of religions seeks to account for the diversity of world religious traditions and to discover appropriate responses to this phenomenon. This particular theology attempts to understand the doctrines of other religions and to evaluate the relationship between the Christian faith and the beliefs of other religious traditions. Paul Tillich, in his study of the history of religions, realized that 'every individual doctrinal statement or ritual expression of Christianity receives a new intensity of meaning'.[17] This means that the future of Christian theological endeavour lies in the attitude Christianity is going to adopt towards religious pluralism. This linking of systematic theology with the history of religions, in positive engagement, is crucial for revitalizing the self-understanding of Christianity. Tillich draws our attention to the fact that religious pluralism is the context for Christian faith and practice.

ARE NON-CHRISTIANS SAVED?

In 1964, Joseph Ratzinger preached a sermon entitled 'Are non-Christians Saved?' It is important to examine this homily as it foreshadows his later teachings, as prefect and pope, on the theology of religions. He writes:

> We are no longer ready, no longer willing, to think that eternal corruption should be inflicted on people in Asia, in Africa, or wherever it may be, merely on account of their not having 'Catholic' marked in their passport.
> ... Yet if we are honest, we will have to admit that this is not our problem at all. The question we have to face is not that of whether other people can be saved and how. We are convinced that God is able to do this with or without our theories, with or without our perspicacity, and that we do not need to help him do it with our cogitations. The question that really troubles us is not in the least concerned with whether and how God manages to save *others*.
> The question that torments us is, much rather, that of why it is still actually necessary for us to carry out the whole ministry of the Christian faith – why, if there are so many other ways to heaven and to salvation, should it still be demanded of us that we bear, day by day, the whole burden of ecclesiastical dogma and ecclesiastical ethics?[18]

Ratzinger sees religious pluralism as a problem and a challenge that should encourage the church to continue with its missionary endeavours, so that all might be saved through the Christian gospel. This means that Christians are responsible for spreading the message of Christ, especially when many people in the world remain unconvinced of the gospel. It is not our problem to know if non-Christians are saved or not. According to Ratzinger, Catholics just need to bear witness to Christ in all aspects of life.

The years from 1992–2002 were the time in which the CDF under the charge of Cardinal Ratzinger investigated several theologians writing on religious pluralism and the theology of religions. On 6 August 2000, the declaration *Dominus Iesus* was published by the CDF. It is obvious that the document, though not written by Ratzinger, represents his own theological thought. Its main concern was to combat inappropriate, pluralistic theologies with fundamental Christological and ecclesiastical orthodoxy.

On 14 September 2000, Ratzinger sent a letter to the presidents of the Bishops' Conferences explaining the purpose and authority of *Dominus Iesus*. He wrote:

> The declaration presents the principal truths of the Catholic faith in these areas; such truths require, therefore, irrevocable assent by the Catholic faithful; the text also refutes errors, clarifies some ambiguities and points out important questions that remain open to theological investigation and debate. Since it is a document of the Congregation for the Doctrine of the Faith, the declaration has a universal magisterial nature.[19]

Ratzinger's thinking on the theology of religious pluralism is clearly reflected in *Dominus Iesus* and his further insights on this topic are found in *Truth and Tolerance*. The essays in *Truth and Tolerance*, mostly from the 1990s, together with his more recent comments and elaborations, are actually reaffirmations of his basic Catholic orthodoxy on those questions raised by religious pluralism. In *Truth and Tolerance*, Ratzinger indicates that there was 'a cry of outrage from modern society but also from great non-Christian cultures such as that of India: this was said to be a document [*Dominus Iesus*] of intolerance and of a religious arrogance that should have no more place in the world of today'.[20] It is in the context of this tense situation that Ratzinger's collection of essays was published. It reaffirms the fundamental Christological and ecclesiological orthodoxy expressed in *Dominus Iesus*. However, *Dominus Iesus* appears to be incompatible with the Second Vatican Council's teaching on other religions.

THE SECOND VATICAN COUNCIL ON OTHER RELIGIONS

For the first time in the history of the Catholic Church, during the Second Vatican Council, her teaching on other religions takes on a positive note. It has taken the church many centuries to acknowledge the wisdom and goodness of other religions. Here I would like to discuss two documents which have had a great impact on the Catholic understanding of other religious traditions: *Lumen Gentium* and *Nostra Aetate*. *Lumen Gentium* first teaches that 'all men are called to be part of this catholic unity of the people of God which in promoting universal peace presages it. And there belong to or are related to it in various ways, the Catholic faithful, all who believe in Christ, and indeed the whole of mankind, for all men are called by the grace of God to salvation.'[21] It then offers an explicit teaching on Muslims by highlighting common ground: 'In the first place amongst these there are the Muslims, who, professing to hold the faith of Abraham, along with us adore the one and merciful God, who on the last day will judge mankind.'[22] The document suggests that there is saving efficacy in Islam because Muslims have acknowledged the creator who will come in judgement one day.

After the Muslims, *Lumen Gentium* also teaches that the divine presence is found in all God-seekers, other believers in God, even if it is 'in shadows and images' that they seek the unknown God. Therefore, those who through no fault of their own, 'do not know the Gospel of Christ or His Church, yet sincerely seek God and moved by grace strive by their deeds to do His will as it is known to them through the dictates of conscience' will also be saved.[23] Here we see Paul's speech in Athens, as presented by Acts 17, having a great influence on the Second Vatican Council's approach to other religions. It suggests that all human beings are called by God's grace to salvation (cf. 1 Tim 2:4).

Lumen Gentium also teaches that 'Whatever good or truth is found amongst them is looked upon by the Church as a preparation for the Gospel.'[24] Here Gerald O'Collins cautions us against thinking that this 'preparation for the Gospel' means people will enjoy the gifts of grace and truth only if they accept the gospel and baptism.[25] The Second Vatican Council never states this. In *Lumen Gentium*, we are told that non-Christians can move from an implicit to an explicit knowledge of God and that they can also move from shadow and images to light.

Further, *Lumen Gentium* also maintains that through the church's effort, 'whatever good is in the minds and hearts of men, whatever good lies latent in the religious practices and cultures of diverse peoples, is not only saved from destruction but is also cleansed, raised up and perfected unto the glory of God, the confusion of the devil and the happiness of man.'[26] In other words, those who are converted to Christianity already possessed elements of revelation inherited from their former religion. Nothing is lost or wasted. In fact, there is some continuity between their old religion and their new-found

Christian faith. God's self-communication always includes revelation, regarding the truth of the gospel, and salvation, regarding the influence of grace. The two cannot be separated.[27]

Nostra Aetate first considers the 'riddles of the human condition' and how different religions strive to respond to it. Then it reflects on the merits of Hinduism and Buddhism in their response to the human condition.[28] More importantly, this document also maintains that the Catholic Church rejects nothing that is true and holy in these religions. The church believes they reflect a ray of truth that enlightens all men and women, and thus encourages its members to dialogue with adherents of other faiths so as to learn from them. This means looking at their doctrines, 'precepts for life' and 'sacred doctrines'. The church acknowledges positively some aspects of Hinduism and Buddhism, the two religions which existed before the coming of Christ.

Besides commenting favourably on these two Asian religions, Hinduism and Buddhism, *Nostra Aetate* devotes an entire article to the Muslims which shows the importance of understanding and conducting dialogue with them. The document acknowledges major features in their understanding of God: 'They [Muslims] adore the one God, living and subsisting in Himself; merciful and all-powerful, the Creator of heaven and earth, who has spoken to men; they take pains to submit wholeheartedly to even His inscrutable decrees, just as Abraham, with whom the faith of Islam takes pleasure in linking itself, submitted to God.'[29] The declaration reveals its respect and esteem for the religious and moral life of the Muslims, the way they worship God in prayer, fasting and almsgiving. In his encyclical, *The Joy of the Gospel*, Pope Francis teaches that 'Our relationship with the followers of Islam has taken on great importance, since they are now significantly present in many traditionally Christian countries, where they can freely worship and become fully a part of society.'[30] Francis respects the Muslim's commitment to righteous living and compassion towards those in need. At the same time, he expects Muslims to respect the rights of Christians to worship and practice their faith in Islamic countries.

RATZINGER'S POSITION

The standard typology in the Christian theology of religions consists of exclusivism, inclusivism and pluralism. Exclusivism has been the church's predominant attitude throughout its history. It regards other religious beliefs as false. In the Catholic Church we have often interpreted the axiom, *Extra Ecclesiam nulla salus* (outside the church there is no salvation) in an ahistorical manner.

Inclusivism regards the Christian faith as the fulfilment of other religions. This approach has been adopted by the Catholic Church since the Second Vatican Council. Traditional non-Christian religions are seen as genuine expressions of human beings' longing to answer the most fundamental question regarding their human existence. Religious pluralism holds all legitimate religions to be the same in that they can help us to reach God or find salvation.

In Ratzinger's exploration of world religions, he deals with the challenges of understanding spiritual truth and at the same time he defends the truth of Jesus Christ as the only saviour of the world. He sums up Christianity's attitude towards other religions in terms of preparation and rejection. This means that Christianity has both positive and negative relationships with other faiths. As a preparation, Christianity is linked with other religions in the covenantal relationship and believes that other religions also speak of God and lead people to him.[31] This places Ratzinger in the inclusivist category. As a rejection of other religions, he believes that faith in Jesus Christ is the only way to salvation, and he also believes in the indivisibility of Christ and the church. Revelation may occur in other religions, but salvation is to be found in Jesus Christ as proclaimed by the Catholic Church. This makes him an exclusivist.

As an inclusivist, Ratzinger stresses that Christians must be aware of what divides them from others and also what unites them with other believers. Christianity is a historical faith, 'a path whose direction we call progress and whose attitude we call hope'.[32] A Christian has hope because he believes that all the sufferings and conflicts in the world will ultimately turn into something positive. There will be the transformation of the world into the heavenly city of Jerusalem, at the end of time.

Ratzinger argues that pluralism of religions cannot be the final word in history. He advocates an inclusivism that is not an absorption of one religion by another, but an encounter that transforms pluralism into plurality. Regarding faith, Ratzinger says revelation offered in Christ springs not from one single culture, but from intervention from above and, thus, does not 'absorb' anything. It provides space for all the great spiritual experiences of humankind as foreshadowed in Pentecost – the many languages and cultures understand each other in the one Spirit. They are not absorbed but brought together in harmony.[33]

Thus we see Ratzinger supporting the inclusivist position regarding the theology of religions while being critical of both Barth's exclusivism and Hick's pluralism. (See note 31, p. 279). In one sense, Ratzinger is closer to what Gavin D'Costa calls the 'restrictivist inclusivists' who uphold the specific nature of Christian faith, with Christ as the norm and baptism as the normal means to salvation. Restrictivist inclusivists acknowledge that not everyone has the opportunity to hear the gospel and so God also provides other channels: 'natural law inscribed in the universe'; 'in the heart through conscience'; or 'the good, true and beautiful *elements* within non-Christian religions'. Other religions are not accepted per se as means of salvation, but act at best, as preparation (*preparatio*) for the gospel. 'Christ is ontologically and causally exclusive to salvation, not epistemologically.'[34] In another sense, he is also closer to the 'open inclusivism' which Paul Griffiths suggests the Catholic Church should adopt.

Against pluralism, Ratzinger tells us that if one religion is as good as another, then there is no basis for having mission. He reminds us that we must continually purify our conscience and move forward towards the truth. He says that the apostles were looking for the 'hope of Israel' and discovered it in the person of Jesus Christ. They did not just accept the religious belief inherited from their cultural milieu, but continued to seek God with an open heart. Ratzinger stresses that there is a dynamic impulse inherent in Christianity – it is not just made up of structures and ideas, but is a living faith that continues to develop within the church. Our conscience and the silent presence of God in our religion guide us along towards salvation.[35] This means that we have to continue searching for God's will which is not fossilized in dogmas and institutions.

Ratzinger's inclusivism is based on his idea that cultures penetrate one another and are capable of relating to each other meaningfully – there have always been intercultural exchanges and fusion throughout history. Thus inclusivism is inherent in the cultural and religious history of mankind.[36] In *Many Religions – One Covenant*, Ratzinger argues that it was the encounter with the non-Christian world that served as a catalyst for Christian unity. It was inevitable that Christians would become aware of other religious beliefs. After all, the gospel was proclaimed to people who already possessed a religious tradition. Christians could not overlook the fact that they were addressing a world deeply influenced by other world religions. Ratzinger reminds us that the religiosity of these people actually put to shame the 'tired faith of Christians'. These people were not just 'non-Christians', they had something valuable to offer to Christians. It was wrong to destroy their unique religious culture. There is even an obligation for Christians 'to understand them from within and bring into Christianity the inheritance that was theirs'.[37]

In view of the above, we see Ratzinger opting for an open inclusivism that asserts the possibility that truths taught by other religions might not yet be explicitly known to our own religion. This means that Christians have something to learn from other religions. Griffiths believes the church should adopt an open inclusivism to deal with the question of truth raised by religious diversity. Griffiths also suggests that the church ought to adopt a 'modalized open inclusivism'. This means accepting the fact that other religions can teach truths that are important and that some of these are not yet taught or understood by the church.[38] Although Joseph Ratzinger makes the exclusive claim that only in Jesus Christ can we find salvation, he is an inclusivist in that he believes divine revelation may occur in other religious traditions.

PLURALISM AS A PROBLEM

In Catholic theology after the Second Vatican Council, we witness a reversal of a narrow ecclesiocentrism. The council has acknowledged that non-Christian religions can be bearers of saving values and truths, but it did not consider them to be a means of salvation. The council also did not spell out the theological implications of religious pluralism. Thus, many theologians venture to construct a 'hermeneutically oriented theology', with the church's new historical experience as the starting point, in order to reinterpret God's plan of salvation.[39] While not claiming to know the reason why God chooses so many, diverse ways of manifesting himself, these theologians attempt to interpret 'an apparently insurmountable pluralism' in the light of Christian revelation. Claude Geffré believes that religious pluralism is neither the result of human blindness over the centuries nor the indication that, after two thousand years, Christian mission has been defeated, but that pluralism 'corresponds to a mysterious divine design'.[40]

Ratzinger, however, sees pluralism as a problem and a challenge for the church and theology. At the same time, he admits that pluralism in 'the interplay of Church, politics and society is a fundamental value for Christianity which teaches 'the relative value of all political and social achievements'.[41] The church must be critical of all political and social absolutes because the freedom to have different social and political options must be safeguarded in the interests of the faith. Ratzinger affirms that faith signifies an ultimate bond with God and helps a person to live his life 'with norms for his concrete action in society'. Thus, our centre of unity is not to be found in social or political praxis, but in the binding force of truth which alone can set us free: 'the bond to the truth is a release of politics from sacral bonds'.[42] Thus, for Ratzinger, pluralism is necessary for faith in the sense that it safeguards the unity of the church in the face of growing political dictatorship.

Instead of pluralism, Ratzinger prefers to emphasize unity and harmony. He accepts pluralism in the secular world, but he is rather sceptical towards religious pluralism in the church for fear that it would lead to relativism. While he admits to pluralism in theology, Ratzinger insists that theologians must work within the context of the church. He insists that theologians must always acknowledge the unity between the Old Testament, New Testament and church dogma: all these elements combine together in our living faith and increase 'the excitement and fecundity of inquiry'. Ratzinger urges theologians 'to seek the inner unity and totality of the truth' in the structure of our faith.[43] This is more stimulating and productive than dismantling it. Our faith is far richer if we connect it to the ancient belief rather than let it remain in 'splendid isolation'.[44]

Ratzinger points out that in the primitive church, there was the concept of *symphonia* as an expression of the 'synthesis between unity and multiplicity' found in the early Christian community. This *symphonia* can be divided into four levels. The first level is found in the Bible itself, in the Old and New Testaments, with its plurality of prophets and apostles.[45] The second level is found among the Christians themselves, a kind of unity that comes as a gift from the Holy Spirit, which alone can bring together diverse elements in the church. The third level of *symphonia* is the unity between creation and the creator, between human beings and God, which allows communion between us and the divine.[46] The fourth level is the idea that the person is a plural being in search of integration and harmony that comes only from God. This symphony will not suppress the multiple dimensions of the human person, but will draw them into unity.[47]

Ratzinger speaks of the difference between a disintegrative pluralism and a fruitful pluralism in relation to theology. A disintegrative pluralism occurs when theologians are not able to accommodate the tension inherent in the entirety of faith. Theology becomes impoverished and narrowed and cannot be reversed by the 'proliferation of juxtaposed partial Christianities rising and falling in succession'.[48] Faith and theology have their own voice, but the voice of theology must depend on faith and be ordered towards it. Theology must explicate faith. If it ceases to expound faith, it ceases to be theology. There must be unity in faith, but theology can be pluralistic. Ratzinger calls 'fruitful theological pluralism' the bringing together of the different historical expressions of faith without cancelling multiplicity while still giving proper recognition to the 'organic structure of truth which transcends man'.[49]

When Ratzinger considers great theologians such as Newman, Guardini and Congar, he realizes how rich and truly contemporary their message is. These writers believed pluralism happens, not because it is willed, but because each of them seeks nothing but the truth. These masters, he says, testify that pluralism happens 'when everyone wants the truth with all his power and in his own epoch'. Ratzinger says that to desire the truth, we must 'accept as the voice and the way of the truth the greater understanding which is already present as a prior given in the Church's faith'.[50] This means not making one's understanding the measure of truth, but welcoming the voice of truth present in the faith of the church.

Ratzinger believes this approach can be a guiding principle for African, Latin American and Asian theology. He says French theology is great because it seeks to find the truth and to express it adequately and for this reason it is both French and universal. For theology to be fruitful, it must be freed from ulterior motives. We reach the pinnacle not by affirming, setting forth or raising ourselves, but by drawing closer to the truth which is never monotonous or exhaustive.[51] Although our minds can only behold truth in fragments, truth has the power to unite us. Ratzinger believes pluralism is great only when it is directed towards unity.[52] This means that the many theologies must serve a common tradition. Ratzinger's theology is essentially ecclesiocentric and this makes him cautious about interreligious dialogue.

INTERRELIGIOUS DIALOGUE

Related to religious pluralism is the issue of interreligious dialogue, which is an important feature in the church's understanding of mission and proclamation. Ratzinger's attitude towards interreligious dialogue differs from John Paul II. In his encyclical *Redemptoris Missio*, John Paul affirms that the 'Spirit's presence and activity affect not only the individuals but also society and history, peoples, cultures and religions'.[53] This means that John Paul acknowledges the mysterious working of the Spirit in other religions. Ratzinger, however, is much less willing to recognize the working of the Spirit in other religious traditions. The declaration *Dominus Iesus*, issued by the CDF under his prefecture, states: 'If it is true that the followers of other religions can receive divine grace, it is also certain that *objectively speaking* they are in a gravely deficient situation in comparison with those who, in the Church, have the fullness of the means of salvation.'[54]

Critics of *Dominus Iesus* find this point objectionable. Jacques Dupuis rightly argues that the 'gravely deficient situation' of the 'others', taught by *Dominus Iesus*, sounds offensive, especially when they also 'possess an authentic religious faith in the practice of which they find their way to God and discover the meaning of human life. Comparisons can be odious and Christians should not indulge in them readily.'[55] Dupuis also laments that Christians and even church authorities have the tendency to compare what is best in one's tradition to what is worst in others. This double standard needs to be corrected so that we can have a more positive evaluation of other religious traditions.[56] Ratzinger, given his conviction on the truth of Catholic Christianity, does not view it this way.

Some Catholics were scandalized when world religious leaders, Buddhists, Muslims, Jews and Hindus prayed together with John Paul II in Assisi in 1986 and again in 2002. Joseph Ratzinger appeared sympathetic to some of these critics. He believes that the seriousness of faith was being undermined on such occasions.[57] While making an effort to say something positive about other religions, in the spirit of the Second Vatican Council, Ratzinger's emphasis on evangelization, the necessity of conversion to Jesus Christ, in *Dominus Iesus*, is done at the expense of interreligious dialogue. Thomas P. Rausch says the declaration fails to communicate the sense that entering into dialogue with another religious tradition can itself be part of witnessing to Jesus Christ and a way of approaching the mystery of God's truth.[58]

Ratzinger is cautious about interreligious dialogue because he insists that it is about truth and not mere tolerance. He thinks that pluralists seek harmony in interreligious dialogue at the expense of doctrine, surrendering the truth and thus, 'baptizing' relativism.[59] Ratzinger insists on having some criteria of truth in order to do the right thing. The search for truth does not mean that we have the truth and others are searching for it. The quest for truth means that everyone is involved. This has relevance even for those who are Christians. The fruit of dialogue is learning: we live by faith, but we still do not know the entire truth. Ratzinger urges us to search for truth, but not to ignore the "indispensable elements" of Christian revelation. He also calls us to 'dwell in Christ, but remain vulnerable to an unpredictable dialogue that may actually change us'.[60]

Many theologians stress tolerance, harmony and equality, but Ratzinger is worried that such a liberal view ignores the differences in belief. Truth becomes relative and changeable according to each situation, and 'religious practices detachable from broader worldviews'.[61] Francis Xavier Clooney remarks, 'Oddly, Benedict's analysis aligns him with subaltern and postcolonial critics who insist that the West keeps distorting the religions and cultures of the wider world to maintain its own hegemony.'[62]

What is Christianity's position in the dialogue of religions? According to Ratzinger, the Christian faith has a mystical and an apophatic aspect, and thus he argues that encounters with the great religions of Asia will remind Christians of this dimension of their faith and will make them more tolerant.[63] He reminds us that God reveals and also conceals himself in Jesus Christ; the incarnate Word and the crucified One far surpass all human words. There is a connection between truth and defencelessness, between truth and poverty.[64]

Ratzinger warns us that in the dialogue of religions we cannot expect unification; this is not possible within our historical time nor is it even desirable. He gives us three criteria to follow in interreligious dialogue. First, in our encounter with other religions, we must not renounce the truth: 'Scepticism does not unite people. Nor does mere pragmatism.' The renunciation of truth and conviction makes man into a mere tool and 'robs him of his greatness.'[65] Thus, Ratzinger insists that we must respect the beliefs of others and be ready to look for the truth in them however strange it may appear to us. Such truths can correct us and deepen our own faith. He says too that we must also allow our narrow understanding of truth to be broken and acknowledge that we never possess the whole truth about God.[66]

Second, Ratzinger says we must look for what is positive in other religious traditions and what contains the precious pearl of truth. However, religions can also be perverted and destructive.[67] We must be ready to accept criticism of ourselves and our own religion. Ratzinger warns that Christians can succumb to sickness and become superstitious. Thus, our faith must always be purified on the basis of truth, 'that truth which shows itself, on the one hand, in faith and, on the other hand, reveals itself anew through dialogue, allowing us to acknowledge its mystery and infinity'.[68] This comes close to the view of O'Leary who writes:

> although truth is an obstacle to dialogue when each of the partners believe themselves to be its sole possessor, nonetheless religions which forfeit their truth-claims hardly deserve to survive. Interreligious theology thus requires a concept of truth which is both firm and flexible, compatible both with a historical relativisation of all religious discourse and an affirmation of the referential objectivity of dogmatic language.[69]

Third, Ratzinger teaches that mission and dialogue must go hand in hand. Dialogue is not a conversation without any direction; it must seek to find the truth.

We will meet people who are religious and try to relate to them meaningfully. The proclamation of the gospel must be a 'dialogical process'.[70] This means opening up the hidden depths in the religion of others. Dialogue of religions is listening to the Logos who points us to the unity we share.[71]

In Ratzinger's writing, *Many Religions – One Covenant*, we can see him adopting a kind of open inclusivism, as advocated by Griffiths, regarding the question of truth in the face of religious pluralism. Ratzinger recognizes and admits that other religious traditions can teach the church truths that are of great significance and which it has not yet realized fully. Griffiths says 'it is part of Catholic orthodoxy to think that the deposit of faith contains implicitly everything of religious significance; but this is compatible with the claim that the Church may learn what some of these implications are from those outside its boundaries'.[72] Although Ratzinger insists on the uniqueness of Christ and the universality of the Christian religion, he is quite disposed to accept truths found in non-Christian religions not yet explicitly taught by the church.

Following the teaching of St Augustine, Ratzinger states that Christianity is related to that divine presence that can be perceived by reason. Christianity is *religio vera* (true religion) in the sense that it is not based on legends but on rational knowledge.[73] Thus, he thinks that Hick is wrong to reduce religion to myth only. According to Ratzinger, Christianity is the worship of the 'true God' and enlightenment is part of this religion; it embodies 'the victory of demythologization, the victory of knowledge … and the victory of truth'. It appears to be intolerant because it refuses to accept relativism and the inter-changeability of gods or to be used for political purposes. Christianity is not just one religion among others, but the victory of perception and truth.[74]

Ratzinger believes that the Christian faith is convincing and its success in the early years after its foundation was due to its linking of faith to reason. It is the synthesis of reason, faith and life that makes Christianity a *religio vera*.[75] This idea of synthesis of reason and faith is clearly a Hellenistic concept and this brings us to Ratzinger's Eurocentric view regarding Christianity.

CHRISTIANITY: A EUROPEAN RELIGION?

Regarding the question of whether Christianity is a European religion, Joseph Ratzinger has highlighted the fact that Christianity did not originate in Europe, but in the Levant, a strategic crossroads where East meets West. He also stresses that it was not just geographical contact, but a spiritual encounter between Asia, Africa and Europe. Hence 'interculturality' shaped Christianity, while Christianity also appropriated many things from the Greeks in terms of their ways of thinking and speaking. In this sense, Ratzinger says, Christianity has become European.[76]

This emphasis on the European connection in Christianity is forcibly brought out in his lecture as pope, in Regensburg, in 2006:

> This inner rapprochement between Biblical faith and Greek philo-sophical inquiry was an event of decisive importance not only from the standpoint of the history of religions, but also from that of world history – it is an event which concerns us even today. Given this conver-gence, it is not surprising that Christianity, despite its origins and some significant developments in the East, finally took on its historically deci-sive character in Europe. We can also express this the other way around: this convergence, with the subsequent addition of the Roman heritage, created Europe and remains the foundation of what can rightly be called Europe.[77]

According to Ratzinger, it was no accident that the early apostles went to Macedonia, to the Greeks, who were the leading intellectuals of the day. The early Christians had to encounter the best minds in Europe – found among the Greeks – and began to absorb many of their ideas. He believes it was part of God's plan that Christianity was cast in Hellenistic thought patterns and expressions. The Regensburg address is also a brief history of modern Euro-pean philosophy rooted in the Old and New Testaments, in Greek and Roman thought. For Ratzinger, Europe is not just another continent, but a cultural destination where reason and revelation met and a symbiosis worked out.[78]

Ratzinger also notes that the Greek version of the Old Testament produced at Alexandria (the Septuagint) is more than a simple (and in that sense really less than satisfactory) translation of the Hebrew text: it is 'an inde-pendent textual witness' as well as a distinct and important step in the history of revelation. Thus for Ratzinger, the relation between faith and reason cast in the Hellenistic mould is part of biblical revelation; it is 'part of the faith itself'.[79] This again means that the confrontation between Christian revelation and Greek philosophy did not happen by chance, it was providential.

In this lecture, Ratzinger traces the process of the 'de-Hellenization of Christianity' that emerged during the Reformation. He speaks about the attempt to develop Western thought beyond the synthesis between Christian faith and Greek reason and to reject metaphysics in favour of *sola scriptura*. This separation of faith and reason was also present in the Protestant liberal theology of the nineteenth and twentieth centuries. Now pluralist theologians are arguing that the early synthesis of faith and reason under Hellenistic influ-ence is not binding on other cultures. Ratzinger writes:

In the light of our experience with cultural pluralism, it is often said nowadays that the synthesis with Hellenism achieved in the early Church was an initial inculturation which ought not to be binding on other cultures. The latter are said to have the right to return to the simple message of the New Testament prior to that inculturation, in order to inculturate it anew in their own particular milieux. This thesis is not simply false, but it is coarse and lacking in precision. The New Testament was written in Greek and bears the imprint of the Greek spirit, which had already come to maturity as the Old Testament developed.[80]

What Ratzinger means here is that the church sought to 'inculturate' itself into other cultures on the basis of reason, something that all cultures have in common. According to James Schall, 'this reason is what was learned from Greek philosophy', but not identified with Greece itself. Such confrontation of Bible and Greek thought was 'the first multicultural effort, the hellenization of the Christian understanding of itself'.[81] In this Regensburg lecture, Ratzinger insists that we must not attempt to get rid of this initial dynamism of the faith because 'the fundamental decisions made about the relationship between faith and the use of human reason are part of the faith itself; they are developments consonant with the nature of faith itself'.[82] This means that there is no such thing as pure Christianity – it comes clothed in Greek reason, as taught by Catholic tradition.

Ratzinger insists that any attempt to accommodate the local culture within the Christian faith must be done with great caution. However, we must differentiate between what is really the original local tradition and what is actually a false claim to universality, in that it is simply European. However, he does not fail to remind us that what is European can also be universal as well.[83] Ratzinger thinks that it is not possible to conceive of Christianity independent of any culture because he fears that 'such a transcultural vision of Christianity' could result in a loss of authentic Christian identity.[84] This means that we must accept the Hellenistic-Roman cultural expression of Christianity that comes to us as God-given. Thus Ratzinger seems to presume that Western culture is the normative standard for Christian theology.

Claude Geffré also says there is no such thing as pure and abstract Christianity. The Christian message has always been 'inculturated' from the beginning of the church. It has adopted the dominant culture of its place and origin – Semitic thought and Greek culture. Geffré believes in a fruitful and creative encounter between Christianity and non-Western cultures that are inseparably linked to their religious traditions.[85] The question now is whether

Christianity should adopt the dominant culture as well as religious values of any new place where it is planted. I agree with Geffré that it is wrong to conceive of inculturation in terms of a Christianity that ceases to be Western in order to become African, Chinese or Indian. It is important, I believe, to retain the best of Semitic spirituality and Hellenistic thought in the process of adapting the gospel to our own local cultures.

GIVING PRECEDENCE TO WESTERN THOUGHT

Joseph Ratzinger's 'privileging' of Greek philosophy must be seen in the context of his criticism of modernity and the three waves of de-Hellenization: 'The thesis that the critically purified Greek heritage forms an integral part of Christian faith has been countered by the call for a de-Hellenization of Christianity – a call which has more and more dominated theological discussions since the beginning of the modern age.'[86] This is related to his criticism of relativism and pluralism. In a debate between Joseph Ratzinger and Jürgen Habermas in *Le Monde* (27 April 2005), Cardinal Ratzinger was reported to have said, 'if all positions are of equal intellectual merit, then cannibalism is only a matter of taste.'[87] He was commenting on the logical consequence of relativism.

In his interview with Vittorio Messori, Ratzinger defended the universal significance of Christian thought as it has evolved in the West. He said, 'there is no way back to the cultural situation which existed before the results of European thought spread to the whole world.'[88] James V. Schall argues that Ratzinger's defence of Europe is likewise the defence of reason. Europe's spiritual and intellectual crisis affects the rest of the world. Schall says: 'For the other cultures to flourish properly, they too need to be what they potentially are—an infusion of this inner rapprochement that, like revelation and reason, is, in principle, universal and not simply European.'[89]

Concerned Christians, in African and other Third World countries, are urgently asking for Christianity to become an expression of their local faith so that it can fully and completely enter into their own identity. Ratzinger, however, does not think that we can discard the cultural expression that Christianity hitherto exhibited. According to him, the desired African theology is at present more 'a project than a reality ... very much of what is regarded as "African" is really a European import and has far less to do with actual African traditions than the classical Christian tradition has.'[90] As we have seen earlier, he has also remarked that there is really no Asian theology that reflects a genuine understanding of Eastern culture. Giving precedence to Western thought, in its historic synthesis of faith and reason, makes Ratzinger reluctant to accept non-Western modes of thinking in principle.

In his Regensburg Lecture, Ratzinger regards Europe as the locus of this mutual acceptance of faith and reason. As a German, he is very concerned about the current spiritual crisis in Europe – aggressive secularism and the decline of Christianity. This is understandable. However, Christianity is also a universal religion. Ratzinger thinks that what is European can also be universal, especially the Greek emphasis on reason and faith. After all, Christianity is a faith that seeks understanding. This presupposes that every culture values reason as a way to conduct our human affairs.

CHRISTIANITY IN ASIA: 'A STUNTED BONSAI'

A somewhat different scenario is presented by Aloysius Pieris, who claims that Christianity's long-term contact with Greek culture in the first five centuries 'coincided with the rise of Christianity as a political *power*'. He observes that the more powerful one becomes, the less one feels the need for dialogue.[91] He agrees with Ratzinger that Christianity became Western through contact with Greece and entered Europe through Rome. The spread of Christianity in other European countries coincided with the spread of the Roman Empire. Pieris argues that 'the church seems to have lost its incarnational praxis due to its authoritarianism'. He likens the church to a tree rooted in the centre of the Roman Empire, its 'branches spreading all over Europe and swallowing the weeds and brambles of primitive cultures'.[92] This means there is nothing divinely sanctioned about Christianity's alliance with Greek philosophy and Roman law – it is a question of power and expediency.

Aloysius Pieris argues that the Greco-Roman models of inculturation are not applicable in Asia, for four reasons. First, the patristic tradition does not regard other religions as valid paths towards salvation. The early church fathers believed that 'only the *culture* of Rome and the *philosophy* of Greece were worth being assumed by the church – that is, capable of being redeemed by Christ from the diabolical grip of pagan religion'. Second, inculturation here often means that religion is separated from culture and philosophy. In the South Asian context, Pieris argues, this is unthinkable.[93]

Third, the Greco-Roman model accepted by the church is based on the 'instrumental theory' of inculturation adopted by Western theology.[94] This means Greek philosophical thought was taken out of its original spiritual context and used as a scaffold for Christians to articulate their doctrines. In the Asian context, this policy cannot work because to remove a philosophy out of its proper context is to render it meaningless. Pieris says, 'To employ a dead philosophy to construct a Christian doctrinal system is an intellectual feat that can at most satisfy only the person who indulges in that exercise.'[95] He also thinks that using a non-Christian culture to support Christianity is also misleading – a kind of 'theological vandalism'.[96]

The final reason that 'the Greco-Roman model of inculturation succeeded in Europe but fails in Asia' is because 'the historical circumstances surrounding the early church in its early Mediterranean phase differ drastically from those of twentieth century Asia'. The emperor-centred religion of Rome was on the decline as its imperial power was reduced by barbarian attacks and more of its citizens turned to the new faith. Thus it was through inculturation that the church was able to save the Greco-Roman culture from becoming obsolete. In Asia, however, the reverse is happening. Pieris claims that 'the imperial religion now in crisis is colonial Christianity, whereas so-called pagan religion is regaining vitality ... as a current of contemporary spirituality that is passing through the length and breath of the post-Christian West'.[97] Hence, Pieris thinks that the urgent call for inculturation is a desperate attempt to give an Asian face to a church that is failing to take root in Asian soil. Since people are afraid to get rid of the 'Greco-Roman pot', Christianity has been growing for four centuries in Asia like a 'stunted bonsai'.[98]

TRADITION AND TRADITIONALISM

There may be some merit in Aloysius Pieris' radical criticism of the Greco-Roman model of inculturation, but it is wrong to 'throw the baby out with the bath water', as it were. I propose that we should preserve the spirit of Greek philosophy 'at its best', while discarding what is merely accidental to the Hellenistic culture. Thus we should abandon a tradition when it has become an idol.

Tradition becomes an idol, according to Jaroslav Pelikan, 'when it makes the preservation and the repetition of the past an end in itself'.[99] This means that we should appropriate the best of Hellenistic tradition found in Christianity and at the same time be open to what is good and true in other cultures. This is in keeping with the spirit of the Second Vatican Council: the ancient substance of the faith is one thing, but the way in which it is presented, while still preserving the same meaning, is another.

We can accept the traditional Western formulation of faith found in Christianity when that tradition 'does not present itself as coextensive with the truth it teaches'. It is a genuine tradition that we can embrace only when it presents itself as 'the way that we who are its heirs must follow if we are to go beyond it – through it, but beyond it – to a universal truth that is available only in a particular embodiment, as life itself is available to each of us only in a particular set of parents'.[100] This means that we should preserve the 'insight' of tradition, the inner wisdom ever present in the human spirit. Pelikan says it is traditionalism that gives tradition a bad name because 'Tradition is the living faith of the dead, traditionalism is the dead faith of the living'.[101]

There have been attempts to present Christianity in local cultures with limited success. To be sure, many people, starting with the ancient Chinese, have an exclusive conception of their own culture and tradition. Perhaps we should be free to use the philosophies of Asia to explain and extend Christianity as long as they do not disagree with previous normative formulations in neo-Platonic philosophy. This means that we should keep the insights of the Greek heritage in Christianity while trying to express the faith in a meaningful way for our native culture. Although this goes against what Ratzinger said at Regensburg, it is in keeping with our tradition. It is also an important distinction to make because it allows us to construct an understanding of Christianity that is intelligible to Asians.

Beyond the ambiguities of what is written in scripture regarding religious pluralism, the church fathers, on the whole, were very harsh in their judgement on pagan religions of their times. They regarded these religions as idolatrous and superstitious. However, we need to place them within their own historical context. Although they were critical and pessimistic about the pagan religions of their time, they were very positive towards the wisdom of Greek philosophy. The early church fathers recognized in the wisdom of the Greek philosophers reflections of the Logos or the Word of God. This idea is found in Justin, Clement of Alexandria and Origen, for example.

As we have seen, Joseph Ratzinger, steeped in patristic studies and influenced by the early fathers' teaching of the Logos, displays an open inclusivism regarding truth found in other religions. He acknowledges that there may be divine revelation in non-Christian religions, but insists that they are not vehicles of salvation. At the same time, giving precedence to Western thought, in his theology, makes him rather critical of theologies operating from a different intellectual framework. Ratzinger's inclusivist position on religious pluralism naturally reflects the official teaching of the Catholic Church and the ambiguity found in scripture. This brings us to his understanding of the church, which we will discuss next.

Chapter 3

Ecclesiology

The point of departure for Joseph Ratzinger's theology has always been ecclesiology. Most of his writings deal with ecclesiology in one way or another. In his doctoral dissertation, he began with an ecclesiological topic exploring the themes of the people and household of God in the writings of St Augustine of Hippo. Ratzinger's understanding of Christian anthropology, the relationship between nature and grace and his Bavarian background, with a strong sense of the church being at the heart of the community, shaped his understanding of ecclesiology. The Second Vatican Council's understanding of the church also affected Ratzinger's own ecclesiology both in the formative and reactive sense. Thus not only did Ratzinger have a significant impact on the Council's understanding of the church, he was also deeply influenced by it and continued to reflect and write on ecclesiological issues.[1]

This chapter attempts to examine Ratzinger's writings on the church, focusing on the Ratzinger-Kasper debate, to highlight an essential feature of Ratzinger's ecclesiology – the ontological and temporal priority of the universal church – and its significance. Ratzinger's understanding of the church can be described as 'ecclesiology from above' as opposed to 'ecclesiology from below'.[2] This chapter proposes to show that Ratzinger's ecclesiology is distinctly normative in character and thus he is reluctant to accept alternative ecclesiological paradigms. Steeped in biblical exegesis and patristic writings, Ratzinger seeks to correct what he perceives to be an erroneous interpretation of the Second Vatican Council regarding the nature of the church.

A number of documents from the Congregation for the Doctrine of the Faith (CDF), signed by Cardinal Ratzinger as prefect, show an attempt to declare as normative his particular ecclesiological vision. Motivated by his perception of how the church should respond to the social, cultural and intellectual challenges posed by contemporary society, his writings on ecclesiology reveal an apologetic stance. Believing that the church is not a human construction, but a gift from God, Ratzinger takes a negative view of pluralism and is bent on correcting theologians who present any different ecclesiology he thinks is a threat to the faith of ordinary believers. He takes a centrist approach to ecclesiology and believes that, 'All roads lead to Rome.'

This chapter concludes that Ratzinger's ecclesiological blueprint may not be adequate for the church to respond effectively to the challenges arising from the various forms of pluralism in our postmodern society. The church would be better served by being open to other ecclesiological visions, without losing sight of the authority of scripture and the traditions of the church.

In spite of criticism, the ecclesiology of Ratzinger has also been supported by many, including Maximilian Heinrich Heim, who has undertaken an important and detailed study on this subject in his book *Joseph Ratzinger: Life in the Church and Living Theology*. There are many educated Catholics who find great encouragement from Ratzinger's efforts to restore the church to its original mission in this turbulent time – 'a restoration of theological faithfulness and a vision for a renewed Christendom'. Ratzinger's vision of the church is seen as a renewal through both the mind and heart, as well as through various church movements.[3] He rightly believes that the church is in constant need of reform.

ECCLESIA SEMPER REFORMANDA

Joseph Ratzinger has frequently discussed his preference for a smaller and purer church, but critics claim that Ratzinger 'represents a backward-looking and intransigent form of ecclesiology that is exclusivistic and life-denying'.[4] This is not exactly a fair judgement because Ratzinger, like Augustine and Luther before him, maintains that the church needs constant renewal – *Ecclesia semper reformanda* – a sentiment also expressed by the Second Vatican Council. However, Ratzinger has his own view of renewal, and some would call it restoration.

Real reform, according to Ratzinger, is not about making structural changes to the church. It is about personal admission of sins and shortcomings. He reminds us that the church is not ours but Christ's. Hence, reform and renewal cannot be just efforts to erect new structures. Real reform means to reform ourselves as individuals. Ratzinger tells us that saints reformed the church in depth, not by grand plans, but by reforming themselves. What the church needs, he insists, is not management but holiness.[5]

Thus, for Ratzinger, renewal for the church means a new orientation to Christ who is its origin. Renewal is 'never a glorification or a new edition of the past in the sense of *restoration*'.[6] In his interview with Vittorio Messori, however, Ratzinger considered restoration desirable, 'if by *restoration* we understand the search for a new balance after all the exaggerations of an indiscriminate opening to the world, after the overly positive interpretations of an agnostic and atheistic world'.[7] Here, Ratzinger is critical of the erroneous interpretation of the Second Vatican Council which resulted in the indiscriminate opening to the values of the world.

ORIGIN OF THE CHURCH

Lumen Gentium, the Second Vatican Council's Dogmatic Constitution on the Church is, for Ratzinger, an important document for understanding the nature of the church. He believes this is not just a matter of ecclesiological theory, but a deep awareness of what the church is. He stresses that 'it is Christ, not the Church, that is the 'Light' of all peoples'. Thus, the church is only healthy to the extent that its attention is focused on Christ. The church is the organism of the Holy Spirit that 'makes the mystery of the Incarnation present in our lives'. Ratzinger stresses the importance of 'interiority' in the life of the faithful. This means that the church grows '"from within," from intimate communion with Christ, through faith, hope and love, as these are at work in the spiritual, and especially the sacramental, life'.[8]

Regarding a contemporary understanding of the church, Ratzinger criticizes the kind of liberalism that promotes a Marxist-oriented interpretation of the Bible. This reading includes the opposition between priests and prophets, which eventually comes to symbolize the class struggle. In this interpretation, Jesus is transformed into a symbol of the suffering proletariat. The eschatological character of the gospel points to a classless society and the 'Kingdom' now becomes the classless society. As a result, ecclesiology takes on a new meaning that fits neatly into the dialectical framework set up by the biblical division between priests and prophets.[9] This develops into the 'popular church' against the 'official church'. Jesus is identified with the popular church serving the Kingdom of God against institutions and their oppressive power.

Ratzinger regards this interpretation, not as a theology, but as an ideology that arose from a particular philosophy of a certain period.[10]

Alfred Loisy, for example, asserts that Jesus proclaimed the Kingdom of God, but what came was the church. Ratzinger rejects this liberal and social-ist interpretation that separates the Kingdom of God from the church. He insists that it was Jesus himself who gathered an eschatological community for that kingdom, which gave birth to the church. Thus, he reverses the dictum of Loisy by stating that 'the Kingdom was promised, what came was Jesus'.[11] Against a liberal and Marxist-oriented interpretation of the Bible, Ratzinger proposes to come to the truth by looking at 'the internal continuity of the Church's memory'. This means that through the church's sacramental life and in the proclamation of the Word, the church preserves the word and action of Jesus in its memory.[12]

Ratzinger admits that the church can be led more deeply into the truth and understand new dimensions of it, but he is reluctant to accept alterna-tive ecclesiological models that go against his own theological presuppositions. Ratzinger thinks that new interpretations can 'assail the identity of the Church's memory' and replace it with a new mode of thinking that is destructive to its nature. He thinks that it is necessary to remove the ideological elements from the dominant interpretation of a given period. The base memory of the church will be the standard for judging historical accuracy, by which Ratzinger means sticking to the biblical text, plus additional new experiences gained through time, as opposed to private opinion.[13]

Referring to the Gospels of John (11:52) and Matthew (12:30), Ratz-inger asserts that Jesus' mission is to gather new people. At this early stage, we see two elements that are important for understanding the church. Ratz-inger writes: 'First, the dynamism of unification, in which men draw together by moving toward God, is a component of the new people of God as Jesus intends it. Second, the point of convergence of this new people is Christ; it becomes a people solely through his call and its response to his call and to his person.'[14]

To be members of God's family, 'people must first lay down their grown-up autonomy and acknowledge themselves as children before God (cf. Mk 10:24; Mt 11:25)'.[15] This is because God is the father of his family and Jesus is the master of the house. The other observation that Ratzinger makes is the request for a special prayer, by the disciples, for the community. A special prayer is 'a badge of their community' and this request signifies the disciples' awareness of having become a community, with Jesus as its head. Ratzinger

regards this as the primitive cell of the church – 'a communion united principally on the basis of prayer'.[16]

Ratzinger traces the origin of the church's self-description as *ecclesia* to the
Old Testament. The Greek term *ecclesia* originates from the Old Testament
origin *qahal*, which means 'assembly of the people'. Such assemblies, in which
people organized themselves for cultic celebration and which served as legal
and political entities, existed in Greek and Jewish cultures.[17] In Greece, the
males decided and determined what was to be done in such a gathering, while
in the assembly of Israel, men and women, gathered 'to listen to what God
proclaims and to assent to it'. This biblical idea of popular assembly can be
traced to the 'convocation on Sinai' and was 're-enacted after the Exile by Ezra'.
A *qahal* coming from God became the centre for Jewish people. Consequently,
the nascent church, which traces its origin back to the Old Testament, regards
itself as *ecclesia*.[18]

Commenting on the Pauline doctrine of the church as the Body of Christ,
Ratzinger asserts that this conception does not exhaust itself in sociological
or philosophical interpretations. He insists that the roots of the Pauline idea
of the Body of Christ are entirely based on biblical tradition. First, there
is the Semitic idea of 'corporate personality' in which 'the "I" is constituted
in relation to the "thou" and the two mutually interpenetrate'.[19] The Pauline formulation has three additional roots: the eucharist, communion and
nuptiality.[20]

Time and again, Ratzinger stresses that the origin of the church is not a
human decision. The church is the fruit of the Holy Spirit that 'overcomes
the Babylonian world spirit'. While the human's 'will to power, symbolized in
Babel', aims at domination, subjection and uniformity, and sows hatred and
division, the Spirit of God is love because he brings about recognition, creates
unity and accepts the 'otherness of the other'. Hence, the many languages
become comprehensible.[21]

The image of Pentecost, found in the Acts of the Apostles, shows the
harmonious relationship between plurality and unity. Ratzinger explains that
in this sense the Holy Spirit is opposed to the spirit of the world. The spirit of
the world is one of domination, while that of the Holy Spirit is one of love.[22]
The church accepts many languages and cultures, and in faith, they understand and enrich one another; it exists in 'manifold and multiform particular Churches'. It is precisely in this way that the church is one. This means
that initially there exists one universal church that speaks in all tongues –
ecclesia universalis. This universal church later spreads to different localities,
but these particular churches still remain the 'embodiments of the one and

only Church': 'The temporal and ontological priority lies with the universal Church; a Church that was not catholic would not even have ecclesial reality.'[23] This particular view of Cardinal Ratzinger was contested by Cardinal Walter Kasper, as we shall see later.

In the Acts of the Apostles, Luke presents the 'path of the Gospel from the Jews to the Gentiles'. He depicts the fulfilment of the command of Jesus to be witnesses 'to the ends of the earth' (Acts 1:18). Ratzinger writes:

> Paul's arrival in Rome marks the goal of the path that began in Jerusalem; the universal – the catholic – Church has been realized, in continuance of the ancient chosen people and its history and taking over the latter's mission. Thus Rome, as a symbol for the world of all the nations, has a theological status in Acts; it cannot be separated from the Lukan idea of catholicity.[24]

Thus in Ratzinger's ecclesiological vision, all roads lead to Rome.

THE CHURCH IN CAPTIVITY

Fundamentally, Ratzinger's assessment of contemporary culture vis-à-vis the church is negative and pessimistic. He views the relationship between the church and the world as confrontational and this has been one of the most consistent themes in his writings. Related to this understanding of the ills and challenges of contemporary cultures is Ratzinger's idea of the church in a 'situation of Babylonian captivity' in the modern world. This is when mistrust and division rule and where people are divided into progressives and conservatives in a fragmented church. Ratzinger thinks that the church has been contaminated by cultural and intellectual novelty.[25] The fault lies in what he believes to be a wrong understanding of the Second Vatican Council or a misguided interpretation of the Council's texts:

> It would seem that in our efforts to understand the Church, efforts which at the Council finally developed into an active struggle for the Church, and into concrete work upon the Church, we have come so close to the Church that we can no longer see it as a whole: we cannot see the city for the houses, or the wood for the trees ... The perspective of the present day has distorted our view of the Church, so that in practice we see the Church only under the aspect of adaptability, in terms

of what can be made of it. Intensive efforts to reform the Church have caused everything else to be forgotten.[26]

For Ratzinger, the efforts to change the structure of the church have done more harm than good. He asserts that reform originally meant repentance, a spiritual transformation. A person becomes a Christian through repentance and this also applies to the church throughout history. The church is kept alive by fighting against ossification and comfortable lifestyles that go against the truth. Thus, reform cannot be disassociated from repentance. We cannot achieve salvation by changing others or accommodating the times. In spite of many 'useful innovations' since the Second Vatican Council, Ratzinger believes that the church has become 'a caricature of itself'. Too much emphasis on external features has reduced the church itself to a place of secondary importance.[27]

Ratzinger acknowledges that behind all these frantic efforts to change the machinery of the church lies the crisis of faith: '"The death of God" is a very real process, and today reaches right into the heart of the Church. It looks as if God were dying within Christianity. For where the resurrection becomes the experience of a message that is felt to be cast in out-of-date imagery, God ceases to be at work.' This means that the church was not originally designed to be an efficient machine, to 'provide a critique of society' or to initiate revolution.[28]

Thus, according to Ratzinger, the church is in 'Babylonian Captivity' because it has reduced all its theological attributes to an entirely political entity. It is no longer seen as a 'reality of faith', but as a human construction.[29] The scandals of history arose when human beings believed only in the achievements of power and failed to trust in the Holy Spirit. Ratzinger laments that the theology of the church has been influenced by sociological theory that is used to interpret ecclesial structure and the sacramental principle has been taken over by the democratic principle.[30]

As prefect of the CDF, Cardinal Ratzinger did all he could to rescue the church from captivity. He stressed that the church's true mission lay in the prayer life of the ordinary faithful and in a return to the fundamentals of faith. This also implies a renewed emphasis on the teaching authority of the church over all believers, including Catholic theologians, some of whom were suspected of promoting ideas that prolonged the 'Babylonian Captivity'.[31] These include new threats in the forms of religious pluralism and relativism. One of the first tasks of Ratzinger's effort to protect the church from erroneous teachings was to correct the misunderstanding of the expression, 'people of God', by criticizing the sociological and political aspects of this term.

THE CHURCH AS THE PEOPLE OF GOD

Joseph Ratzinger says the Second Vatican Council introduced the concept of the 'people of God' as an ecumenical bridge. The idea of reform became an important feature of this concept of church as people of God. There is also the idea that the church has not reached its final destination and its hope still lies ahead. Thus the 'eschatological' implication of the concept of church became clear. The phrase expresses the historical nature of the pilgrim church:

> the unity of the history of God with men, the inner unity of the People of God that transcends the boundaries even of the sacramental states of life, the eschatological dynamic, the provisional nature and broken-ness of the Church, which is always in need of renewal, and finally the ecumenical dimension as well, that is, the various ways in which being joined and related to the Church are possible and real, even beyond the confines of the Catholic Church.[32]

Ratzinger admits that the expression people of God does occur in the New Testament frequently, but only in a few passages does it refer to the church, and when it does designate the church, it also refers to the people of Israel. Thus, according to Ratzinger, people of God does not refer to the church in the New Testament. Only in the 'christological reinterpretation of the Old Testament' can it refer to the church. As we have seen, the normal term for the church in the New Testament is *ecclesia*, which in the Old Testament means assembly of the people to hear the word of God. The word ecclesial-church is also the New Testament 'variation on and transformation of the Old Testa-ment "People of God" concept'. It implies the notion that only a new birth in Christ can create a new community.[33]

The expression people of God is not an empirical concept because we cannot regard God as our ancestor, for that would be blasphemy. Ratzinger argues that we become people of God, only by 'incorporation into Christ' – 'Christology must remain the centre of the teaching about the Church'. At the same time, the church is thought of in terms of the sacraments of baptism, Eucharist and holy orders. In short, the church is a sacrament and we are the people of God only by virtue of the crucified and risen Christ.[34] Thus, the concept of the church as people of God conveys the historical nature of the church, the unity of God's people and the eschatological dimension. It conveys the provisional and fragmentary nature of the church, ever in need of renewal. It also expresses the ecumenical dimension in which communion in the church can exist beyond the boundaries of the Catholic Church.[35] This concept can also lead to a dangerous interpretation, Ratzinger warns:

> commentators very soon completely handed the term 'people' in the concept 'People of God' to a general political interpretation. Among the proponents of liberation theology it was taken to mean 'people' in the Marxist sense, in opposition to the ruling classes, or more generally, it was taken to refer to popular sovereignty at long last being applied to the Church.[36]

This led to the debate on church structures and the expression people of God came to mean democratization, in the Western sense. Ratzinger opposes politicizing a concept that had come from an entirely different context. He argues that the expression people of God implies a relationship with God. It is therefore a 'vertical relationship'. The crisis in the church is reflected in this expression. It is a 'crisis of God' because we have abandoned the essentials. Thus, all that is left is a struggle for power that is prevalent in the world.[37]

Not only does Ratzinger seek to correct a wrong interpretation of the Council's ecclesiological vision, he also wants to stress the Second Vatican Council's conception of local churches. In his ecclesiology, Ratzinger moves from an emphasis on the church as the mystical body of Christ to the church as the sacrament of salvation. This leads to an understanding of the importance of the Eucharist as the foundation of the church.

EUCHARISTIC ECCLESIOLOGY

Joseph Ratzinger has said:

> that the separation of the doctrine of the eucharist and ecclesiology, which can be noted from the eleventh and twelfth centuries onwards, represents one of the most unfortunate pages of medieval theology … because both thereby lost their centre. A doctrine of the eucharist that is not related to the community of the Church misses its essence as does an ecclesiology that is not conceived with the eucharist as its centre.[38]

He teaches that the institution of the Eucharist is the 'making of a covenant' and thus it is the 'concrete foundation of the new people'. This means that the people come into being through the Eucharist's covenantal relationship with

God. Jesus brings his disciples into his communion with God and also into his mission, to draw all people, at all times and places, to himself. These followers of Christ become a 'people' through communion in the Eucharist.[39]

The Old Testament theme of covenant is appropriated by Jesus and receives a new meaning – 'communion with Christ's Body'. Thus, the church, the people of the new covenant, takes its origin from the Eucharist. As mentioned earlier, Ratzinger says the church is regarded as the people of God, only through its communion with Christ. It is only this relationship with Christ that allows men and women to gain access to God. Ratzinger writes:

> the Eucharist, seen as the permanent origin and centre of the Church, joins all the 'many', who are now made a people, to the one Lord and to his one and only Body. The fact already implies that the Church and her unity are but one. It is true that the many celebrations in which the one Eucharist will be realized also point ahead to the multiformity of the one Body. Nevertheless, it is clear that these many celebrations cannot stand side by side as autonomous, mutually independent entities but are always simply the presence of one and the same mystery.[40]

Influenced by Henri de Lubac, Ratzinger asserts that the church as the mystical body of Christ refers to the Eucharist. St Paul and the early fathers also connected the idea of the church with the Eucharist. Eucharistic ecclesiology implies that Jesus' Last Supper is the event that founded the church:

> the Eucharist joins human beings together, not only with one another, but also with Christ, and that in this way it makes people into the Church. At the same time this already determines the fundamental constitution of the Church: Church lives in eucharistic communities. Her worship service is her constitution, for by her very nature she is service of God and therefore service of men, the service that transforms the world.[41]

The Mass is the church's form through which it develops the new relationship of multiplicity and unity. This means that the ecclesiology of local churches has its origin in the formulation of the Eucharistic ecclesiology.[42] Thus, we see Ratzinger's ecclesiology seeking to clarify the role of local churches through an understanding of the church as a sacrament of salvation and the Eucharist as the foundation of the church. Aidan Nichols sums up the significance of Eucharistic ecclesiology when he writes:

The value of a eucharistic ecclesiology is that it derives the ministerial, and therefore governmental, structure of the Church from the pattern of her eucharistic life and in so doing suggests how we should understand the relation of the local church, which celebrates the Eucharist in a particular place, to the universal Church, the *Catholica*. The Eucharist is always celebrated by a particular group, yet that which is so celebrated is, in fact, the Eucharist of the whole Church. The local church, therefore, manifests the plenitude of the Church – yet only in the measure of its communion with all the other churches.[43]

Ratzinger again emphasizes that the church is not a human construction. We can only receive the church from where it is really present: 'from the sacramental communion of his Body as it makes its way through history'.[44] This leads to his preference for an ecclesiology of *communio*.

ECCLESIOLOGY OF COMMUNION[45]

Joseph Ratzinger teaches that the concept of communion lies 'at the heart of the Church's self-understanding'. This implies the union of each person with the Trinity and with the rest of humanity. Rooted in faith and begun as a reality in the church on earth, it is 'directed towards its eschatological fulfillment in the heavenly Church'.[46] This concept of communion must be understood in the biblical sense and in the biblical context, communion has theological, Christological, soteriological and ecclesiological characteristics.[47]

There is also this sacramental dimension as acknowledged by St Paul: 'The cup of blessing which we bless, is it not a communion in the blood of Christ? The bread which we break, is it not a communion in the body of Christ? Because there is one bread, we who are many are one body ...' (1 Corinthians 10:16–17). Thus, the ecclesiology of communion forms the basis for Eucharistic ecclesiology. Ratzinger writes:

In the Eucharist, Christ, present in the bread and wine and giving Himself anew, builds the Church as His Body and through His Risen Body He unites us to the one and triune God and to each other. The Eucharist celebrated in different places is universal at the same time, because there is only one Christ and only a single body of Christ. The Eucharist comprehends the priestly service of 'repraesentatio Christi' as well as that network of service, the synthesis of unity and multiplicity which is expressed in the term 'communio'.[48]

Communion has two dimensions: the vertical that is communion with God and the horizontal that is communion with one another. Christians must understand that communion is a gift from God given to us through the paschal mystery. Ecclesial communion is both invisible and visible. The invisible reality refers to our communion with the Father, through Christ, in the Holy Spirit. The visible reality is our communion with one another, as sharers in the divine nature, in the passion of Christ and in the same faith. In the church on earth, there is this close relationship between the invisible and visible aspects of communion. The link between these two dimensions of communion, invisible and visible, 'constitutes the Church as the *Sacrament* of salvation'. From this sacramentality, Ratzinger argues, the church is open to missionary and ecumenical work. It is sent out to the world to realize the mystery of communion which is essential to its nature: 'to gather together all people and all things into Christ; so as to be for all an *"inseparable sacrament of unity"*'.[49]

Another important point that Ratzinger makes is the idea that the church is a communion of saints. This communion fosters unity among the members of the church when they are members of one body. The invisible element means that communion exists not only among those still living, but also among those who have died in Christ, in the hope of rising again. Ratzinger writes:

that there is a *mutual relationship* between the pilgrim Church on earth and the heavenly Church in the historical-redemptive mission. Hence the ecclesiological importance not only of Christ's intercession on behalf of his members, but also of that of the saints and, in an eminent fashion, of the Blessed Virgin Mary's. *Devotion to the saints*, which is such a strong feature of the piety of the Christian people, can thus be seen to correspond in its very essence to the profound reality of the Church as a mystery of communion.[50]

Ratzinger's understanding of communion became the official ecclesiology when he was prefect of the Congregation for the Doctrine of the Faith. Meanwhile, the word 'communion' was interpreted differently by different people. Ratzinger says that like the expression people of God, the word 'communion' became a slogan, its meaning distorted and devalued when people only emphasized the horizontal aspect and abandoned the vertical dimension. In this case the ecclesiology of communion was reduced to a concern with relations between the local churches and the universal church. The egalitarian emphasis on equality in communion was gaining popularity. In 'Eucharist, Communion and Solidarity', Ratzinger expressed his concern clearly:

> It was unavoidable that this great fundamental word of the New Testament, isolated and employed as a slogan, would also suffer diminishment, indeed, might even be trivialized. Those who speak today of an 'ecclesiology of communion' generally tend to mean two things: (1) they support a 'pluralist' ecclesiology, almost a 'federative' sense of union, opposing what they see as a centralist conception of the Church; (2) they want to stress, in the exchanges of giving and receiving among local Churches, their culturally pluralistic forms of worship in the liturgy, in discipline and in doctrine.[51]

In this erroneous understanding, according to Ratzinger, communion is seen as 'emerging from a network of multiple communities'. He is opposed to the horizontal idea of communion, with its emphasis on the idea of 'self-determination within a vast community of churches', that dominates the thinking of the church.[52] Ratzinger admits the need to correct the imbalance and excessiveness of Roman centralization, but he also reminds us that questions of this sort should not distract us from the main task of proclaiming Christ to the world. He rightly asserts that the church should not be proclaiming itself but God.[53]

At the same time, Ratzinger insists that communion is related to the universal church, with its ecclesial hierarchy and papal primacy. Thus, there are criteria to be met by Christian communities in order to be qualified as a 'valid church'. These criteria centre on the requirements of 'valid ministerial orders, including a valid episcopate, and the celebration of a valid Eucharist'. Above all, for Ratzinger, communion with Rome is an important prerequisite.[54] It is no surprise that he insists on the ontological priority of the universal church.

Joseph Ratzinger was highly criticized for his assertion concerning the priority of the universal church: 'The universal Church in her essential mystery is a reality that ontologically and temporally is prior to every particular Church.' He replies to the criticism by saying that 'the ontological priority of the universal Church—the unique Church, the unique Body, the unique Bride—vis-à-vis the empirical, concrete manifestations of various, particular Churches is so obvious to me that I find it difficult to understand the objections raised against it'.[55] Those objections are possible only if we look at the church with its shortcomings and not as something willed by God. For Ratzinger, these oppositions are 'theological ravings' by people who see the church only as a human institution. He sarcastically remarks that nowadays, any theologian concerned about his reputation feels the need to criticize all documents from the CDF. Thus, 'in this case one has abandoned not only the ecclesiology of the Fathers, but the ecclesiology of the New Testament and the understanding of Israel in the Old Testament as well. It is not just the later deutero-Pauline letters and the Apocalypse that affirm the ontological priority of the universal Church to the particular Churches.'[56] We will now examine in greater detail this contentious issue which involves Ratzinger's highly publicized debate with Cardinal Walter Kasper.

THE PRIORITY OF THE UNIVERSAL CHURCH

When the ecclesiological concept of communion is applied analogously to the relationship between the universal church and particular churches, Ratzinger strongly asserts the priority of the universal church. He dismisses the idea that the particular church is a subject complete in itself. According to Ratzinger:

> In order to grasp the true meaning of the analogical application of the term *communion* to the particular Churches taken as a whole, one must bear in mind above all that the particular Churches, insofar as they are *'part of the one Church of Christ,'* have a special relationship of *'mutual interiority'* with the whole, that is, with the universal Church, because in every particular Church *'the one, holy, catholic and apostolic Church of Christ is truly present and active.'*[57]

Consequently, Ratzinger insists that the universal church is not merely the sum of all the particular churches or a federation of churches. It is also not the result of the communion of all the churches, but 'it is a reality *ontologically and temporally* prior to every *individual* particular Church'. The universal church is the mother and not the offspring of the particular churches.[58]

In its original and first manifestation, the church is universal. The local churches that have arisen in different places are particular expressions of the one unique Church of Jesus Christ. 'Arising *within* and *out of* the universal Church, they have their ecclesiality in it and from it.'[59] Ratzinger argues that the relationship between the universal church and the particular churches is a mystery and cannot be compared to any human organization. We become members of the one, holy, catholic and apostolic church through faith and baptism. However we 'do not belong to the universal Church in a *mediate way*, *through* belonging to a particular church'. Instead, we belong to the universal church in an '*immediate way*' although we enter it through a particular church. Ratzinger says 'from the point of view of the Church understood as communion, this means therefore that the universal *communion of the faithful* and the *communion of the Churches* are not consequences of one another, but constitute the same reality seen from different viewpoints'.[60] This means that when one becomes a Catholic through a particular church, one automatically belongs to the one, holy, catholic and apostolic church.

THE RATZINGER–KASPER DEBATE

Joseph Ratzinger's strong assertion of the priority of the universal church led to a prolonged debate between him and Cardinal Walter Kasper. In a series of exchanges, Kasper accuses Ratzinger of reversing the traditional order of priority. This is because 'the local church is neither a province nor a department of the universal church; it is the church at a given place'.[61] Kasper says he has reached this position regarding the relationship between the universal church and particular local churches through his pastoral experience. He analyses the question in terms of praxis and not doctrine.[62] Kasper accuses Ratzinger of approaching the problem from a purely abstract and theoretical point of view, without taking into consideration the actual pastoral situations.

Walter Kasper is particularly against the assertion of Ratzinger that: 'in its essential mystery, the universal church is a reality ontologically and temporally prior to every individual church'.[63] He contends that the Congregation for the Doctrine of the Faith identifies the one, holy, catholic and apostolic church with the universal church in a way that excludes the particular churches. Another serious problem with Ratzinger's assertion of the ontological and temporal priority of the universal church is the unspoken assumption that 'the Roman church is *de facto* identified with the pope and the curia'.[64]

Unlike Ratzinger, Kasper believes that the problem of the relationship between the universal church and the local churches cannot be approached by theoretical deduction because the church is a concrete reality. Like Ratzinger, he starts off with scripture, but arrives at a different conclusion. Kasper writes:

In the letters of Paul, the local church is clearly and firmly at the center. When in his principal letters Paul uses the word 'church' (*ecclesia*) in the singular, he refers to a particular church or to a given community. When he speaks of 'churches' in the plural, he refers to several local assemblies. For Paul, the one church of God comes to life in each local church. Thus there is the church of God in Corinth and so forth. The church of God is present in each of them. In the captivity letters (which in the opinion of many scholars are not by Paul), this meaning of *ecclesia* recedes into the background and the universal church as a whole comes into focus.[65]

Likewise, Kasper also asserts that in the Gospel of Luke, the word *ecclesia* refers to a domestic and local community. The early church was developed from local communities, presided over by a bishop; 'the one church was present in each and all, they were all in communion'. Kasper acknowledges that the See of Rome, 'presiding in charity', was the guiding and leading authority in determining orthodoxy. For the Eastern Church, this authority of Rome did not include jurisdictional power.[66] Thus Kasper concludes that the ecclesiology of the first millennium neither stressed the primacy of the universal church nor the local churches.

Kasper argues that the CDF document, 'On Some Aspects of the Church Understood as Communion', signed by Cardinal Ratzinger, 'went beyond the limits of the council's doctrine, which is that the universal church exists "in and from" the local churches. The Congregation asserted that the local churches exist "in and from" the universal church.'[67] Kasper thinks that Ratzinger's doctrine of the primacy of the universal church is based on a highly questionable understanding of the Pentecostal event in the Acts of the Apostles. This is because the Pentecostal event does not refer to the universal church, but to the gathering of the Jewish people living outside Israel, which will eventually become a church of all nations, through the guidance of the Holy Spirit.[68]

Ratzinger finds support for his understanding of the ontological primacy of the universal church in a theory about the pre-existence of the church in the words of Paul who speaks about the heavenly Jerusalem (Hebrews 12:22 ff.). Kasper admits that this was a widespread opinion held by the early fathers and evident in the Jewish Torah as well as in Platonic philosophy. Although the pre-existence of the church is an important theological doctrine for a correct understanding of ecclesiology, Kasper insists that it is not an argument to support the ontological primacy of the universal church.[69]

Kasper claims that the Pauline texts about the pre-existence of the church do not support the idea of the primacy of the universal church, but they do support his argument, and that of many others as well, of the simultaneous pre-existence of the universal church and the particular churches. This is because the pre-existent church exists in and from the particular churches. Quoting Henri de Lubac, Kasper says that the universal church cannot have a separate existence, or even exist, outside the particular churches: 'God does not love empty abstractions. He loves concrete human beings of flesh and blood. God's eternal saving will intended the incarnation of the Logos in view of the concrete church composed of people of flesh and blood.'[70]

Kasper also admits that this debate about the primacy of the churches is not a contest over Catholic doctrine, but it is a conflict between theological opinions and underlying philosophical assumptions. Influenced by Bonaventure, Ratzinger proceeds from Plato's teaching on the primacy of ideas as a universal concept. Kasper, more of a Thomist, follows Aristotle's approach and looks upon the universal as existing in a particular concrete reality.[71] Both the Platonic and Aristotelian schools were accepted as part of the Catholic tradition. Bonaventure and Thomas Aquinas were respected as doctors of the church and venerated as saints. If such pluralism and diversity were accepted in the Middle Ages, Kasper argues, Ratzinger should be more flexible in accepting differences of opinion.[72]

The motive behind Kasper's objection to the ontological and temporal priority of the universal church, Ratzinger believes, is related to Roman centralism and the role of bishops. He insists that the CDF never dreamed of identifying the universal church with the pope and the Roman curia. Thus, the fear of Roman centralism is unfounded. In response to this 'attack', Ratzinger writes:

> The church of Rome is a local church and not the universal church—
> a local church with a peculiar, universal responsibility, but still a local
> church. And the assertion of the inner precedence of God's idea of the
> one church, the one bride, over all its empirical realizations in particular
> churches has nothing whatsoever to do with the problem of centralism.[73]

This means, according to Ratzinger, that the identification of the ontological priority of the universal church with the pope and the curia makes no sense because ontological priority is only an expression of the 'inner priority of unity' of the church. It has nothing to do with Roman centralism.

Kasper admits that the transformation of Ratzinger's thesis of the ontological priority of the universal church into 'the priority of inner unity' can be accommodated in both Platonic and Aristotelian paradigms. Kasper writes: 'The fact that unity as a transcendental determination of being makes variety and multiplicity possible to begin with is a fundamental insight of both Platonic and Aristotelian–Thomistic metaphysics, which thereby stand in opposition to the postmodern principle of absolute pluralism.'[74]

Both theologians agree that the one Church of Jesus Christ exists 'in and from' the local church and the local churches exist 'in and from' the universal church.[75] Kasper is concerned that Ratzinger's universal church is just an abstraction without any historical foundation. Ratzinger thinks that Kasper's ecclesiology reduces the church to a sociological entity, a church without depth. Ratzinger insists on a sequence: the universal church comes first, then the local church. But Kasper argues that one does not step out of the local church into the universal church (or vice versa): 'Because of simultaneity and perichoresis, one is already in the universal Church when one is in local church.'[76] Thus Kasper denies the ontological priority of the universal church.

The debate took place when Walter Kasper was secretary and later president of the Pontifical Council for Promoting Christian Unity. During this period, Joseph Ratzinger was prefect of the Congregation for the Doctrine of the Faith. Their theological positions can be understood as reflecting their ecclesial functions: Kasper is concerned with ecumenism and Ratzinger is concerned with the doctrine of the faith. Nonetheless, the debate between these two distinguished German theologians highlights ecclesiological complexities and tensions. It is clear that Ratzinger's theological approach is to strengthen the unity or universality of the church, which he thinks is threatened by pluralism. As prefect of the CDF, his preferred ecclesiological model became normative and binding on all Catholics, including theologians.

Ratzinger has the tendency to label theological positions which differ from his as ideologies or slogans. He unfairly associates Kasper with the 'sociological reductionism' and 'ecclesiological relativism' of Leonardo Boff's theology.[77] Many question the propriety of Ratzinger comparing Kasper's ecclesiology with Boff's understanding of the church. Boff and Kasper inhabit different ecclesiological planets.[78] Kasper's ecclesiology goes beyond sociological–empirical reductionism. A criticism like that coming from Cardinal Ratzinger as prefect of the CDF is not only inappropriate, but reveals his reluctance to accept ideas from a different theological framework, even if they come from no less a theologian than Cardinal Walter Kasper.

MANICHEAN INFLUENCE

Critics are concerned that the church has become increasingly reactionary in recent years and that Ratzinger's ecclesiological outlook 'fosters an exclusivistic mentality' in the church. It is an ecclesiology that perceives the church as a separate entity vis-à-vis the world. It is a church that has to fight against the corrupting influences of the present time.[79] In this regard, Eamon Duffy describes Ratzinger's view of the church–world relationship as Manichean in outlook, 'the lurid and simplistic world of easy dualisms'. Ratzinger sees, in the atheistic culture of Western contemporary society 'signs of the return of dark forces' in the form of the 'liberal–radical ideology'.[80] Since the 1960s, there has existed a 'scandalous optimism', an 'uncritical openness to the world', which Ratzinger believes must be abandoned.[81] Duffy asserts that this kind of worldview ignores the experience of the Pauline communities and all Christian communities, who understand the church as a place where 'sin, error and sheer human cussedness co-exist alongside grace and truth'.[82]

Duffy insists that there cannot be the 'sort of simple church/world dualism' that Ratzinger perceives because the 'Church *is* the world'. All the church's thinking and its institutions are conditioned by the secular world and are thereby 'implicated in the relativism and imperfection of the created order'. The authoritarian and hierarchical model of the church favoured by Ratzinger did not descend from heaven but is shaped by social, cultural and political forces, derived from the Roman imperial government. These influences are still prevalent in the church. Duffy claims that 'even the most unequivocally spiritual concerns and activities of the Church are rooted in worldly paradigms'.[83] Duffy also argues that Ratzinger's rejection of liberal modernity in Catholicism 'is not the rejection of the "world" by the Church, but the repudiation of one form of "worldliness" in favour of another. Ascetic, aristocratic, authoritarian, corporatist, over against liberal, democratic, bourgeois, individualistic'. Duffy cautions us against accepting Ratzinger's deification of one polarity and demonizing of the other.[84] The authoritarian and hierarchical model of the church fits well with what Roger Haight describes as 'ecclesiology from above' in contrast to 'ecclesiology from below'.

ECCLESIOLOGY FROM ABOVE

Roger Haight's analysis of 'ecclesiology from above' offers an accurate description of Ratzinger's understanding of the nature of the church. This ecclesiological, ideal type is characterized by the attempt to define 'the essential nature and structure of the church that transcends any given context'. It is an 'a-historical' view of the church in which its essence 'is determined by those constitutive elements that transcend its particular instantiations, and these can be grasped precisely by abstracting from those individualizing particulars which characterize the church wherever it is, but are precisely not of its defining substance'. This method tends towards exclusivism because in defining the church, it sets forth 'the limits or frontiers beyond which is non-church or a defective embodiment of it'.[85]

An ecclesiology from above is one that looks upon the authority of the magisterium, tradition and scripture as absolute. Haight argues that such ecclesiology 'presupposes the intelligibility of the doctrinal language about the church, and it appeals to its normative character'.[86] This kind of ecclesiological vision tends to see the church standing against the world. Haight says: 'in contrast to the world in its secularity, the church defines the sphere of the sacred ... Implicitly, the church represented a social reality that was in some measure set apart from the world, usually in some sense "above" it'.[87]

In ecclesiology from above, the development of the church is based on a doctrinal account of history that is different from critical history: 'God's providence in history led to the church; God more or less "directly" founds the church in the work of Jesus Christ; and God as Spirit animates and directs the development of the church from its beginning at Pentecost'.[88] Haight's account of ecclesiology from above is clearly reflected in Joseph Ratzinger's writings on the church. Ratzinger's understanding of the church means that it is beyond criticism and thus, it takes on a special authority in its own right.

Another feature of ecclesiology from above is its 'christocentrism'. In Haight's view, 'this means that the church, even when it is not considered constitutive of the salvation of all, is the summit of all religious forms, and the single, normative religion that is superior to all others because the church is constituted by Christ as its center. In short, in an ecclesiology from above, christocentrism has a tendency to become ecclesiocentrism'.[89] The final aspect of Haight's description of ecclesiology from above is the hierarchical structuring and ordering of the church itself: 'the levels of power and authority have their foundation in God, and they descend'.[90]

Ecclesiology from above is similar to what Nicholas Healy calls 'blueprint ecclesiologies'. Healy says, 'Ecclesiology is not about the business of finding the single right way to think about the church, of developing a blueprint suitable for all times and places. Rather, I propose that its function is to aid the concrete church in performing its task of witness and pastoral care within what I will call its "ecclesiological context"'.[91] Ratzinger, however, believes there is a blueprint that is universal and timeless for the church to build on. Unfortunately, he writes: 'the Church of the post-conciliar period is a huge construction site ... where the blueprint had been lost and everyone continues to build according to his taste. The result is evident'.[92]

The late Cardinal Carlo Martini had 'painfully witnessed, in the last two decades of the twentieth century, the triumph of universalistic ecclesiologies (endorsed by Pope Benedict) that have barred the ways towards real collegiality and reduced the authority of the episcopal conferences. The tragedy of unfit bishops that mishandled the clergy sex-abuse crisis was a severe punishment for that.'[93] In his last interview, Martini lamented that 'the Church is 200 years behind the times.'[94] In contrast to ecclesiology from above, 'ecclesiology from below' provides a good balance to complement the 'merely theological' ecclesiology favoured by Joseph Ratzinger.

ECCLESIOLOGY FROM BELOW

Ecclesiology from below refers to a method in which one examines the church from its 'concrete, existential and historical' perspectives.[95] It takes a 'genetic approach' in the sense that it is attentive to the church's origin as a historical organization. By applying the tools of social and historical analysis to examine the nature of the church, it acknowledges that the church is an organization susceptible to social forces from within and without. To understand the full reality of the church, it is therefore crucial to understand the social and historical situations.[96] Despite the use of social-historical analysis, Haight insists that ecclesiology from below is still a theological discipline and therefore, 'it cannot be reduced to conclusions that can be generated by history or sociology alone'. At the same time, it is also important to understand how the historical and social aspects of the church relate to its theological dimensions. Haight claims that 'this church is experienced religiously or theologically, because in it and through it people recognize the presence and activity of God'. Likewise, 'when symbols pointing and referring to God are used to illumine the full reality of what is going on in the existence of church, a theological imagination and judgment are at work'. Thus, theological judgements include the fact that God, as Spirit, is active and at work in the church, and Christ is present in the preaching of the Word and in the sacraments.[97]

As this ecclesiology from below emphasizes the concrete realities of culture, the conditions of the poor and interreligious dialogue, it is more suited for meeting the challenges of postmodern society. Characterized by its historical consciousness, an awareness of globalization and appreciation of pluralism, such an understanding of the church embraces the reality and value of other churches and religions. It is more attentive to human suffering, the plight of women, secularization and individualism, all of which result in a decreased participation in the life of the church.[98] Wary of 'theological reductionism', ecclesiology from below avoids 'the exclusive use of biblical and doctrinal language in the interpretation of the Church' but emphasizes the church as an interdependent 'empirical, human, and historical community'.[99]

Haight also believes that 'a pneumatocentric church adhering to Jesus Christ as its norm opens up to a good deal of pluralism'.[100] In other words, a Spirit-centred ecclesiology allows recognition of legitimate pluralism in church teaching and structures. In addition, as the Spirit 'blows where it wills' (John 3:8), free from all constraints, it is present and active throughout human history.[101] We contend, with such a delineation, that an ecclesiology from below suits the Asian churches better than the top-down approach discussed earlier.

ECCLESIOLOGICAL REVOLUTION

Moving away from the speculative debate on the nature of the church, Aloysius Pieris calls for an ecclesiological revolution. He says: 'there is no church that is not local'. However, this does not mean that 'all local churches *in* Asia are necessarily local churches *of* Asia!' [102] What Pieris means is that our local churches are actually institutions, imported from another continent, struggling for centuries, without much success, to adapt themselves to the local culture. They are actually Asian branches of local churches from Rome, Canterbury, and so on.

To evangelize Asia, Pieris insists that local churches *in* Asia must become local churches *of* Asia. He has observed that a local church *in* Asia is usually a wealthy church working *for* the poor. But to become a local church *of* Asia, the church could only be a poor church working *with* the poor. In order to become local, the church must first be evangelized to become good news to Asians. This also means that the local churches *of* Asia must work with other great religions, not as competitors but as collaborators.[103]

Pieris argues that the 'local church's mission to the poor of Asia is total identification ... with the monks and peasants', who have kept for us 'in their *religious socialism*, the seeds of liberation that *religion* and *poverty* have combined to produce'. The local church must 'remove the cross from the steeples where it has stood for four centuries and plant it once more on Calvary'.[104] This means that the church must come down from its pedestal and be planted in the midst of the suffering people. Pieris also asserts that 'the local church *in* Asia needs yet to be "initiated" into the pre-Christian traditions under the tutelage of our ancient gurus, or it will continue to be an ecclesiastical complex full of "power" but lacking in "authority"'.[105] Thus, the church should listen and learn from other ancient religions and also from the poor of Asia.

NOT A ONE-WAY STREET

The communion ecclesiology of Joseph Ratzinger, with its 'top down' approach, has greatly influenced Catholic teaching and policy.[106] This kind of ecclesiology is a reaction against liberalism, various forms of pluralism and relativism, which Ratzinger perceives as threats to the church. Quoting Christopher Duraisingh, Gerard Mannion states: 'Forms of pluralism are seen as dangerous to the very identity and integrity of the church; therefore, greater and centralized teaching authority and clearer and uniform formulations of truth are seen by some as urgent for the very survival of the church.'[107] However, a rigid, official, ecclesiological model is not adequate enough for the church to respond to the challenges of the postmodern world.[108] Without altogether discarding this curial ecclesiology, the church would be better served by taking into consideration an ecclesiology from below. Such an ecclesiological paradigm as described by Roger Haight is reflected in the writings of Aloysius Pieris, Leonardo Boff, Edward Schillebeeckx, Peter Phan and Jacques Dupuis, among others. As we have seen, such an ecclesiology is more responsive to the challenges posed by pluralism and globalization.

Ratzinger may think that all roads lead to Rome but other theologians believe that the Asian churches do have something important to teach the Church of Rome and the church universal. It is not a one-way street from Rome to the other local churches. There should be mutual learning and teaching between the Church of Rome and the other local churches. Thus, there should also be mutual correction and encouragement among all the local churches, including the Church of Rome. Only in this way can we dispel the widespread misconception in some countries, such as China, that the Christian church in Asia is a foreign enterprise that takes orders from a foreign power, just as they did in the days of colonialism and imperialism.

In this chapter, we have discussed Ratzinger's writings on ecclesiology, his thought on the ontological priority of the universal church over local churches, which has deep implications for the Catholic Church's relationship with the other Christian churches and the effort to achieve unity. Instead of taking a critical stance towards our separated brethren and regarding them as dissenters, we need to adopt an ecclesiology that allows us to work closely with the other Christian communities in the building of God's Kingdom. The focus of the next chapter will be on Ratzinger's understanding of other Christian communities.

Chapter 4

Ecumenism

Joseph Ratzinger's theological approach to ecumenism is closely tied to his fundamental ecclesiology, which we have examined in the previous chapter, and the developments in the church since the Second Vatican Council. In his writings on Christian unity, Ratzinger has maintained a certain consistency in his attitude towards other churches: that the Catholic faith is superior to other paths. Explicitly or implicitly, he has always held that the way towards the fullness of salvation is to be found only in the Roman Catholic Church.[1] For Ratzinger, the ultimate aim of Catholic ecumenical endeavour is the transformation of the separated Christian churches into authentic, particular churches in communion with Rome.

In ecumenical endeavours, while he was still prefect of the Congregation for the Doctrine of the Faith, Joseph Cardinal Ratzinger's preference was for a slow, 'realistic and theologically attentive, approach'. As a result, he was very critical of shortcuts towards unity. In recent years, Ratzinger has been frequently associated with an 'ecumenical winter'.[2] Critical of the various approaches to ecumenism that relied on sociological or political models, Ratzinger believed it was unlikely that full Christian unity would happen in the near future. However, as Pope Benedict XVI, he confirmed his commitment to Christian unity as a priority in his pontificate.

Ratzinger's understanding of ecumenism is based on his insistence on the priority of Logos over ethos and the priority of the universal church over particular churches, and it is conditioned by his critical attitudes towards pluralism and relativism. His approach to Christian ecumenism is also influenced by his concern over the decline of Christianity in Europe. However, as we shall see, the situation in Asia is different in many ways.

This chapter seeks to review Joseph Ratzinger's writings on the ecumenical situation, focusing on the Anglican and Orthodox Churches. It proposes a practical and broader approach to ecumenism in view of the fact that Christianity is a minority religion, existing among ancient and diverse religious traditions in the Asian continent. Pastoral involvement in the lives of the faithful is particularly urgent in Asia where the majority of people live in poverty and lack the basic necessities of life. While agreeing with Ratzinger that ethos without Logos cannot endure, ecumenical efforts must not be too dogmatic and abstract, but must be directed to the welfare of people. We will first examine Ratzinger's negative assessment of the ecumenical situation and the various ecumenical paradigms that have been adopted.

ECUMENISM FROM BELOW

The positive feeling about ecumenical effort, generated by the Second Vatican Council, did not last long once its resultant initiatives had been translated into official forms. Ratzinger thus remarks that 'very soon after the initial conciliar enthusiasm had waned, the alternative model of "grass-roots ecumenism" cropped up, which tried to bring about unity "from below" if it could not be obtained "from above".[3] This kind of approach had the unfortunate consequence of splitting the church into 'grass-roots church' and 'official church'. Ratzinger claims that in spite of its popularity, 'grass-roots ecumenism' eventually divides congregations. This kind of politically motivated ecumenical activity that seeks to replace traditional ecclesiastical divisions with progressive Christianity would only contribute to more divisions and splinter groups, each recruiting members for its own party.[4]

This 'grass-roots ecumenism' or 'ecumenism from below' believes that authorities should be left out of ecumenical activity because eventual reunion of churches would only strengthen the hierarchy's traditional position, and thus stop the development of the popular church.[5] Ratzinger is critical of such an approach because it seeks to bypass the ordained leadership and appeal directly to the laity. Besides, the church authorities would be forced to accommodate the wishes of the people. There is also the danger that the hierarchy and the faithful would be divided, and thus ecumenism from below would violate the notion of communion.

Ecumenism from below also has the tendency to focus on praxis at the expense of doctrine. Ratzinger believes that a Christianity that defines itself in terms of social involvement is not able to produce long-term unity and an established church life. People remain in the church, not because of social or political commitment, but because they think that the church can give answers about the meaning of life here and about the hereafter. Ratzinger argues that 'religion still enters into people's lives, especially when the things that neither they nor anyone else can control intrude on their lives, and then the only thing that can help is an answer that comes from the One who is himself beyond us'.[6] This means that neither the popular church nor the official church, acting in isolation, can bring about effective ecumenical action.

Furthermore, Ratzinger does not believe that the ecumenical unity of the church can be built on a sociological model inspired by neo-Marxism: 'it is no longer just a question of institutional ecumenism against "base" ecumenism but of the ecumenism of a Church man can construct against that of a Church founded and given by the Holy Spirit'.[7] Such a perception suggests that Ratzinger has a Platonic cast of mind – his 'typical impulse is to see meaning as already given and fixed' and he is also reluctant to accept new interpretations or viewpoints.[8]

ECUMENISM FROM ABOVE

Another ecumenical strategy that Ratzinger criticizes is the Fries-Rahner project. This model suggests that once church authority has decided on a closer relationship with other Christians, Catholics would just follow, given the tradition and structure of the Catholic Church. This 'ecumenism from above' calls on church leaders to dispense with normal criteria for entry into the Catholic Church. Such a dispensation would allow new members gradually to integrate into the life of the church and their initial reservations about Catholicism would disappear. Surprisingly, Ratzinger thinks that such a strategy, as advocated by Karl Rahner, is too dependent on a gross exaggeration of papal power and episcopal authority. He is doubtful that such official ecumenism will work in the Catholic and Protestant Churches because it does not correspond to their understanding of the church.[9]

The 'ecumenism from above' proposed by H. Fries and Karl Rahner, in Ratzinger's opinion, is 'a forced ride to unity'. It is impossible to direct the various Christian denominations towards unity like a military exercise where the importance lies in the marching together and 'individual thought is of lesser importance'.[10] In the Fries-Rahner project, ecumenical effort implies building a bridge to all denominations, especially to those Christian communities that were established after the Reformation. Ratzinger is particularly against

Rahner's thesis of 'epistemological tolerance', which is fundamental to this offi-cial ecumenism.[11] This model implies that 'in no particular Church may any proposition be rejected and excised from the profession of faith, which is a binding dogma in some other particular Church'.[12] The fundamental weakness of this formula is that it avoids the question of the truth of the faith. For Ratz-inger, church unity should be based on 'the unity of fundamental decisions and fundamental convictions' and not on 'unity in action'.[13] However, this does not mean that unity in action is unimportant. In fact, it is one of the crucial tasks in our endeavour to promote Christian unity, as I shall be discussing later in this chapter on practical ecumenism.

ECUMENISM FROM THE SIDE

Consensus ecumenism is also criticized by Ratzinger because it inverts the relationship between consensus and truth: instead of truth creating consen-sus, now it is consensus that creates truth. The confession of faith becomes an 'achievement of consensus'. Praxis creates truth, and thus action becomes the 'actual hermeneutic of unity'.[14] Ecumenism also transcends the limits of Christian churches and becomes an 'ecumenism of religions'. Since praxis is given prominence, Christianity and other religions are judged by their contri-bution to the liberation of human beings, justice and peace, as well as ecolog-ical concerns. Hence, these ends become the core of religious belief.[15] This approach goes against Ratzinger's belief in the priority of orthodoxy over praxis.

Connected to its stress on praxis, consensus ecumenism also focuses on the Kingdom of God in place of Christology and ecclesiology. Consensus ecumenism leaves open the question of God, as the emphasis is now on the 'primacy of action'. Ratzinger argues that this means that the doctrine of God's nature is no longer primary. It is a pluralistic understanding of religions that disregards the difference, for example, between Christian Trinitarian belief and Buddhist nirvana. Ratzinger is critical of this kind of religious pluralism that treats all religions as equally valid paths towards salvation. He thinks that such pluralist theology deprives religious beliefs of their contents. Ecumen-ism, in this sense, is concerned, not so much with convergence, as with the coexistence of Christians and adherents of other religions.[16] This emphasis on action rather than on the truth of the faith worries Ratzinger because his concern is with orthodoxy.

ORTHOPRAXIS AND ORTHODOXY

The emphasis on praxis in religions, Ratzinger believes, has become a dominant ideology that cannot last long: 'Ethos without logos cannot endure; that much the collapse of the socialist world ... should have taught us.'[17] He also admits that in the sphere of pluralism, some elements of unity are possible while division still exists. Although Ratzinger rejects the priority given to praxis over Logos, he acknowledges the need to work for a better world. Thus, the important subject matter of ecumenical dialogues is to determine what the commandment of love means, in practice, at this present time.[18]

In commenting on the path of ecumenism today, Ratzinger warns of the danger of pluralism and relativism regarding the Christian doctrine. He writes: 'Whenever the distinction between the personal, revealed God, on whom we can call, and the non-personal, inconceivable mystery disappears, then the distinction between God and the gods, between worship and idolatry, likewise disappears.'[19] We cannot work out an ethic without Logos because without a standard of judgement, we end up in an 'ideological moralizing'. The neglect of what is distinctively Christian and the internal conflict of churches, lead to new oppositions that can be violent. Ratzinger thinks that the disregard for religious content, for the sake of unity, will actually lead to more sectarianism and syncretistic tendencies.[20] To avoid this situation, ecumenism must always be seeking after unity in belief and not just work for unity of action.[21]

Ratzinger believes that theological dialogues must continue in a much more relaxed way and be less oriented towards success: 'it is enough if many and varied forms of witnessing to belief thus develop, through which everyone can learn a little more of the wealth of the message that unites us'. We must be ready to face a 'multiplicity of forms' without developing 'self-sufficiency'. We do not make the church: it is shaped by Christ in word and sacrament.[22] Ecumenism is 'really nothing other than living at present in an eschatological light, in the light of Christ who is coming again'. This means that our ecumenical efforts are only provisional and it is only in Christ that we are journeying towards unity.[23]

Ratzinger proposes an ecumenism that involves the people's experience of faith, the study by theologians and the doctrinal teaching by bishops. It is a process where interpenetration and maturity of insight will gradually enable Christians to unite at a deeper level. Theological unity as found in John 17 is the work of the Holy Spirit and not the result of human negotiating skills. Ratzinger argues that even joint theological statements remain on the level of human understanding and do not pertain to the act of faith. If we recognize the limits of 'ecumenical negotiations' then we will not be disappointed. The most we can achieve is a good relationship in some areas but not unity itself. Ratzinger laments that the success of ecumenical efforts just after the Council has made many people understand ecumenism only in political terms, as in diplomacy.[24]

To sum up, Ratzinger rejects the primacy of orthopraxis over orthodoxy because truth is compromised and consensus determines what is valid. Thus, praxis becomes the criteria of what is true. He suggests that we should learn 'praxeological patience', which means we must accept the necessity of division.[25] Ultimately, this can be overcome only through the conversion of everyone to the truth that is in Christ.

THE QUESTION OF TRUTH

The question of truth is fundamental to Joseph Ratzinger's theology, as he insists that 'ecumenical' does not mean concealing the truth so as not to offend others.[26] He believes that 'full truth is part of full love'. This means that Catholics must not look upon other Christians as opponents against whom they must defend themselves, but must recognize them as brothers and sisters with whom they can speak and from whom they can also learn. Ecumenical means that we give proper attention to the truth that others hold. It means to consider the whole and not to single out some aspects for condemnation or correction. Thus we have to present the 'inner totality of our faith' in order to let other Christians know that 'Catholicism clearly contains all that is truly Christian'. For Ratzinger, to be a Catholic 'is not to become entangled in separatism, but to be open to the fullness of Christianity'.[27]

The real differences between churches concern the confession of faith, the creed and the understanding of the sacraments. The other differences do not really matter because they do not divide the core of the church. However, division within the central sphere threatens the church's existence and its very being. In this regard, Ratzinger distinguishes between human and theological divides. Human division is the 'silent divinization' of our own ideas and works – it is a widespread temptation of human beings. In most religious schisms, such divinization of human thinking plays an important role in the conflict. Ecumenism requires us to liberate ourselves from such subtle distortions. Ratzinger believes that differences between different Christian communities can remain, but they should not distract themselves from the nature of the church.[28]

While Ratzinger recognizes that we can tolerate differences, he insists that we must not be indifferent to the truth. It is, thus, important to distinguish between human tradition and divine truth.[29] Hence, the first task of ecumenism, according to him, is to recognize what is variable and what cannot be changed because it forms the heart of the church. Theological reflection alone does not bring about reconciliation and at the same time it is the non-theological factors that produce division. The worst scenario is when those who defend their own ideas present them as coming from God himself.[30]

Truth cannot be determined by majority vote: either something is true or not. Ratzinger is opposed to consensus ecumenism: 'it is not consensus that offers a basis for the truth, but the truth that offers one for consensus.'[31] This means that authority comes from truth, not from agreement by many people. The Anglican, John Macquarrie, however, has argued that 'truth is not something at which one arrives, but more of an ongoing process, involving the interplay of different views which sometimes agree, sometimes conflict, sometimes correct each other, but which defy all attempts to subsume them into a single truth.'[32] This means that the fullness of truth belongs only to God and we can share this fullness, only at the end of time. Joseph Ratzinger, on the other hand, believes that the church already possesses the authority to teach the truth.

We will now examine Ratzinger's writings, on Anglican and Orthodox Churches, which serve to highlight the differences between them and the Roman Catholic Church and the difficulties in achieving unity.

ANGLICANISM

Joseph Ratzinger maintains that the Anglican Church is not ready for full communion with the Catholic Church. The Anglican Communion appears to be episcopally structured on the same model as Orthodoxy, but in practice Anglicanism operates on a principle of dispersed authority. This means that no person or institution can speak on behalf of the entire Anglican Church. The Anglican–Roman Catholic International Commission (ARCIC) documents seem to suggest that the only obstacles between the two churches are the First Vatican Council teaching on papal infallibility and the dogmas on

Mary, from the nineteenth century. Ratzinger, however, claims that the real issue is the question of authority in the church: 'dogmas are only the most tangible symptoms of the overall problem of authority in the Church'. Ultimately, it is how we view the structure of Christianity that affects our attitude towards matters in the church as a whole.[33]

The problem in the Anglican Church, according to Ratzinger, is who decides what conforms to scripture. ARCIC declares that neither its church leaders nor councils are free from errors. The commission also asserts that the general councils have erred. It also states that only those judgements that are faithful to scripture and tradition are protected from error. There must also be reception but the commission points out that 'reception does not create truth or legitimize the decision'.[34] Ratzinger points out that the ambivalence and lack of direction in these declarations is due to the lack of a central authority in the Anglican Communion. This makes cooperation with the Catholic Church difficult because the Anglican Church itself is divided and lacks a unified voice to speak on behalf of all its local churches.

Ratzinger is also critical of ARCIC's understanding of authentic church teaching as 'manifestly a legitimate interpretation of biblical faith'.[35] Dogmas formulated before the Reformation were not a manifestation of a legitimate interpretation of the Bible. If they were so, there would be no need for councils or a teaching authority to determine what is truly revealed by God. What is manifested must occur in the context of life experience. Authority cannot be transferred to what is manifested by history because then there will be different interpretations. In the light of this, Ratzinger claims that in the New Testament and in the life of the early Christian communities, it is the universal church that teaches.[36]

In the Catholic Church, apostolic succession safeguards the authenticity of tradition. The universal church extends itself into the nature of the local churches. This means that the local churches must be in communion with the universal church. Ratzinger finds it necessary to correct the error found in the report of ARCIC that states: 'The Second Vatican Council allows it to be said that a Church out of communion with the Roman See may lack nothing from the viewpoint of the Roman Catholic Church except that it does not belong to the visible manifestation of full Christian communion.'[37] He insists that it is wrong to claim the support of the Second Vatican Council for such superficial unity which consists of a loose confederation of sister churches.

Joseph Ratzinger argues that the 'romantic idea' of provincial churches restoring the structure of the early church goes against the historical reality and actual experiences of the early Christian communities. While he admits that the early church did not have Roman primacy in practice, he claims that it did have the 'living forms of unity in the universal Church that were not mere formalities but constitutive of the very nature of provincial Churches'.[38] As noted in the previous chapter, he emphasizes the priority of the universal church over the local churches. Ratzinger, therefore, regards the Anglican Church as a defective embodiment of the universal church because it lacks communion with Rome. For him, the question of authority is related to tradition and only the universal church can provide an adequate medium for the interpretation of scripture.

The Anglican Church is essentially a national church.[39] Ratzinger asserts that a national church contradicts the New Testament's idea of 'church' because it has the 'tendency to particularize Christianity':'modern nationalism has deformed legitimate ecclesiastical provincialism and turned it into a cloak for ethnic separatism'.[40] Once the universal church disappears as a concrete reality, it becomes a political tool in the hands of the government. The church loses its power as its entire structure is altered.[41] Ratzinger is also critical of the so-called 'Parliament of Churches', an ecumenical council that would harmonize pluralism and 'promote a Christian unity of action'. He believes no union would result from such a model, but the very impossibility of unity would become 'a single common dogma'.[42] This means that he is particularly against the idea of ecclesiological pluralism.

Quoting William Ledwich, Ratzinger writes that, 'Jesus did not found a Catholic party in a cosmopolitan debating society, but a Catholic Church to which he promised the fullness of truth.'[43] This implies that the Anglican Church, reduced to a religious parliament in England, can hardly be called a branch of the Catholic Church. The Anglican Church has become a national religion 'structured on the principles of liberal tolerance, in which the authority of revelation is subordinate to democracy and private opinion'.[44] Sociologists of religion readily identify the Church of England as a civic religion. Ratzinger refers to John Henry Newman and the Tractarians who wrote about the place of authority in the church and the value of dogma, as opposed to the right to private judgement in religious matters.[45]

In view of possible unity, Ratzinger insists that the Anglican Church must clarify the relationship between its episcopal and political authority, which was the original cause of its separation from the Catholic Church. He admits that there have been misguided developments in papal primacy and thus the theological core must always be brought to light. However, the primacy of the universal church must not be weakened to the extent that its theological reality is dissolved. At the same time, there must be variations in the practice of primacy: 'the ways of putting the office into practice are subject to alteration and must always be tested afresh by the principle'.[46]

Ratzinger objects to describing the Anglican and Catholic Churches as 'our two traditions'. In other words, he disagrees with different forms of church being seen as different traditions and that divisions are of secondary importance in the theological sense – they are just differences in the realization of common Christianity. There is a trend to substitute 'tradition' for 'confession'. This is misleading and erroneous, according to Ratzinger, because when 'confession' becomes 'tradition', 'the question of truth is replaced with conciliatory concern for what history has brought about'.[47] He writes:

> lurking behind the new concept of tradition was the elimination of the question of truth. The difference between the Churches is reduced to a difference of 'traditions' (customs). This puts the ecumenical debate on a completely new track: it is no longer man's great struggle for the truth; rather, it is the search for compromise in the matter of tradition, for an equilibrium between the customs.[48]

This implies that if the differences in churches are due to different traditions and not different confessions, we need not discuss the question of truth. Theology, then, becomes diplomacy.

Furthermore, if the difference between the Catholic and Anglican Churches is a matter of tradition, what then is the meaning of tradition? Ratzinger points out that the ARCIC documents do not say what tradition means to both parties.[49] For him, tradition means 'above all that the Church, living in the form of apostolic succession with the Petrine office at its centre, is the place in which the Bible is lived and interpreted in a binding way'.[50] This means that there is an historical continuity in the interpretation of the church's teaching, a fixed standard that is open to further understanding.

Joseph Ratzinger is very critical of how the word 'tradition' is being misused in Protestant circles as, for example, in the Lima Documents on Baptism, Eucharist and Ministry (BEM). It seems that they have decided that 'Scripture – torn to pieces by the disputes among confessions and exegetes' – can no longer serve as a foundation. They decided to depend on 'tradition', not in the Catholic sense, but as a kind of custom, the actual form of Christian life that each confession embraces. Ratzinger writes: 'in this it is completely unimportant to ask when and how a tradition arose. The fact that it could and can sustain church life gives it its right in the ecumenical quest. Thus what is factual – the existence and persistence of a practice – acquires a hitherto unknown weight.' It follows that in some African countries, baptism can take the form of laying-on of hands, without water.[51] In some other 'traditions', it is customary to give children just a blessing to link them to the church. According to Ratzinger, such customs no longer belong to Luther or Calvin, let alone the Catholic or Orthodox principle of tradition.[52]

Catholic theology stresses the unbroken identity of the apostolic tradition firmly established in the unity of the church, expressed in the ecclesial imposition of hands during priestly ordination. Without the church, the imposition of hands has no meaning. Ratzinger teaches that 'the sacrament is the sacrament of the Church, not a private way to the beginnings of Christianity'.[53] In this regard, he argues that the difference between Protestants and Catholics is not just a question of sacrament and sacramentality, it goes deeper, into the problem of scripture and tradition. The 'essential character of the word and the essential character of the Church cannot be present if 'there is a break with the concrete continuity of the Church that celebrates the Eucharist with the bishops'.[54] This implies that the gospel cannot be found in *sola scriptura*, in isolating scripture from the church.

Both the Lutheran and Anglican Churches accepted the creed and dogma formulated before the Reformation. Ratzinger claims that it is not *sola scriptura* in the strict sense. These Protestant churches acknowledge a certain tradition established before the Reformation; they accept only a tradition that is found in the texts from the past. This means that the living voice of the church 'is minimized in theology by the demand for testing against Scripture, while in practice it is reduced to the sphere of mere discipline, which is thereby cut off from its true foundations'.[55]

Clearly, Ratzinger has foreseen great obstacles in efforts to have dialogue with churches that do not have a centralized authority and a clear understanding of tradition. The tone of his writing on dialogue with the Anglicans sounds discouraging and pessimistic.

The difficulties for Anglican–Catholic ecumenism at the present time are not so much about doctrinal matters, but, more significantly, about the decision of the Anglican Church to ordain women and about the issue of sexual morality. When the Episcopal Church in the United States decided to ordain women, the Vatican allowed entire Episcopalian parishes to enter into communion with Rome while retaining much of the Anglican liturgy and tradition. However, when the Church of England allowed women to be ordained and several English Anglicans requested similar concessions from Rome, the petition was rejected. Only individual Anglican priests were accepted into the Catholic Church. The priests were re-ordained, which means that the Anglican orders were not accepted as valid. This is based on Leo XIII's *Apostolicae curae* that declared Anglican ordinations to be 'absolutely null and utterly void'. Ratzinger claims that this declaration – the non-validity of Anglican orders – is in fact an infallible teaching of the church.[56] It therefore follows that Anglican priests would have to be re-ordained if they want to remain as priests in the Catholic Church.

On 4 November 2009, Joseph Ratzinger, as Pope Benedict XVI, issued his Apostolic Constitution *Anglicanorum*. This Apostolic Constitution introduces a new church structure that will allow former Anglicans to enter into full communion with the Catholic Church while maintaining aspects of their liturgical distinctiveness and Anglican ethos. This Apostolic Constitution is seen by many as an attempt by the pope to poach Anglicans who are unhappy with the decision of their church to ordain both women and openly active homosexuals, while others see it as public recognition of many aspects of Anglicanism that are fully compatible with the Catholic faith.[57]

Ratzinger highlights what he perceives to be the weaknesses and untenable positions of the Anglican as well as the Lutheran Churches. Their lack of central authority makes it difficult for them to discuss issues with the Catholic Church on behalf of the entire church. Their refusal to be in communion with the universal church weakens their identity and power to exercise their authority. Besides, as already mentioned, these Protestant churches regard as traditions only those creeds and dogmas that existed before the Reformation. This means that they place their faith only in the old texts and are, thus, cut off from the living voice of the church that has continued since the sixteenth century.

THE ORTHODOX CHURCH

In his letter to the Metropolitan Damaskinos of Switzerland on 20 February 2001, Joseph Ratzinger expresses his understanding that the Orthodox Church and the Catholic Church belong to one another. Therefore, none of the doctrinal disputes are insurmountable.[58] Ratzinger thinks that the obstacle that stands between the two churches is not so much a question of doctrine as the remembrance of old hurts that keeps the two communities apart: 'the power of the confused tangles of history seems to be stronger than the light of faith that ought to be transforming them into forgiveness.'[59] This means that both churches need a purification of memory to begin the process of healing that will eventually lead to unity.

Many people believe that the main obstacle to the full restoration of unity between the Catholic Church and the Orthodox Church lies in the 'pope's primacy of jurisdiction'.[60] Ratzinger thinks this is a 'problem of language'. The pope's jurisdiction over the whole church is based on honour, not in the worldly sense, but in the sense of service and obedience to Christ. The pope presides over the church, in charity. This *agape*, expressed fully in the Eucharist, is connected to the theology of the cross, which is the most profound manifestation of God's love for us, in Jesus Christ.[61]

Joseph Ratzinger also claims that without the primacy of the pope's jurisdiction over the whole church, the Catholic Church would long ago have split into national churches or into groups practising various different rites. This would make it impossible to have a general view of the ecumenical situation. The primacy of the pope makes possible the steps of reconciliation towards unity. Ratzinger believes that the problem of autocephalous churches ('self-headed' Eastern Orthodox churches whose primates do not report to higher authorities) shows 'the necessity for an instrument of unity' which must also be 'correctly balanced with the independent responsibility of the local Churches'.[62]

Orthodox believers were offended when Ratzinger asserted that it is not appropriate to refer to the Orthodox Church and the Roman Catholic Church as two 'sister Churches'. He explains that the term 'sister Churches' refers to particular churches only. For him, it is a matter of setting right the relationship between the plural churches and the one singular Church.[63] This suggests that the Catholic Church is not on the same level as the other churches. In the *Credo* we confess that there is only one Church of Christ which, of course, exists in reality, in many particular churches. At the same time, these particular churches form parts of the one Church. Therefore, according to Ratzinger, to speak of the Orthodox Church and the Catholic Church as sister Churches would be 'setting up a plural above and beyond which no singular is apparent. A dualism would remain at the ultimate level of the concept of "Church," and the one Church would thus become a phantom, a utopia, whereas bodily existence is the very thing that is essential to her'.[64]

As we have seen in the previous chapter, Ratzinger laments that the term 'universal Church' is very often misinterpreted in instances where he insists on the ontological and temporal precedence of the universal church over the particular churches. To interpret this definition as favouring Roman centralism is 'complete nonsense', according to Ratzinger. He adds that the local Church of Rome is a local church that is entrusted 'with a special responsibility for the whole Church, but she is not herself the universal church'.[65]

Maintaining the ontological and temporal priority of the universal church over the particular churches is 'not a declaration that the local Church of Rome should seek to acquire as many privileges as possible', Ratzinger insists.[66] It is not a question of the distribution of power, but about the mystery of the church. He writes:

> this is strictly a matter of theology, not of juridical questions or of Church politics: the fact that God's idea of the Son's one bride, eschatologically oriented toward the eternal wedding feast, is the first and the one essential idea of God that is at stake in matters to do with the Church, while the concrete realization of the Church in local Churches constitutes a second plane that is subsequent to the first and always remains subordinated to it.[67]

For the Orthodox Church to be in communion with Rome, Ratzinger suggests that the only condition is that they accept the teachings of the primacy of the pope during the first millennium:

> Rome must not require more from the East with respect to the doctrine of primacy than had been formulated and was lived in the first millennium ... Rome need not ask for more. Reunion could take place in this context if, on the one hand, the East would cease to oppose as heretical the developments that took place in the West in the second millennium and would accept the Catholic Church as legitimate and orthodox in the form she had acquired in the course of that development, while, on the other hand, the West would recognize the Church of the East as orthodox and legitimate in the form she has always had.[68]

Ratzinger stresses the importance of apostolic succession in preserving the unity of the church. Both the Catholic Church and the Orthodox Church have accepted that the church came into existence through the scriptures. The bishops, 'by virtue of their sacramental consecration and the ecclesial tradition', personify this unity of the church. This church unity, Ratzinger claims, is based on the concept of *successio apostolica*, an intrinsic part of the structure of the church, as expressed since the second century.[69] He writes:

> The apostolic succession is not a purely formal power; it is part of the mission for the gospel. That is why the concepts of succession and tradition were not separated in the early Church and why Vatican Council

II is justified in linking the two closely together. The *successio*-structure is the expression both of the link with tradition and of the concept of tradition in the Catholic Church. On this question, there is, so far as I can see, no essential difference between the Catholic Churches of East and West.[70]

The structural unity between the two churches has not been destroyed. Perhaps this is the reason why Ratzinger says that Rome should not demand that the East accepts the doctrine of papal jurisdiction other than the one formulated during the first millennium.

Ratzinger understands the Orthodox Church's aversion to papal primacy, but he thinks that they developed an incorrect interpretation of the Petrine office. According to the Orthodox point of view, the development of *monarchia papae*, papal monarchy, destroyed the ecclesial structure, and, as a result, the primitive church was replaced by something different. This means that the Western Church is no longer under the bishops in their collegial unity. Instead, the church has become a 'centrally organized monolith' and the idea of a 'perfect society' has replaced the idea of succession. According to Ratzinger, the Orthodox Church has developed the mistaken idea that, in the Catholic Church, 'the faith that was handed down no longer (so it seems) serves as the normative rule – a rule that can be newly interpreted only with the consensus of all the local churches'. The Eastern Church has, thus, held that in the Catholic Church, the will of the supreme pontiff creates a new authority.[71]

This understanding by the Orthodox Church was reinforced in 1870 by the Catholic teaching on the primacy of jurisdiction, exercised by the bishop of Rome. On the one hand, only tradition serves as a valid source of the law.[72] On the other hand, the source of the law appears to come from the will of the sovereign who creates new laws that are binding to all. The Orthodox Church thus believes that the sacramental structure of the church has been replaced by a new concept of law, the papacy, which is not a sacrament but only a juridical institution that 'has set itself above the sacramental order'.[73] Thus, the Eastern Church must reject papal authority. However, the decision of Joseph Ratzinger to step down from the chair of St Peter shows that the Catholic Church understands the papacy not as a sacramental order but as an administrative function.

The Orthodox Church also contends that the Roman Catholic understanding of papal primacy, with its insistence on the universal jurisdiction of the papacy, goes against the Eucharistic foundations of the church.[74] Since the Eucharistic communities are 'wholly the body of Christ' under their bishops, they are 'fundamentally equal and may not be subordinated to one another'. The Orthodox Church admits that, historically, Rome played a prominent role among the five ancient patriarchates: Rome, Constantinople, Alexandria, Antioch and Jerusalem. However, it disagrees with the Catholic understanding of the role of the patriarch in Rome.[75] This means that the Orthodox Church is opposed to the Catholic tradition of papal primacy, with its strong emphasis on the universal jurisdiction of the pontiff. It believes that the authority of the patriarch was 'an expression of synodality' and 'bound to the communion of Churches'.[76] It has rejected the notion of Roman primacy that assumes a 'supra-episcopal authority', as well as 'any primacy understood as a power over other local bishops and their Churches'. Instead, for the Orthodox Church, the essential form of primacy lies in the synod of bishops. Simply put, primacy lies in the episcopacy to which it belongs.[77]

According to Joseph Ratzinger, the removal of the anathema of 1054 reflects a holy and historic responsibility that goes beyond mere courtesy.[78] It is an important historical action involving 'the dialogue of love and the theological dialogue'. Quoting the Metropolitan Meliton's words, Ratzinger states that the act of reconciliation brings 'no modification whatever in the status of dogma, in the existing canonical order, in the liturgy or in the life of the Church ... It does not mean a restoration of the sacramental community.'[79]

The fundamental aim of the event was the restoration of ecclesial love – 'a community of love between bishopric and bishopric, between Church and Church'. Ratzinger claims that this ecclesial love 'is not yet a sacramental community but possesses in itself the necessary dynamism to become such. It is to be regarded as an actual ecclesial union that binds churches as churches.'[80] This restoration of love means that we must forget the past, as St Paul says (Philippians 3:13). Memory has the dangerous power of causing 'the poison of yesterday to become the poisoning of today'. Thus, Ratzinger says that 'reparation of the past can take place through a purification of memory'. This means amending our past mistakes through the concept of forgetting; the purification of memory that will serve to heal the wounds. In practical terms, both churches erase from memory the excommunication that took place in the past. Forgetting is forgiving.[81]

As we have seen, Ratzinger has written substantially on the subject of ecumenism. He is well acquainted with the ecclesiology of the Anglican, Lutheran and Orthodox Churches. Aware of the painful history that exists in the relationship between the Catholic Church and the other Christian communities, Ratzinger maintains a cautious and realistic attitude towards the prospect of unity in the near future. Rejecting the primacy of orthopraxis over orthodoxy, he stresses the importance of truth in our search for common ground in ecumenical endeavours. In spite of his sceptical attitude towards various models of ecumenism, Ratzinger acknowledges that plurality of churches has a legitimate existence within Christianity. This means that he is ready to accept the multiplicity of churches, provided they are united under one universal church.

UNITY THROUGH DIVERSITY

According to Joseph Ratzinger, diversity is healthy and even desirable once the 'poison of hostility' has been removed. Studying Augustine's interpretation of the Pauline statement, 'there must be factions' (1 Corinthians 11:19), Ratzinger argues that even though divisions and factions are human realities, they are also part of 'divine arrangement'. We do all we can, through penance and sacrifice, to heal the divisions, but it is God who will ultimately draw all people to himself.[82] By this, he means that partitions and factions are a divine necessity in order to yield a greater good, through purification. Eventually, in God's time, this division will disappear, resulting in a more profound unity.

Not adverse to plurality and diversity, Ratzinger has personally experienced how Catholics and Protestants can live together peacefully in his homeland. In Germany there is a healthy and fruitful coexistence between Protestants and Catholics. Initially, there had been great hostility between the two churches, but gradually they developed into 'a positive factor for the faith on both sides'. This may explain why St Paul speaks about the necessity of factions. Ratzinger questions: 'Could anyone really imagine an exclusively Protestant world? Is not Protestantism instead, in all its declarations, precisely as a protest, so completely connected with Catholicism that it would be scarcely imaginable without it?'[83] Lamentably, Ratzinger does not argue that the converse is true: Catholicism needs Protestantism to remind itself of the need for constant reformation and purification based on the Word of God.

According to Ratzinger, the Catholic understanding of plurality is different from the Protestant idea of independent national churches such as the Anglican Church, or a federation of churches such as the Lutheran Church. In fact, from the beginning, Catholic theology has recognized the plurality of churches. This means the acceptance of a multiplicity of churches existing within the framework of one visible Church of God. These particular churches are in close communion with one another as they help to build up the one church. The unity is born of a 'vigorous multiplicity'. Thus, there exists a Church of God in Athens, in Corinth, in Rome: the members of each local community assembled together, with the bishop presiding over the Eucharistic celebration. All these churches in different localities partake of the 'essence of the Church', and are truly a 'Church'. For Ratzinger, one essential element of being a church is that it must not exist in isolation, but must be in communion with the other churches, and together they form the one church.[84]

Plurality of churches had a legitimate existence within the church, but unfortunately, in the course of history, this plurality eventually disappeared, taken over by a centralized system. In the process, the local church of Rome began to absorb all the other local churches so that unity became uniformity.[85] This plurality of churches had 'no room *within* the Church' and 'was developed *outside* of it in the form of autonomous separate Churches'.[86] The Catholic Church, since the Second Vatican Council, has tried to remedy this situation with its ecumenical endeavours.

Ratzinger admits that the Catholic Church is not yet prepared to accept the phenomenon of multiplicity in unity. It is a renewal that involves a process of opening up which takes time.[87] He asserts that there is the one Church that is identified with the historical continuity of the Catholic Church. Although Catholics cannot demand that all the other churches be absorbed into Catholicism, they can hope that 'the hour will come when "the Churches" that exist outside "the Church" will enter into its unity'.[88] Ratzinger also says that they must remain 'in existence as *Churches*', changing only those features that unity demands.[89]

The Catholic Church considers itself the Church of Christ, in spite of its 'historic deficiency'. It also recognizes the plurality of churches that should exist within it but, today, this plurality can only exist outside.[90] As we have seen, Ratzinger recognizes the valid existence of the plurality of churches under one universal church, but he is opposed to the present plurality of denominational churches, which is a particular characteristic of Protestantism. Ratzinger is also realistic enough to accept that division among churches not only represents the evil tendency in human beings, but can also be a divine necessity. This is because separation is necessary for our purification. 'Unity in diversity' or 'a reconciled diversity' is, thus, an acceptable formula for Joseph Ratzinger, in our ecumenical endeavours.[91] He has in mind the Uniate rites in the Eastern model.

THE EASTERN MODEL

While Joseph Ratzinger argues that it is presumptuous for Catholics to demand that all the other Christian churches be incorporated into the Catholic Church, he hopes that they will eventually enter into communion with Rome. They could remain in existence as 'churches' modifying only those features which unity demands.[92] Here Ratzinger's position appears to be that the various Protestant denominations might eventually be received into full communion as Uniate rite churches. They would be like the Eastern rite churches, in union with Rome, while at the same time retaining their own distinctive spiritual, liturgical and canonical traditions.

This uniate model could be the basis for reunion between the Catholic Church and the Anglican Church, for example. It would replace the existing denominationalism with a visible unity among the churches. At the same time, it would guarantee that the rich heritage of the various Christian traditions would be preserved.[93] This could be the goal for the next stage of the ecumenical movement. Perhaps Joseph Ratzinger would agree with the observation of Edward P. Echlin:

> Since Vatican II there has been a development towards pluralism underway in the Church of Rome. The uniformity promoted before the council is yielding to a comprehensiveness that augurs well for the convergence of Christian churches. When Rome embraces her sister churches in full communion it seems certain that these churches will be, in the celebrated phrase of Malines, 'united not absorbed.' Such unity— in a coexistence in full communion—will be a preliminary step leading to even wider unity and Catholicity.[94]

Thus, unity is not to be identified with uniformity in ecumenical dialogue. It is the duty of Christians to defend the legitimate interests of pluralism against the forces of uniformity. However, maintaining a healthy pluralism in unity is a complex process. There is always this tension existing between unity and division. Paul Tillich has observed:

> neither the ecumenical nor any future movement can conquer the ambiguity of unity and division in the churches' historical existence. Even if it were able to produce the United Churches of the World, and even if all latent churches were converted to this unity, new divisions would

appear. The dynamics of life, the tendency to preserve the holy even when it has become obsolete, the ambiguities implied in the sociological existence of the churches, and above all, the prophetic criticism and demand for reformation would bring about new and, in many cases, spiritually justified divisions. The unity of the churches, similar to their holiness, has a paradoxical character. It is the divided church which is the united church.[95]

Joseph Ratzinger supports the idea of a 'fruitful pluralism' and acknowledges the positive aspect of division. Thus, he says that the way to promote unity through diversity is not to impose on the other party anything that threatens his or her core identity as a Christian. This means that Catholics should not try to force Protestants to recognize papal authority, the sacraments, and so on, and Protestants should not pressure the Catholic Church to allow inter-communion based on Protestant understanding of the Eucharist; such respect for the 'otherness' of the other, which is inherent in the division, would not delay unity but, rather, is a prerequisite for it.[96]

Ratzinger rightly says that this kind of tolerance and acceptance can produce charity and closeness, whereas urgent insistence can only create tension and aversion. Ultimately, we must leave God to do what is actually his business – Christian unity.[97] While I agree with Ratzinger's cautious approach towards ecumenism in the Western context, in Asia we need to engage in practical or secular ecumenism as the situation requires Christians to respond urgently to the social and economic needs of the people.

PRACTICAL ECUMENISM

Asia is a vast and diverse continent where various religious beliefs, including different branches of Christianity, continue to flourish. In spite of modernization and rapid economic development, Asia is steeped in religious traditions. At the same time, the gap between the rich and poor is growing rapidly, and the majority of people are struggling because of a lack of the basic necessities of life in many parts of the continent. Hence, a practical or secular ecumenical approach that strives for the common good, in the midst of religious pluralism, is more appropriate and meaningful here. For example, Christians from different denominations, including Roman Catholics, can cooperate in charitable and social work.

Practical ecumenism implies 'a unity with true existential foundations, rather than one that has come about as the blueprint devised by a high-powered ecclesiastical commission'.[98] Thus, it is not ecumenism from above. Although Joseph Ratzinger insists that ethos without Logos is not sustainable, as evidenced by the collapse of socialism, he has admitted that an ecumenism of praxis has value in that it fulfils Christ's commandment to love. However, focusing on practical ecumenism does not imply that we are indifferent to the truth. In fact, we uphold the truth as defined in Matthew 25:31–46.

Given the present situation where impasse in ecumenical dialogue is inevitable, practical ecumenism also has the advantage of setting 'realistic intermediate goals', in keeping with what Ratzinger has suggested. While doctrinal or liturgical differences may be intractable, charitable works, as a means of witnessing the gospel, can be readily organized by different churches in harmony with one another. Likewise, Ratzinger also insists that the different churches can jointly address the 'great moral questions of our time'. This can be done through joint testimonies of faith before a world torn by doubts and fears. These small efforts should emphasize the common features of Christian living which exist despite divisions. Working together in these modest projects shows that separation no longer equates to opposition, as Ratzinger has pointed out.[99] Christians will be challenged to understand and accept members of other churches as brothers and sisters in Christ.

Ecumenical effort aimed at fostering unity among Christian communities is meaningful when churches are willing to work together on the practical tasks of helping the poor, visiting prisoners, alleviating poverty and suffering, and so on. In short, Christians should be united in the building of a better world. John Macquarrie argues that the basis of this practical ecumenism 'is not a nicely worked out ecclesiology or even a doctrine of redemption but simply that natural morality which is common to all men by virtue of their humanity'.[100] This means that we do not have to force adherents of other faiths to be baptized or call them 'anonymous Christians'. It is enough that they have 'the law written on their hearts' (Romans 2:15). Macquarrie rightly asserts that this non-exclusive practical or 'secular' ecumenism is 'the recognition that all humanity is the creation of God' and 'has a share in that image of God that is perfectly expressed in Christ'.[101]

Practical or secular ecumenism first seeks the unity of humankind rather than the unity of the churches. It reminds Christians that what will remain at the end of time will not be the church, but the Kingdom of God – 'gathering up both church and world in an eschatological unity'. Therefore, our primary aim should not simply be ecclesiastical unity, but the unity of the world. Once we focus on the unity of the world, the unity of the church may come more quickly as a 'provisional stage on the way'.[102] Augustine Cardinal Bea writes that the church as it is, is a society which is also perfectly human, 'feels itself intimately linked with all mankind, and co-operates in the achieving of unity for mankind'.[103]

Similarly, Konrad Raiser, the former general secretary of the World Council of Churches, stresses social concerns above doctrinal issues. In so doing, he indicates that ecumenical effort should be directed to addressing social problems such as economic inequality, sexism and other injustices rather than debating theological issues and ministry. Raiser thinks that previous ecumenical efforts were too philosophical and theological.[104] At the same time he fears that this newer ecumenical model, which seeks to bring Christians from different confessions together, could lead to a denial of Christ's divinity and his unique salvific role. This is also Joseph Ratzinger's concern. However, there is no concrete evidence to show that Christians would deny the salvific efficacy of Christ or his divinity just because they are too involved in charitable and social work.

Practical ecumenism safeguards the diversity of churches. Ratzinger is right to be cautious about ecumenical efforts and the rush to unity because of his worries over serious doctrinal differences. Therefore, I think it is appropriate that various churches begin by coming together to work on common social projects to alleviate the sufferings of the poor and marginalized. It is also important to understand ecumenism as 'the science of bridge-building, a science of dialogue across different groups'. This means that, eventually, ecumenism will include not just Christians, but people of other faiths and even those who have none.[105]

Ans Van der Bent rightly insists that there must be dialogue between the church and the world; though the church is not of the world, it is in the world to serve and minister to it. He stresses 'service within the world'. While the church is discovering the world, it should also help the world to discover the church.[106] The church must re-evaluate its structure with a view to dealing with problems such as secularization, poverty, the environmental crisis and threats to justice and peace. Facing the same problems in the world draws churches closer together. This will help them to deepen their theological investigation and work out a plan that allows common action.[107] Quoting José Miguez Bonino, Ans Van der Bent writes:

The churches cannot address society as if they were outside it, untouched by its struggles, unspotted by its sins and injustices, exempt from responsibility. The churches can only be *credible* if they recognize their involvement and, in the necessary reforms that they demand for society, endeavour to make the corresponding reforms in themselves. By recognizing their mutual accountability, this need for internal purification can be a part of the ecumenical dialogue and praxis.[108]

There is already enough ecumenical, doctrinal and ethical consensus among most of the churches to deal with problems such as torture, the foreign debt of developing countries, refugees and so on.[109] It would, therefore, seem appropriate to start from this common basis, namely, our social commitment to the world. Practice cannot be separated from doctrine. According to Ans Van der Bent, 'only a deep solidarity with the threatened and broken world will reveal how narrowly the social teachings of the churches are still defined'.[110] Our churches are still so caught up with doctrinal purity and ecclesiastical rectitude that they are neglecting Christ's command to serve the poor and the oppressed. Critical of the Roman Catholic claim that the sole church of Christ 'subsists' in the Roman Catholic Church, Ans Van der Bent thinks that this implies that other churches do not have the authority to produce valid social teachings.[111] For him, 'the fullness of the church subsists in its manifestation of Christ's redemption of the entire human race'.[112] His interpretation maintains that the main ecumenical work for all churches is to be involved actively in the pastoral task of bringing about a better world for all.

CONCERN FOR EUROPE AND ASIAN REALITIES

In spite of the many criticisms of Ratzinger's approach to ecumenism, there are those who interpret his writings on these issues as openness to other Christians and non-Christians. These supporters acknowledge Ratzinger's consistent commitment to ecumenism and his positive evaluation of other faiths, suggesting that his critics are not sharp enough to understand his nuanced statements and critical stance.[113] A good example is Ratzinger's Regensburg Lecture in which he addressed the interdependency of faith and reason, but which many misconstrued as a speech against Islam. He has been critical of the various ecumenical models, but he is also committed to promoting

Christian unity in a gradual manner. He is willing to enter into a dialogue with Protestant theology:

> Catholic theology requires that there be, despite all divisions and antithesis, a common theological motive; that, whether they accept or reject each other's view, the two sides be sensitive and responsive to each other. Second, it should likewise be clear that Catholic theology must not regard its role in this dialogue to be that of trying to agree with whatever is currently the strongest position of the other side but must rather look, in its own way, for whatever common ground there may be and, in doing so, not be afraid to learn from its partner.[114]

Ratzinger rightly advocates a search for a common ground and a willingness to learn and be corrected by the other.

Be that as it may, Ratzinger's ecumenical approach is influenced by his concern over the decline of Christianity and his hope for a united Christian Church to combat the threat of aggressive secularism in Europe. Ratzinger believes that for Europe to build a humane society, it must return to its original Greek roots and Christian heritage. This means that Europe must rediscover the objective and eternal values that stand above politics and must stress the rule of law. In view of this, he emphasizes the Greek concept of *eunomia* – the enactment of good laws and the maintenance of civil order.[115] Ratzinger thinks that Christian values can help to halt the decline of European civilization. Thus, with a view to rebuilding Europe, Christian unity can play a significant role.

This ecumenical concern of Ratzinger's may be justifiable and timely given the present situation in Europe. However, the challenge for the churches in Asia is to be united so as to fight against poverty and oppression, and promote justice and peace, as part of witnessing to the gospel of Jesus Christ. Ratzinger reflects on the true and the good. Such reflections, however, always take place in a particular culture. John Paul II called for a dialogue between faith and culture, and the Second Vatican Council recognized the need for 'accommodated preaching', but to Ratzinger this smells of relativism.

Although Christianity in Europe has slowly been made irrelevant by the surge of secularism, the West continues to exercise authority and control over the churches of Asia. In the Catholic Church, the papacy and the magisterium maintain strict control over the local churches in Asia. In the various Protestant denominational churches in Asia, economic support from mother churches in the West is still crucial for their functioning and even for their survival. Thus K. M. George rightly says: 'while the spiritual vitality of the Western churches is probably drying up, their institutional power over the churches of the South is still going strong.'[116]

Asian theologians, from both Catholic and Protestant churches, have been calling for a rediscovery of Asian Christian identity. To achieve this, the churches in Asia must shed their Western trappings. There is an obvious gap between the 'theological understanding of identity and the ecclesiastical–institutional reality of our churches'. This poses an obstacle to Asian ecumenism.[117] Perhaps a more appropriate approach to ecumenical endeavour in Asia lies in the various branches of Christianity coming together, putting aside their doctrinal differences, and making a concerted effort to deal with the problems related to poverty, justice, peace and ecological issues. Christian churches also need to unite in a major push to preach the gospel in the face of aggressive secularism. In the next chapter we will examine Ratzinger's response to this threat against the faith.

Chapter 5

Secularism

Joseph Ratzinger seeks to unite the Christian churches in Europe as a strategy to halt the rise of secularism in Western society, as mentioned in the last chapter on ecumenism. Secularism relegates religion to the private domain, insists that the state remains neutral in religious affairs and, hence, promotes religious pluralism. This chapter examines Ratzinger's characterization of this onslaught on church and religion as an aggressive ideology. It attempts to trace the relationship between secularism and Christianity. It also examines the influence of Western Enlightenment and Marxism on the development of secularism.

In addition, this chapter focuses on the dialogue between Jürgen Habermas and Joseph Ratzinger in *The Dialectics of Secularization*. However, beyond making some brief speculative remarks, this dialogue offers little reflection on how non-Western modes of thought can shed light on understanding our secular age. In view of the growing religious pluralism in the West, the conflict between secularism and Christianity has somewhat abated. Meanwhile, some people have discovered that Eastern philosophies such as Confucianism, Taoism and Buddhism may have something to contribute to our post-secular society.

This chapter concludes with Ratzinger's call for a 'healthy secularism' that can help to build a society where different traditions, cultures and religions flourish. This would seem to indicate that Ratzinger is not against secularism in itself, but only when it becomes a threat to the Christian community.

SECULARIZATION AND SECULARISM

Secularization and secularism look somewhat similar in spelling, leading none-too-careful writers to use the two terms interchangeably. It is important, though, to note that they carry different meanings and connotations. Seculari-zation refers to a historical process that traces the advancement of scientific truths and principles from the mid-seventeenth century. The modernization of society that gradually pushed the role of religion out of public life was dominated by scientific discoveries and the principle of evidence-based truths.

Secularism, on the other hand, is a worldview where gods, divine revela-tion, religious dogmas and supernatural practices have no role in civil society. Each individual is free to follow his or her natural inclination in matters of worship and prayer, but that individual cannot impose this set of beliefs on others. Religion is thus a private matter which must not impose itself on the government of the day. The outcome is the strict separation between the state and religious institutions, and people of different religious beliefs and those without any religion are equal before the law.[1]

THE THREAT TO THE CHURCH

It is well known that Ratzinger has always been concerned with the threat of aggressive secularism and relativism, as revealed in many of his writings and addresses. His preoccupation with this profound problem is not really a reactionary stance. It is more the position of a priest who is deeply concerned about the secularization, not only of Western society, but of the church itself, in that many Catholic schools and institutions have lost a sense of being Cath-olic. In his address to the plenary members of the Council for Culture entitled 'The Church and the challenge of secularization', Ratzinger says:

> This secularization is not only an external threat to believers, but has been manifest for some time in the heart of the Church herself. It profoundly distorts the Christian faith from within, and consequently, the lifestyle and daily behaviour of believers ... They live in the world and are often marked, if not conditioned, by the cultural imagery that impresses contradictory and impelling models regarding the practical denial of God: there is no longer any need for God, to think of him or to return to him.[2]

In addition to this denial of transcendence inherent in secularization, Ratz-inger also laments the 'death of God', taught by intellectuals, that results in selfish individualism. We are thus in danger of 'drifting into spiritual atro-phy and emptiness of heart'. To counteract this tendency, he encourages us to appeal to the lofty values of existence that give meaning to life: the dignity of the human person, the equality of men and women, and the meaning of life and the afterlife.[3]

Apart from this address in 2008, in the first speech of his historic state visit to the United Kingdom in September 2010, Joseph Ratzinger, as Pope Benedict XVI, urged Britain to maintain its respect for religious traditions and warned against 'aggressive forms of secularism'. He said, 'Today, the United Kingdom strives to be a modern and multicultural society ... in this challenging enterprise, may it always maintain its respect for those traditional values and cultural expressions that more aggressive forms of secularism no longer value or even tolerate.'[4]

In November 2010, the pope surprised Spain with strong words against what he described as 'aggressive secularism' on the part of the government. Since 2004, the government had legalized gay marriage, relaxed abortion legislation and eliminated compulsory religious education in schools. He said, 'The renaissance of modern Catholicism comes mostly thanks to Spain. But it is also true that laicism, a strong and aggressive secularism was born in Spain, as we saw in the 1930s ... This dispute is happening again in Spain today. The future of faith and the relations between faith and secularism have Spanish culture as its epicenter.'[5]

As we shall see, Ratzinger is not against secularity per se, but rather secularism as an ideology that marginalizes God and does not allow breathing space for Christianity. In fact, Ratzinger has argued that the secular tradition is necessary to correct the extremes and temptations of religion. Since the Second Vatican Council, the church has come to recognize the secular, neutral state as a positive value and cultural achievement. Martin Rhonheimer says that it is significant that in Benedict XVI's Christmas address to the Roman curia on 22 December 2005, he referred positively to the 'model of a modern state' originated by the American Revolution. He also distinguished this American model from the Jacobin model of the French Revolution which no longer allows the church any freedom.[6]

One thing is clear, like John Henry Newman, Joseph Ratzinger is unquestionably opposed to the liberal spirit of secularism and relativism that has adverse effects on the church and its faithful. In the next section we will explore the relationship between secularism and Christianity.

THE CHRISTIAN ORIGIN OF SECULARISM

Although Joseph Ratzinger is critical of the aggressive secularism that threatens the religious life of people, I have argued that secularism is a blessing in disguise in that it helps the church to purify itself and to be more faithful to the gospel.[7] In many ways, secularization was more a threat to the church than to the Christian faith.[8] In fact, secularism has its roots in Christianity. Owen Chadwick claims that the Reformation 'baptized' the secular world by levelling the differences between the clergy and the laity.[9] This implies that all secular callings are also a vocation from God. Furthermore, it was Christian conscience that made Europe secular by teaching people to be tolerant and inclusive. Gradually, the West allowed religious pluralism to flourish and abolished state religion.

According to Peter Berger, it was the Reformation in the sixteenth century that started the process of secularization when the reformers placed sole emphasis on scripture and private interpretation of the Bible. Research and advanced studies in scripture, by Protestant scholars in the eighteenth and nineteenth centuries, led to the 'disenchantment of the world'. The Protestant Reformation had ignited a resurgence of secularizing forces previously kept in check by Catholicism. Chadwick writes: 'If the drama of the modern era is the decline of religion, then Protestantism can aptly be described as its dress rehearsal.'[10] Many intellectuals, including theologians, think that modern society has no place for religious beliefs which are perceived as superstitious and primitive. It seems that a truly modern person must be 'godless' and the unfolding of history is a secularizing process in which human beings try to get rid of the gods.[11]

In the context of mission, Vinoth Ramachandra asserts that Christianity had a 'powerful secularizing thrust' in its attitude towards local language and culture in the sense that it stood in stark contrast to Muslim and Hindu notions of eternal, divine tongues', regarding Arabic and Sanskrit respectively. The Christian mission destroyed the powerful myth of Christendom and led to the successful separation of church and state, of religion and territory. Eventually, the modern secular culture resulted in the 'rejection of Christianity on the basis of Christian social and cultural achievements'. Hence Henrikus Berkhof writes: 'Secularization is a child of the gospel, but a child who sooner or later rises against his mother.'[12] Thus, the notion of secular has a Christian origin.

If secularization has a Christian origin, we can say that the church has unwittingly given birth to secularism and now it is trying to control this rebellious child with little success. This child in turn has been adopted by modern societies that have forgotten their Christian origin. It was Jesus himself who said, 'Render to Caesar the things that are Caesar's, and to God the things that are God's' (Mark 12:17). This could perhaps be said to be the original source of secularism. Therefore, it is not surprising that secularism is flourishing in Europe, in the heart of Christendom.

One of the main features of secularization is the distinction it makes between the public and private sectors in society. It is a distinction that applies to all aspects of life, both tangible and intangible. It follows then that religion belongs exclusively to the private domain and has no place in the public life of the nation. This is to safeguard the people against the intolerance of the state and to assure that the state remains neutral in religious matters. At the same time religion or the church cannot intervene or interfere in public affairs. In this way, secularization liberates science and learning from religious influence. This process of secularization already existed even before we coined the word for it.[13] This banishment of God from the public arena, in secularism, is also a legacy of the Enlightenment.

THE ENLIGHTENMENT

In his introduction to Joseph Ratzinger's *Christianity and the Crisis of Cultures*, Marcello Pera recognizes that the rationality of the Enlightenment bore marvellous fruit, for without it, there would not have been many of the great scientific, technological, economic and political advances that changed the lives of many in Europe.[14] However, in Ratzinger's opinion, these advances were also accompanied by scourges such as 'marginalization, the triumph of subjectivity, and the imprisonment of the divine, of the sacred, of God in a ghetto' and, in Europe, the banishment of God from the public square.[15] Ratzinger writes:

> This same rationality [of the Enlightenment] leaves its imprint on all the world today in a much deeper way, thanks to the technological culture that science has made possible. Indeed, in a certain sense, scientific rationality is imposing uniformity on the world. In the wake of this form of rationality, Europe has developed a culture that, in a manner hitherto unknown to mankind, excludes God from public awareness. His existence may be denied altogether or considered unprovable and uncertain and, hence, as something belonging to the sphere of subjective choices. In either case, God is irrelevant to public life.[16]

Ratzinger admits that the Enlightenment has a Christian origin and has drawn attention to its Christian values. Since the Second Vatican Council, the church has also tried to establish a harmony between Christianity and the Enlightenment by reconciling itself with modernity. Martin Rhonheimer says

Western Enlightenment is a prodigal son of Christianity in whom the father recognizes himself. After due correction and reconciliation, perhaps incomplete, this son acquires the right to live in the father's house. Rhonheimer also thinks that it was Christian culture which gave rise to the modern secular state. Christianity may be necessary to prevent the secular political culture from turning into 'an all-absorbing monism' that is hostile to religion.[17]

Influenced by the Enlightenment, contemporary philosophies are characterized by their anti-metaphysical element that denies the existence of God. Thus Ratzinger writes: 'They are based on a self-limitation of the positive reason that is adequate in the technological sphere but entails a mutilation of man if it is generalized. The result is that man no longer accepts any moral authority apart from his own calculations.'[18]

The philosophy of the Enlightenment is incomplete because it deprives itself of its original sources. This radical detachment from its roots will eventually lead to treating human beings as no different from other living things.[19] As a result, secularization, influenced by this philosophy, which was originally a positive development, turns against itself, resulting in people losing their identity and experiencing alienation. Joseph Ratzinger highlights this theme when he speaks of the crisis of catechesis in *Handing on the Faith in an Age of Disbelief*:

> In the technological world, which is a self-made world of man, one does not immediately encounter the Creator; rather, initially, it is only himself that man always encounters. The fundamental structure of this world is feasibility, and the manner of its certainty is the certainty of what can be calculated. Therefore even the question of salvation is not geared to God, who appears nowhere; rather, once again, it is geared to the ability of man, who wants to become the engineer of himself and of history ... For him, creation is silent with regard to morality; it speaks only the language of mathematics, of technological utility.[20]

MAN IS THE MEASURE OF ALL THINGS

Joseph Ratzinger vehemently rejects the Enlightenment's motto – 'Man is the measure of all things' – a theory which has convinced the West of our human ability to build a world of justice and reason. According to this motto, everything is possible for human beings. We do not need God. Discoveries and scientific and technological advancements have followed, but, unexpectedly, disillusionment, alienation and scepticism have also arrived. Commenting on technology and scientific advancement, Ratzinger says it is not the method but the power of its success that threatens to destroy the earth. This has resulted in the unification of 'technical' civilization, which in turn has caused 'the fragmentation of the philosophical consciousness and the dissolution of its specific content, namely, the question of truth'.[21]

One way out of the above situation, Ratzinger asserts, is to make philosophy 'wholly "positive"', which means that only what is empirical and scientifically proven is acceptable. Thus, the question of the truth of God, of spiritual things, is abandoned. But 'pure positivism' is unbearable in the long run and so truth becomes the product of human beings and is replaced by practical results. Truth, too, is produced 'scientifically'.[22] This implies that human beings can create an ideal future solely with their practical skills and expertise and with no need of divine assistance. As mentioned earlier, Ratzinger believes that this Enlightenment thinking with its anti-metaphysical trait is incomplete because it is divorced from its original source. This is related to the neglect of ontology, the stress on the Being as foundation, which is one of the great philosophical concerns of Ratzinger, in view of the threat of aggressive secularism as well as theological and religious pluralism.

ON METAPHYSICS

Joseph Ratzinger raises this issue in *The Nature and Mission of Theology*, where he claims that philosophy and theology cannot do without ontology. It seems that contemporary philosophers and theologians are both hostile to ontology. This is the reason why they are 'indissolubly dissociated', because the ontology which they deny could give them a solid foundation.[23] Ontology would give them a common ground on which to base dialogue. Philosophy and theology need this dimension of thought if they are to work together. Faith and philosophy confront the basic question of human death. Such a question implies the need to live meaningfully while at the same time it lets people find their origin and destination. Ratzinger writes: 'Death, the one question which it is impossible to ignore forever, is thus a metaphysical thorn lodged in man's being ... Faith hears the answer because it keeps the question alive.' When Christian faith speaks about the resurrection, it is not talking about an unknown future, but 'the comprehension of man's being within the whole of reality'.[24]

In view of the above, Ratzinger argues that the fundamental problem concerning justice and hope, the relationship between history and ethos, though formulated differently from time to time, has remained essentially the same throughout history. The relationship, however, can progress in the exchange of question and answer in philosophical and theological reflections. The dialogue of human thought, from the perspective of faith, gives us one aspect, and from the perspective of philosophy, another.[25] Consequently, both must remain in mutual relationship to give us a full picture of reality.

Ratzinger argues that faith furthers an ontological claim when it asserts that there is a God who has power over us all, as it implies that God, as the creator and saviour of the whole universe, reaches beyond the specific religious community that proclaims him. The prophets of Israel see in God, 'the primordial creative ground of all reality'.[26] God is the creator and saviour, not only of one specific community but of the whole world. Ratzinger believes this is a breakthrough in thinking about God because it does not just perceive him as a symbolic representation, in a particular religion. It is an appeal to our reason, as is evident in the writings of the prophets and wisdom literature in the Old Testament, which proclaim the true God in contrast to man-made idols. Hence, the faith of Israel goes beyond a particular people's way of worship, but rather is put forth as a universal claim. Ratzinger asserts that it is universal because it is rational.[27]

Christianity is a universal religion on the basis of the above claim. It is this critique of religion, found in the very heart of Israel, that resulted in the successful synthesis of secular Greek thought and the Bible, which the early church fathers sought to achieve.[28] Thus, the universality of faith makes missionary endeavour 'meaningful and morally defensible'. It is only this kind of faith that directs itself beyond the symbolism of a specific religion towards an answer that appeals to people's common sense. The question of God thus requires that theology take a philosophical position in debate. At the same time, philosophy 'must open itself to faith's claim on reason'.[29]

Ratzinger believes this to be an anthropological problem. If a human being's spiritual life is to remain intact, if his spiritual life is not to be allowed to disintegrate into a 'flat rationalism' dominated by technology or 'dark irrationalism', then faith and reason must be brought into a proper relationship.[30] The 'wave of esotericism' we are now witnessing is caused by human beings' inability to integrate into 'positivistic rationalism', resulting in the resurgence and even the flourishing of superstitions. Positivism doubts man's capacity to know the truth and confines knowledge to what can actually be produced and verified. Meanwhile, outside this scientific domain, irrational forces dominate and human beings become servants of 'inscrutable powers'.[31]

The Christian faith, on the other hand, responds to the primordial questions of man with respect to his origins and goals: 'What can I know? What may I hope for? What is man?' Incidentally, these primordial questions also constitute the essential core of philosophy. Thus, faith is related to truth. Only if a human being is capable of truth can he find freedom.[32] This understanding of Being as the foundation in metaphysics, however, is essentially a medieval, European way of thinking, which is untenable in our pluralistic world according to Gianni Vattimo, who presents us with a different perspective.

POSTMODERN PLURALISM

Unlike Joseph Ratzinger, Gianni Vattimo believes that, in twentieth-century philosophical thinking, it is no longer possible to think of Being (ontology) as the foundation because Europeans have come to recognize that there are other cultures that cannot be considered 'primitive' just because they fall behind the West in terms of 'progress'.[33] He asserts that the pluralistic world in which we live cannot be based on an ideology that seeks to unify 'at all costs in the name of a sole truth'. This would also go against the ideals of democracy.[34] Vattimo also claims that 'since God can no longer be upheld as an ultimate foundation, as the absolute metaphysical structure of the real, it is possible, once again, to believe in God ... not the God of metaphysics or of medieval scholasticism', but the 'God of the Bible'. Once we discover that the idea of Being as the eternal structure of metaphysics is untenable, 'we are left with the biblical notion of creation, namely with the contingency and historicity of our existing'. Translating this in secular and philosophical terms, Vattimo argues that in our experience of postmodern pluralism, 'we can think of Being only as event, and of truth ... as a historical message that must be heard and to which we are called to respond'.[35]

The church must accept the influence of modernity, Vattimo insists, and this means recognizing 'the profoundly Christian meaning of secularization'. The Christian's vocation consists of 'deepening its own physiognomy as source and condition for the possibility of secularity'.[36] Secularization is seen as a 'purification of the Christian faith' – a return to the 'faith's authentic essence'.[37] Vattimo makes this startling assertion that 'secularization is the way in which kenosis, having begun with the incarnation of Christ ... continues to realize itself more and more clearly by furthering the education of mankind concerning the overcoming of originary violence essential to the sacred and to social life itself'.[38]

One of the features of Christianity is a universalism, 'the awareness of a plurality of cultures and of a lay space where these can confront one another'. To become a true partner in cultural dialogue, Vattimo says, 'Christianity cannot put aside this essential feature of its heritage and identity; it must present itself as a bearer of the idea of secularity for the sake of its own specific authenticity.'[39] He thus calls for the development of Christian, lay vocation. This implies acknowledging the secularized character of Christianity and, also, recognizing this essential feature of the Christian faith as being unique, in comparison to other religious traditions. Christianity can take part in interreligious dialogue by referring to its 'specific lay orientation' which is not emphasized as much in other cultures and religions.[40]

In view of our pluralistic and multicultural societies, Gianni Vattimo argues that Christianity can recover its universalizing function only by stressing its missionary inclination as 'hospitality' and establishing its laity.[41] This means that in interreligious dialogue, Christians should be ready to acknowledge that others might be right. It is the 'principle of charity' realized in the form of 'hospitality in the dialogue between religions and cultures'. It includes listening and giving voice to others.[42] In other words, the new mission of Christianity should be moving from emphasis on universality to understanding the particularities of other faiths with the view of establishing a dialogue.

So far we have discussed Ratzinger's view of secularism, which is linked to the Enlightenment project by its anti-metaphysical element. Ratzinger insists on the importance of ontology in the study of philosophy and theology in order to counteract the atheistic ideology of modern society. This brings us to the most influential atheistic philosophy in the secular world – Marxism.

MARXIST PHILOSOPHY

During his recent trip to Cuba, in March 2012, Joseph Ratzinger claimed that Marxism no longer corresponds to reality.[43] It is no surprise that Ratzinger is very critical of Marxist philosophy and its influence on liberation theology. Owen Chadwick claims that at the heart of European secularism lies the theory of Marxism.[44] For Marx, religion is the 'opium of the people' and not 'opium for the people', as amended by Lenin. The idea was not new, but the phrase was. Chadwick argues that, when not taken out of context, Marx's phrase is not contemptuous of religion. His language is poetic, 'Religion is the sight of the oppressed creature, the heart of a heartless world, the soul of a soulless government.'[45]

Marx did not make an intellectual assault on religion like that of the Enlightenment. His main question was whether religion was desirable, or not, for society, not whether religion was true or false. For him, there was no need to argue about religion because it was the outcome of a failed social structure which ended in a capitalist society. Marxist historians claim that the social causes of secularization are most important because social changes are 'the necessary context of intellectual changes'. They examine material production and the history of production and state that in order to change people's ideas, we must change their living and working conditions. A social revolution is needed to abolish religion.[46]

Marx believed that religion 'formulates alienation' for 'it is the soul of alienation'.[47] The first form of religious alienation is detachment from our 'natural instincts'. The second form is the 'divine justification of social evil' by promising the poor and oppressed better things in the afterlife. Hence, heaven and hell are necessary to a society based on class. In a society without alienation, no one would need religion. Marx always believed that 'criticism of all society begins with criticism of religion'.[48] It follows that revolution must overthrow religion because it is part of the evil social system.

There is a close relationship between Marxism and Christianity. Alasdair MacIntyre viewed Marxism as a kind of Christian heresy.[49] Chadwick asserts that the whole idea of alienation is based on Christian and Jewish axioms. In addition, Marxist determinism is similar to Calvinist predestination and Marxism has a powerful eschatology – his view of the future is 'apocalyptic in its force'. Chadwick argues that 'religion without a god may still be religion'.[50] It follows that atheism can have a religious origin. Marx had used religious language to describe a non-religious process in his early writings. Consider this phrase of Marx, 'The religion of working men is religion without god because it seeks to restore the divinity of man.'[51]

Joseph Ratzinger views Marxism fundamentally as a philosophy that denies the existence of God in its effort to create a perfect society. He explains that the Frankfurt school and the entire neo-Marxist movement advanced the idea of truth as praxis. Suddenly theology became relevant, in both the university and society, when it adopted the idea that truth was produced by the method of praxis. Thus, 'practical theology' provides us with the framework where 'the struggle for a more human future on the basis of memories preserved in the history of faith' becomes the starting and end point of theological reflection. This gives theology an opportunity to become scientific and practical in the modern sense. However, Ratzinger thinks this approach is ironic and even incomprehensible because it seems that 'overnight theologians and their communities became the most effective representatives of the neo-Marxist movement'. He considers it 'a curious paradox' that only Marxism could revive an 'ailing theology' and make it into a real science. At the same time, religious passion restored a scientifically and politically exhausted Marxism. To Ratzinger, this is 'like the blind leads the blind, both shall fall into the ditch'.[52] For him, there is no compatibility between Marxism and theology.

In 'Eucharist, Communion, and Solidarity', a lecture given at the Eucharistic Congress of the Archdiocese of Benevento, Italy, on 2 June 2002, Ratzinger said that many were convinced that the Marxist socialist system was able to achieve human equality and eliminate poverty. However, he believed that an ideology that denies the existence of God can bring only horrors and massacres. Ratzinger claimed that the liberal model of the market economy under the influence of Christian social ideas has been quite successful in some parts of the world. But he was sad to see that in places such as Africa, 'clashing power blocs and economic interests have been at work', and particular powers and ideologies seek to expand and dominate the market. Therefore, Ratzinger argued that 'without God things cannot go well'.[53]

Marxism, like liberal capitalism, attempts to create a perfect society. According to Ratzinger, the worldviews of both are basically materialistic: 'they hold that matter is primary, spirit being but the product of matter, so that if the material conditions are improved, so will the human spirit'. Their worldviews deny the sacredness of the human person, since persons can be discarded in the public interest. Ratzinger believes this 'loss of the transcendent evokes the flight to utopia'. This can result in violent revolution when people fight against the imperfections of a society that fails to deliver what it has promised.[54]

Be that as it may, Marxism is closely related to Christianity, like a kind of Christian heresy as mentioned earlier. Essentially, Marxism was not a denial of God, but a reaction to a church that persuaded people to accept their suffering and injustice willingly, in the hope of a better future, in the afterlife. Marx and his followers believed economic, social and political liberation could be achieved without Christianity. Paradoxically, the secularization of society may provide opportunities for religion to renew itself. In the next section we will discuss Ratzinger's dialogue with Habermas. The two men make very exciting debating partners because the general public views one as the personification of the Catholic faith and the other as the personification of liberal and secular thinking.

DIALECTICS OF SECULARIZATION

The Dialectics of Secularization by Jürgen Habermas and Joseph Ratzinger is a good place to examine, in depth, Ratzinger's thoughts on secularism. This book is a transcript of their dialogue on an agreed subject: 'The pre-political Moral Foundations of a Free State'. Ratzinger posed this provocative question to his audience at the Catholic Academy of Bavaria: Is religion 'an archaic and dangerous force that builds up false universalisms, thereby leading to intolerance and acts of terrorism?'[55] The context for the question was a debate between himself, then prefect of the Congregation for the Doctrine of the Faith, and Jürgen Habermas, a liberal, secular philosopher who proclaimed himself to be 'tone-deaf in the religious sphere'.[56] Ratzinger did not deny the fact that religion could be an archaic and dangerous force and Habermas did not defend his own commitment to a neutral, universally accessible reason as defence against the claims of any revealed religion.

FOUNDATIONS OF THE SECULAR STATE

Habermas admits that free, secular states have arisen, as in the case of his native Germany, from a 'common religious background and a common language'.[57] However, he is more concerned with whether such states, as they exist today, are able to justify their commitment to neutral, non-religious principles of reason. He thinks that regardless of whether citizens are themselves motivated by a particular ethic or perceived revelation, the liberal state can 'satisfy its own need for legitimacy in a self-sufficient manner'.[58] Its uniting bond is the 'democratic process itself – a communicative praxis ... exercised only in common and that has as its ultimate theme the correct understanding of the constitution'.[59] Habermas says democracies can maintain legitimacy without having to ground themselves in any singular worldview or metaphysical understanding. He admits, however, that democracies do demand the solidarity and the commitment of their citizens to the process itself.[60]

As the trend for globalization moves society beyond the confines of a particular political system, it frees the global economy from many political constraints. However, there is no law to guarantee human rights in the globalized world and the secular state faces destabilization as people increasingly feel compelled to act in their own self-interest. Therefore, many people are losing hope in this process of globalization. Habermas does not say the secular forces of communicative reason do not work in a global and pluralistic society. He is simply saying that these forces should be treated 'undramatically, as an open, empirical question'.[61] He admits that reason has its limits and we must become aware of them. Consequently, reason cannot claim to know what 'may be true or false in the contents of religious traditions'.[62]

In view of the above, Habermas acknowledges the feasibility of alternative claims and admits that there is something to learn from religious traditions, something which reason does not provide. Religions, he says, have kept alive and continue to reformulate contextual interpretations of redemption, of 'salvific exodus from a life that is experienced as empty of salvation'.[63] This task cannot be performed by secular philosophers alone. Regarding 'the substance of biblical concepts accessible to a general public that also includes those who have other faiths and those who have none', secular societies must learn to transpose these concepts into a context that is relevant for everyone. For example, the biblical idea of man in the image of God can be translated as referring to the dignity of all human beings.[64] In other words, secular philosophers must learn to appreciate that religious traditions have a contribution to make. The bonding of a secular democratic process with a society depends on the faith and commitment of the people whose religions play an important part in their lives.

Jürgen Habermas, a methodical atheist, agrees that the heart of European culture is Christian in origin. It also depends on Christianity for its nourishment.[65] In *Times of Transitions*, he writes:

> Christianity has functioned for the normative self understanding of modernity as more than a mere precursor or a catalyst. Egalitarian universalism, from which sprang the ideas of freedom and social solidarity, of an autonomous conduct of life and emancipation, of the individual morality of conscience, human rights, and democracy, is the direct heir to the Judaic ethic of justice and the Christian ethic of love .... To this day, there is no alternative to it. And in light of the current challenges of a postnational constellation, we continue to draw on the substance of this heritage. Everything else is just idle postmodern talk.[66]

Like Joseph Ratzinger, Habermas also regards political philosophy, which has given birth to secularism in Europe, as having been influenced by the covenantal theology of the Old Testament and Hellenistic philosophy. The liberal secularism of modern Europe thinks it has freed itself from religious faith, but, in actual fact, it has merely suppressed or forgotten its religious roots. Ideas such as liberty, conscience and human rights, which are fundamental for liberal secularism, are continually nourished by its religious roots.[67] Likewise, Gianni Vattimo would even say the secularizing trend in modern Europe consists not only in exposing the errors of religion, but also in the survival of these errors in some degraded forms. It follows that 'a secularized culture is not one that has simply left the religious elements of its tradition behind, but one that continues to live them as traces, as hidden and distorted models that are nonetheless profoundly present'.[68]

FRIEDRICH NIETZSCHE AND LEO STRAUSS

According to Gary Glenn, Jürgen Habermas's acknowledgement of the Christian roots of European secularism reflects not only Ratzinger's conviction, but also that of Friedrich Nietzsche who opposes Christianity.[69] In *Twilight of Idols*, Nietzsche writes:

> If you give up Christian faith, you pull the *right* to Christian morality out from under your feet. This morality is simply *not* self-evident ... Christianity is a system, a view of things that is conceived as a connected *whole*. If you break off a major concept from it, faith in God, you break up the whole as well; there are no necessities left to hold onto any more. Christianity presupposes that human beings do not know, *cannot* know, what is good and evil for them: they believe in God, who is the only one who knows it. Christian morality is a commandment; its origin is transcendent; it is beyond all criticism, all right to criticism; it is true only if God is truth – it stands and falls with faith in God.[70]

Therefore, according to Nietzsche, if the New Testament God is rejected, secular morality would be groundless, inconsistent and incoherent. Western society's continued preference for some of the political and moral fruits of Christianity such as tolerance and humanness are now without any foundation and also lack the energizing spirit to sustain the personal and political sacrifices needed for stability. Nietzsche teaches that the only consistent inferences from the rejection of the Christian God are that the strong would do what they like to the weak and that without that 'God', there would be no rational basis for sacrificial love.[71]

Agreeing with Nietzsche, Leo Strauss claims European relativism (rather than secularism) tends to be liberal rather than ruthless because it is inconsistent. At times it prefers Judeo-Christian values instead of the strict dictates of secularism. It follows, therefore, that 'the inconsistent reliance on Christian morality, while jettisoning the Christian God, shows that its secularism is liberal or "post Christian"'.[72] It would be rational to condemn or suppress evil, but relativism teaches that such knowledge of good and evil is not available and, hence, we must tolerate it. However, Strauss observes that, 'Absolute tolerance is altogether impossible; the allegedly absolute tolerance turns into ferocious hatred of those who have stated most clearly and most forcefully that there are unchangeable standards founded in the nature of man and the nature of things.'[73] Strauss claims that 'liberal relativism has its roots in the natural right tradition of tolerance or in the notion that everyone has a natural right to the pursuit of happiness as he understands happiness; but in itself it is a seminary of intolerance'.[74] Such an assertion agrees with Ratzinger's analysis that the more relativism becomes the accepted norm of thinking, the more it becomes intolerant.[75]

THAT WHICH HOLDS THE WORLD TOGETHER

It is interesting to note that Ratzinger did not put forward his own religion or any metaphysical basis as the legitimizing force behind Western democracies. He agrees with Habermas that the adherents of secular reasoning and those with religious convictions should learn from each other. He also demands something more active, something as revolutionary to secular democracies as secular democracies are to the European churches. He provides a brief analysis of the dynamics of power and law. He says that the law cannot be the arm of the strong because law is the only thing built strongly enough to oppose those with power. It offers strength to those who are weak. Law is the 'antithesis of violence' because the true function of the law is equality for all.[76]

Ratzinger argues that 'revolt against the law, will always arise when law itself appears to be no longer the expression of a justice that is at the service of all, but ... the product of arbitrariness and legislative arrogance'.[77] He asserts that democracy is the most appropriate form of political order only when the law is the expression of the common interest of all'.[78] However, total consensus is hard to achieve among human beings and the vagaries of the majority can be blind and unjust.[79] While Habermas has great faith in democratic systems of law, Ratzinger thinks they are hard to sustain because of pluralism and globalization. Doubting the reliability of reason, Ratzinger is afraid that religious believers will no longer come to trust in the protection of secular systems.

As to whether religion is to be blamed for the acts of terrorism and intolerance that occur when conflicting worldviews collide, Ratzinger admits that it is often true. As to whether religion should be placed under the guidance of reason, Ratzinger asserts that reason has taken humanity not only as far as the atomic bomb, but even further, to the point where 'man is now capable of making human beings, of producing them in test tubes ... man [has become] a product ... he is no longer a gift of nature or of the Creator God'.[80] One could debate the advantages and disadvantages of genetic engineering, but it is hard to argue with Ratzinger's point that the pace of the effort is out of control and that the sense of life being a gift is disappearing. Thus he rightly asks: 'Does this then mean that it is reason that ought to be placed under guardianship? But by what or by whom?'[81] Ratzinger's position is a balanced one: that reason and religion should restrict each other by setting boundaries for each other.

Ratzinger does not say that religious belief can be the saviour of a world gone astray nor does he believe that the answers are to be found in a debate between secular reason and religion. He goes further than Habermas and suggests that the classic debate between a 'neutral' secular reason and a Christian-dominated worldview in the West is not even a universal debate. Both are global in their reach but are 'de facto not universal'.[82] Ratzinger admits that there are 'pathologies' in religion, but he believes pathologies are also found in secular reason.[83] He agrees with Habermas that secular reason and the Christian religion need to learn from each other because of the necessary relationship between faith and reason.

DIVERGENCE AND CONVERGENCE OF VIEWS

Ratzinger and Habermas have radically different worldviews, but what is interesting is that both of them have expressed a willingness to learn from the other and to hope for something that neither of them has yet experienced. Inherent in their respective positions is the commitment to pursue something new as well as the commitment to redeem what is old. Both men explore how a liberal state can transcend its majoritarian relativistic foundations. Habermas thinks that a state with a neutral worldview can generate its own view and give legitimacy to the people so that they can begin to vote, relate sincerely to one another and share a will that can be democratically realized.

Contrary to Ratzinger, Habermas thinks that no religion or exterior source is required to establish these values in the community. The state is legitimate because the citizens assist in formulating the laws and shaping the political culture. The process of democracy yields 'the fruit of a socialization in which one becomes accustomed to the practices and modes of thought of a free political culture'.[84] Habermas claims that political liberalism can establish the values a state needs from within the community, except when it faces 'external threats' such as capitalism. According to him, capitalism may lead to isolation of people from one another within society, people acting on the basis of their own self-interest, and so on, and the state would lack the values to counteract the situation.[85] Habermas admits that religion can provide the resources needed to fight such external threats and suggests that philosophy could secularize some useful religious concepts, such as the dignity of the person, in order to provide a common ground.[86]

It is intriguing to find in this dialogue that it was Habermas who suggested that religion ought to play a greater role in public life and even more surprising to hear Ratzinger proclaiming that religion, unchecked by rational critique, can become an ideology with terrible consequences. Both men are sceptical of the absolute claims of science and agree that, even in our pluralistic world, 'philosophy must continue to seek to salvage truth or succumb to a postmodern collapse into relativism, and the shared pragmatic recognition of the vital epistemic and discursive contributions that spiritual worldviews can positively contribute to the organization of civil society in light of a deflated and overly rationalistic conception of human nature'.[87] They are aware of the threat to human solidarity, of a globalized world with its relentless capitalism and they also agree that the state with the help of religion can revive some forms of solidarity.

POLYPHONIC RELATEDNESS: EAST AND WEST

Since secularism is most developed in Europe, Habermas and Ratzinger offer little reflection on the way in which non-Western cultures could contribute to a better understanding of our post-secular age. This absence is all the more striking when Ratzinger himself has said:

It is important that both great components of the Western culture learn to *listen* and to accept a genuine relatedness to these other cultures, too. It is important to include the other cultures in the attempt at a polyphonic relatedness, in which they themselves are receptive to the essential complementarity of reason and faith, so that a universal process of purifications (in the plural!) can proceed.[88]

In view of Ratzinger's call for a 'polyphonic relatedness', Jonathan Bowman suggests that non-Western modes of thought must be regarded as equal partners in this dialectic (between secularism and Christianity) and viewed as 'authoritative sources of potential redaction of Enlightenment and Christian ideologies'.[89] Bowman calls for an ambitious, 'multi-faceted purification' of secular ideology, using Eastern religious teachings: the Confucian 'notion of the rectification of names', the Taoist 'idea of truth disclosure' and the Buddhist 'practice of right speech'.[90] However, in spite of the call for a polyphonic relatedness, the dialogue focuses only on the European scene. Jürgen Habermas, the champion of the Frankfurt School of Critical Theory, naturally speaks of human rights, and Joseph Ratzinger, schooled in the patristic tradition, speaks of natural law.

HUMAN RIGHTS AND NATURAL LAW

Habermas argues that there is a need to translate spiritual values into secular language, given the fact that the world has been badly battered by market forces and growing government interference in the public sphere. Market forces seek to increase their capital while an expanding governmental bureaucracy seeks to increase its power. As mentioned earlier, one example of the possible translation of the spiritual into the secular is the reference to the Judeo-Christian notion of the human being created in the image of God, which in turn is translated into the notion of the dignity of the human person. This forms the basis of human rights.

Ratzinger, on the other hand, points to the natural law as the moral basis of the modern state. Although he does not grant equal weight to claims about truth in all religions, he believes the situation created by globalization and the mass media can provide a means of utilizing other traditions as a check on the claims to universality made by Enlightenment proponents and, in my opinion, also found in some aspects of church dogma. Such an attempt might lead to a new version of universally held values. Ratzinger writes: 'Ultimately, the essential values and norms that are in some way known or sensed by all men will take on a new brightness in such a process, so that that which holds the world together can once again become an effective force in mankind.'[91] In spite of their differences, both Habermas and Ratzinger share the same insight that spiritual influence in the public sphere can help people discover the truths about human nature.

ROLE OF RELIGION IN SOCIETY

Habermas' view in this dialogue demonstrates that he recognizes the importance of the religious dimension, which includes tolerance between the church and state, in his political–ethical project.[92] He rejects the transformation of science as an alternative religion.[93] Habermas admits that the modernization project started by the Enlightenment has become the victim of a society that can lose its ability to control things. What he means is that when the dynamics of a globalized economy and markets in general are 'clearly outside the control of consensual rational judgments ... [the] citizens become "depoliticized," but they seem to show indifference to the glaring inequalities' between people in different parts of the world.[94] He also admits that we are entering into a post-secular phase where societies are becoming more open to the questions of the spirit because they have developed the habit of critical enquiry. Hence, Habermas writes: 'there is a ready audience for the theory that the remorseful modern age can find its way out of the blind alley only by means of the religious orientation to a transcendent point of reference'.[95]

The interesting point to note here is that Habermas is willing not to acknowledge just the continued existence of religion in our secular societies, but also to take up the 'cognitive challenge' of this phenomenon.[96] Perhaps the most surprising thing that Habermas articulates is the concession he gives to religion when he says:

> [W]e find in sacred scriptures and religious traditions intuitions about error and redemption, about the salvific exodus from a life that is experienced as empty of salvation ... This is why something can remain intact in the communal life of the religious fellowship – provided of course they avoid dogmatism and the coercion of people's consciences – something that has been lost elsewhere and that cannot be restored by the professional knowledge of experts alone.[97]

In this, Habermas implies that there are 'societal pathologies' and people whose lives have gone astray. He speaks of 'the failure of individuals' plans for their lives' and 'the deformation and disfigurement of the lives that people share with one another'.[98] It is clear that Habermas disapproves of those who wish to keep religion out of the public sphere for he believes, 'it is in the interest of the constitutional state to deal carefully with all the cultural sources that nourish its citizens' consciousness of norms and their solidarity'.[99] He advocates mutual understanding and tolerance in a society that allows space for religious discourse. In spite of growing secularism, Habermas understands that religious fellowship is here to stay.

PURIFICATION OF REASON AND RELIGION

The position of Ratzinger regarding secularism is made even more interesting by the fact that he did not begin his response with a comment on religion. Instead, he gave an analysis of the state of the world today: globalization, increased human potential for construction and destruction, and the problem of relativism, which weakens the possibility for a common ethical ground. Few would disagree with him that power should be subordinate to the law. However, in practice, this is not so easy because injustice can be committed by majority vote and diverse cultures may not agree on the norms for civil rights.[100]

Regarding the abuse of both reason and religion, Ratzinger proposes that reason should accept that it has limits and be willing to listen to the great religious traditions of humanity. At the same time, Christianity, which currently is not yet capable of establishing a set of universally acceptable principles, must go through a critical and cleansing process of rational enquiry.[101] Ratzinger writes: 'Religion must continually allow itself to be purified and structured by reason; and this was the view of the Church Fathers, too.'[102] This implies that religion and reason are correlated: both are called to engage in mutual purification and healing.

Ratzinger has clearly stated that the two branches of Western civilization – Christianity and scientific rationalism – can gain acceptance only by acknowledging the multicultural nature of our pluralistic world. A renewed spiritual culture can be established through a two-pronged dialogue that takes into account the 'apprehensions of these alternative cultures towards both Christianity ... and ... scientific rationalism'. However, the fact remains that these two branches are only intelligible to and accepted by a small section of humankind. They are far from universal. Non-Western cultures, spiritual in their nature, are very suspicious of 'domineering rationalism' and 'crass materialism'.[103]

According to Virgil Nemoianu, Ratzinger is not a political conservative, but more like a kind of 'moderate social democrat'.[104] Nemoianu believes that there are few places left in the world where reason can find a home other than inside the Catholic Church. Thus, it is understandable that faith and reason become the basis for building bridges to thinkers such as Habermas who, although 'tone deaf in the religious sphere', still seek connection with the religious traditions of the world.[105]

Ratzinger, for his part, believes that reason and religion must purify one another. In fact, they need each other. He admits that Christianity and scientific rationalism are only accepted by a small percentage of people in the world – it is not as universal as we think. This means that we must interact with non-Western cultures. Ratzinger acknowledges that the secular is a legitimate sphere with its own autonomy, privileges and limits. He is not against secularism as such, but only as an aggressive ideology that systematically seeks to discredit religion.

HEALTHY SECULARISM

From *The Dialectics of Secularization*, we can see that Ratzinger's understanding of secularism is nuanced and balanced. He does not say Christianity could be the saviour of our broken world and that it would get rid of the malaise of humankind. However, he is fighting against an aggressive ideology that threatens our freedom and pushes God out of human existence. The secularism experienced in Western society is no longer a neutral influence that opens up space for religious freedom; it is being transformed into an ideology that penetrates politics and does not allow a Christian vision to exist. Thus, the Christian faith runs the risk of being something purely private and disfigured.

In an interview in *La Repubblica*, the Italian daily, on 19 November 2004, Ratzinger said, 'We must defend religious freedom against the imposition of an ideology which is presented as if it were the only voice of rationality, when it is only the expression of a "certain" rationalism.' In this interview, Ratzinger recognized that a just secularism allows freedom of worship and that the state should not impose religion but, rather, allow space for religious belief. It allows various religions to be co-builders of society. Whereas, when secularism is transformed into an ideology, to speak of God is seen as an attack on the freedom of unbelievers: God has been marginalized in the world of politics.[106]

Christianity cannot regard itself as being in conflict with secular reality because 'God so loved the world that he gave his only Son, that whoever believes in him should … have eternal life' (John 3:16). Secular reality is not unknown to the Christian faith. Pope Paul VI said the church 'has an authentic secular dimension, inherent to her inner nature and mission, which is deeply rooted in the mystery of the Word Incarnate, and which is realized in different forms through her members.'[107] Perhaps the tension in Western society is not a conflict between religion and the secular, but between those who search for deeper meaning in life and those who believe that the human life has no meaning beyond this earthly existence. Perhaps the conflict is actually between faith and the ideology of secularism, which believes that there is no answer to the fundamental questions concerning life and death.[108]

In his address to the new ambassador to the Holy See of the Republic of San Marino, Ratzinger asserted that a condition of 'healthy' secularism is needed 'for building a society where different traditions, cultures and religions may peacefully co-exist'. He says we will go into a blind alley if we completely separate public life from traditions. Therefore, 'it is essential to redefine the sense of a secularism that emphasizes the true difference and autonomy between the different components of society' and also to preserve the specific competences of each component, in working towards the common good. This healthy secularism suggests that it may be possible for each sector of society to be governed according to its own rules, but secular society must not neglect the fundamental ethical base in human beings.[109]

In sum, a healthy secularism that Joseph Ratzinger supports should include a separation of church and state, as well as a neutral stance towards religion, which is required in a pluralistic society. This means that no religion is given a privileged status, there is equality between people of different religious beliefs, and people have the freedom to believe or not to believe. A healthy secularism should also maintain a harmonious relationship between the adherents of different faiths, hence the importance of engaging in interreligious dialogue at all levels.[110] Secularism is not just an end in itself, but can be a means towards democracy and religious pluralism. If such is the case, the secularist principle of separation of church and state should include equal participation of all citizens in the democratic process as well as free exercise of their religion.[111]

AN EXCEPTIONAL PHENOMENON

José Casanova reminds us that the term 'secularization' has its root in Western Christian discourse, that of *saeculum*, just as the term 'religious' is derived from Western secular modernity. These categories evolved within the European context as the result of the interaction between Christianity and Western culture. This recognition should allow a 'less Eurocentric comparative analysis of patterns of differentiation and secularization in other civilizations and world religions'.[112] Casanova argues that the secularization of Western Europe is not a universal but an exceptional phenomenon, unlikely to be repeated in other parts of the world. It is particularly a European, 'Christian and post-Christian historical process'.[113]

Furthermore, through Western colonial expansion, the process of secularization became globalized and entered 'into dynamic tension with the many different ways in which other civilizations had drawn boundaries between "sacred" and "profane," "transcendent" and "immanent," "religious" and "secular."'[114] Casanova argues that in other civilizations, the transcendent is not necessarily religious and the secular is not necessarily profane. As such, we need to be more open to non-Western analysis of the secular dynamics and be critical of Western secular categories in order have a better understanding of this complex phenomenon.[115]

Casanova's theory of secularization confirms Joseph Ratzinger's observation that aggressive secularism is a European phenomenon that strikes at the heart of the Christian faith and poses a threat to the Western church. Ratzinger also fears that this threat may spread to the rest of the church. However, the spread of secularism has not led to a decline of religious belief and practice in Asia. In fact, various religious beliefs are flourishing in Asia as can be seen by the many temples, mosques and churches there. Even in communist China, where the government pursues an atheistic policy and persecutes underground churches, Christianity continues to spread. According to the 2007 Chinese Spiritual Life Survey conducted by Fenggang Yang and the Institute for Religion at Baylor University, only fifteen percent of the Chinese population can be regarded as 'pure atheists'.[116] This suggests that the church must rethink and reformulate its doctrines and policies regarding pastoral care and mission in Asia.

In this chapter we examined Ratzinger's concern for the rise of aggressive secularism in Europe and its negative effect on Christianity. Secularism is related to relativism because the confinement of religious beliefs to the private sphere implies that all religions are equally valid as paths to salvation. Besides the widespread rise of secularism, the rise of religious pluralism has led to interest in Eastern religions and philosophies such as Confucianism, Taoism and Buddhism in the West. Ratzinger associates religious pluralism with relativistic thinking regarding one's faith. In the next chapter we will discuss Ratzinger's warning against the dictatorship of relativism.

Chapter 6

Relativism

Joseph Ratzinger sees relativism, a product of secularization, as the greatest doctrinal threat in Western societies. In Asia, relativism includes a 'negative theology' that denies the uniqueness and universality of Jesus Christ as the saviour of the world and Christianity as the one and true religion. Ratzinger's encounters with different forms of relativism such as National Socialism (Nazism) and Marxism early in his life made him very much aware of their inherent danger. His classical and humanistic education in Munich led him to a profound reverence for the past, present and future of humanity as the place for the incarnated Logos.[1]

In this chapter, we shall examine the nature of relativism as understood by Ratzinger, who is not against relativism per se, but only when it becomes absolute and imposes itself on ethics and religion. There is also a tendency in Ratzinger's writings to equate religious pluralism with relativism, which results in his dismissal of theology not grounded in the Western philosophical–theological tradition. However, in our contemporary pluralistic society, there are some who think that relativism is a positive thing in that it denies fundamentalism, allows one to explore different options in life and avoid past mistakes. Thus, in view of the universal nature of our church, relativism is a welcome feature. In this regard, the ideas of Richard Rorty, Tissa Balasuriya and other critics will be discussed in relation to Ratzinger's warning against the dictatorship of relativism.

The complete abolition of relativism was never Ratzinger's idea because he believes it also possesses some legitimate forms. Relativism can be positively used as a philosophical tool in the search of truth. As pope, he writes:

In this process of innovation in continuity we must learn to understand more practically than before that the Church's decisions on contingent matters – for example, certain practical forms of liberalism or a free interpretation of the Bible – should necessarily be contingent themselves, precisely because they refer to a specific reality that is changeable in itself.[2]

Ratzinger is only against the attempt by some people to make relativism be the rule unto itself. He does not question relativism in all its forms, but only focuses on its effects on faith and morals. However, he is especially worried that relativism has become the dominating influence in theology. In its destructive forms, relativism has resulted in distorting the Christian faith: 'Thus, for example, if religious freedom were to be considered an expression of the human inability to discover the truth and thus become a canonization of relativism, then this social and historical necessity is raised inappropriately to the metaphysical level and thus stripped of its true meaning.'[3]

It is clear that Ratzinger's chief preoccupation was relativism in the areas of ethics and religion. Thus he would choose this topic as the keynote of his homily, preached to the College of Cardinals on 18 April 2005, at the Mass before they entered the conclave from which he himself was elected as pope:

Having a clear faith, based on the creed of the Church, is often labelled today as a fundamentalism. Whereas relativism, which is letting oneself be tossed and swept along by every wind of teaching [Ephesians 4:14] looks like the only attitude acceptable to today's standards. We are moving towards a dictatorship of relativism which does not recognize anything as for certain and which has as its highest goal one's own ego and one's own desires.[4]

Perhaps this was the occasion when a good many Catholics heard the word 'relativism' for the first time because it was printed in all major newspapers in the world. But Ratzinger had spent his life analysing and opposing relativism in many of his writings and speeches. There is no discontinuity between Cardinal Ratzinger and Pope Benedict, who has remained consistent in naming the dangers of relativism, as we shall see. George Weigel has observed that Ratzinger did not use the phrase 'dictatorship of relativism' to be provocative. He used it as a matter of fact and wanted the voting cardinals to know where he stood regarding the church in the modern world.[5]

THREAT OF RELATIVISM

Ratzinger traces the threat of secularism to relativism specifically, a problem typical of modernity. It is the notion that absolute truth cannot be grasped by the human mind. Relativism is not just a philosophical flaw, but a serious political problem as well. His analysis of relativism has as its point of departure the conscience.[6] Relativism implies an infallible conscience, which means that actions are acceptable as long as we are true to our conscience. The different choices that we make concerning a particular issue show that a single truth does not exist, and thus relativism flourishes. Thus it seems that there is a plurality of truths, and therefore we cannot criticize the positions of others if they are true to their consciences. If each person has a differing viewpoint, we no longer try to determine which is right, but label or categorize them as progressive or conservative. The danger here is that truth is abandoned and all that is left is the image. If we cannot convince others that our view is true, we then try to persuade others that it is the best by perfecting the image, which some politicians are expert in doing. Ratzinger believes this 'relativistic outcome of the subjective conscience drains the political realm of any moral obligation'.[7] In his early life, growing up in Nazi Germany where truth was determined by its leaders, Ratzinger realized the importance of defending the truths of the Christian religion.

Another serious threat is that relativism leads to the elevation of science and technology, a world obsessed with nuclear weapons, cloning, stem-cell research, and so on. Human beings begin to think that they are the masters of nature. Ratzinger thinks a secularized, technology-savvy and relativistic world does not possess enough 'moral energy' to provide the restraints that people need.[8] Man seeks to realize all that he desires to the extent that progress is worshipped as a religion. This modern fascination with science and technology, Ratzinger has observed, is related to the pursuit of realizing a utopia on earth. This reminds him of the horrors of Marxist regimes that attempted to perfect humans, observing that 'wherever politics tries to be redemptive, it is promising too much'.[9] This notion of an earthly paradise is actually 'a secular artefact of religion'. When people no longer believe in heaven, they try to build it on earth.[10]

In view of this, Ratzinger perceives the collapse of socialism and communism as a failure of utopianism and a parallel increase in relativism. Utopianism is essentially non-relativistic because it has a particular goal. If utopianism and religion are both rejected, there is nothing left except to embrace relativism where everything and anything goes. Ratzinger warns against the dictatorship of relativism, a condition related to postmodernism, which has also influenced the study of anthropology, literary studies, philosophy and religion.

THE POSTMODERN CONDITION

A foremost Marxist literary critic, Terry Eagleton, seems to articulate the concern of Ratzinger when he asserts that postmodernism refers to a form of contemporary culture and implies a style of thought suspicious of classical notions of truth, reason, ultimate ground of being, and so on.[11] Eagleton says postmodernism 'scoops up something of the material logic of advanced capitalism and turns this aggressively against its spiritual foundations... It is as though it is urging the system, like its great mentor Friedrich Nietzsche, to forget about its metaphysical foundations, acknowledge that God is dead and simply go relativist.'[12] Eagleton also asserts that postmodernism does not envisage an optimistic future as it promotes cultural relativism, scepticism, pragmatism and localism, distaste for ideas of solidarity and disciplined organization.[13]

Postmodernism teaches 'the notions that everything is a "text," that the basic material of texts, societies and almost anything is meaning, that meanings are there to be decoded or "deconstructed," that the notion of objective reality is suspect'. As such, postmodernism favours relativism and is hostile to the idea of a unique, objective and transcendental truth. Relativism believes truth is elusive and subjective.[14]

The Enlightenment was keen to deny religious transcendence and to affirm the orderly system of nature. However, all organisms and societies within that system had their own internal, functional system of knowledge and thus the Enlightenment was also relativistic. But the vision was considered unique, which contained within itself relatively valid systems. According to Kant, everything inside nature was subject to its law, but knowledge itself and morality were outside it. Thus, inside nature there was no room for reason but only causation. But nature, as a uniquely orderly system, was the construction of a reason determined to subsume all phenomena to a system. Kant consigns all of nature to causality and when this is applied to culture, relativism results.[15]

Kant's ethics are reduced to the obligation to be rational, which means 'orderliness', to make no exceptions and to unify them in an orderly system. His ethics applies to cognition as well, and in exploring the world, all information is treated alike. Thus there is no privileged source of enlightenment. Ernest Gellner says 'the essence of sin is the making of exceptions ... there is no and can be no Revelation'. The cognitive ethics of the Enlightenment shares with monotheistic exclusive scriptural religion the belief in the existence of a unique truth. It repudiates the idea that this unique truth comes from a privileged source and could be definitive: 'it shares with hermeneutic relativism the repudiation of the claim that a *substantive*, final and definitive version of the truth is available'.[16] Only its procedure is considered absolute, all ideas are relative. Thus the idea that there is a unique and final message delivered at one place and one time, to be accepted as a matter of faith, violates the rules of cognitive ethics. Gellner admits that for those of us who are committed to this viewpoint, it constitutes our worldview and it is the only one we have.[17]

The idea that there are no objective standards of belief comes from Nietzsche, among others, when he asserted that 'God is dead'. People have stopped believing in the Christian God. This is particularly true in Europe. Darwin's theory of evolution also challenged the idea of a divine design in the natural world. Furthermore, the two world wars shattered people's belief in a benevolent God. The enormous growth in knowledge of other cultures and acceptance of cultural diversity has led people to question their own knowledge and belief system, as well as what kinds of conduct are acceptable. The technology of mass destruction applied repeatedly with great success threatens our belief in the objectivity of moral values. Underlying such social and historical uncertainties are deep philosophical problems about the legitimacy of belief.[18]

Postmodern critics, such as François Lyotard, advise against accepting the concepts of reality, truth and morality. In *The Postmodern Condition*, he declares that philosophical discourses consist of nothing but 'metanarratives' – total philosophies of history or the quest for a universally valid philosophy for humanity. When implemented, these metanarratives tend to end in failure, like Marxism in the Soviet Union. The postmodern condition implies that we must overcome our Enlightenment legacy by abandoning the quest for truth.[19]

POSTMODERN FEATURES

Virgil Nemoianu gives nine features of postmodernism and five of them are relevant to our discussion here. First, there is the modification of gender relationship which includes the undermining of the traditional family.

Nemoianu believes this is the most powerful form of postmodern relativization to the extent that it attempts to modify human nature as we traditionally know it. Second, there is the tension between globalism and multiculturalism. Globalism is centralizing, and it attempts to seek a common destiny for humankind. Multiculturalism, on the other hand, is based on differences such as race and culture, among others. Third is the rise of relativism and scepticism as the guiding norm of conduct in all areas of life, or what Ratzinger would describe as the 'dictatorship of relativism'. This implies placing all values under interrogation and doubt. Macronarratives disappear and the principles of Nietzsche replace those of Aristotle and Aquinas as the intellectuals influencing the conscience of society. Fourth is relativization and questionableness of the past which lead to discontinuity and rupture in history. Fifth, religions do not disappear but appear in different forms. Here the spiritual-mystical dimension of religion replaces the dogmatic–theological one. Syncretism, pantheism and mysticism adapted to contemporary society are the features of this new mode of religious expression.[20]

André Malraux claims that 'the twenty-first century will be religious or will not be at all'. This means that we are in a situation in which there is a serious disequilibrium between technical–scientific progress and the spiritual progress of humankind. Thus it is urgent that we work to re-establish the balance and cooperation between the two. The speed in one direction and the slowness in the other can destroy us. Humanity is in danger of destroying itself as can be seen in the moral and social malaise that advanced countries experience. There is a general lack of purpose and vitality in these countries, which results in violent conflicts without solution and hope. These postmodern features indicate a state of disorder and chaos, of levelling and 'indifferentiation'. This applies to social interrelationship, to the 'destructuring of human groups and to the contempt and ignorance of religious values and cultural–literary accomplishments.'[21]

Nemoianu says postmodernity is not a diabolical condition, but it is a dangerous one. We must not demonize it but learn to deal with it. He also claims that the Roman Catholic Church is in good shape to deal with the crisis of postmodernity because of its rational discipline and the quality of its pontiffs, who have been exceptional in the last hundred years. As an institution, Nemoianu asserts that the Catholic Church's involvement in social and political affairs remains healthy, although not always successful.[22] It is clear that Ratzinger is prepared to deal with this crisis in Western Europe, as can be seen by his warning against relativism in his homily on 18 April 2005 and on other occasions.

RELATIVISM AND LIBERATION THEOLOGY

When the Soviet Union collapsed and communism was no longer a prevalent ideology in the West, Ratzinger perceived the rise of liberation theology and interest in religious pluralism as relativism in disguise. In 1996, Ratzinger told the Latin American bishops that the demise of European Marxism would likely 'reinforce an already potent tendency in the non-Marxian West towards a thoroughgoing relativism as the prevailing philosophical *Weltanschauung* of our time'.[23] The relativism which he believes would replace Marxism as the main threat to the church is a European phenomenon – 'Europe's post-metaphysical philosophy'.[24]

In his first major text on this topic, 'Relativism: The Central Problem for Faith Today', a speech addressed to the presidents of the Doctrinal Commissions of the Bishops' Conferences of Latin America in Guadalajara, Mexico (1996), Ratzinger warned that liberation theology was a threat to the faith of the church. It was a challenge because it seemed to offer a practical and plausible response to the fundamental question of Christian redemption. In this Latin American theology, the word 'redemption' was replaced with the word 'liberation'. Ratzinger says, 'If sin exerts its power over the structures and impoverishment is programmed beforehand by them, then its overthrow will come about not through individual conversions but through struggle against the structures of injustice'.[25]

This struggle is thus political by nature and redemption becomes a political process guided by Marxist ideology. Faith becomes praxis, a concrete task that people take into their own hands. Ratzinger thus defines liberation theology as being faith in praxis, a political action to realize salvation on earth. He calls it 'a phenomenon with an extraordinary number of layers' that strives to be a universal with its emphasis on Christian living based on scripture and the signs of the times.[26] Liberation theology seeks to be established scientifically and to become the absolute arbiter of Christian thought, going beyond the borders of Latin America into other Third World countries.[27]

The pragmatism that is implied in the theology of liberation tends to democratize the church. This is because relativism seems to promote tolerance. The problem with this notion, according to Ratzinger, is that faith is no longer considered as coming from God, but as a decision made by the majority in the community:

> The faith, together with its praxis, either comes to us from the Lord through his church and the sacramental ministry or it does not exist

in the absolute. The abandonment of the faith by many is based on the fact that it seems to them that the faith should be decided by some requests, which would be like a kind of party program: whoever has power decides what must be part of faith.[28]

Democratization will threaten the very foundations of the church. The catholicity of the church is not just geographic and chronological, but diachronic and extends across time to include all people, past, present and future. Thus Ratzinger says that, 'one cannot ascertain the *sensus fidelium*, or "sense of the faithful" merely by taking into view what a majority of Catholics thinks today. One must consider what the testimony of the church has been throughout the ages.'[29] What constitutes the real majority behind church pronouncement might appear to be a few people holding leadership positions, but in actual fact, it is the decision of the 'saints' extending throughout the centuries of the church's life.

Ratzinger states that, 'it is the function of the magisterium to uphold the testimony of every generation of believers over against the tyranny of the present. It is in that sense ... that the magisterium reflects a genuinely democratic principle: it honors the witness to the faith of Catholics from every era of church history.'[30] This means that authoritative truth comes from the revelation of God. Democratic processes, a kind of relativism, cannot be compared to revelation.

RELATIVISM AND DEMOCRACY

After the collapse of totalitarian regimes in Europe in the years between 1945 and 1989, there was the belief that democracy, in spite of its shortcomings, was the only suitable system of government because it protected freedom, justice and the good of the majority. Relativism becomes the philosophical basis of democracy as it embraces positive values such as tolerance and freedom. This means that no one can claim to know the right way forward. Relativism is also appealing to many people because 'it draws life from all the ways acknowledging each other as fragmentary attempts at improvement and trying to agree in common through dialogue, although the advertising of perceptions that cannot be reconciled in a common form is also part of this.'[31] Thus a free society is supposed to be relativistic.

Ratzinger asserts that 'the modern concept of democracy seems to be inseparably connected with relativism, whereas relativism appears to be the real guarantee of freedom, precisely of the essential core of freedom as well: freedom of religion and freedom of conscience'.[32] Thus he declares that 'the modern concept of democracy seems indissolubly linked to that of relativism'. A 'consistent relativism' means that 'there is ultimately no other principle governing political activity than the decision of the majority, which occupies the position of "truth" in the life of the state.' If moral truth is reducible to whatever the majority decides, democracy 'is not defined in terms of its contents, but in a purely functional manner'.[33]

Hence public life in such a society depends on 'acknowledging each other as fragmentary attempts at improvement and trying to agree in common through dialogue'. Although Ratzinger agrees that in the political realm, what is relative cannot be absolute, there are nevertheless rights that have absolute validity.[34] He also warns that 'a democracy without values, in fact, turns into a tyranny of relativism with the loss of its own identity, and in the long run can degenerate into open or insidious totalitarianism, as history has frequently shown'.[35]

In political philosophy there are two opposing positions. The first one is the radically relativistic position which excludes the concept of the good and true from politics because it endangers freedom; natural law is rejected as being 'metaphysically dubious'. And thus 'there is ultimately no other political principle than the decision of the majority, which replaces the truth in the life of the state'. The second position is that 'truth is not the product of politics (of the majority) but rather precedes it and illumines it'. This understanding is important, according to Ratzinger, when applied to ecclesiology where: 'Praxis does not create truth, but rather truth makes praxis possible'.[36]

Jeffrey Stout criticizes Ratzinger's understanding of democratic procedure by arguing that what democracy contributes to the discussion of the relativity of ethical concepts is not the gravely mistaken notion that however the majority decides to apply a concept is necessarily correct. It actually means that 'the wise, fully informed, disinterested representative of a moral tradition' is not necessarily to be found in the teaching of the church. Stout insists that in a democracy there must be a freewheeling discussion of moral issues in which all are encouraged to participate. Ethical wisdom can be found in ordinary people who take their moral tradition seriously.[37] There is also this democratic suspicion that those holding powerful positions, be it in the church or secular organizations, are as likely to have a corrupting influence as to have an edifying effect on one's application of moral concepts. The church is free to organize itself to inculcate its values to converts and children. But Stout rightly argues that the church cannot expect its authority to be honoured by all the citizens in the country. In political discussion, moral authority must be a publicly earned entitlement, and not given to some persons because of the positions they occupy.[38]

RELATIVISM AND RELIGIOUS PLURALISM

Ratzinger recognizes that in society, there must be some relativism in the way we organize our life. The problem starts when relativism becomes absolute and sees itself as being unlimited. What is worse, as far as Ratzinger is concerned, is that this absolute relativism is being applied to ethics and religion, for example, in the pluralistic theology of religions.[39] Relativism ignores the search for truth; people now substitute practice for truth and that is why the whole axis of religion is displaced. The declaration, *Dominus Iesus*, signed by Ratzinger as prefect of the CDF, states that: 'The Church's constant missionary proclamation is endangered today by relativistic theories which seek to justify religious pluralism, not only *de facto* but also *de iure (or in principle)*. As a consequence, it is held that certain truths have been superseded; for example, the definitive and complete character of the revelation of Jesus Christ.'[40]

To lay claim to truth for one religious belief appears to be presumptuous today, Ratzinger laments. The focus is now on the 'kingdom' or 'regnocentricity' which all religions must move towards. Hence, it is not necessary for all religions to move closer to one another, but towards the centre which is the kingdom. This movement towards the kingdom will 'serve as an instrument for the construction of the future'.[41] But Ratzinger believes that this will deprive religions of their content.

When Ratzinger speaks of relativism in theology as being the attenuation of Christology, he has in mind John Hick, who employs the Kantian distinction between phenomenon and noumenon. Hick refuses to acknowledge the historical truth of the incarnation and also denies that 'there is a binding and valid truth in history in the figure of Jesus Christ and the faith of the church'. He thinks that people who believe in this doctrine are seen as representatives of a fundamentalism that constitutes a 'real attack on the spirit of modernity' which promotes tolerance and freedom.[42] Ratzinger criticizes such a view as he states, 'to return to Hick's thinking, faith in the divinity of one concrete person, as he tells us, leads to fanaticism and particularism, to the dissociation between faith and love and it is precisely this which must be overcome'.[43] This attenuation of Christology that Ratzinger writes about is also called *low* Christology, which relativism promotes. Its primary focus in understanding the person of Jesus Christ is not in his divinity, but his humanity. Once Jesus is separated from Christ, he cannot be any more a source of truth than Buddha or other religious geniuses.

Ratzinger's warning against religious pluralism is not simply an authoritarian desire to maintain Catholic orthodoxy, it has to do with his early life experience according to John Allen:

> He witnessed that in Nazi Germany, when mistaken ideas about human nature led to the disasters of the Second World War, including the horrors of the Holocaust. His concern for maintaining the truths of the faith is therefore not simply an authoritarian desire to police the limits of acceptable thought; it has much deeper roots.[44]

MISSION AND DIALOGUE

Another effect of this dogma of relativism is that mission will be rendered obsolete because all people will come to God according to their own religious and cultural heritage. Missionary activities will be seen as presumptuous and the arrogant attitude of one particular culture that imagines itself to be superior to those whom they are going to convert.[45] Relativists hold that the belief that Jesus Christ is one valid and binding truth is fundamentalist. It is an 'assault upon the spirit of the modern age and, manifested in many forms, as the fundamental threat to the highest good of that age, freedom and tolerance'.[46] In order to overcome this arrogance, relativists propose to dialogue. But Ratzinger says this kind of dialogue is not constructive because there is no mutual respect for the truth. He writes,

> In the relativist meaning, *to dialogue* means to put one's position, that is, one's faith, on the same level as the convictions of others, without recognizing in principle more truth in it than that which is attributed to the opinion of the others. Only if I suppose in principle that the other can be as right or more right than I am, can authentic dialogue take place … dialogue must be an exchange between positions that have fundamentally the same rank and therefore are mutually relative.[47]

Ratzinger believes that dialogue and mission need not be antithetical, but must penetrate each other. Dialogue is aimed at discovering the truth together, but he insists that dialogue is useless if the dominant philosophy in our modern times is relativism. According to Ratzinger,

> It [relativism] prescribes itself as the only way to think and speak – if, that is, one wishes to stay in fashion. Being faithful to traditional values and to the knowledge that upholds them is labeled intolerance, and relativism becomes the required norm. I think it is vital that we oppose this imposition of a new pseudo-enlightenment, which threatens freedom of thought as well as freedom of religion.[48]

The declaration *Dominus Iesus*, signed by Ratzinger as prefect of the CDF, regarding the unicity and salvific universality of Jesus Christ and the church, issued on 6 August 2000, states that:

> The Church's constant missionary proclamation is endangered today by relativistic theories which seek to justify religious pluralism, not only *de facto* but also *de iure (or in principle)* ... The roots of these problems are to be found in certain presuppositions of both a philosophical and theological nature, which hinder the understanding and acceptance of the revealed truth ... On the basis of such presuppositions, which may evince different nuances, certain theological proposals are developed – at times presented as assertions, and at times as hypotheses – in which Christian revelation and the mystery of Jesus Christ and the Church lose their character of absolute truth and salvific universality, or at least shadows of doubt and uncertainty are cast upon them.[49]

The declaration stresses the necessity of Christ and the church for the salvation of humankind:

> With the coming of the Saviour Jesus Christ, God has willed that the Church founded by him be the instrument for the salvation of *all* humanity (cf. *Acts* 17:30-31). This truth of faith does not lessen the sincere respect which the Church has for the religions of the world, but at the same time, it rules out, in a radical way, that mentality of indifferentism 'characterized by a religious relativism which leads to the belief that "one religion is as good as another."' If it is true that the followers of

other religions can receive divine grace, it is also certain that *objectively speaking* they are in a gravely deficient situation in comparison with those who, in the Church, have the fullness of the means of salvation.[50]

EASTERN RELIGIONS

Relativistic theology of religions appeals to Indian philosophy because of the family resemblance between the post-metaphysical European mind and the traditional negative theology of India, which tends to set aside the uniqueness of Christ. This theology seeks to classify Jesus as just one of the saviour figures in history – a manifestation of the Logos rather than the Logos himself.[51] Thus in view of the importance we place on interreligious dialogue these days, relativism appears as the true philosophy of humanity itself.

Hence, if truth cannot be grasped, Christianity can be abandoned in favour of other exotic Eastern religions, all directed to experiencing the Absolute through a new gnosis, like the Gnosticism in the ancient world, which utilized biology, psychology and physics. Ratzinger asserts that as God retreats from the Western world, the gods return, promising us 'a moment to sense the pleasure of infinity and to forget the misery of finite existence. The more the pointlessness of political absolutisms becomes obvious, the more powerful will be the attraction of irrationalism, the renunciation of everyday reality.'[52]

In India, with the support of Western philosophical thought, Christian theology tends to set aside the image of Christ from its exclusive image in order to place it on the same level as other Indian saving myths. The historical Jesus is no more the absolute saving figure, but one among many. Ratzinger has observed that in the encounter with cultures, relativism appears to be the real philosophy of humanity. He concludes that in the age of globalization:

> Anyone who resists [relativism] not only opposes democracy and tolerance – the basic imperatives of the human community – but also persists obstinately in giving priority to one's Western culture and thus rejects the encounter of cultures, which is well known to be the imperative of the present moment. Those who want to stay with the faith of the Bible and the Church see themselves pushed from the start to a no-man's-land on the cultural level and must as a first measure rediscover the 'madness of God' (1 Cor. 1:18) to recognize the true wisdom in it.[53]

In the past, people searching for meaning in life were concerned with absolute truth in religion. However, Ratzinger believes, 'at a time when we have learned to doubt even whether we can know the transcendent at all, and when we are extremely uneasy about the potential for intolerance when claims of truth are made in this area, it seems that the future must belong only to mystical religion'.[54] People are not interested in the doctrinal aspect of faith, but exotic oriental beliefs which emphasize the experience of the Other rather than knowing the Other. Ratzinger writes:

> individual religions are relativized; for all the differences and, yes, the contradictions among these various sorts of belief, the only thing that matters, ultimately, is the inside of all these different forms, the contact with the ineffable, with the hidden mystery. And to a great extent people agree that this mystery is not completely manifested in any one form of revelation, that it is always glimpsed in random and fragmentary ways and yet is always sought as one and the same thing ... Associated with this relativizing is the notion of a great peace among religions, which recognize each other as different ways of reflecting the One Eternal Being and should leave up to the individual which path he will grope along to find the One who nevertheless unites them all. Through such a relativizing process, the Christian faith is radically changed.[55]

This relativizing process alters our understanding of the figure and role of Jesus Christ. This relativistic interpretation means that Jesus is not the Son of God, but only one who has experienced God in a special way. He is perceived as the enlightened one and not fundamentally different from other enlightened figures such as Buddha or Socrates.[56]

Eastern religions promote mysticism; the individual has little value and therefore 'there is no uniqueness of persons, the inviolable dignity of each individual person has no foundation, either'.[57] Ratzinger is not totally opposed to oriental religions because he thinks that behind this fascination with mystical religion there is a deep spiritual need to rediscover the mysterious aspect of our faith. God remains shrouded in mystery, fully unapproachable because of our sinfulness. Ratzinger also sees a common ground for dialogue with the negative theology of oriental religions. He has observed that 'the mystical dimension of the concept of God, which the Asian religions bring with them as a challenge to us, must clearly be decisive for our thinking, too, and for our faith'.[58] Ratzinger has also reminded his reader of the apophatic dimension of the Christian faith.[59] The modern encounter with the religions of Asia will remind Christians of the mystical aspect of their faith.

CRITIQUES OF ANTI-RELATIVISM

David Bloor claims that criticism of relativism is based on the false assumption that a relativist is an absurd fool who does not believe in the reality of an independent material world:

> All too often, attacks on relativism proceed on the assumption that a relativist is someone who, absurdly, does not believe in the reality of an independent, material world. Relativism is assimilated to philosophical 'idealism' – the theory that reality is just a projection of thought and has a mental rather than material basis. The encounter with the relativist is then framed in terms of an alleged 'realist/ relativist' controversy. This is a false dichotomy, but it has great polemical utility and makes it easy to present the relativist as a fool. The absolutists can thus go on their way without too many questions being asked about their own position.[60]

Bloor says, 'the truly dangerous people abroad in the world today are all absolutists. It is the dictatorship of absolutism, and the war of absolute against absolute, that is to be feared.' We must cherish our customs, traditions of law and morality, but not treat them as absolutes because they are human artifacts and conventions. Thus it is important to have a sceptical, historical awareness and, above all, to cultivate a relativist sensibility.[61]

Concerning the question of truth which forms the essential core of Ratzinger's theological discourse, Gianni Vattimo argues that we must be freed from our last idolatry, the adoration of Truth as our God. We need more relativism to accomplish this task. According to him, 'Christians live in multi-religious and multicultural societies, and the idea that salvation comes only through the church is not simply uncharitable; it risks our rendering any peaceable (and thus Christian) kind of life with our neighbours impossible.'[62] Vattimo also says that if we believed what Ratzinger told us about truth, 'we would need laws against the free exercise of Protestant and non-Christian practices, against the display of non-Christian religious symbols, against the education of non-Catholic children in non-Catholic schools, against construction of mosques, synagogues, temples, Protestant chapels'. Given Jesus' command to love, to be meek and not to judge others, Vattimo asks, might it not be necessary for any genuine Christian to be relativistic?[63]

Referring to Ratzinger's comment about Christians being tossed about by different ideological waves, Jeffrey Stout replies that although conformism is a danger to the moral health of any free society, 'it is not, however, a distinctively modern problem, and its connection with relativism is unclear'. Church leaders have been known to enforce conformity in their own ways based on their own understanding of moral and religious commitments. But, Stout says, 'ecclesiastical might does not make right'.[64] Nonetheless, one understands why a prelate like Ratzinger, concerned with the continued authority of his church and moral teachings of its members, might want to stress that its doctrines were definitive, not open to reconsideration or reinterpretation. Thus Barbara Herrnstein Smith says, 'One can also understand why, to reinforce that emphasis inspirationally, he [Ratzinger] might invoke, as looming on the horizon, the dictatorship of a relativism identified as skepticism toward orthodox ideas'.[65]

THE RELATIVISM OF RICHARD RORTY

Richard Rorty confronts the view of Ratzinger that a dictatorship of relativism threatens society. He believes we are much better off without the notion of moral obligations grounded in the structure of human nature. For Rorty, religion is a private matter, and to bring it out into the marketplace is dangerous business. This does not necessarily betray a philosophical hostility towards religions, but reveals a commitment to the principles of liberty and freedom of conscience.[66] Rorty characterizes Ratzinger's warning against the 'dictatorship of relativism' as a 'Platonic way of thinking'.[67]

While Ratzinger disparagingly criticizes the relativists' habit of being carried away by every wind of doctrine, Rorty sees relativism as being open to new possibilities and a willingness to consider all options about what might increase the welfare of human beings. He believes being open to doctrinal change is the only way to avoid past mistakes. Rorty defines relativism simply as the 'denial of fundamentalism'. He claims that this is better than the thesis put forward by Ratzinger who says relativistic ethicists hold 'every moral conviction is as good as every other moral conviction', a thesis which no philosopher has ever tried to defend.[68]

While Rorty agrees with Ratzinger that politics should not try to be redemptive, he thinks redemption was a bad idea in the first place because human beings do not need to be redeemed, they are not degraded beings. But they need to be made happier because as clever animals, human beings have learned to cooperate with one another.[69] He admits the Christian inspiration behind political idealism, but thinks we do not have to transcend our 'ego and its desires'.[70] Rorty remains firm in his secularist stance. But he thinks he is spiritual because he has 'an exalted sense of new possibilities opening up for finite beings'.[71] There is some merit in looking at relativism as a denial of fundamentalism as suggested by Rorty. He sees relativism as a positive thing that enables one to be open to new possibilities and to consider various options to increase the welfare of people.

In an interview with Vittorio Messori, Ratzinger speaks of a 'crisis of original sin', an evolutionist hypothesis which relates to a certain 'Teilhardism' in theology. In this crisis, original sin is understood as 'natural deficiencies' of human beings, who will move from imperfection to perfection and complete realization. Salvation is perceived as moving towards the future, the 'necessary development to the better'. This implies that 'there has never been a "redemption" because there was no sin on account of which man would need to be healed, but only ... a natural deficiency'.[72] Ratzinger claims that this crisis is only a symptom of our inability to understand the reality of our own selves, God and the world.

Ratzinger believes we must remain faithful to 'the common human experience of contact with a truth that is greater than we are'. He believes such an idea is the result of the confusion between truth and power. As a relativist, Rorty is convinced that there never was a truth that is greater than we are. He sees the conflict between fundamentalism and relativism as a contest between 'two visionary poems': one offers a vertical ascent to something beyond mere humans and the other is a horizontal progress towards greater cooperation among people.[73]

However, Ratzinger acknowledges that there is a difference between relativism and a justified level of pluralism. There is no such thing as one correct political option: 'What is relative, the construction of a freely ordered common life for men, cannot be absolute'.[74] In the political sphere, Ratzinger admits that the view that one single correct option does not exist is, to a great extent, true. The construction of a free society cannot be absolute; it has to be relativistic. Nonetheless, he also reminds us that even in politics, there cannot always be absolute relativism: there are things that are wrong and can never become right, and there are also things that are right and can never become wrong. Complete political relativism is also undesirable because innocent life must be protected and the state must be granted substantial autonomy to fulfil this duty. Without autonomy, the state may be trapped in religious ideology.[75]

AN ASIAN APPROACH

Tissa Balasuriya, coming from an Asian perspective, asserts that while relativism makes one's wish the ultimate value, there is also the danger that those who claim to possess the absolute and full truth want to impose it on others. Balasuriya proposes a middle way where there are norms that are binding, but without the absolute claim to truth.[76] A universal institution like the Catholic Church needs some definite doctrines and accepted ways of life. On the one hand, there is the fear of individualistic and hedonistic relativism which we have seen in Ratzinger's many writings and addresses. On the other hand, Balasuriya says that an acceptable teaching of the church cannot be one that claims to be absolute. Thus he argues that what is needed are some universal norms that follow human reason, natural law and the requirement of the common good.[77] The church likewise should seek 'normative norms that are not absolutely absolute' because the world of multi religions, philosophies and cultures requires a more gentle and flexible understanding of life and its values than a dominance of self-righteous absolutism.[78]

Balasuriya argues that the Asian approach to the analysis of problems does not generally limit itself to a view of truth and righteousness as either right or wrong. It is one of 'both – and' rather than 'either/or'. There are thus shades of colour or different routes up the mountain, so to speak, like the *yin* and *yang* in Chinese philosophy. Life is not conceived as merely linear, but cyclical and involves dynamic continuity from one stage to another, or even from one life to another. Asian religious traditions do not support a punishing transcendental god who condemns anyone for eternity.[79]

Asian thought does not deny a transcendent or divine being, according to Balasuriya, but it would question whether the transcendent can be fully known by us and whether our limited view of the divine excludes others. The transcendent is not definable in our categories or in our philosophical limits of monism or dualism. The divine is not a system, but a principle or an intuition in oriental thinking. To claim the monopoly of divine knowledge would be to create a god according to our own design and needs. Balasuriya claims that Asian approaches would be more consonant with Jesus' teaching in parables than would Christologies defined in Greek philosophical categories or Roman legal structures. Therefore, in this historical context, the Christian mission can be rethought in a way that is better appreciated in the Asian context.[80]

Balasuriya claims that Asians would question why they should be converted to Christianity if their spiritual heritage is so gravely deficient as stated in *Dominus Iesus*. Perhaps it is the official church's interpretation of the gospel that is gravely deficient. If that was the case, Asians would have to suffer the unjust world order set up by the Christian West and be told that the religions of their ancestors are not up to standard. The Christian faith would only be 'adding insult to the injury of the centennial past'. Thus Asians have much difficulty in accepting the claims of orthodoxy from an institution that excludes the vast majority of humanity from the benefits of divine revelation and the possibility of salvation.[81]

According to Balasuriya, the present trends of secularization and de-Christianization reveal an implicit rejection of the claims of the church to be the unique guardian of the gospel of Christ. His hope is that the church would have the grace to realize the limitations of its claims of possessing the absolute truth, would be humble and willing to learn from other religions and even from secular humanity. The mission of the church in Asia should be characterized by humility in thought and action. Our mission should include the acceptance of the core values of all religions concerning the basic issues of the moral life of individuals and societies. It is on this basis that we can organize our society at the local and international level. In this way religions can work together for the common good.[82]

In doing this, we need not dilute the gospel message. On the contrary, we would be challenged to live out the beatitudes. We would become better disciples of Jesus and, likewise, persons of other faiths could be invited to live the core message of their religions. We would all be called to conversion, self-purification and loving our neighbours, which is the core value of all world religions. Balasuriya believes this would serve the best interests of the church. The mission of the church would be better understood as a humble service that leaves the question of the eternal salvation of persons to God, whatever their religion. Thus a way has to be found to reconcile the message of the gospel with the respect due to other faiths and to the universal salvific will of God.[83]

Perhaps Balasuriya has a point in stressing that Asians have a different approach in analysing a problem, and that the oriental perception of the divine operates on different premises. But I disagree with Balasuriya's claim that Asians would not want to be converted to Christianity because the church says that their spiritual heritage is gravely deficient. I would argue that it is precisely the fact that they find Christianity more fulfilling, rational and humane that would cause them to embrace the faith.

In sum, Ratzinger believes that modernism dominated by relativism and scepticism can be overcome by the Christian teachings of Jesus as the only true saviour of the world who sets people free by this truth and love. He is convinced that tolerance, reason and freedom are not only compatible with truth, but they are also compatible with one another. Ratzinger also strongly supports interreligious dialogue as long as it does not lead to a religious pluralism that believes all religions are one and the same, different paths towards the one divine reality, a position advocated notably by John Hick and Paul Knitter. Interreligious prayer is possible only if the participants agree about the nature of God, the nature and subject of prayer. Such common prayer sessions must not lead to relativism or a denial of the uniqueness of Jesus Christ in the Christian faith.

On the occasion of the presentation of *Dominus Iesus*, Ratzinger made it clear that in a pluralistic society that portrays relativism as the one true and humane philosophy, it is necessary to defend the core of the Christian faith. This means there is a universal and binding truth in history, which became flesh in Jesus Christ, and was handed down to us through the faith of the church.[84] This fact tells us that not all religions are equally valid ways to salvation, even though seeds of truth and goodness may be found in them. Thus, the claim to the uniqueness of the revelation of Jesus Christ must not be compromised and we should not weaken our missionary zeal in proclaiming Jesus as the way, the truth and the life (John 14:6).

Contemporary relativism has manifested itself not only in modern philosophy and world politics, but also in Catholic theology and the life of the church. Under the guise of pluralism and adaptation, it has affected the faith and relativized the truth about Jesus Christ as the unique saviour of the world. Ratzinger became acutely aware that under the name of ecumenism and interreligious dialogue, Catholic understanding of Christology and Christian anthropology were being altered and weakened. Thus, he thinks it is very important to restate the true meaning of Christian revelation as found in Jesus Christ.

Ratzinger is against absolute relativism regarding matters of religious beliefs, but he acknowledges the value of relativism in politics.[85] His preoccupation with relativism was not so much a reaction against postmodernity, as it was the position of a priest deeply concerned with the secularization of his church. However, Ratzinger equates religious pluralism with relativism, which he thinks is destructive. Perhaps this is the reason why he has such a negative attitude towards theologies coming from the Asian continent. Pluralism implies a variety of viewpoints and perspectives concerning the same reality, but it is not relativism.

Chapter 7

Europe

Unlike many theologians in the post-Second-Vatican-Council period, Ratzinger was not 'principally a globalist'.[1] His primary concern was and still is the decline of Christianity in Europe. In fact, long before Ratzinger spoke out against aggressive secularism and the dictatorship of relativism threatening the fabric of European society, he had written about the decline of the West and the need to regain its Christian roots and identity, in order to survive the crisis and make itself relevant to the rest of the world. He believes that modernity has denied religion any influence in the public sphere and thus is responsible for promoting aggressive secularism, consumerism and hedonism in Europe. This prompted Lieven Boeve to write: 'The primary intuition that the present pope takes as his point of departure is that the crisis of Europe and the crisis of Christianity in Europe are inherently related.'[2]

Joseph Ratzinger believes that the origins of most problems in the world can be traced back to their European roots. James Schall, summarizing Ratzinger's position, states: 'Scratch a world problem and more often than not a European thinker will be involved.'[3] The root problem originated in Europe before it became global and it became a world problem because it was an 'unresolved European problem'.[4] Thus, resolving the European problem could be the beginning of saving the world. Ratzinger reminds us that the focus on Europe was evident as far back as St Paul's journey to Macedonia, which was providential and not accidental. This journey resulted in a close relationship between Jerusalem and Athens, 'the place where the initial inspiration for what we now know as Europe was hammered out'. Christianity, because of Greek influence, became a 'religion of reason, of *logos*'. Ratzinger, therefore, believes that the world can be revived intellectually and spiritually by first guiding Europe back onto the right path.[5]

This chapter attempts to examine critically Joseph Ratzinger's writings on the crisis in Europe, which is characterized by the clash between Christianity and radical Enlightenment thinking that excludes God from the public sphere. In modern times, Western Europe has become one of the most secular societies in history. Since Ratzinger believes in the powerful and universal influence of Western culture, he fears that the aggressive secularism and the decline of Christianity in Europe may affect the ordinary faithful in other parts of the world. This chapter seeks to show that such a pessimistic view of contemporary European culture is rather one-sided and is conditioned by his own theological vision, influenced by St Augustine and St Bonaventure.

This chapter also proposes an alternative way of understanding the role of Christianity in the face of growing pluralism in European societies. It calls for a separation of Christianity from the influences of Christendom that are still present in Europe. It is understandable that Joseph Ratzinger is distressed about the decline of the Christian faith and the church's influence in Europe. However, this chapter will present the argument that the Christian faith has the ability to adapt itself to modernity and also to renew itself in different forms. While Ratzinger has written positively about multiculturalism, he has failed to acknowledge the flourishing immigrant churches among Africans, East Asians and Latin Americans in Western Europe. First of all, we will examine Ratzinger's definition of Europe.

THE FOUNDATIONS OF EUROPE

Joseph Ratzinger claims that 'Europe is a geographical term only in a secondary sense: Europe is not a continent that can be defined solely in geographical terms but is rather a cultural and historical concept.'[6] That Ratzinger defines Europe in such intellectual and cultural terms has far-reaching implications for the way he views the West's present and future condition. To him, European culture is connected with certain ideas, actual events and a particular way of life that is distinctive. This means that in the future other cultures could come and occupy the European continent, but such cultures could not be truly European if they were not built on Europe's historical and cultural foundations.[7]

The two cultural foundations of Europe that Ratzinger has identified are Christian faith and Western, rational, philosophical tradition that has its roots in Ancient Greece. He explains that while Europe was once a Christian continent, it was also the birthplace of that 'new scientific rationality that has given us great possibilities and equally great threats'. Ratzinger admits that Christianity did not originate in Europe, but 'it was precisely in Europe that Christianity received its most historically influential cultural and intellectual form, and it therefore remains intertwined with Europe in a special way'.[8] Robert Spaemann writes:

> If Europe does not export its faith, the faith that – as Nietzsche puts it – 'God is the truth, that the truth is divine,' then it inevitably exports its lack of faith, that is, the conviction that there is no truth and no justice and that the good does not exist ... Without the idea of the unconditional, Europe is nothing more than a geographical concept – besides being a name for the place where the destruction of man began.[9]

Thus, Ratzinger sees the old continent abandoning its cultural and religious heritage, and severing itself from its Christian foundations by adopting a 'radicalized form of reason and freedom'.[10]

A CLASH OF CULTURES

The crisis began when Europe developed a culture, previously unknown in the history of humankind, that excluded God from its public life.[11] A breakdown between the two interdependent cultural foundations ensued. Since the age of the Enlightenment, Europe's rational philosophical tradition has taken a destructive turn: a radical Enlightenment against Christianity. By developing 'autonomous reason that is honed to the strictest Enlightenment demands' and excluding religion, Europe has in fact turned against the finest tradition of the Enlightenment.[12]

Thus, we have witnessed, in Western Europe, a conflict between Christianity and Enlightenment thinking. Ratzinger explains: 'Although, on the one hand, Christianity found its most influential form in Europe, we must also say, on the other hand, that Europe has developed a culture that most radically contradicts, not only Christianity, but the religious and moral traditions of humanity as well.'[13] In other words, a culture has developed in Europe in which God has disappeared from public awareness as a result of denial or privatization of religious belief.

This modern godless culture, according to Ratzinger, is defined by the rights of freedom: 'Its starting point is freedom, which it takes to be a fundamental value that measures everything else: the liberty of religious choice, which includes the religious neutrality of the state.'[14] This freedom that is meant to avoid intolerance becomes strangely contradictory to itself – it becomes, paradoxically, the intolerance of political correctness. Such political correctness seeks to impose its own view as the absolute one and is intolerant of other opinions.[15] Ratzinger believes freedom that comes from a godless culture is no freedom at all. When reason is cut off from its roots in the divine, it loses its sense of direction. The notion of freedom developed by this radical Enlightenment in Europe also cannot coexist with God because it views God as limiting and enslaving.[16]

In contrast to Joseph Ratzinger's negative attitude towards the legacy of the Enlightenment, Werner Ustorf stresses that the Christian faith is always in 'constant conversation' with the past and, in the European context, this refers to the Enlightenment. We can only work within the bounds of the culture to which we belong.

Thus, Christianity, in this cultural context, must deal with the influences of the Enlightenment and post-Enlightenment. Ustorf makes the interesting point that other forms of Christianity, in Africa or Asia, for example, have been able to flourish and develop outside the influence of the Enlightenment. He rightly asserts that the challenges posed by the Enlightenment and post-modernity are not crucial issues in most forms of Christianity, and issues such as poverty, war, marginalization and environmental problems are much more urgent. The Christian discourses nowadays are very diverse, but not mutually exclusive. They help to 'critique and correct one another'.[17] What this means is that different forms of Christianity are taking shape in various cultures and at different times.

Ustorf also points out that the Enlightenment provided a new perspective from which to understand Christ in the West – 'an indigenization of Christianity in Western terms'. He meant, by this, that the Enlightenment introduced new cultural and religious elements into the Christian narrative and, thus, like any other form of Christianity, syncretism. Unlike Joseph Ratzinger, Werner Ustorf thinks that what is important 'is not the religious and cultural content of the faith, but its direction towards Christ'.[18] This means there is no fixed or static pattern of Christian life and thought and, therefore, we cannot expect to return to the form of Christianity that the West had previously experienced.

THE PLACE OF CHRISTIANITY IN THE EUROPEAN CONSTITUTION

As evidence of this conflict between religious conviction and secularism, Joseph Ratzinger explores the public debate regarding the place of explicit references to God and Christianity in the proposed new constitution of the European Union. The debate reveals Western Europe's reluctance to acknowledge God publicly or to affirm its Christian roots. He claims that this exclusion, this wish to be open to Europe's present-day multiculturalism, is based on a mistaken notion of tolerance. He assures us that mentioning Europe's Christian roots is not offensive to non-Christians, since it merely represents a reference to a historical and normative fact. Muslims are not offended by references to the Christian moral foundation of Europe, but rather by the secularist denial of God. Jewish citizens will not be offended either because Europe's Christian roots go back to Mount Sinai.[19]

Sharing Ratzinger's concern, Baroness Sayeeda Warsi, the first female Muslim cabinet minister in Britain, claims that the voice of faith is somehow not heard and people of faith do not have enough courage. She asserts: 'Aggressive secularism is pushing faith out of any public place. Europe would not try to erase the church spires on our horizons; then why would you try to erase our religious history or the role of Christianity in the development of values of our nations? Europe needs to be more in tune with its Christian identity.'[20]

Furthermore, Ratzinger laments that the majority of Europeans naively believe that Europe can sustain itself solely on the basis of a culture of rationalism, science and technology. These Europeans 'presuppose the idea that only radical Enlightenment culture, which has reached its full development in our time, is able to define what European culture is'. Beside this rationalistic culture, other religious cultures are only allowed to coexist as long as they subordinate themselves to this Enlightenment ideology.[21]

The banishment of Christian roots from Europe has not led to greater tolerance with respect to other cultures. In fact, we are confronted by an absolute expression of a mindset and lifestyle that 'stands in radical contrast ... to the other historical cultures of humanity', Ratzinger argues.[22] The tension that characterizes our modern world is not caused by the conflicts among different religious cultures: it is between those who deny that God is the root of life and the great religious traditions, 'the clash between this radical emancipation of man and the major cultures of history'.[23] It follows that the refusal to mention God in the draft of the European constitution is not the expression of tolerance for non-theistic religions and agnosticism, but the expression of a mindset bent on erasing God from the public sphere of life. Ratzinger writes: 'Relativism, which is the starting point of all of this, thus becomes a dogmatism that believes itself in possession of the definitive knowledge of reason and of the right to regard everything else as a mere stage of humanity's development that has been fundamentally superseded and that is best treated as a pure relativity.'[24]

Louis Dupré, a native of Belgium and professor of philosophy of religion at Yale University, has also been critical of the failure of writers of the proposed preamble to the European constitution to acknowledge Christianity as a European heritage. Agreeing that the past models are no longer appropriate for the future, Dupré recognizes that 'the foundation of the new Europe needs a more inclusive base. Yet if Europe's spiritual identity is to be preserved, it must remain firmly attached to the principal values of its tradition.'[25] These values include the 'care of the soul' or a 'high respect for the inner life'. Dupré, however, admits that 'as for the common Christian faith that forged such a strong bond among Europe's peoples, many Europeans have lost it and most recent immigrants never had it.'[26] He also argues that Europe must not be satisfied with just political, economic and scientific integration:

> Europe's political and economic unification must be accompanied by a strong awareness of a distinctive cultural and spiritual identity. This is the reason why the dispute over Europe's Christian heritage is so important. In writing the preamble to the EU Constitution, the most significant element in the European tradition must not be erased.
>
> Today Europe needs a strong spiritual reintegration as well as a political–economic one. The former requires that it assimilate essential parts of its spiritual heritage: the Greek sense of order and measure, the Roman respect for law, the biblical and Christian care for the other person, the *humanitas* of Renaissance humanism, the ideals of political equality and individual rights of the Enlightenment.[27]

Dupré views this European heritage in terms of a single cultural body with different dimensions, a 'unity of spirit in a variety of expressions', which he wishes to see explicitly mentioned in the European constitution.[28] Like Ratzinger, Dupré recognizes the need for a more inclusive cultural base for the new Europe in view of multiculturalism, but, at the same time, he still advocates a sort of spiritual identity that will unite the people.

DIALECTIC OF ENLIGHTENMENT

Interestingly, Ratzinger's severe criticism of the radical Enlightenment ideology finds support in the works of two Marxist philosophers: Max Horkheimer and Theodor W. Adorno. In *Dialectic of the Enlightenment*, they speak about the total self-destruction of the Enlightenment. The Enlightenment aimed at liberating humankind from fear and yet the 'fully enlightened earth radiates disaster triumphant'.[29] According to the dictates of the Enlightenment, 'whatever does not conform to the rule of computation and utility is suspect' and thus, 'Enlightenment is totalitarian'.[30] Hence, whatever cannot be reduced to numbers becomes illusion – 'modern positivism writes it off as literature'.[31] Enlightenment is like a dictatorship in which the dictator manipulates people as far as he can. Consumerism is promoted and consumers' needs become the excuse for manipulation and domination by technology: 'No mention is made of the fact that the basis on which technology acquires power over society is the power of those whose economic hold over society is greatest'.[32] In other words, the rationality in technology entails domination and control through standardization and mass production, thereby sacrificing individuality and creativity.

The Enlightenment absolutizes itself and places importance only on things that are calculable and measurable. In Ratzinger's opinion, such an agnostic and material society cannot survive for long. He summarizes the dissolution of the moral realm as the 'privatization of morality' and its reduction to the 'calculation of what will be successful'. This dissolution will make society immoral because it attaches no value to what gives human beings dignity.[33] A symptom of this, in our modern society, is the pathological concern for the protection of our 'physical integrity' coupled with a 'diffused indifference to the moral integrity of the human person'. For Ratzinger, this results in a negation of human beings as human beings, and the 'negation of freedom and of human dignity'.[34]

THE DEATH OF GOD

In a prophetic manner, Joseph Ratzinger has written: 'The Islam that is sure of itself has to a large extent a greater fascination for the Third World than a Christianity that is in a state of inner decay'.[35] Such an assertion reminds us of Friedrich Nietzsche, a philosopher Ratzinger often cites and criticizes. Nietzsche wrote about the lukewarm faith of Christians in Europe. Clearly

Ratzinger is worried that the Christian faith in the West is moving in this direction. He is greatly influenced by Henri de Lubac, whose writing on atheist humanism finds echoes in many of Ratzinger's critiques of contemporary Western culture. In his *Memoirs*, Joseph Ratzinger recalls the impact of Henri de Lubac's book, *Catholicisme: Aspects sociaux du dogme* (1938), on his own thought. He also cites it in his encyclical *Spe Salvi*.

God, according to Nietzsche, is 'nothing more than the mirror of man'; in certain rare moments, a person becomes aware of certain intense feelings such as love and power, and he ascribes them to a 'superhuman being'.[36] He divides his nature into two spheres: the 'ordinary weak' man and the rare powerful God. Thus, through his own making, he is cheated of his best qualities: 'Religion is a matter of adulteration of the personality.' Therefore, according to Nietzsche, we need to 'regain possession of those lofty and proud states of the soul' that we have mistakenly given to God. He believes this process of 'self-despoilment and self-debasement' is carried out, to the extreme, in Christianity. Nietzsche believes that God is an 'undesirable guest' who can live only in the mind of man. In order to get rid of him, we need to trace the origin of this idea in the human mind. It is this 'historical refutation' that will carry weight.[37] Man alone can free himself from the idea of God, 'by an act of will'. Faith in God as taught by Christianity, serves to discipline the human person. It therefore follows that the human being needs to get rid of faith so that he can exalt himself and proclaim 'the death of God'.[38]

The expression 'the death of God' is a fundamental category in Hegel's philosophy. Hegel applied it to Christ who died and rose again and also to human reason, 'which must pass through the moment of negation in order to join the universal spirit'.[39] However, for Nietzsche, 'the death of God' means that we must make a decision – 'it is our preference that decides against Christianity – not arguments'. The death of God is something willed by the individual himself. Nietzsche adds, 'It is we who have killed him. We are the assassins of God.'[40]

Henri de Lubac recognizes the noble principles and sound intuitions behind the modern thoughts of these atheistic philosophers, whose criticism and analysis of society have been insightful and accurate. These atheistic humanists were able to grapple with the social and spiritual problems that people faced. However, the world they present can no longer be called Christian in any sense and 'the God they reject is ... a mere caricature of the God we worship'. According to de Lubac, many people who were attracted by these atheistic philosophies did not comprehend their real significance – they have an 'imposing grandeur' that 'masks the horror that were their purchase price'.[41]

Few people were able to see the final outcome of these godless movements to which they were attracted. De Lubac warns that the denial of God is a threat to humankind. We can either retreat back to the barbarism of the Middle Ages or we can rediscover God in the church which 'sets before us, the living God who made us in his own image'.[42]

De Lubac laments that forms of atheism such as 'critical atheism, liberal atheism, atheism resulting from laicism' are still with us. These varieties of atheistic philosophy have preserved a number of original Christian values, but having been cut off from their original source, they are powerless to sustain them. Virtues such as justice and liberty, without divine backing, do not constitute true humanity. These virtues become unreal when no longer seen within the context of faith in the living God; they become 'empty forms' without God's sustenance. De Lubac says, without God, even truth and justice become idols.[43]

The influence and effect of atheistic humanism can be seen today in the two errors of Europe that, in Ratzinger's opinion, must not be repeated. They are: 'nationalism' and the 'exclusiveness of technical reason and the destruction of the ethos'. According to him, these two 'sins' have led Europe to fall from grace. Rather than the model of a nation state that exalts itself, Ratzinger calls for a political entity that is more inclusive – a 'cultural fellowship' that embraces all humanity.[44]

EXALTATION OF ONE'S NATION

Joseph Ratzinger defines nationalism as the 'modern radicalization of tribalism' which has left a bloody path through the centuries.[45] In Europe, nationalism took on a new dimension in the nineteenth and twentieth centuries. First of all, an exaltation of one's own nation had taken place among European peoples in the sense that each nation wanted to impose its own beliefs, which it sincerely believed to be genuinely humane, on the rest of the world. It was a curious combination of nationalism and universalism. There was also an attempt to use the Christian religion in the national interest – one's own brand of Christianity was regarded as purer than everyone else's.[46] Instead of dominating others, Ratzinger urges each nation state to subordinate its national interest to the common good of humanity: 'Correct European universality must mean that the individual states transcend and overcome themselves.' The goal should be that 'everything exists for all' and 'no one is a stranger anywhere.'[47]

Ratzinger calls for European countries to grow together into a European community because the nations of Europe are 'no longer autonomous entities that make claims of hegemony vis-à-vis other states but are elements of a greater polymorphic community in which all are related to each other as givers and receivers'.[48] He is proposing, in other words, that European countries should overcome nationalism and ideological divisions. Ratzinger advances an analysis of Europe's crisis of faith which is strikingly similar to that of the English historian, Christopher Dawson (1889–1970). According to Dawson, European nationalists and racists believe that they are vastly different from other races. Nationalism and racism deny the unifying force of Christianity that has created a 'supranational spiritual community' from different nationalities. Dawson also insists that we must recognize the historic role of the church, as the 'inspiration for the community of nations called Europe', so that we can solve the problems we are facing.[49]

THE EXCLUSIVENESS OF SCIENTIFIC RATIONALITY

Joseph Ratzinger believes that the 'absolutization of scientific–technical civilization' and the promise of earthly utopia have led Europe to fall from grace because they have resulted in the exclusion of the divine from the shaping of history and human life.[50] Mistrusting science and technology, Ratzinger believes that this 'exclusiveness of the technical reason' played a significant role in the disintegration of moral values and the banishment of God from the public sphere. Europe has been very successful in the technological and economic fields, but it lacks the moral energy to deal with other aspects of life. Ratzinger writes: 'I see a paradoxical synchronicity here: the victory of the post-European technical–secular world ... and its faith that are the basis of its identity, has in fact already disappeared from the scene and that the hour of the value systems of other worlds ... has now come. In the very hour of its most extreme success, Europe seems to have become empty from within.'[51] In other words, Christianity, the cultural heritage of Europe, which contributed so much to Western civilization, is declining, at a time when Europe is most prosperous and advanced.

This departure from religious–ethical tradition and the emphasis on scientific rationality appear to be a European phenomenon. Ratzinger warns that a world order founded on technological rationality could turn out to be 'a utopia of terror'.[52] While he affirms rationality as a fundamental trait of the European spirit that has dominated the world, he claims

that this rationality turned destructive when it was cut off from its foundations and when it made technological capability the only standard by which
we measure our human conduct.[53] As a result, we are now threatened by a
'new paganism' in the advanced Western countries and elsewhere. Ratzinger
laments that many people in the West have excluded God, the foundation of
all good things, from their lives. They consider God as too distant and vague,
and start to turn to other powers that are more accessible. Ratzinger writes:
'The decomposition of the Christian synthesis facing us must ultimately also
lead to a disintegration of man himself'.[54] What Europe and the rest of the
world need now are 'corrective elements' taken from their own cultural and
ethical traditions to prevent the destruction of humanity.[55]

Generally, the church has always been wary of technological innovations
and scientific advancements. Joseph Ratzinger's critical attitude towards the
advancements of the technical world falls within this tradition. In many ways
the church considers technical progress a blessing as well as a curse. Pius XII
was optimistic about the arrival of 'technoscience', but Paul VI highlighted the
gap between scientific advancement and the moral development of humanity.
John Paul II spoke against nuclear weapons and medical procedures that affect
birth, and he strongly emphasized ethics in his reflections on technology.[56]
This brings us to Ratzinger's criticism of the 'myth of progress' with its over-
emphasis on scientific rationality and the attempt to create a utopia on earth.

THE MYTH OF PROGRESS

Progress, in the post-Hegelian sense, presupposes a 'mechanistic interpretation of history' in which freedom is equated with the removal of ties and
human progress is seen in terms of technical ability.[57] Ratzinger is critical of
such understanding of progress because personal freedom and ethical responsibilities are seen as a hindrance to progress. He writes: 'ultimately, there exists
the "technologistic" variant of the belief in progress, which sees man's progress
in the growth of technical ability as such'.[58] Critical of the myth of progress
because it 'squanders the forces of today on an imaginary tomorrow',[59] Ratzinger argues that this myth of progress is related to the attempt to construct
a perfect society, an attempt undertaken by the communists with disastrous
results.

Influenced by St Augustine who understood that, in spite of its achievements, the Roman Empire could perish, Joseph Ratzinger worries that

European culture, too, may perish. He argues that this reality should make us realize that no one can construct a definitive and perfect form of society: 'The future always remains open, because human life lived in common always revolves around human freedom and therefore always has the possibility of failure.'[60] Trying to construct the definitive society is wrong because it excludes the absolute criterion that is God. Accordingly, we must discard the myth of 'innerworldly eschatologies.'[61] This myth of progress has led Helmut Kuhn to state: 'With the triumph of Hegelianism in Germany … the philosophy of history has taken the place of ethics, and the good has been identified with what is up to date.'[62] Since then, ethics has been separated from politics.

Joseph Ratzinger argues that the threefold association of belief in progress, the 'absolutization of scientific–technical civilization' and the promise of a new humanity was developed into a political myth in Marxism.[63] Even after the collapse of Marxism, the exclusion of God is a real threat that continues to be felt in the Western world.[64] Ratzinger sees the crisis of Marxism as a question put to the Western world regarding the myth of progress. He is convinced that it is 'the power of the spirit, the power of convictions, of suffering and of hopes' that has brought about the collapse of Marxism in Europe. In Ratzinger's opinion, this means that materialism, which seeks to reduce the spirit to a 'mere superstructure of the economic system', has been defeated.[65] Thus, for him, progress does not mean having more material wealth, nor being independent from ethical imperatives.

Unfortunately, Europe has not learned a lesson from the collapse of communism, Ratzinger laments. The collapse of communism came about not just because of its 'false economic dogmatics' but, rather, because of its 'contempt for man and because they [communist regimes] subordinated morality to the needs of the system … The real catastrophe that the Communist regimes left behind is not economic. It consists in the devastation of souls, in the destruction of moral consciousness.'[66] Former communists have become economic liberals, but the moral and religious issues underlying the collapse of communism have not been revealed in the course of analysis.[67] Ratzinger thinks that, by putting the emphasis on technocracy and the right to self-determination without spiritual foundation, Europe has lost its values because it has rejected Christianity. The remedy he proposes is that, 'Today, at this precise hour in history, Europe and the world need the presence of God … As Christians, we are responsible for maintaining the presence of God in our world, for it is only this presence that has the power to keep man from destroying himself.'[68]

To sum up, Joseph Ratzinger contends that Europe has been deeply influenced by the 'master narrative of progress and emancipation'. It has forgotten what it is to be truly human. The major ills of our time, such as AIDS, drugs, terrorism, ecological crises and so on, have resulted from a wrong conception about the foundation of humanity. Ratzinger believes that truth and freedom are not self-made but revealed and given by God.[69] By this, he means that the truth of humanity is revealed in the Christian understanding of anthropology that can be regarded as a 'synthesis of the major ethical intuitions of humankind'.[70] Ratzinger also laments that this new Western civilization has created its own truths as well as 'new moralities' which are claimed to be practical and situational.

NEW MORALITIES

Joseph Ratzinger is convinced that 'man's Being contains an imperative; the conviction that he does not himself *invent* morality on the basis of calculations of expediency but rather *finds* it already present in the essence of things'.[71] Lamenting that 'purely functional rationality' has given birth to a new set of moral values that are pragmatic and relativistic, he writes: 'In a world based on calculation, it is the calculation of consequences that decides what is to count as moral or immoral. And so the category of the good, which Kant had put front and centre, disappears. Nothing is good or evil in itself, everything depends on the consequences that can be foreseen for a given action'.[72] Ratzinger thinks that these new moralities not only contradict Christianity but also the religious tradition of humankind. He contends that, in the wake of the collapse of Christianity in Europe, the new values that have emerged are inadequate to unite people effectively because they lack divine support. This 'new moralism' includes key concepts such as justice and peace, as well as conservation and creation, but Ratzinger asks: 'What, in fact, does "justice" mean? Who defines it? What is conducive to peace?' Such morality is misguided, its basic thrust is wrong, it lacks a 'serene morality' and it values 'political utopia', at the expense of the dignity of the individual.[73]

These new moral values manifest themselves in the decline in birth rates. Institutions that support marriage and children are also rejected. Europe is infected by fear of the future. Children, our future, are seen as a burden rather than a source of hope.[74] Ratzinger, however, teaches that marriage and the family, together constitute an integral element that characterizes European identity:

Monogamous marriage, as the basic structure for the relationship between a man and a woman and as the cell for the construction of civic society, has been formed by biblical faith. It has given Europe – East and West – its specific 'face' and its specifically human character, precisely because one must struggle again and again to realize the form of fidelity and of renunciation that monogamous marriage by its nature requires. Europe would cease to be Europe if this basic cell of its social construction were to disappear or to be changed in its essence.[75]

While wary of the risk of confronting the issues of marriage, divorce and cohabitation, Ratzinger is also critical of homosexual partnership because they are not open to the formation of a family with children, which is in direct contradistinction to the moral history of humankind.[76]

Besides the emergence of these new moralities, Joseph Ratzinger has also observed a self-deprecation in the West which is 'pathological'. He admits that it is laudable to try to understand foreign values, but one must also learn to see that which is great and pure in one's own culture. More importantly, if Europe is to survive, it requires a 'critical and humble acceptance' of self and faith in God who is near us.[77]

Ratzinger writes: 'Certainly we can and must learn from that which is holy to others, but it is our obligation both in relation to them and to our own selves to nourish our own reverence for the Holy One and to show the face of the God who has appeared to us, the God who cares for the poor and the weak.' Failing to do this will result in denying the identity of Europe and depriving others of the opportunity of knowing God. The present 'absolutely profane character' in the West is foreign to many cultures. In fact, multiculturalism can help us to recognize our own Christian roots.[78]

It is evident from his writings on Europe that Ratzinger regards Europe as much more than an economic, political or legal entity: 'it constitutes, for its citizens, an entire living space, a way of being together by different peoples that is founded on a mutual ordering of faith and reason. And this mutual ordering of faith and reason is the real spiritual foundation on which authentic European culture rests and that marks what Europe really is.'[79] It follows that social arrangements, even if they physically take place in Europe, are not truly European if they do not have this mutual ordering of faith and reason.[80] What Europe needs now, if it is to survive, Ratzinger urges, is a recovery and reaffirmation of its own cultural and religious roots, and that means the mutual ordering of faith and reason.

FAITH AND REASON

In spite of the decline of Christianity and the emergence of new moral values in Western Europe, Joseph Ratzinger is hopeful for a spiritual regeneration because the Christian vision of reality is still a potent force in the West. He admits that the relationship between the two visions of reality – religious and secular – is close and tense at the same time. Although Christian and secular cultures are non-universal, these two great Western cultures exert a powerful influence on the world and on every other culture.[81] Ratzinger believes that faith and religion still have many things to teach people in our modern scientific age. There is a 'necessary correlation between faith and reason … called to purify and heal one another'. They need each other and must acknowledge one another's roles in human existence.[82]

The affirmation of the correlation between Christian faith and Western, secular, rational thought is not a 'false Eurocentrism' because, according to Ratzinger, 'these two determine the situation of the world in a way unparalleled by any other cultural forces'.[83] Christian and Western secular cultures must also engage in a dialogue with other cultural traditions so that they will be open to learning from the 'Western complementarity of faith and reason'.[84] He believes that reason given by God can retain its 'evidential character' only when the entire culture maintains its Christian tradition. Therefore, when reason is severed from the religious faith of its historical culture, it becomes blind.[85] Such an isolation of reason from faith leads to cynicism and the destruction of humankind. Consequently, the real problem we have today is reason's blindness to the spiritual dimension of life.[86] Tracey Rowland puts it this way: 'From Benedict's perspective the suicide of the West began when people stopped believing in the Christian account of creation and started to sever the intrinsic relationship of faith and reason.'[87]

Ratzinger believes that the Christian faith is the 'most universal and rational religious culture … it offers reason the basic structure of moral insight which, if it does not actually lead to some kind of evidential quality, at least furnishes the basis of a rational moral faith without which no society can endure'.[88] However, reason that severs itself from God loses its sense of direction and is susceptible to the powers of destruction. Without this 'absolute point of reference', human beings become the 'hopeless prey of the forces of evil'. Christians must also fight the temptation to reduce reason to the 'rationality of production'.[89] This means that we do not order our lives solely according to the dictates of the market, focusing only on our material well-being. Finally, we can have a healthy religion only when our reason is open to God and when we do not push morality into the subjective realm.[90] Besides this mutual ordering of faith and reason, Ratzinger calls for a rebuilding of Europe based on Christian values.

CONSTRUCTION OF EUROPE ON CHRISTIAN ETHOS

Joseph Ratzinger claims that the Christian ethos, which is the 'ethos of purified reason', must form the basis of political realism. According to him, politics is more than just practicality; it is a moral issue and the aim of politics is justice and peace using the law to regulate the exercise of power.[91] The basic principles for establishing justice, valid throughout the ages, are to be found in the Ten Commandments and the teaching of Christ in the New Testament. Ratzinger writes:

> The emergence of Europe after the collapse of the Greco-Roman world and the mass migration of peoples was the work of Christianity. It is indisputable that it was Christian faith that gave birth to Europe in that period. In the same way, the restoration of Europe after the Second World War has Christianity as its root, and this means that it has responsibility before God as its root... If we wish to build up Europe today as a stronghold of law and of justice vis-à-vis all men and cultures, we cannot withdraw to an abstract reason that knows nothing of God, a reason that itself belongs to no culture but wants to regulate every culture according to its own criteria.[92]

Ratzinger claims that, even now, Christian truths and values must be the foundation on which Europe is to be constructed. This means that we have a responsibility before God because Europe is not just an economic entity, but a 'community of law, a stronghold of law' for all humanity.[93] Christian values allowed reconciliation to happen after the injustices that took place during the Second World War. This shows that we must create a space for God if we are to remain humane.[94]

Europe's fundamental spiritual foundation has been shaken due to 'the dissolution of the primal certainties of man about God, about himself, and about the universe – the dissolution of the consciousness of those moral values that are never subject to our own judgment – all this is still our problem. In a new form, it could lead to the self-destruction of European consciousness.'[95] Ratzinger suggests that a concrete way to rebuild Europe on Christian values is to guarantee human rights and dignity, now and in the future. There must be laws to protect the value and dignity of human beings and to guarantee freedom and equality, in addition to the basic principles of democracy and the rule of law in society. These fundamental principles must be guaranteed in the European Constitution.[96]

In European culture, the good is received from a higher tradition: Judaism and Christianity received from God the Ten Commandments from which the modern concept of human rights was formulated. If Europe exports only its technology and rationality without Logos and ethos, it will destroy humanity's great ethical and religious traditions, as well as the foundations of human existence, including Europe itself. For Ratzinger, this is Eurocentrism in the negative sense. He calls upon Europe to teach the world the 'inner origin of its rationality' – 'the recognition of the Logos as the foundation of all things, a glimpse of the truth that is also the criterion of the good'. Then, through a 'process of giving and receiving', Europe can unite all the great traditions of humanity so that 'no one is a stranger to anyone else'.[97]

In the same vein as Arnold Toynbee, Ratzinger believes that the fate of a society always depends on 'a creative minority'. As a creative minority, Christians can 'help Europe regain the best elements of its inheritance. It will allow Europe to serve the whole of mankind.'[98] To accomplish this, Christians and non-Christians must ensure the creation of a moral foundation based on Christian principles. Establishing common convictions will be possible only if we live our own inheritance vigorously and purely. This will make its inherent power of persuasion visible and effective in society as a whole.'[99]

As Christianity is no longer the dominant force in Europe and autonomous reason has taken over as the measure of all things, Ratzinger urges Christians, non-Christians and even non-believers to live as if God does exist, to live as if there were a higher authority and to accept a basis for measuring things that is greater than human reason. This may help Europe to regain its soul. The Enlightenment project attempted to present a world without God, resulting in disaster.[100] Just as Pascal challenged his non-believing friends to assume the possibility that God existed, so must Christians.[101] Thus, Ratzinger concludes that, just as the notion of *esti Deus non daretur*, even if God did not exist, served as an ethical base for peaceful coexistence at a time of religious conflict, it is possible to hold the notion of *si Deus daretur*, as if God existed, to realize the same goal.

The construction of a society based on Christian values is related to Joseph Ratzinger's understanding of democracy. Democratic societies in Europe reveal that rationality and freedom require a moral foundation that cannot be self-generated. While democracy represents the best system in governing, it is not a value in itself, not even an ideal. This is because majority decisions, in a representative democracy, can be detrimental to minorities.[102] Ratzinger writes: 'The state is not itself the source of truth and morality. It cannot produce truth from its own self by means of an ideology based on people or race or class or some other identity. Nor can it produce truth via the majority.'[103] Thus, in Ratzinger's opinion, the crisis in Europe has to do with its distorted understanding of the meaning of freedom, democracy and rationality. Freedom has been reduced to individual self-determination, democracy means the protection of this freedom by the majority and rationality can be defined as functionality and effectiveness.

THEOLOGICAL VISION

Joseph Ratzinger is determined to build up a countercultural church in opposition to the secularizing trend in Europe. He also places his trust in the church that he believes is the guardian of truth, capable of reviving the European spirit. This theological vision of Joseph Ratzinger has to do with his understanding of St Augustine and St Bonaventure. Influenced by Augustine, Ratzinger sees the world in dualistic terms: conflict and contrast between Christian notions of truth and freedom and contemporary Western culture. This means that faith must be presented as 'countercultural, as an appeal to nonconformity'. Ratzinger believes that only the gospel will save us, not philosophy, science or even scientific theology.[104]

The model for this task, according to Joseph Komonchak, is 'the effort to preach the gospel in the alien world of antiquity and to construct the vision Christian wisdom manifest in the great ages of faith before philosophy, science, and technology separated themselves into autonomous areas of reflection and activity'. This 'Bonaventuran' theological vision refers to the final stages of Bonaventure's intellectual journey when he responded to the cultural challenge of his times with an anti-intellectual, anti-Aristotelian kind of piety.[105] Ratzinger is, thus, combating modernity with this anti-intellectual and anti-secular vision.

With such a theological vision rooted, not only in Bonaventure, but in Augustine and Plato as well, Ratzinger has never been enthusiastic about *Gaudium et Spes*, a document of the Second Vatican Council. It is an optimistic text, on the church in the modern world, based on an 'incarnational approach' inspired by the Dominican theologian, Marie-Dominique Chenu, who emphasized reading the 'signs of the times' so that the church could proclaim the message of Christ meaningfully to the world at large. Ratzinger found this text, *Gaudium et Spes*, conceding too much to the world.

He criticized the draft for not stressing the reality of sin in the world, for confusing the natural and supernatural, and for its ambiguous notions of 'world' and 'church'.[106] He was afraid that, in *Gaudium et Spes*, dialogue was taking the place of the proclamation of the faith.[107]

According to Komonchak, Ratzinger favours the Augustinian distinction between science and wisdom that offers 'a deeper epistemology than that of Aquinas, and greater emphasis on the Cross as the necessary point of contradiction between church and world'.[108] This suggests that, when analysing the European situation, Ratzinger tends to see things in black and white: Christian faith versus the godless Enlightenment ideology. As we have discussed in previous chapters, Ratzinger's opposition to theological dissent and his reluctance to accept theological pluralism had its roots in this theological outlook. Komonchak writes:

> Ratzinger wanted the church again to be able to pose as a real alternative, a set of meanings and values that can stand at a critical and redemptive distance from contemporary culture. It is the importance of their [sic] being an ecclesial – not simply a theological or intellectual – response to today's challenges that led him to insist on internal unity. It is the church, and not theology, that would provide a real alternative; and theologians were often perceived as in fact and, because of their defense of public dissent, in principle preventing the unity that is required for the church's effective redemptive service in the world.[109]

Such a position means that Ratzinger is sceptical about having a genuine dialogue with the world, fearing that it might compromise the church's proclamation of the gospel. Apart from this reluctance to enter into dialogue with the world and the harsh treatment given to dissident Catholic theologians, Ratzinger's perception of the decline of Christianity in the West is one-sided in that he focuses only on white people of European stock without taking into consideration the influx of Christian immigrants from developing countries. Besides, has Christianity really been banished, almost to the point of extinction or is Europe really as godless as Joseph Ratzinger seems to imply?

IS CHRISTIANITY VANISHING IN EUROPE?

Philip Jenkins argues that Christianity has not disappeared in Europe. In fact, there are signs of its growth within secular society. He writes: 'the recent experience of Christian Europe might suggest not that the continent is potentially a graveyard for religion but rather that it is a laboratory for new forms of faith, new structures of organization and interaction, that can accommodate themselves to a dominant secular environment'.[110] Although multiculturalism is positively assessed by Joseph Ratzinger, he does not mention the growth of immigrant churches among Africans, East Asians and Latin Americans in Western Europe. Jenkins says that even if we accept the pessimistic view that most Westerners are turning away from Christianity, these new immigrant churches represent a kind of religious revival. European Christianity is neither dead nor dying. We have seen new movements within churches and also flourishing immigrant churches.[111]

The idea of Christian Europe now becoming secularized has prompted Anton Wessels to ask: 'Is Europe Christian?' and to 'what extent it has been de-Christianized today?'[112] A balanced response comes from Delumeau: 'the God of Christians was much less alive in the past than has been thought and today he is much less dead than is claimed'.[113] Recent conflicts with Islamic extremism have forced secular-minded Europeans to realize that many of their values are rooted in Christianity. In fact, Jürgen Habermas, the 'purest secularist', has said that 'Christianity, and nothing else, is the ultimate foundation of liberty, conscience, human rights, and democracy, the benchmarks of Western civilization: "To this day, we have no other options. We continue to nourish ourselves from this source. Everything else is postmodern chatter."'[114]

AN ESSENTIALIST APPROACH

By reducing a diverse continent like Europe to two fundamental features – the Christian faith and Western philosophical tradition – Ratzinger takes an essentialist approach in his analysis of a reality that is highly complex and dynamic. His definition of Europe suggests a 'cognitive "filtering out" or abstraction of certain aspects of a much broader cultural dynamic'.[115] This essentialism, as well as the 'grand narrative' it implies, has been rejected by postmodernism in favour of a 'multiplicity of localized histories'.[116] Richard King argues that the grand narrative 'involves the ascendancy of secular rationality of an ideal within Western intellectual thought, a concomitant marginalization of "the mystical"' East.[117] In other words, if Christianity and Hellenistic thought are fundamental to European identity, non-Western countries are seen as the 'other'. Refuting essentialism by citing Derrida, Patrik Fridlund writes:

> The dominant Western discourse ... works from an idea of a hierarchical axiology in which values are ranked in dichotomised pairs like normal/abnormal, full/empty, proper/parasitic, serious/non-serious, literal/non-literal, centre/periphery, and essence/addition. There is a desire to find the original pure, proper, normal and essential, and only then – afterwards – to see the deviations and the complications in what is held to be the impure, parasitic, and abnormal.[118]

Of course, Joseph Ratzinger is not comparing Europe with the rest of the world in an 'Orientalist discourse'.[119] However, his essentialist position regarding the identity of Europe does overlook other historical, cultural and religious changes in Western society, such as the influx of immigrants.

Most people would acknowledge the Christian heritage of European culture, but the idea of promoting the 'myth of a Christian Europe' in order to exclude other religious and secular traditions is something else. Since the time of Constantine, political and church leaders have found this myth useful in furthering their personal agendas. I am not saying that Ratzinger is promoting the myth of a Christian Europe in order to exclude others, but his vision of Christianity in Europe comes close to recreating a church that is authoritarian and intolerant. I concur with much of his analysis of the crisis in Europe, but his approach towards the core identity of Europe seems to be exclusive and even dangerous, for it does not take into account the growing religious and cultural pluralism in the West.

THE MYTH OF CHRISTIAN EUROPE

While Joseph Ratzinger seeks to debunk the myths of nationalism, technological civilization and human progress, Werner G. Jeanrond seeks to unmask the myth of Christian Europe. In contrast to Ratzinger's understanding of Europe, in cultural and historical terms, and his insistence on its Christian roots, Jeanrond understands the European Union as constituting 'a community of law, and not a community of views of life'.[120] He sees Europe, not so much as possessing a soul, but rather, as offering 'a constitutional space to all its citizens, and legal protection for the development of their respective religious or humanist convictions'.[121]

In view of the growth of Islam in Europe and the intention of Turkey to join the European Union, Jeanrond argues that it may not be appropriate to define contemporary Europe in Christian terms. Europe is characterized by a plurality of religious movements and traditions. All these different religions will shape the structure of a united Europe. The religious future of Europe will not be Christian, but 'radically pluralistic'. Jeanrond thus claims that the myth of a Christian Europe has been revealed as 'a dangerous project'.[122] Aylward Shorter also warns that there is a dangerous tendency, in official church documents, to equate Christian patrimony with Western culture: 'it is a multicultural phenomenon which assists the Church in passing "from one kind of clarity to another" in its developing understanding of the faith. It is a naïve over simplification to identify this patrimony with the culture of Europe, even if that culture is seen to be what it is in reality, a complex phenomenon of astonishing diversity.'[123] Nonetheless, this myth continues to be a powerful force in European culture and politics. Many people still consider Europe a Christian continent, at least historically, in spite of aggressive secularization since the Enlightenment.[124]

Jeanrond claims that the myth of a Christian Europe has been used against Islam, Judaism, Communism and secularism, which are considered to be dangerous 'others'. If this is so, it follows that Christianity, as a common religion, has been employed by its supporters to give the 'European project a strong internal identity'. This myth suited the church hierarchy as well as politicians at various times.[125] The result of such an 'integrationist Christian Europe' meant *others* were excluded or marginalized. Besides, this project of a united Europe sought to organize 'the faithful into a monist system of one ruler, one religion and one people, a system which in its secularised form even inspired Hitler's political vision for Germany and beyond'.[126] Today, however, Europe is characterized by a religious plurality with great diversity even within Christianity itself. Europe has a flourishing Jewish community and a growing Muslim population. This new religious landscape thus calls for interreligious dialogue and cooperation in various social fields.[127]

Europe is not a 'Christian property' or an exclusive 'Christian space', Jeanrond insists.[128] The future of Europe is the concern not only of Christians, but of others who are living on the continent. Since we are aware of the danger of nationalism, as predicted by Joseph Ratzinger, any attempt to embrace a religious myth or ideology, in order to unify Europe, is inappropriate. Christianity should not be used to fill the gap created by the collapse of ideologies after 1989. Jeanrond insists that Europe does not have a soul, but a space where people of different religious traditions and secular beliefs live and work together.[129]

In Europe, the three Abrahamic religions – Judaism, Christianity and Islam – have their own political visions and ethical systems, and Christianity is no longer the most dominant force in Western society. Present-day Europeans are rather sceptical about religious beliefs and the church has been weakened by sexual scandals and corruption. Furthermore, Christianity is no longer seen as a religion that promotes peace and understanding.[130] Consequently, it is not surprising that contemporary Europeans will seek sources, other than churches, to satisfy their spiritual needs. They will not be content to accept religious traditions and doctrines handed down by religious authorities, although they will still seek religious services when required. In trying to satisfy their religious needs and aspirations, Europeans will practise 'syncretistic selection' based on their 'individual insights'. But one thing is clear, according to Jeanrond, the future of Christianity in Europe will be 'more colourful, more diffuse, more pluralistic than its past'.[131] At the moment, he thinks it is important to expose the dangers of the myth of a Christian Europe. Jeanrond's argument highlights the differences between Christianity and Christendom.

CHRISTENDOM VERSUS CHRISTIANITY

In 321, Emperor Constantine proclaimed Christianity the religion of the Roman Empire and thus Christendom was born. After three centuries of periodic persecution by the state, Christianity finally allied itself with secular forces. Later, the Roman elite as well as the masses became Christian and other religions were banned. From then on, a strong relationship between church and state, as well as between church and society, was forged. For the next 1,500 years, Christendom became the context in which Christians lived out their faith. According to Hugh McLeod, 'they lived in a society where there were close ties between the leaders of the church and those in positions of secular power, where the laws purported to be based on Christian principles, and where, apart from certain clearly defined outsider communities, every member of the society was assumed to be a Christian'.[132] The downside to this marriage between altar and throne was that the church lost its freedom.

There have always been Christians who saw the partnership between church and state as detrimental to Christianity itself. Christendom meant that the church was under the control of the state. It also meant that the church had to compromise by approving customs and values that were against Christian principles. Since the Reformation in the sixteenth century, there have been people in Western Europe who have wanted the church to remain independent of the state and Christians to refrain from forcing their beliefs on others.[133] Since the nineteenth century, religious tolerance has been advocated for practical reasons and on the grounds that everyone has the right to follow their own conscience.[134]

Hugh McLeod asserts that Christianity and Christendom can and must be separated. For three centuries, Christianity was able to flourish before it became Christendom. In China there are many Christians, but there has never been a Christendom. Although Christendom was just a phase in European history, it lasted for more than a thousand years, and we are still under its influence.[135] Many people would be happy to see the end of this particular era, but some, like Joseph Ratzinger understandably lament the decline of Christian values in Western Europe. What Ratzinger has witnessed in Europe, namely the decline of Christianity as a dominant influence on society, is an inevitable process of history due to the nature of the Christian faith itself. Christianity has adapted well to modernity and even at times allowed itself to be neutralized. According to Yves Lambert, Christianity, in the beginning, succeeded in becoming an autonomous religion, but later became 'the instrument of symbolic legitimisation of the socio-political order'.[136] This shows that Christianity was able to adapt to changes in society, probably because Christians are taught to render 'to Caesar the things that are Caesar's, and to God the things that are God's'(Mark 12:17).

Following Bellah, Lambert asserts that our present situation represents a stage of religious development which is very different from that of 'historic religion'. Gordon Melton writes:

> During the twentieth century, the West has experienced a phenomenon it has not encountered since the reign of Constantine: the growth of and significant visible presence of a variety of non-Christian and non-orthodox Christian bodies competing for the religious allegiance of the public. This growth of so many religious alternatives is forcing the West into a new situation in which the still dominant Christian religion must share its centuries-old hegemony in a new pluralistic religious environment.[137]

What we have today is a transformed landscape: it is accepted that one cannot prove or disprove the existence of God by means of reason. New conflicts such as genetic manipulation and euthanasia have arisen, but they do not seem to affect the faith itself. Individual freedom has led people away from God, but it has also given rise to the adoption of a more personal faith and new religious practices.[138]

Perhaps the greatest challenge that Christianity now faces is globalization and religious pluralism. Yves Lambert claims that the impact of modernity on religion is the 'loss of the monopoly of religions in the symbolic field', such as 'conceptions of life and the world'. These conceptions are now influenced by other religions and secular sciences.[139] Due to the pluralistic nature of European society, not everyone shares the same Christian values. We are now witnessing the transformation of Christendom into Christianity in Western Europe, resulting in Christians becoming the creative minorities. Perhaps this minority status will enable Christians to be united and to live the gospel more faithfully.

The crisis faced by mainstream Christianity may be a sign that Christendom is dead and that we are witnessing a spiritual revival. Jonathan Bonk argues that 'Christendom from its earliest days found it impractical to follow the *ways* of Jesus – to actually reflect the mind of Christ – as demonstrated by its violent politics, aggressive and self-centred economics, and fierce militarism.'[140] In fact, the conversion of the pagan world to Christianity took place first on the battleground. Christianity has its origin in war – *Christus victor*! The Christian God has revealed himself as a 'God of war' and a conqueror.[141]

It is generally agreed that a people is defined primarily by shared memory. Bonk, however, thinks that the mere recollection of its Christian roots and identity will not be sufficient for the salvation of Europe. Perhaps Europe has never been saved in the gospel sense. Bonk makes this cutting comment:

> Old Christendom was violent, and powerful neo-Christendom still prefers violence as an effective means of insisting that its will be done on earth. While old Christendom, since World War II, has enjoyed a relative moratorium on war, time and circumstance will doubtless change that situation, perhaps in the not-too-distant future. As for neo-Christendom, it is disheartening to observe how utterly reliant on violence and its terrible instruments this great society and its institutions have become... Neo-Christendom is no mere victim, but the primary beneficiary, of violence around the word.[142]

Many would agree with Jonathan Bonk and desire to see the end of Christendom and its influences. But how can we transform the violence of Christendom to peaceful living according to the gospel? Lamin Sanneh, taking his inspiration from the poet T. S. Eliot, advocates a Christian state in which 'the church can have the sort of relation that is not a concordat or a reciprocal one'. This is possible only when the rulers have received a Christian education, so that they can act in a Christian way without imposing their beliefs on others.[143]

Sanneh thus calls for the creation of a Christian community that recognizes the 'primacy of ethics and a code of Christian conduct'. It could be achieved only with 'a sense of moral accountability to God'. The community of Christians would have a 'composite and cumulative effect' on the pluralistic society that includes people of exceptional ability from different religious traditions.[144] It follows that Christians, with their common belief and system of education, can influence each other and collectively form the conscience of society. Sanneh's idea of a Christian state may find support from Joseph Ratzinger, who believes that a creative minority should include Christian leaders capable of helping to revitalize Europe through the establishment of a Christian, moral foundation in society.

BEYOND A CHRISTIAN PERSPECTIVE

As we have seen, due to Joseph Ratzinger's Augustinian background, he tends to see things in stark contrast: the church versus the world. But I argue that faith and the church are not always in opposition to the world. They actually participate in influencing the world and are, in turn, influenced by the world. Worldly processes have religious and human significance in that God saves us in our particular historical context. Lieven Boeve has argued that 'while his [Ratzinger's] critique of radical Enlightenment thinking is likely to disturb some observers, it is not likely to convince the majority on account of its massive oppositional character... The socio-cultural evolutions that have taken place in the West would seem to be too complex to be captured by a simple opposition: "belief–unbelief".'[145] In other words, according to Boeve, Ratzinger simply reduces the problem of European identity to the ancient debate between Christianity and the atheistic ideology of the Enlightenment.

The real situation in Europe is more complex than Ratzinger's black and white analysis because the relationship between the Christian faith and the modern world is not just polemical but reciprocal. Europe cannot simply be understood, in its totality, by just looking at things from a Christian perspective. No single tradition, not even modern secular culture, can survive forever. Furthermore, today's European society is characterized by the ascendancy of cultural and religious pluralism as a result of massive immigration from Asia, Africa and other parts of the world. The situation demands that the future of Christianity in Europe be evaluated. It is incumbent upon Christians to respect others and be open-minded towards their beliefs while remaining rooted in their own tradition. They can afford to be critical of others whose religious convictions run contrary to theirs without imposing their views on the rest of society.[146] This means that Christians can contribute to the future of Europe along with non-Christians, including those with no religion.

So far we have explored Ratzinger's educational, cultural and religious background to reveal his Eurocentric bias, particularly in his ecclesiology, ecumenical theology and attitude towards religious pluralism with its evil twins of relativism and secularism. In the following chapters we will look at alternative approaches in contrast to Ratzinger's normative theology, which I believe are more relevant and workable in the Asian context, which is characterized by poverty and religious diversity. We will discuss the works of Tissa Balasuriya, Jacques Dupuis, Peter Phan, Hans Küng and Paul Knitter, whose works were investigated and censured by the CDF. Their dissenting voices provide a different way of doing theology and also of being church.

Chapter 8

Tissa Balasuriya OMI

We have seen in Chapter 6 how the Sri Lankan priest, Tissa Balasuriya, challenged Cardinal Joseph Ratzinger's understanding of relativism and criticized the church document, *Dominus Iesus*, from an Asian perspective. He was investigated by Rome in 1994 for charges related to religious pluralism and relativism in one of his books. His case is an example of a certain harshness that the Congregation for the Doctrine of the Faith under the direction of Ratzinger wielded in dealing with dissident theologians labouring in the field of religious pluralism. The CDF accused Balasuriya of deviating from the integrity of the truth of the Catholic faith in his book, *Mary and Human Liberation*. For this offence, he was excommunicated in January 1997. The severity of the punishment meted out to him by the CDF made Balasuriya a type of celebrity among Third World theologians. Many were sympathetic towards him and dreaded what the CDF might do next to those specializing in the areas of religious pluralism and interreligious dialogue.

Mary and Human Liberation is not so much about Mariology as about Western theologies and the missionary enterprise. Even so, Balasuriya was accused of challenging fundamental Catholic beliefs, such as original sin and the immaculate conception, as well as allegedly embracing religious pluralism and relativism. The most serious charges according to the *Notification* were that Balasuriya relativized Christological dogma and failed to acknowledge the uniqueness of Christ as Saviour as well as the role of the church in the economy of salvation. As we have seen, Joseph Ratzinger had spent his entire theological career thus far fighting against the 'dictatorship of relativism', which he deemed as the gravest threat to the gospel since Marxism. The punishment of Balasuriya demonstrates that he viewed the religious intuition of Asia as a variation of Western relativism and as a challenge to Catholic orthodoxy. In Ratzinger's view, anything that sounded like religious relativism was unacceptable to the Catholic Church. Eventually, after a year, Balasuriya signed a 'statement of reconciliation' and the excommunication was lifted on 15 January 1998.

This chapter examines the key aspects of Balasuriya's book, *Mary and Human Liberation*, which were censured by the church (CDF). It reviews the *Notification*, which published his *latae sententiae* (meaning his excommunication has automatically taken place) and the international outcry from within and outside the Catholic Church.

By revisiting the case of Balasuriya, this chapter seeks to understand the difficulties and dangers of those working at the 'frontiers' of Christian faith who often have to deal with the power and politics of the ecclesiastical establishment. Revisiting this case also reveals to us that the church, like any other human institution, is liable to make mistakes and needs to be more transparent in its investigation of theologians who are suspected of having strayed from orthodoxy. The CDF needs to adopt a more just and humane procedure in carrying out its duties. The story of Balasuriya's excommunication and reconciliation also brings home the importance of dialogue within the church, the right of theologians to dissent, and the need for the church to be open to theologians operating from a non-Western paradigm.

BIOGRAPHICAL SKETCH

Born on 29 August 1924 in Kahatagasdigiliya, Sri Lanka, into a middle-class Catholic family, Sirimevan Tissa Balasuriya joined the Congregation of the Oblates of Mary Immaculate (OMI) in 1945 and made his religious profession in 1946. Prior to entering the religious life, he studied at the University of Ceylon and received a BA in economics and political science. It was at the university that he was awakened to the systematic exploitation of the poor throughout his country. He studied philosophy and theology at the Gregorian University for the licentiate degree and was ordained in Rome in 1952. In 1962, he left for Oxford University, where he obtained a diploma in agricultural economics. He also studied theology, catechetics and sociology at the Institut Catholique in Paris.

Returning to Sri Lanka, Balasuriya taught at Aquinas University and later became its rector from 1964–71. It is widely acknowledged that he played a major role in the development of that institution. He resigned from the university to start the Centre for Society and Religion to promote interreligious dialogue with Hindus, Buddhists and Muslims. He was also a founding member of the Ecumenical Association of Third World Theologians (EATWOT).

Shocked by the official violence in his country involving ethnic clashes between Singhalese and Tamils, Balasuriya, a Singhalese himself, started working in the slums of Colombo and revived a journal called *Social Justice* for the purpose of promoting human rights and economic reforms. At the heart of the civil conflict in Sri Lanka was the fight for democratic pluralism. Balasuriya was at the forefront of this struggle as he stood for pluralism, social justice and working for civil reconciliation among his people. He supported the poor and marginalized against the powerful and was very critical of multinational corporations from the West exploiting a developing country like Sri Lanka.

At the spiritual level, Balasuriya worked to harmonize his Catholic faith with Sri Lankan culture. Critical of the old missionary approach where salvation is accomplished only by conversion and conformity to a form of Catholicism that is essentially 'a form of ecclesiastical colonialism', Balasuriya wanted a church that reflected his native culture and its aspirations.[1] After a long illness, he passed away on 17 January 2013, and his funeral was attended by people from all walks of life, from Catholic priests to Buddhist monks. 'Let us bury only the bones and the flesh of Fr Balasuriya,' said the Bishop of Anuradhapura, who presided at the funeral, 'but let us also keep his words and deeds with us'.[2]

PORTRAYAL OF MARY: A BETRAYAL

With these words in mind, let us now examine some aspects of his controversial book, *Mary and Human Liberation*, a work that led to his excommunication and gained him worldwide recognition. Balasuriya begins his book with a sharp criticism of traditional Marian theology and spirituality that developed around the concept of original sin, which he believes presents an overly negative view of human beings. Traditional dogmas on Mary emphasize the special privileges and graces she received from God, but less her active role in the life and ministry of Jesus. Mary is portrayed as a woman shielded from the trials and difficulties of life. Though loving and motherly, she seemed not to be concerned with poverty, injustice and the exploitation of women in her society. Balasuriya thinks that the church's teaching on her virginity and immaculate conception draws attention to the issue of sexual morality and temptation, leading to an anti-sexual bias, and deflects from the more important issues of injustice and exploitation in a male-dominated society.[3] Balasuriya can be considered the first Asian theologian who called attention to the exploitation of impoverished women in Asia.

This traditional presentation of Mary in popular devotion, in Balasuriya's opinion, betrays what is *actually* depicted in the gospels – Mary as a strong and decisive woman, resisting the social evils of her time and taking an active role in her son's mission. Traditional hymns to Mary neglect the importance of liberation from social evils and also downgrade the value of human sexuality.[4] In this sense, they clearly betray the message found in the Magnificat in Luke 1:46–55.

For Balasuriya, the Magnificat is an example of the call to transform society which traditional Mariology neglects. It seems to me that his Marian theology revolves exclusively around this canticle of social, political and economic liberations. As we shall see, he is actually advocating a theology of liberation, a trend of thinking independently, censured by Joseph Ratzinger in many of its aspects. Even the Hail Mary, the most commonly recited Catholic prayer, is not spared from Balasuriya's criticism. He regards it as lacking in 'liberative dynamic' and has the unintended effect of 'tranquillizing Catholics'.[5]

Regarding Marian shrines in Sri Lanka, Balasuriya would love to see them as helping people to understand better their predicament in an unjust society. He believes Marian shrines and basilicas should be instrumental in proclaiming the message of the Magnificat regarding liberation from oppression and exploitation. Far from being an obedient and submissive girl from Nazareth, Mary must be presented as a mature and committed woman participating in the daily struggles of the common people.[6] This suggests that we should not enshrine her and raise her up on an unreachable pedestal. Mary should be seen as one of us, helping us in our daily struggles for a more equitable society.

The Marian devotion promoted in Sri Lanka is based on a theology that is individualistic and, therefore, in Balasuriya's view, does not contribute to the development of a mission theology and ministry that is relevant to the country. Marian theology is tied to Christology, but it is a theology that is other-worldly in nature, which also affects its spirituality. Thus, Balasuriya encourages local Catholics to develop a theology that does not slavishly follow the European dominant theology and colonization, specifically that of the Portuguese and British.[7]

Balasuriya thinks that the traditional presentation of Mary as a docile and faithful virgin mother can lead to passive and individualistic tendencies which are not in accord with the gospel presentation of Mary as a bold and determined woman. Linked to original sin, Marian spirituality encouraged a sense of dependency and powerlessness among devotees, especially women.[8] This kind of devotion, Balasuriya laments, lacks a clear focus on the social transformation in the area of social justice and peace in our society. The effect of this traditional spirituality leads only to greater conformity to a prevailing unjust social system. In fact, Balasuriya claims that Christians are 'among the worst exploiters' because traditional Marian devotion prevents them from considering the plight of the poor and oppressed.[9] Traditional Mariology is popular but not helpful in leading us to true holiness, where the care for the poor and needy takes precedence. Hence, Balasuriya calls for a new thinking in the study of Marian spirituality in which liberation is the hermeneutic key.

TOWARDS A MARIAN THEOLOGY OF LIBERATION

Balasuriya insists that we must reflect on the life of Mary in the context of Roman imperial rule in which the exploitation of the poor, women and the Jewish race was prevalent in a time of intense social and political upheavals. At the annunciation, Mary's *fiat* was not just a sign of submission to God's will, but showed that God was dependent on a woman to carry out his plan for the redemption of humankind, as some feminist theologians have emphasized. Given the deep 'respect for the mutuality of relationships' between creator and creature,how much more, Balasuriya argues, should there be mutual respect between women and men.[10]

Regarding Mary's visit to Elizabeth, Balasuriya focuses again on the Magnificat: 'My soul glorifies the Lord', and sees in this prayer (Luke 1:51–53) a threefold strategy for action in the area of political consciousness, political structures and power, and in the distribution of material goods. In other words, Mary was proclaiming a *cultural revolution* in which the proud are cast down and the poor are uplifted; a *political revolution* in which power is transferred from the mighty to the masses; and an *economic revolution* in which the hungry are given good things and the rich are sent away empty. Here we see a total reversal of values and structures, a radical message of revolutionary importance.[11]

Unfortunately, Balasuriya contends, the Christian tradition has succeeded in domesticating Mary to the extent that 'she is known as the comforter of the disturbed, rather than as a disturber of the comfortable'. But, in actual fact, her words can be a call to radical action for dismantling unjust structures in society and for the conscientization of people. The Magnificat, Balasuriya maintains, reconciles a revolutionary message with personal love.[12] It is a powerful hymn in which we are called to be active and contemplative at the same time. Liberation theologians find in the Magnificat a great inspiration for the poor in their struggle for justice and freedom.

Not having a decent place to give birth to Jesus, and rejected by many people, Mary shared in the human suffering and pain of childbirth. The gospel presents to us an ordinary mature woman experiencing difficult problems and trials common to womanhood and motherhood. In the Presentation of Jesus (Luke 2:22–40), Mary consciously participated in the redemptive work of her son. Balasuriya reminds us that only a strong and loving woman could accept a sword that would pierce her heart, as is narrated in Luke 2:35–40. In her flight to Egypt, like many political exiles and refugees, Mary experienced the hatred, cruelty and brutality of political rulers of her time.[13] Balasuriya decries the popular devotions that do not emphasize the harsh social and political realities in the life of Mary in their portrayals of the incarnation, the visitation, the nativity, the presentation and flight into Egypt.

Balasuriya argues that it is more important to examine Mary's life in relation to Jesus than to indulge in speculation concerning her preservation from original sin or her virginity. Our admiration should be focused on Mary's ability to reconcile 'deep recollection with an active commitment, along with her Son, and thus 'grow in grace with God and man," along with Jesus [also]' (Luke 2:52). Balasuriya holds that Mary is torn between her love for her only son and her consciousness of the demands of social and political liberation and justice for her people.[14] Mary could not be indifferent to the social and political issues of her time. Otherwise she would not have accompanied Jesus in his public life all the way to the cross and beyond during the early period of the infant church with the apostles.[15] In actual fact, Balasuriya claims, 'She is the first priest of the New Testament, along with Jesus, offering the flesh of her flesh. She participates in the first and foremost sacrifice of the New Testament.'[16]

The problem with traditional Marian theology, in Balasuriya's view, is that Mary is not portrayed as the ordinary human mother of a human son who lived in a human situation similar to that faced by millions of mothers and children in the world.[17] This suggests that Mary is elevated into a heavenly being with no earthly use for ordinary people. For Balasuriya, what is so significant about Mary in our Christian life is not so much that she is a virgin and, conceived immaculately, but that she is closely associated with Jesus of Nazareth in proclaiming the message of human liberation and fulfilment. In other words, Mary shared with her son the building of a new humanity and thus she is an example to all of us.[18] Further, the message of Jesus Christ is concerned principally with the establishment of the Kingdom of God and not primarily a church.

In this controversial book, Balasuriya seeks to offer a reflection from the Third World perspective, in which poverty, the exploitation of women and social injustice are prevalent, in a context in which there is a plurality of religions and cultures in the midst of secularization. He wants to present Mary as an active participant in Christ's mission, which is open to all. It is a Mariology intimately related to Christology and inspired by the Magnificat. This approach is relevant to the struggles of women for equality and justice in a male-dominated society such as Asia where women are exploited and abused. Balasuriya believes that the liberation message of Jesus with Mary can be an inspiration to all women in helping them to raise their consciousness about their rights and dignity.[19]

Balasuriya is critical of the traditional development of Marian theology and spirituality in popular piety because of some of the presuppositions and underlying assumptions that form the basis of such doctrines. He assumes that the Marian doctrines are formulated by a male clergy in order to make the faithful more docile and obedient and thus regards them as ideology masquerading as divine revelation.

THE DOCTRINE OF ORIGINAL SIN

While accepting original sin in the sense of 'the innate human tendency towards evil', Balasuriya is opposed to the idea that human beings are born alienated from God because of the sin of disobedience committed by our first parents. He points out that the doctrine of original sin taught by the church has serious drawbacks. First and foremost, it is not found in the scriptures. In the Old Testament, we cannot find any evidence that sin is transmitted through the generations, although it does mention the universal tendency towards sin. The Old Testament made no statement regarding the inability of human beings, after their fall from a supernatural state, to reach God through repentance. The Jewish people expected a political redeemer for their race, but the Torah was sufficient for them as far as salvation was concerned.[20]

In the New Testament, Jesus never mentioned original sin, but rather repentance, love of God and neighbour (Matthew 25); the teachings of Jesus are summed up in the Sermon on the Mount (Matthew 5—7). Furthermore, the gospels do not teach that baptism is a necessary prerequisite for salvation. The case of Zacchaeus (Luke 19:1–10) reveals that to be saved, one must repent. Balasuriya holds that the doctrine of original sin has 'disastrous consequences' for the Christian mission.[21] This is because the doctrine of original sin and the requirement of baptism for salvation made Christianity an exclusive religion and as a result presented other religious traditions as deficient and invalid. It has led to anti-Christian sentiment in Asia, where there exists a plurality of venerable religious traditions. On top of this, the connection between Christianity and Western colonialism does not improve the image of Christians either.

According to Balasuriya, the New Testament teaches that salvation comes from God through Jesus Christ (Acts 4:12). It also stresses the importance of good will and good works (Matthew 5:16; James 2:24; 1 Peter 2:12). But there is no mention of original sin as taught by scholastic theology. Balasuriya holds that grace coming from Jesus Christ is freely available to all people. This suggests that people need not be Christians or members of a church to experience the grace and salvation given by Christ. He believes this open approach would help to promote dialogue with people of other faiths because Christianity is not presented as an exclusive religion.

St Paul speaks of the need to be justified by faith and fidelity to one's conscience (Romans 1:16–17; Galations 2:16), but Balasuriya argues that there is nothing close to the idea of original sin and the necessity of baptism for the remission of this inherited sin as taught by later theologians. Before St Augustine, there was no common agreement regarding the existence and nature of original sin. It was in the fourth century that Augustine put forward the idea of original sin transmitted to us by our first parents through sexual relations. This was in refutation to the theology of Pelagius, who insisted that humans are free to choose between good and evil. According to Pelagius, even though the grace of God is helpful, it is not necessary. Adam's sin was his personal sin and cannot be transmitted to his children.[22]

Developing his position between the two extreme views of Manichaeism, (which maintained that human beings are by nature evil) and that of Pelagius (who held that human beings could overcome evil by their own free will), Augustine posited the idea that the sin of Adam and Eve is transmitted to all human beings through procreation, which he called 'concupiscence'. Thus, original sin implies that human beings are a fallen race that deserves to be condemned to hell were it not for the grace of God, which has brought us salvation through Jesus Christ. This idea of Augustine became the official teaching of the Catholic Church and was developed further by St Anselm and the scholastics of the thirteenth century.[23]

Balasuriya draws attention to the evolution of this idea of original sin that became church doctrine, a process deeply influenced by the presuppositions of the scholastic theologians. This doctrine eventually led to the proclamation of the dogma of the immaculate conception of Mary. The doctrine of original sin, in Balasuriya's opinion, is unjust to humankind because we are not responsible, in any collective sense, for the sin of Adam and Eve. It is built on European medieval philosophical assumptions of the human person and has dire consequences. For example, the interpretation of Genesis by the church fathers was that woman was the cause of temptation and thus Eve was identified with evil. This understanding denigrated women and promoted male superiority. The doctrine of original sin also degrades human sexuality. Since females are closely related to the body, this doctrine also promotes prejudice against women. Further, this obsession with sexual ethics in Catholic moral theology deflects its attention from the more serious issues such as social injustice and exploitation.[24]

The doctrine of original sin implies that salvation is only accomplished through Jesus Christ, the universal Saviour. The church claims monopoly on salvation through the administration of the sacraments; it has the 'power to mediate salvation beyond this life'.[25] Balasuriya regards this as 'religionism'.[26] He contends that Jesus and Paul emphasize a personal relationship between God and us. In addition, the doctrine of original sin means that other religions are not valid ways to gain salvation and those who have no religion cannot rely on their conscience. Western missionaries preaching Jesus Christ as the only remedy to original sin created much conflict, violence and exploitation, because this pessimistic Western view of human nature is not in accord with Asian philosophy. Balasuriya insists that we must find a way to explain original sin so as not to discredit the role of other religions. In the Asian context, the idea of a loving God who is bent on punishing the entire continent just because they have not been baptized as Christians is simply repulsive and unacceptable.[27]

Regarding mission, Jesus preached that 'the Kingdom of God is at hand, repent and believe in the Good News' (Mark 1:15). What is needed is a change of heart – *metanoia*. Balasuriya tells us that the first Jewish converts in the Acts of the Apostles were baptized without understanding the concept of original sin. Conversion was understood in terms of 'radical social transformation'.[28] But since the church's mission is to convert all persons on all continents, 'Christianity became Church-centred' rather than Jesus-centred, God-centred or human-centred.[29] Again this doctrine plays a significant role in its empha-sis on the need for redemption through Christ brought about by joining the church. It serves the purpose of making the church more powerful because it considers itself infallible in matters of faith and morals. Thus, we can see that the doctrine of original sin, the idea of redemption through Christ only, as well as Christian missionary endeavours led the church to reject other reli-gions and even non-Western cultures.[30]

In his discourse on the doctrine of original sin, Balasuriya wants us to know that church teaching, for the most part, is guided by the presupposi-tions and self-interests of its officials and theologians, who developed them into doctrinal formulations and claimed that they were part of divine revela-tion. The impact of original sin is so profound and deeply embedded in our Christian culture that we must expose its presuppositions in order to reveal its negative consequences, especially concerning the Christian mission.

TOWARDS AN ASIAN THEOLOGY

The controversy around *Mary and Human Liberation* can be traced back to the 1990s movement, led by K. C. Abraham and others, to develop theologies from the context of the developing world. Balasuriya, as a founding member of the Ecumenical Association of Third World Theologians, contributed to this movement by writing his version of theology from an Asian perspective. He asserted that Asian cultural and religious backgrounds could contribute much Christian theology because in Asia many other ancient religions coexist, which calls into question the Christian idea that God's revelation is confined to the Bible alone. Asian theologians are convinced that God's power cannot be limited, which means that the sacred texts of other religious traditions can also be a source of divine revelation. The Christian tradition is only one spiritual tradition among many others and cannot be considered exclusive or unique. Further, it is evident that non-Christian religions have contributed much good and human fulfilment in Asia for many centuries, long before Christianity arrived on its shores.[31]

In his broader work, Balasuriya argues that Asian Christian theology must admit the possibility of other ways of interpreting the origin of the universe, human life and the afterlife. As a foreign religion associated with Western colonialism, Christian teaching is seen as primarily a Western construct built upon a selective interpretation of Scripture. Church doctrine regarding Jesus' divinity and humanity is not intelligible in the context of Hinduism, Buddhism and Islam. Balasuriya considers Christ as the cosmic Lord and therefore he cannot be limited to Jesus as a human person born at a particular time and space.[32] He suggests that we rethink the traditional dogma defined by the Council of Chalcedon (CE 451). Calling for a 'dedogmatization' of theology, he questions the presuppositions behind some of the church doctrines that have a negative impact or influence on the lives of the faithful.[33] He believes that the negative influence of Christian mission in Asia is related to such traditional teachings of the church. Some of these doctrines were little more than ideologies that legitimized the Western missionary approach. For Balasuriya, the commitment to be true followers of Jesus Christ in the context of poverty and the plurality of religions in Asia should lead us to care for the poor and respect people of other faiths. This means the sharing of material and spiritual goods among different religions. In the case of countries under socialist governments in Asia (such as China and Vietnam), Balasuriya calls for greater autonomy and self-reliance for local churches in formulating their own doctrines and in their administration.[34]

Balasuriya calls for a deconstruction and reconstruction of the theological processes dominated by European thinking. This reinventing of theology includes listening to people who are marginalized and oppressed, which would lead to a critical redefining of scripture and tradition that in the past tended to discriminate on the basis of race, gender, social class and other religious beliefs.[35] In relation to these issues, Balasuriya also calls for a rethinking of the questions of original sin, gender relations, as well as the role of Jesus Christ and the church in the economy of salvation. He bemoans the fact that the practice of spirituality in the church has failed to discredit racial and gender discrimination because its understanding of spirituality is based on the 'modern', self-centred and individualistic approach prevalent in the West. Balasuriya desires a spirituality that is more socially oriented and broader in its interpersonal concern and which includes studies and appreciation of other religions and cultures.[36] Without such a shift, he believes that the process of secularization that is happening in the West may spread to Asia, when the educated young start to find the church irrelevant. Therefore, the churches in Asia must find ways and means to make the gospel relevant to this group of people.

Unfortunately, Balasuriya argues, church authorities are reluctant to acknowledge the validity and significance of this call for a rethinking in theology because of their attachment to orthodoxy and traditions that assured them great power and influence. Furthermore, not only are church authorities keen to preserve and protect the faith of the ordinary believers, the faithful are also attached to the pious practices which keep them in subjugation: 'the internalization of one's own subjection to the powerful acquires a legitimation and sacredness'.[37] Critical of the ecclesiastical hierarchy, Balasuriya argues that a traditional Mariology developed in a church that monopolized the sources of grace, and which was dominated by a male clergy, contradicts the spirit of interreligious dialogue because it marginalizes other religions and opposes the spirit of Christian ecumenism. We need to rethink our understanding of Mariology and Christology on both the theoretical and spiritual levels so that they can become relevant to our pluralistic society in Asia and, increasingly, in the West.[38]

INTERFAITH RELATIONS

For Balasuriya, interreligious dialogue is 'a source of theology'.[39] This suggests that through dialogue with other religions, we can understand better God's revelation in history. It is also another means of listening to God and participating in building his Kingdom on earth. In interreligious dialogue, Balasuriya insists that we take into consideration the idea of the divine or absolute in other religions, which is very different from that found in orthodox Christianity. For example, Theravada Buddhists believe that the ultimate reality (or what we might call the 'divine') is unknowable or impersonal and many Hindus see all reality 'pantheistically'. Islam is a strictly monotheistic religion that cannot accept the ideas of Trinity and incarnation in Christianity. In this context, Balasuriya argues, Christians in Asia must rethink their understanding of Jesus Christ and the idea of redemption. From an Asian perspective, it is clear that the Hellenistic and Roman philosophical-theological formulations are not the only way to articulate the mystery of the divine.[40]

To have a better appreciation of other religions, according to Balasuriya, Christians have to be aware of the presuppositions on which their theology and philosophy are built. Religious traditions such as Confucianism, Hinduism, Buddhism, Islam and Christianity have their teachings based on certain presuppositions given by their cultural and philosophical systems. For example, the Western system of logic is based on the principle of non-contradiction and has 'a tendency to be exclusive of opposites'. There is the dichotomy of true and false, leaving no room for a middle or grey area. Many oriental understandings of logic, however, are 'more inclusive and harmonizing'.[41] Of course, Balasuriya is simplifying his point for the sake of illustration; we cannot separate the world so neatly into two distinct modes of thinking: Western dualistic and Eastern non-dualistic systems. In other words, there is a variety within East and West as well as overlap between them. Beyond philosophical and cultural difference, in view of the different presuppositions in each religion, Balasuriya asks, what should be the attitude of Christians towards these other faiths?[42] To answer that question, Balasuriya emphasizes the importance of distinguishing between the core of Christianity (namely the teaching of Jesus in the gospels) and the subsequent development in the interpretation of the scripture by the church. He regards the teaching of Jesus as 'the communication of his primordial spiritual experience.'[43] Balasuriya points out that there is 'hardly anything that is divisive of religions' in the message of Jesus.[44] In other words, other religions will not find the message of the gospel objectionable, because Jesus calls us primarily to love God and our neighbour, a teaching found in or at least compatible with most religious traditions.

Balasuriya believes in the personal acceptance of Jesus Christ as 'our guide in life' and the scripture as divine revelation. However, he reminds us that the teaching of the church concerning how we live our Christian lives must be verified by our own personal experience, because theology developed by different communities is based on different presuppositions. In other words, while God may be absolute, theological statements about God are relative. Balasuriya claims that the church's answer to theological questions can 'claim only a faith that is due to the Church in her teaching power. They are not necessarily answers directly from Jesus.'[45] In fact, conflicts among Christians of different denominations are due to secondary conclusions arising from different presuppositions. The core teaching remains the same. Hence, in interfaith relations, Christians must be aware of their secondary presuppositions that have the tendency of making their religion exclusive or normative.[46] The challenge for Christians is to distinguish between the essential core of Jesus' teaching, which is not relative, and subsequent development and elaboration of his message, which may be. It is a difficult task, Balasuriya admits, because many Christians consider the teaching of the church as the norm of the Christian faith.

However difficult, this task is essential in a society where there is a plurality of religions, and interreligious dialogue is needed to promote peace, mutual respect and understanding. Balasuriya warns that in some Asian countries, there are serious religious and communal conflicts, especially when one religion claims the right to dominate others or claims to be the only true path to salvation.[47] Clearly, a religion that recognizes the equality of all people before God would obviously have a different impact on history from the one that claims for its adherents a special status as 'chosen people'. In order to promote better appreciation of other faiths, we have to understand that the prepositions of one religion are not necessarily more valid than those of other religions. After all, presuppositions in theology concern things that cannot be verified empirically. This leaves us with no alternative but relativism, because human fulfilment achieved through religious belief and practice can be observed in the lives of adherents. 'By their fruits you will know them' (Matthew 7:20). Thus, Balasuriya argues it is possible to discover a critical principle that is valid in interpreting Christian theology as well as valid for interpreting other religions.[48] This principle refers to how much a religion can promote justice, peace and love among its followers.

RETHINKING CHRISTOLOGY AND MARIOLOGY

In view of the plurality of cultures and religions of Asia, Balasuriya calls for a re-evaluation of Christology and Mariology at a deeper level than what is being done in Europe. He thinks that Western theology with its specific presuppositions has had a negative and damaging effect on the people of Asia for centuries and remains an obstacle to interreligious dialogue. He calls for a rethinking of the core teaching of Christianity regarding the nature of salvation, the role of religions and the identity of the various founders like Jesus, Buddha and Muhammad.[49] Balasuriya limits the role of religions to specific functions: offering a path for purification and liberation; offering good models for holiness; forming communities of holiness; providing core values for personal and community growth. He stresses that religious communities and organizations are after all 'this-worldly realities'. Although they emphasize the afterlife, no one knows what happens after death. All we have is faith in God's grace. Religious organizations, Balasuriya asserts, have no influence beyond death.[50]

The Second Vatican Council teaches that God's grace is available to everyone, Christians, non-Christians and even those with no religion. Christians believe in redemption through Jesus Christ, but Jesus did not deny salvation to those of goodwill. Balasuriya points out that the grace and merits of Christ cannot be controlled and channelled exclusively by one particular church or religious organization, which in any case cease to operate beyond this life. The role of religion is to help people to attain human fulfilment and realization as individuals and members of a community, as well as liberation for our Mother Earth.[51] What Balasuriya suggests here is that the church will cease to exist after its earthly journey – only the Kingdom of God will be realized in the fullness of time where all things are gathered in Christ (cf. Ephesians 1:10).

Balasuriya claims that in the Asian context, the doctrine of the 'divine maternity' of Mary raises questions concerning Jesus' divinity. At the same time, he acknowledges that in the Hindu–Buddhist context, Mary as the mother of God can be accepted as one of the deities or goddesses at the popular level. Hinduism, for example, can accept divine manifestations of the Absolute known as avatars and Mary as the mother of God can be understood within that theological framework. This understanding is, of course, different from the Christology taught by the Councils of Nicaea and Chalcedon, which insist on the exclusive nature of Jesus' divinity, which can be an obstacle in the dialogue with Hinduism. With Muslims, the elevated status of Mary will present a greater obstacle – given the strict understanding of monotheism in Islam.[52] This suggests that traditional church teaching on Christ and Mary can cause an impasse in interreligious dialogue. Balasuriya prefers to focus on the mediation of Mary understood as 'atoning and reconciling humanity' with God or as a 'channel of divine grace as mediatrix of graces'. Popular Asian religions, according to Balasuriya, have no difficulty in accepting Mary as a 'mediator and channel of divine favours'.[53]

However, the real obstacle may be linking Mary's status to the idea of an exclusive and unique mediator or saviour, Jesus Christ. Traditional Christology emphasizes the divine nature of Jesus and sees humanity as a fallen race that can be redeemed by Christ alone. Balasuriya points out that this exclusive definition of Jesus is a major issue in Asia, unlike, in Europe and Latin America where majority of people profess at least a cultural Christianity. Aware that we should not dilute our faith for the sake of dialogue, Balasuriya calls for a re-examination of the traditional doctrine of Christ's divinity and exclusivity that might not necessarily originate from scripture or Jesus himself.[54]

Interreligious dialogue, thus, can be seen as an opportunity for Christians to rethink and revaluate traditional theological assumptions. Although these are not directly related to Marian spirituality, the understanding of Christ is crucial for the development of Marian dogma. Balasuriya wishes to see a portrayal of Mary as one who is eloquent in her silence and courageous in her commitment to her son's mission. Readily accepted as a mediator between God and humanity, Mary will be loved and invoked by the people in Asia as well as in the church.[55]

Most of the ideas put forward in *Mary and Human Liberation* are not new. In his earlier work, *Planetary Theology*, published in 1984, Tissa Balasuriya

claims that traditional Christian theology is determined by dominant Western powers, which are capitalist oriented, male and clerical. They interpret
the scripture in a way that suits their interests. With their Western prejudice
and lack of respect for indigenous beliefs, they deny that these other religious
traditions can have salvific features. Further, Balasuriya asserts that traditional Christian theology is also 'culture-bound' and 'implicitly ethnocentric'.
It has unwittingly assisted in European colonialism and, as such, has rendered
many aspects of Christian teaching unacceptable to non-Westerners. Church-
centred, traditional theology often equated the Kingdom of God with the
expansion of the church. It regards the church as an indispensable vehicle to
get people to heaven.[56] This position alienates many people in Asia.

THE STORM BEGINS: *LATAE SENTENTIAE*

A work like this, from a Third World theologian, criticizing the church teaching authorities in no uncertain terms, could not avoid attracting the ire of the
Vatican. Over the last fifteen years, the CDF has acted against theologians'
writings regarding women's ordination, religious pluralism and other issues
in Christology and ecclesiology, and Balasuriya's book touches on almost
all of these issues. Thus, on 2 January 1997, the CDF published a 'Notification on the Work of *Mary and Human Liberation* of Fr Tissa Balasuriya
OMI', signed by Joseph Cardinal Ratzinger and by Prefect and Archbishop
Tarcisio Bertone, Secretary of the Congregation, announcing Balasuriya's
excommunication.

The Notification accused Balasuriya of denying the dogma of original
sin and viewing it simply as a development of Western theological thought.
According to the Notification, this led him to question Mary's immaculate conception, perpetual virginity and bodily assumption. Furthermore, it
charged Balasuriya with 'denying the authority of tradition as a mediation of
revealed truth'. In reducing the Petrine ministry to a question of power, the
CDF claimed that he was in fact denying the infallibility of the pope. The
Notification concludes with this sentence:

> In publishing this *Notification*, the Congregation is obliged also to
> declare that Father Balasuriya has deviated from the integrity of the
> truth of the Catholic faith and, therefore, cannot be considered a
> Catholic theologian; moreover, he has incurred excommunication *latae
> sententiae* (can. 1364, par. 1).[57]

Two things can be gathered here. First, the CDF objected to the fact that Balasuriya had encouraged a religious pluralism and relativism that Ratzinger had labelled as an ideology that mortally threatens the Catholic faith. Second, it objected that Balasuriya questioned the Church's authority to teach divine truth. The CDF held that, as much as the church respected the *sensus fidelium* (sense of the faithful), this did not mean that one could challenge the teaching of the magisterium. *Latae sententiae* meant that Balasuriya had excommunicated himself by persisting in the errors stated in his book and, thus, no formal trial was needed. The only other case of excommunication we know of in the present times is that of the French bishop, Marcel Lefebvre (1906–91), not for heresy but for promoting schism within the church.

Learning of the excommunication, Balasuriya said: 'When this threat of excommunication was made I found it unthinkable. There was no excommunication of a theologian for half a century. I asked myself how they could come to this extreme action, when all they had said was that my response was "unsatisfactory". I felt this was a complete travesty of justice.'[58] Hans Küng, who was himself investigated and censured by the CDF said, 'This is much tougher, perhaps because he is a Third World theologian. It is very serious for this man, and it is very unjust, but it is the consequence of the system. This is the system as it works, and as it will work as long as Catholicism doesn't get rid of a doctrine that says that the pope is always right ... They (CDF) want to menace everyone else who is in this field.'[59]

Charles Curran, also disciplined by the CDF, wrote to Balasuriya to give his support:

> The action against you is so much more radical than the action against me. The Vatican's action against me (and in the case of Hans Küng) was limited to my role as a Catholic theologian and did not affect my canonical identity as a Catholic or even my role in the order of presbyters. The Vatican action now separates you canonically from the church community and from the exercise of priestly ministry ...
>
> Only my identity as a Catholic theologian was attacked by the Vatican, but its action against you destroys the most fundamental identity of your life as a baptized Catholic, a theologian, and a priest. I was hurt by the action against me, but you must be devastated by what has been done to you.[60]

The Balasuriya File, which consists of letters opposing the excommunication of Balasuriya published by *The Tablet* states:

The Congregation for the Doctrine of the Faith's resort to excommunication marks a more ruthless and extreme exercise of its power and a
departure from its previous policy of merely condemning an individual
as unfit to teach Catholic theology. Excommunication is an ultimate
and terrible punishment, which the Vatican hesitates to apply to South
American dictators, Mafia members and IRA bosses who put themselves 'beyond the pale'.[61]

Reaction from outside the Catholic Church was also very strong. For example,
Revd Roy Robinson from the United Reformed Church wrote:

> As for Fr Balasuriya's excommunication, can the Pope really be serious
> in inviting us, the representatives of the Churches of the Reformation,
> to discuss with him the role of the papacy, when he gives us such exam-
> ples of the abuse of papal authority?[62]

The main issue in this affair is not whether Balasuriya's theological ideas are
heretical or not, but, rather, the way he was treated by the church he had
served for so long as a faithful servant. His treatment goes against a natural
sense of justice. The severity of the punishment also calls into question the
way the procedure was carried out. The CDF acted as prosecutor, judge and
jury, pronouncing a sentence to which there was no appeal.

WHAT IS AT STAKE?

By excommunicating Tissa Balasuriya, Joseph Ratzinger was warning those
who work in the field of religious pluralism not to stray from orthodoxy. This
move, however, stifles the spirit of creativity, especially in the promotion of
interreligious relations. This severity of the punishment is likely to prevent
good theology from flourishing. It is ironic that Ratzinger defended the
excommunication of Balasuriya at a press conference by claiming that, 'one of
the greatest challenges for the Church of the third millennium is the search for
an authentic Asian Catholicism ... We are very sensitive to the situation in this
great Asian continent, so decisive for the future of humanity,' he declared. 'We
are very attentive not to quench the flame of the appropriation and creation of
an Asian identity for the Catholic faith.'[63]

The most serious charge against Balasuriya's book was that of relativism
which Ratzinger characterized as 'the central problem for faith today'.[64] He

said that when relativists called for interreligious dialogue, they meant 'putting one's own position, i.e. one's faith, on the same level as the convictions of others without recognising in principle more truth in it than that which is attributed to the opinions of others'. Truth, thus, becomes relativized, which in fact is no truth at all, in Ratzinger's opinion. Hence, truth is being devalued by relativism. Ratzinger insists that there are 'non-negotiables' that Catholic theologians must uphold in the presence of other religions.[65]

The Tablet editorial maintained that Balasuriya 'is not a full-hearted relativist of the sort Cardinal Ratzinger attacked in his lecture ... With or without reservations, no true relativist could have signed the Credo of Pope Paul VI, as he did.' In fact, Balasuriya is more of a pluralist than a relativist. The editorial asserts that 'pluralism springs not from a loss of value, but on the contrary from an absolute respect for the neighbour, and in this sense Christians are the original pluralists. Any theologian who is pluralist in this sense is true to the central Christian requirement.'[66] Unfortunately, Ratzinger equated pluralism with relativism. The excommunication of Tissa Balasuriya is indeed a sad episode in the life of the church. There is cause for lamentation.

'MY GOD, MY GOD, WHY HAST THOU FORSAKEN ME?'

Bradford E. Hinze asserts that when considering those theologians investigated by church authorities, we need to listen to their lamentations because they reveal the conflicts, anxieties and impasse involved in the procedures of the CDF. In other words, lamentation articulates the anguish and pain that some scholars in the church face when they try to be creative and faithful to the Spirit. Seen as offering 'a source of wisdom, renewal and reform in the church', lamentation is 'a privileged site for hearing the Spirit of God who groans in the human heart and the suffering world when something new is struggling into existence and when the Spirit is stifled'.[67] Bradford Hinze discusses ten 'lamentations' of the theologians investigated.[68]

First, the theologians concerned complain that they were never informed of who reported them to the CDF and who examined their work. Did the examiner have the competency and expertise to judge their work? In spite of efforts to humanize and modernize its processes, the CDF lacks proper procedure to investigate errors in theological writings. Its processes are secretive, inquisitorial and unfair to the accused by any modern standards of jurisprudence. The CDF, however, defends its secrecy of the process by maintaining that if the complaints are unfounded, the case is closed and the theologian's reputation will not be affected.[69]

Joseph Ratzinger reports: 'I get many letters from the United States, not only from bishops but from Catholic lay people as well ... the letters provide us with a reflection of typical Catholics. They are people, who are preoccupied with the thought that the Catholic Church would remain the Catholic Church.'[70] Balasuriya disagrees, 'We can no longer accept secret, anonymous denunciations. Those who accuse others to Rome must be subject to reasonable norms of inquiry. If they defame or falsely accuse someone, they should be subject to punishment. This is operative in civil society.'[71]

Second, the theologian being investigated has to keep silent while the case is going on, which means isolating the individual, depriving him of support. There is no transparency regarding the actions of the CDF, and thus it cannot be held accountable and its action cannot be evaluated in public. This imposition of secrecy and silence is painful to the theologian. According to Balasuriya, the theologian has no right to a lawyer; no right to dialogue with the CDF; no right to question the witnesses, who are unknown to him; no right to due process, as in canon law, and no right to appeal to another court.[72]

Third, a frequent complaint is that the theologians' works were not interpreted accurately, for example, that passages from their work are often taken out of context. For instance, Balasuriya complained of the fifty-eight 'unproved generalizations, misrepresentations, distortions and even falsifications' by the CDF, which he tried to clarify. However, his explanations of his position were rejected.[73]

Fourth, the CDF is judging the theologian based on strict and narrow dogmatic propositions. There is little acknowledgement of doctrinal development. Non-infallible teachings are sometimes treated as infallible, a process known as 'creeping infallibilism'.[74] Balasuriya claims that his book makes several distinctions as an attempt to distinguish what Jesus taught and its later development, but they were ignored.

Fifth, the officers of the CDF occupy the roles of investigators, prosecutors and judges. The accused are presumed guilty when they are called up. His accusers acted as his judges. Further, he had no recourse to legal counsel and no third party was appointed to arbitrate or defend him. It seems that this was the custom in the Middle Ages. During the Second Vatican Council, Cardinal Frings of Cologne had argued that the methods of the Holy Office (CDF), as it was then called, were out of touch with modern times and a cause of scandal for people. He said: 'No one ought to be judged and condemned without having been heard, without knowing what he is accused of, and without the opportunity of correcting his views.'[75]

Sixth, the restriction to communicate causes much mental suffering and anguish to the theologians who are investigated. Balasuriya laments that, 'The whole thing seemed designed to force me into a corner, almost to give me a heart attack... they trap you by a combination of forces, psychological, spiritual, theological, social, political and economic, the purpose of which is to bring you down.'[76]

Seventh, the investigation masqueraded as a dialogue. The theologian has to face a group of people who have already reached a conclusion about his or her work. One wonders if Pope John Paul II had himself read *Mary and Human Liberation*. Balasuriya claims that if the pope had read the book and considered all the issues involved, he would not have been excommunicated.[77]

Eighth, there is defamation of character and sometimes the theologian loses his academic position and livelihood. The Cologne Declaration (1989) states that 'The power to withhold official permission to teach is being abused; it has become an instrument to discipline theologians.'[78]

Ninth, there is failure to trust the community of theologians and the faithful. The CDF members proceed as if they were the sole guardians of the faith. In this case, by lifting the excommunication within a year, it seems that the CDF caved in to the demands of the people brought about by the extensive media coverage. Perhaps this is how the sense of the faithful is made known to the church in this day and age.

Tenth, the CDF creates a culture of fear and intimidation. The congregation is fostering a disciplinary culture that is stifling the Spirit. Younger scholars, especially lay theologians, are afraid to be creative in their theological pursuit for fear of losing their jobs. Priest theologians have better support and opportunities made possible by a clerical culture. As we have seen, Balasuriya's own religious congregation, the Oblates of Mary Immaculate, stood behind him during the crisis. Theologians who were rehabilitated after the Second Vatican Council were mostly priests from the religious orders: some, such as Yves Congar OP and Henri de Lubac SJ, were made cardinals later.

THE RIGHT TO DISSENT

In giving the *nihil obstat*, or permission for a Catholic theologian to publish his or her work, Ratzinger makes a distinction between teaching in the name of the church and pure research.[79] But many theologians do not see themselves as church officials teaching in the name of the church. In fact, Balasuriya criticizes church teaching for distorting the gospel. Most theologians accept the fact that the Vatican has the right to question and admonish teachings that harm the faith. However, to silence and excommunicate theologians violates academic freedom.

Concerning the Second Vatican Council's decision to rehabilitate some theologians, Avery Dulles wrote: 'By its actual practice of revision, the council implicitly taught the legitimacy and even the value of dissent. In effect the council said that the ordinary magisterium of the Roman Pontiff had fallen into error and had unjustly harmed the careers of loyal and able scholars.'[80] This meant that the church accepted the right to dissent in theological disputes. Be that as it may, the theologians subjected to discipline complained that the CDF procedure for investigation is flawed; the accusations are unclear; there is a failure to make a distinction between dogma and theological opinion; and only experts who toe the Vatican line are consulted. Clearly there are 'serious deficiencies in the justice of their process', Charles Curran reported.[81] The Catholic Theological Society of America also reported that the procedures used by the CDF to investigate dissident theologians 'fail to honour fundamental human rights and the safeguards in our countries [USA and Canada] necessary to protect these human rights.'[82]

While there is certainly a more humane way to carry out this procedure, we must admit that there will always be tension between theologians and the CDF: the tension created by making the faith more relevant to contemporary society and to specific cultures and the need to protect the faith from distortion. As a bureaucracy, we cannot expect the CDF to be forward looking, promoting cutting-edge theology. Its main function is to protect and preserve Catholic orthodoxy in faith and morals. However, Thomas Reese says that the number of theologians investigated and censured is at an all-time high, even more than the numbers during the Modernist crisis in the late nineteenth and early twentieth centuries. If this rift between theologians and the magisterium continues, Reese believes that the church will lack creative thinking to respond to new questions, needs and opportunities in the new millennium.[83] In other words, the church will make itself irrelevant in the postmodern world and may even cause a schism.

THE STORM SUBSIDES: RECONCILIATION

The reconciliation of Balasuriya with the Catholic Church took place on 15 January 1998 in Colombo, Sri Lanka. In the presence of Nicholas Marcus Fernando, archbishop of Colombo, Osvaldo Padilla, the apostolic nuncio in Sri Lanka, and Fr Marcello Zago, superior general of the Missionary Oblates of Mary Immaculate, Balasuriya signed Pope Paul VI's Profession of Faith. According to an official document from the archbishop's office, he 'regretted the harm caused' by *Mary and Human Liberation* and by 'subsequent events'. He also 'expressed his Catholic faith and recognised the authority of the magisterium [teaching authority] exercised at both the local and universal levels in regard to his writings'. Agreeing to submit his writings on faith and morals for church approval, he also promised to 'abstain from any declaration that is in contradiction to this reconciliation'.[84]

The Oblates' office in Colombo reported that: 'Although the process of reviewing all that led to the excommunication was rather painful, it was an experience of grace and healing, first of all for Fr Balasuriya himself and for all those associated with this moment of open and honest dialogue.' The support he had received from his religious congregation was due to his years of dedicated and generous service. Not an obdurate person, Balasuriya was willing to revise or change his ideas. He says in the *Preface* of *Mary and Human Liberation* that his work 'is open to criticism and correction in a climate and context of a genuine search for the truth'.[85] The case of Balasuriya gives us the opportunity to reflect on the relationship between theologians and the magisterium, the issue of religious pluralism and interfaith relations, and power and politics in the Vatican.

CRITICAL REFLECTION

Distinguished theologians, such as Küng and Curran, were investigated and censured by the CDF and were forbidden to teach in Catholic faculties and seminaries, but, unlike Balasuirya, they were not excommunicated. It is thus intriguing that Balasuriya had to face such a severe punishment. Unlike Küng and Curran, Balasuriya was an Asian theologian from a developing nation. Perhaps church officials have little respect for Asia, or for developing nations, or perhaps he simply did not have the powerful friends in the Vatican that others did. The CDF under Ratzinger wanted to rein in pluralist theologians, and it was a clear warning to others working in this field. More than just questioning the church authorities' exclusive mandate to teach, Balasuriya's ideas stood in stark contrast to Ratzinger's own theological approach.

As we have seen, in *Planetary Theology* (1984), Balasuriya supports religious pluralism and criticizes the ecclesiastical establishment as well. However, this book was never censured. Why? One can only speculate that in the 1980s, the magisterium was not so preoccupied with the errors connected with religious pluralism and that Ratzinger was just settling into his new position as prefect of the CDF. It was only in the 1990s that religious pluralism and relativism became such burning issues.

The trial of Balasuriya involved an exchange of many letters, but there was no opportunity for constructive dialogue on theological issues. Balasuriya was not allowed face-to-face contact with high-ranking officials in the CDF. This was a painful episode regarding the church's treatment of a theologian who laboured to make the gospel more relevant to his people. It makes one wonder how the church can engage in dialogue with other religions when it cannot conduct a proper dialogue within its own ranks. Balasuriya made this astonishing remark: 'In fact, it was through the BBC that I first heard about my own excommunication!'[86]

There may be unconventional ideas in Balasuriya's *Mary and Human Liberation* that need to be investigated, but to excommunicate Balasuriya in this postmodern age seems farcical given the chequered history of the Vatican. Some believed that the massive protest in the media helped to shorten the length of Balasuriya's excommunication. But it is significant that the church sought to reconcile with Balasuriya so quickly.

One can only speculate under what condition and context Balasuriya signed the Profession of Faith. It seems that there was compromise on both sides, the Vatican and Balasuriya. Belonging to a religious congregation like the Oblates of Mary Immaculate helped much in the process of his reconciliation with the church authorities. It could be that realizing its mistake and how badly it had handled the whole affair, Rome was anxious to conclude this sordid episode without losing face. This was hastened by the worldwide outcry and extensive media coverage that were assisted by the internet, where news spreads fast and wide. Perhaps this is how the *sensus fidelium* expresses itself now. It is a new reality that the Vatican needs to understand and accommodate. This means that the Catholic Church has to move out of its premodern ghetto into the global world that is the Information Age where greater transparency is expected.

Chapter 9

Jacques Dupuis SJ

I n Chapter 8, in the case of Tissa Balasuriya, we saw Joseph Ratzinger's concern that relativism is influencing Catholic theology, especially in the area of religious pluralism. He is particularly critical of theologies arising from the Asian context that encourage more openness and inclusiveness towards non-Christian religions. This brings us specifically to the case of the Belgian Jesuit, Jacques Dupuis, a distinguished theologian who worked within the bounds of Catholic orthodoxy. Nevertheless, he was called up by the Congregation for the Doctrine of the Faith, at the time when Cardinal Ratzinger was its prefect, regarding his book *Toward a Christian Theology of Religious Pluralism*.

This chapter seeks to review Jacques Dupuis' book in the light of Joseph Ratzinger's understanding of religious pluralism and Catholic orthodoxy. It includes Ratzinger's position in contrast to Dupuis' theological approach. It concludes that the investigation of Dupuis' book had more to do with Dupuis' conflict with Ratzinger's theological viewpoint than with contravening Catholic doctrines. In fact, the CDF did not ask Dupuis to change a single line, but only to include the Notification in any subsequent editions of the book.

The first sign of trouble for Dupuis came in March 1993 when Ratzinger, addressing a gathering in Hong Kong, called relativism the most serious problem of our time. He said that relativism drains Christianity of its content: 'Church-centeredness, Christ-centeredness, God-centeredness, all of these seem to give way to kingdom-centeredness, the centering on the kingdom as the common task of all religions, under which point of view and standard they are supposed to meet.'[1] In this reference, in a footnote, Ratzinger specially alluded to a journal article written by Jacques Dupuis.[2] Five years later, Dupuis would find himself under a cloud of suspicion.

Jacques Dupuis was one of the first theologians to come under the scrutiny of Joseph Ratzinger, who late in his career as prefect of the CDF, began to focus his attention on the theology of religious pluralism. Thus, in 1998, the CDF began an investigation of Dupuis' work and instructed him to keep silent regarding the investigation and not to spread the ideas in his teaching and writing because they were considered 'controversial'.[3] On 27 February 2001, the CDF published a Notification concerning Dupuis' book, *Toward a Christian Theology of Religious Pluralism*, 'intended to safeguard the doctrine of the Catholic faith from errors, ambiguities or harmful interpretations'.[4] Dupuis, who had devoted his entire life to the church as a priest and theologian, was deeply hurt by the investigation. He died three years later on 28 December 2004.

INDIAN EXPERIENCE: 1948–84

Let us first take a brief look at Dupuis' early life in the Far East, which shaped his theology of religious pluralism. Jacques Dupuis' long years of experience in India and exposure to its non-Christian traditions shaped his theology. Naturally, as a priest, his theology was also shaped by the teaching of the church. As a theologian, he had tried to respond to a world in which Christians were increasingly aware of the nature of different religious paths. This led him into conflict with church authorities in spite of the fact that the Secon Vatican Council document, *Nostra Aetate*, focused on the commonality between the Catholic faith and other religions. It stated that 'the Catholic Church rejects nothing which is true and holy in these religions'.[5] Dupuis took this seriously and sought to identify the significance of other religions in God's plan for humankind. He was able to see the issues of revelation and salvation in a more complex and broader perspective than he found in the church's teaching of the time. Dupuis was convinced that divine revelation was not limited to the Judeo-Christian tradition, but also extended to other religious traditions. Joseph Ratzinger, however, believes that Abraham's history is the history of all nations because salvation comes from the Jews.[6]

Jacques Dupuis was born in Belgium in 1923 and entered the Society of Jesus in 1941. As a young Jesuit scholar, he volunteered for missions in India. It was at St Xavier's College, Calcutta, that Dupuis made his first contact with non-Christian students. They attracted him with their goodness and piety which had been taught to them by their parents, who were, for the most part, Hindu. It seemed clear to Dupuis that 'God had revealed himself in and through their Hindu faith.[7] Thus, he began to reflect seriously on the variety of religions in the world. It was obvious to him that these religions were not simply superstitions. In an interview with Robert Blair Kaiser, a writer for *Newsweek*, Dupuis said he would not presume to know what God had in mind at the point in time when these religions began: 'I don't know … And I don't think Ratzinger knows either.'[8]

Dupuis was ordained in 1954 and from 1960–84, he was professor of systematic theology at the Jesuit-run theological faculty, Vidyajyoti Institute of Religious Studies, in New Delhi. In 1984, he became professor of Christology at the Pontifical Gregorian University in Rome. He also edited *Gregorianum*, the Gregorian University's journal. As an advisor to the Pontifical Council for Interreligious Dialogue, he played an important role in the writing of *Dialogue and Proclamation*, the Vatican's 1991 guidelines on interreligious dialogue, a subject at the heart of John Paul II's pontificate.

In 1997 Dupuis published his book, *Towards a Christian Theology of Religious Pluralism*. As mentioned earlier, the CDF, headed by Cardinal Ratzinger, investigated this book. As a result, Dupuis cancelled his classes for the first semester of 1998/99 at the Gregorian University so that he could concentrate on responding to the charges brought by the CDF and, in fact, wrote nearly 200 pages in reply. Dupuis became professor emeritus in December 1998 and turned seventy-five in the same year. He continued to edit *Gregorianum* until 2003. At the heart of Jacques Dupuis' theology was the belief that although Jesus is the Saviour of humankind, God also works in other religions. Dupuis never denied the primacy of Christianity and his theology was distinctly Trinitarian in character. Dupuis believed that in every authentic religious experience, the triune God of Christian revelation was present and operative.

His last book, *Christianity and the Religions: From Confrontation to Dialogue*, was dedicated to Cardinal König and prefaced with a quotation from Joseph Ratzinger about the need for men in the church who are obedient and humble in their quest for truth. In this book, Dupuis clarified some matters. For instance, he introduced the term 'inclusive pluralism',[9] which means that adherents of other religions can be saved because their faiths contain 'elements of truth and grace'. Thus, these other religions have a positive meaning in God's overall plan of salvation. He qualified the 'complementarity'[10] between Christ and Christianity, on the one hand, and world religions, on the other, as 'asymmetrical'.[11] He also clarified what he meant by the Word-to-be-incarnate (*Verbum incarnandum*) and the Word incarnate (*Verbum incarnatum*).[12] Dupuis' words in the postscript reveal him as a faithful servant of the church: 'I once more submit my efforts and endeavors to the consideration of my theological peers and to the judgment of the church's doctrinal authority.'[13]

In an interview in London, Dupuis summed up his theology of religious pluralism: 'In a sense we must be prepared to recognise the word of God in the sacred books of those other religious traditions. It remains true, of course, that the fullness of divine revelation is found in Jesus Christ. And the reason for this is that Jesus Christ as the Son of God made man can express the mystery of God more deeply than the prophets of the Old Testament and the prophets of the other religious traditions.'[14]

Dupuis also mentioned his experience in India: 'I went through a conversion by living for so many years in India. If I had not lived in India for 36 years, I would not preach the theology that I am preaching today. I consider my exposure to Hindu reality as the greatest grace I have received from God in my vocation as theologian.'[15] Dupuis stressed the concrete environment in which he lived out his faith and practised his theology. Ratzinger, however, emphasized the ecclesial aspect of life when he says: 'theology can remain historically relevant only if it acknowledges this living environment' of the church and participates in it. He regards the church as the 'vital milieu' of the theologian. Besides rigorous scholarship, Ratzinger insists that the theologian must participate in the 'organic structure of the Church' with prayer and contemplation.[16] Although Dupuis did not deny the church as the living milieu of theology, Ratzinger stressed this ecclesial context more.

Toward a Christian Theology of Religious Pluralism is an attempt by Dupuis to give an 'organic treatment' to salvation history that is Christocentric.[17] This means maintaining the Christian identity while engaging in interfaith dialogue and conversation. He insists that the theology of religions must be studied within one's personal perspective on faith and within 'the presuppositions which faith implies'. This theology 'interprets the data in the perspective of a personal commitment to a religious faith'.[18] Although theology must necessarily be 'confessional', Dupuis argues that a Christian theology must adopt a global outlook that incorporates, in its vision, the entire religious experience of humanity. This means that its horizon must be 'universal'.[19] At the same time, Dupuis maintains that religious faiths differ from each other substantially, and thus, it is not possible to have a universal theology. We must acknowledge the 'plurality and diversity of beliefs and the mutual acceptance of the others in their otherness'. Thus the model he proposes is not one of mutual assimilation, but of 'interpenetration and cross-fertilization of the various traditions in their diversities'.[20]

In a similar way, Joseph Ratzinger also maintains that only when 'cultures are potentially universal' and are open to others can 'interculturality' take place and lead to 'fruitful forms'.[21] The tendency towards openness of all men to each other is hidden in our souls and 'touched by truth'.[22] Ratzinger asserts that we cannot see all religions as superstitions, but, at the same time, it is also wrong to think that all religions are good and equally valid as paths to salvation.[23]

DE FACTO AND DE JURE

Jacques Dupuis asserts that religious pluralism 'has its roots in the depth of the Divine Mystery itself and in the manifold way in which human cultures have responded to the mystery'. He insists that differences must not only be tolerated but welcomed and celebrated with thankfulness because they are 'a sign of the superabundant riches of the Divine Mystery which overflows to humankind and ... an outstanding opportunity for mutual enrichment, "cross-fertilization," and "transformation" between the traditions themselves'.[24] Religious pluralism is not only a reality (de facto) but must also be accepted in principle (de jure).[25] Hence, it has a place in God's plan of salvation, and commitment to one's faith is compatible with openness to others. Dupuis also argues that, in the final analysis, a theology of religions must be a theology of religious pluralism.

Dupuis acknowledges that religious pluralism persists, due in part to the failure of Christian mission, especially in Asia. He also believes that religious pluralism can be welcomed as a positive thing as it shows the superabundant generosity of God in that he reveals himself to humankind in diverse ways. Therefore, theology must assign to the plurality of religions a positive meaning in God's overall plan for humanity. The multiplicity of religions in the world is not an obstacle to be removed, but rather a richness to be celebrated and enjoyed by all.[26] Following Edward Schillebeeckx's thinking, Dupuis believes Christianity has a positive relationship with other religions. Christianity can maintain its uniqueness and at the same time affirm the positive nature of other religious traditions.[27]

The principle of religious pluralism is based on the richness and diversity of God's revelation to humankind. According to Dupuis, there is only one divine plan for humanity, but it is multidimensional: 'it belongs to the nature of the overflowing communication of the Triune God to humankind to prolong outside the divine life the plural communication intrinsic to that life itself'. Therefore Dupuis teaches that it is not incidental that God spoke in many and diverse ways before speaking through his son (Hebrews 1:1). The Christ-event does not make obsolete 'the universal presence and action of the Word and the Spirit'.[28]

Although religious pluralism manifests God's superabundant love for us, Dupuis stresses that we must maintain the 'constitutive uniqueness and universality of Jesus Christ'.[29] The Christ-event is 'constitutive' and 'relational'.[30] What Dupuis means is that the death and resurrection of Jesus Christ opens the way for all of us to reach God, but the uniqueness of Christianity must not be construed as absolute. Only God's saving will is absolute. The death and resurrection of Jesus Christ are at once particular in time and universal in meaning. They are unique, yet related to all the other divine revelations made to humankind in our salvation history.

Truth and grace in other religions are not just stepping stones, they represent extra advantages for humankind. Dupuis believes they operate throughout the entire history of God's relationship with his people and not just in the Christian religion. The truth of Christianity is neither exclusive nor inclusive, 'it is related to all that is true in other religions'.[31] Thus, the Christian theology of religions studies the complementarity and convergence of various religious traditions in the light of the mystery of the divine Trinity as revealed in Jesus Christ. The final goal of Christianity and other religions is the 'eschatological fullness of the Reign of God'.[32]

Some people have mistaken Dupuis' definition of religious pluralism *de jure* for the Hickian one which holds that, in principle, all major religions are equally valid paths to salvation.[33] Religious pluralism, in principle, according to Dupuis, means acknowledging that God's presence is available to people through the 'spiritual riches' that their religions embody and express. This does not mean that all the great religious traditions are equally valid channels of salvation. The presence and activity of the Spirit touch the cultures and religions of humankind everywhere. Thus, the Spirit's activity in various religions implies 'some kind of religious "pluralism" which exists in principle'. Therefore, Gerald O'Collins insists that we need to differentiate between the 'pluralists' and the kind of 'pluralism' that Dupuis accepts.[34]

Unfortunately not everyone appreciates the fine analysis and distinction that Jacques Dupuis attempts to make in his writings on religious pluralism. William Burrows remarks that critics of Dupuis, most of whom had never worked outside Europe, could not grasp the impact of globalization and the end of Western domination and thus interpreted him only in the light of 'Post-Kantian aspects of the Enlightenment' and European conflicts with secularism. Hence, they could not comprehend the deep implications involved in Christian engagement with other religious traditions.[35] In fact, church authorities reacted critically towards theologians who were involved in inter-religious relationships without explicitly upholding magisterial teaching. In this regard, David Tracy is right when he asserts: 'Every pluralism is some-times considered a positive reality by participants but sometimes not, espe-cially not, by authorities within the tradition.'[36] As a result of Jacques Dupuis' book, *Toward a Christian Theology of Religious Pluralism*, the CDF issued a warning in the form of a declaration – *Dominus Iesus*.

UNIQUENESS OF JESUS CHRIST

In September 2000, the CDF issued the document *Dominus Iesus*, signed by Cardinal Joseph Ratzinger, which drew attention to the difficulties that religious pluralism could cause for the missionary endeavour of the church. The text speaks of the problem and danger of relativizing the missionary proclamation of the church and insists on the unique and universal salva-tion brought about by Jesus Christ. Besides the warning, the declaration also invites theologians 'to explore if and in what way the historical figures and positive elements of these religions may fall within the divine plan of salva-tion.'[37] Bradford E. Hinze claims that this is the most important document that deals with the issues of religious pluralism and relativism in Christology and ecclesiology.[38]

Although *Dominus Iesus* does not criticize any author by name, it is quite clear that it is referring to Jacques Dupuis' work because at the time when this CDF document was presented to the public, a Notification on Dupuis' book had already been prepared. It became obvious that the CDF's declaration was referring to Dupuis' book, when it stated:

> The Church's constant missionary proclamation is endangered today by relativistic theories which seek to justify religious pluralism, not only *de facto* but also *de jure (or in principle)* … Christian revelation and the mystery of Jesus Christ and the Church lose their character of absolute truth and salvific universality, or at least shadows of doubt and uncertainty are cast upon them … Not infrequently it is proposed that theology should avoid the use of terms like 'unicity', 'universality', and 'absoluteness', which give the impression of excessive emphasis on the significance and value of the salvific event of Jesus Christ in relation to other religions.[39]

The document asserts: 'Jesus Christ has a significance and a value for the human race and its history, which are unique and singular, proper to him alone, exclusive, universal, and absolute.' Also 'it is precisely this uniqueness of Christ which gives him an absolute and universal significance whereby, while belonging to history, he remains history's centre and goal: "I am the Alpha and the Omega, the first and the last, the beginning and the end" (Rev 22:13).'[40] Dupuis laments that while affirming Catholic identity, the document also attempts to deny the authenticity of other religions. He asks, 'Does the Catholic doctrine of the complete character of the revelation of Jesus Christ need to deny a priori the existence of some divine revelation elsewhere?'[41] Dupuis finds the exclusive mentality of the document objectionable.

Dominus Iesus characterizes the theology of religious pluralism as 'relativistic attitudes toward truth itself, according to which what is true for some would not be true for others; the radical opposition posited between the logical mentality of the West and the symbolic mentality of the East.'[42] Perhaps this is what the Notification meant by ambiguities and errors in Dupuis' work: Eastern philosophical presupposition of subjectivism and the tendency to interpret scripture outside tradition and magisterial teaching. Theologians who hold such views have difficulty accepting the Christ-event as definitive in history. The Notification accuses some theologians, for example, of uncritically absorbing ideas from a variety of philosophical contexts without regard for truth. *Dominus Iesus* sums up very well Ratzinger's fears about religious pluralism and relativism.

We will now examine *Toward a Christian Theology of Religious Pluralism*, focusing on Dupuis' call for a shift from ecclesiocentrism to Christocentrism and then to Theocentrism.

SHIFTING PARADIGMS

When speaking about the paradigmatic shift in the debate over the theology of religions, Dupuis thinks that the term 'paradigm' is better than 'model' to express the change in the understanding of human salvation. Models do not exclude each other; they complement each other and need to be combined in order to give us 'a comprehensive view of the reality concerned'. However, a paradigm is the opposite, in the sense that it opposes and excludes others. It deals with the principles of interpreting reality. For example, one cannot hold a Ptolemaic and Copernican worldview at the same time. Thus, if one paradigm is no longer operative, we have to move on or 'shift' to another one.[43]

First, Dupuis speaks of the paradigmatic shift in theological discourse from ecclesiocentrism to Christocentricism: this means a radical 'decentering' of the church and focusing on the mystery of Christ. In other words, it is Jesus Christ and not the church that is at the centre of the Christian mystery.[44] Hence, a 'broad Christocentric perspective' replaces a 'narrow ecclesiocentric approach'.[45] With regard to the theology of religions, this paradigmatic shift from exclusivism to inclusivism requires a distinction to be made between the roles of Jesus Christ and the church which cannot be both on the same level in the economy of salvation. Jesus Christ alone is 'the mediator between God and human beings' according to the gospel. Therefore, Dupuis claims that 'a theology of religions cannot be built on an ecclesiological inflation that would falsify perspectives'.[46] What this means is that membership in the church cannot be used as a criterion for the salvation of souls. Ratzinger, however, thinks this decentring of the church is the effect of the dogma of relativism. He fears that this would deprive Christianity of its content and eliminate missionary endeavours to convert people to Catholicism.

Second, there is the shift from Christocentrism to Theocentrism. This means God alone stands at the centre. One can believe in pluralism in the sense that people can and do find salvation through various religious traditions and also accept, as Dupuis does, that the one, universal, constitutive mediation of salvation comes through Christ. Dupuis reports that, at the heart of the paradigmatic shift, is the Christological question: the contention that a person is saved through faith in Jesus Christ, but not that Jesus Christ is the only way for all human beings to be saved. In other words, Jesus Christ is the saviour of Christians, but other ways to be saved are available to non-Christians.[47] Dupuis does not share the view that all religions, including Christianity, despite their differences, have the same validity and equal value.

Some link this second shift to the pluralism of John Hick. However, Dupuis is too sophisticated and meticulous a theologian to apply Hick's pluralism to this paradigmatic shift without qualification. Ratzinger characterizes Hick's pluralism as 'relativism in theology' and a 'revocation of Christology'. Ratzinger claims that Hick rejects the identification of the historical Jesus of Nazareth with the living God as a myth; Jesus is relativized by Hick and reduced to one religious figure among others. This means there is no 'absolute person in himself, within history', so there can only be 'ideal figures' or models that, in themselves, direct our attention to the divine reality that cannot be known.[48] Ratzinger fears this will lead to a denial of the church, its sacraments and dogmas.[49] He accused Hick of denying transcendence, but Hick responded by saying that Ratzinger's judgement was wrong and not based on a proper study of his writings.[50] Hick actually does hold that the divine reality cannot be known in itself – a position that, in practice, means that the transcendent, divine reality can be set aside and ignored.

THE PNEUMATOCENTRIC MODEL

There is also a shift from the Christocentric model to focus on the Word and the Holy Spirit, the 'Logos and the Pneuma'. Advocates of this move believe that in every event and in every circumstance, it is the Word of God that saves and not specifically the incarnated Jesus. Dupuis argues that 'The Christ' is just a title and 'a title does not save'.[51] In the prologue to the Gospel of John, we learn that the Logos existed before the incarnation. In the same way, the Spirit of God was present before the Christ-event. Thus, Dupuis says we need to move beyond the narrow Christological perspective and build a new theology of religions based on a pneumatocentric model unconfined by the particularity of history: the economy of the Spirit transcends space and time.[52]

The Spirit 'blows where he wills' (John 3:8); it is present throughout human history and remains active today inside and also outside Christianity. The Spirit also inspires people in their own religious traditions. Discussing the position of Paul Knitter, Dupuis asks: while Christians are assured of salvation by the Christ-event, can followers of other religions receive this assurance from their own traditions through the 'immediate autonomous action of the Spirit of God?'[53]

The Holy Spirit is the 'point of entry' into the lives of people, which God uses to communicate with them. Dupuis also claims that the model centred on the Holy Spirit cannot be separated from the Christological model. In spite of the fact that the Spirit is present before and after the Christ-event, Christian faith stresses the distinction between these two phases although they are 'complementary and inseparable'.[54] This means that pneumatocentrism and Christocentrism constitute two inseparable aspects of the divine economy.

When we discuss shifting paradigms and modes of contradiction, we employ the categories and models of the Western way of thinking. Dupuis insists that we must move beyond this European way of categorization in order to build a theology of religions that is founded on 'harmony, convergence and unity'. This means that we must abandon talk of uniqueness in order to discover the 'singularity of each religious tradition' and also the 'positive significance of the plurality of those traditions'.[55] Ratzinger, however, steeped in

European tradition, prefers to see Christianity as a unique religion, based on divine revelation and influenced by Greek philosophy and Roman laws, and to see the church as an essential component of that revelation.

CONVERGENT PATHS

Jacques Dupuis argues that a Christian theology of religious pluralism must be an 'interfaith theology'.[56] We must be truly committed to our faith while at the same time taking a universal perspective and opening ourselves to all human experiences of the absolute. The relationship between Christianity and other religions cannot be viewed 'in terms of contradiction and opposition between realization here and stepping-stones there'. It must be viewed in terms of 'interdependence, within an organic whole of universal reality', between the diverse ways that human beings encounter the Divine mystery.[57]

The Trinitarian Christology proposed by Dupuis implies that Jesus Christ must not be a substitute for the Father and, thus, interpretation of faith must be 'God-centred'. Jesus is the way and the truth, according to the Gospel of John (14:6), but 'never the goal or the end'.[58] The mystery of God is 'made known' to us only through the incarnate Son (John 1:18). Dupuis maintains that although Jesus is close to the Father by virtue of the incarnation, the two remain distinct. There is an 'unbridgeable distance' between the Father and Jesus in his humanity. 'God stands beyond Jesus'; he is at the centre of the Christian mystery, not in the 'absolute sense', but in the order of the economy of God's relationship with his people in history. What Dupuis means is that although there is a unique closeness between God and Jesus by virtue of the incarnation, God the Father and Jesus in his humanity are not on the same level.[59]

Some critics accuse Dupuis of making a 'personal distinction between the eternal Word of God and the historic Jesus of Nazareth'. With reference to this, Gerald O'Collins says Dupuis likes to make a distinction but not a separation between the two natures of Christ and their respective functions. The Word of God (Logos) was present and active everywhere both before and after the incarnation and it was not overshadowed by Jesus taking a human form. Dupuis stresses that the Word of God is identical with Jesus of Nazareth.[60] We must 'distinguish between the divine and human actions' but not between two personal agents. There is only one divine plan of salvation and not two economies of salvation. All people are called to share in the one life of the Trinity through the activities of the Son and the Holy Spirit.[61]

Dupuis also proposes a Spirit Christology that extends 'beyond the resurrection to illustrate the relationship between the action of the risen Lord and the economy of the Holy Spirit'. In building a theology of religious pluralism, the universal presence and action of the Holy Spirit must be affirmed and followed as a guiding principle. Christology does not exist without pneumatology, nor can it be allowed to develop into a 'Christomonism', Dupuis argues.[62] Furthermore, the action of the Spirit is not confined to the risen body of Christ. While the Spirit continues to work in total communion with the glorified Christ after resurrection, it also exercises its mission towards those outside the Christian faith, through Jesus' mediation. To maintain that the Spirit's saving action takes place exclusively through Christ's glorified body is a kind of 'Christomonism' that Eastern theologians have renounced.[63]

As opposed to their Western contemporaries, the Eastern theologians have a theology that stresses the role of the Holy Spirit in the divine economy of salvation. It emphasizes the distinct roles of the Son and the Spirit. What is more, this 'relationship of order' between the Son and the Spirit exists without any subordination of one to the other. In addition, Dupuis stresses that while the Son and the Spirit are distinct, they also complement each other in the economy of salvation. He writes, 'The Christ-event is at the center of the historical unfolding of the divine economy, but the punctual event of Jesus Christ is actuated and becomes operative throughout time and space in the work of the Spirit.'[64]

Thus, a theology of religious pluralism must be able to hold in 'constructive tension', the particularity of the historical Christ-event and the universal action of the Holy Spirit. It will then be able to show that God's revelation in human cultures and religious traditions outside Christianity does not imply two channels of salvation, Christology and pneumatology, with one for Christians and the other for non-Christians.[65] It follows that Jesus Christ and the Holy Spirit form one divine economy of the divine–human relationship. This is similar to the idea of John Paul II who taught that the Spirit operates beyond the visible boundary of the church in the world's cultures and religions.

Dupuis says the historical Christ-event must not be allowed to obscure the fact that the Trinity, with its distinct and correlated functions, is also operating in the divine economy. The Trinitarian mystery implies the existence of unity and plurality at the same time; there is diversity and communion of persons in the Godhead. The Christ-event must be seen within 'the manifold modality of the divine self-disclosure and manifestation through the Word and the Spirit'. God's inner life overflows outside the Godhead. Thus, 'One God – One Christ – Convergent Paths' means that the Christ-event assures us that God has diverse ways of reaching humankind; these diverse paths tend towards a 'mutual convergence' in the divine mystery which constitutes our final goal and destination.[66]

Dupuis' interpretation maintains that the activity of the Spirit reaches and enriches non-Christians in and through their own religious beliefs and practices. Since non-Christian religions contain elements of truth and goodness, the Spirit of God is also present in them and so their adherents can obtain salvation by following the dictates of their own religions. Although the teachings of the Second Vatican Council state that non-Christians may be saved, the church has not, as yet, recognized that there are 'salvific structures' in other faiths. The document *Nostra Aetate* is silent on this issue. The church does not give any straightforward answer as to whether non-Christian religions have salvific structures. Ratzinger agrees that the elements of truth and goodness in other religions offer paths towards salvation, and do so only through the Spirit of Christ, but the religions themselves are not capable of saving the believers. This particular distinction that Ratzinger makes leads him to view religious pluralism as a kind of relativism. It is a relativism that implies that all authentic religious traditions offer paths of salvation.

HISTORY AND COVENANTS

The idea that salvation begins only with the vocation of Abraham is misleading, according to Dupuis. In the same way as Karl Rahner, Dupuis believes that world history coincides with salvation history.[67] Human history is the story of God's relationship with humankind. God wills all human beings to be saved (1 Timothy 2:4). Karl Rahner bases his belief in the universality of divine revelation on an analysis of the existential condition of human existence, which he calls the 'supernatural existential'.[68] This means that salvation history cannot be confined to the Judeo-Christian tradition because other religious traditions also have their own 'prophetic words interpreting ... divine interventions in the history of peoples'. God's gifts to his people are not limited to Israel; they are extended even to Israel's enemies.[69]

Dupuis warns us not to interpret the Christocentrism of salvation history as a Christomonism. The centrality of the Christ-event actually enhances the universal presence of the Word and the Spirit throughout salvation history, in the many religions of humankind. John Paul II affirmed that the Holy Spirit was present in every historical situation, before and after the Christ-event. The 'Logos-Wisdom and the Spirit' were operative in pre-Christian times.

Later, they were understood as 'two distinct persons within the mystery of the Triune God': one was the Son who became incarnate in Jesus Christ, and the other was the Spirit of Christ. Dupuis says that the two divine persons were 'present and operative in the pre-Christian dispensation without being formally recognized as persons'. The Prologue to St John's Gospel affirms this, and St Irenaeus develops the concept of the universal presence of the divine Logos before the Christ-event. Thus, the Logos was present throughout the history of humankind and culminated in the incarnation of Jesus Christ.[70]

Dupuis is not saying anything unorthodox by maintaining this, because John Paul II, in his encyclical *Redemptoris Missio*, explicitly confirmed the universal presence of the Spirit. In his theology of religious pluralism, Dupuis attempts to combine the universal action of the Word and Spirit in one economy of salvation with the Christ-event. In line with the teaching of Rahner, Dupuis asserts that the 'Logos' pre-incarnational action is oriented toward the Christ-event' and the Spirit is actually the '"Spirit of Christ" from the beginning of salvation history'.[71] Dupuis insists that there is one divine economy in which the actions of the Word, Spirit and Christ-event are inseparable.

In addition, Dupuis argues that a theology of religious pluralism must express the universal presence of the Word and Spirit outside the Judeo-Christian tradition and indicate that Jesus is not just the founder of Christianity, but the '"refounder" of the universal covenant'.[72] The various covenants are diverse ways of God relating to his people through the Logos.[73] Therefore, Dupuis believes it is wrong to view the covenant of Noah as merely a setting up of natural religion, as Catholic theology teaches.[74] We must see the covenant with Noah as containing supernatural revelation and, thus, as a true event of salvation with a 'Trinitarian rhythm'.[75] Dupuis writes: 'The covenant with Noah thus takes on a far-reaching significance for a theology of the religious traditions of peoples belonging to the "extrabiblical" tradition'. Hence, non-Christians are also covenantal peoples or 'peoples of God'.[76]

Dupuis also makes it clear that extrabiblical traditions bear the imprint of the Trinity. He says, as we search for '"traces" of the Trinity (*vestigial Trinitatis*) in creation and ... in the spiritual activity of human being', we can also discover these vestiges in non Judeo-Christian traditions.[77] Other religious traditions, Dupuis argues, are also 'symbolized by the Noachic covenant, and keep, *mutatis mutandis*, an enduring value'. Just as the coming of Christ has not suppressed the law in the Mosaic covenant, neither has the cosmic covenant with Noah been suppressed by the Christ-event.[78]

In light of the above, Jacques Dupuis teaches that divine revelation is not limited to biblical history but extended to the entire history of salvation. He believes that divine revelation is 'coextensive with the history of salvation' and is extended to the whole of world history. Therefore, the prophetic figures and written and oral teachings of other religious traditions also manifest a 'word spoken by God' to their followers and to all humankind.[79] This is because 'God wills that the other religions perform functions in his plan' for the salvation of humankind – a plan which will be fully disclosed only at the end of time. Dupuis says a theology of the 'Word of God in history' must be both 'Trinitarian and Christological'. It should search for the 'signs of God's action' and the 'imprint of the Spirit' in other religious traditions, and look for traces in their 'sacred books and the oral traditions … and the living memory of those traditions'.[80]

According to Dupuis, the uniqueness and universality of Jesus Christ are neither absolute nor relative, but 'constitutive' in the sense that the Christ-event affects us all. They are also 'relational' in the overall plan of God's design for humanity and, thus, the 'other religious traditions represent true interventions and authentic manifestations of God' in history. Therefore, all genuine religious beliefs form an integral part of our salvation history culminating in Jesus Christ.[81] However, at the same time, the Christian faith must also claim, a 'constitutive uniqueness' for Jesus Christ, for it is in him that the 'historical particularity coincides with universal significance'.[82]

The idea that salvation history begins with the Noachic covenant runs contrary to Ratzinger's reading of the Old Testament. Unlike Dupuis, Ratzinger treats Abrahamic history as the starting point of our salvation history. Ratzinger believes that, although there are many religions, there is only one covenant. This means that Abraham's history, the history of Israel, is also the history of all humankind. The mission of Jesus is to merge all the various histories of nations into the history of Israel. Thus, 'the history of Israel should become the history of all' and 'Abraham's sonship is to be extended to the "many."' This implies that nations can share the promises made to Israel by 'entering into the community of the one God' whose will is truth for all.[83] Hence, all nations become the chosen people of God, with Israel, through following God's will and through 'acceptance of the Davidic kingdom'. For Ratzinger, salvation comes from the Jews alone.[84]

WAYS OF SALVATION

As we have seen, Jacques Dupuis claims that Jesus Christ is unique not in the absolute or relative sense, but in the 'constitutive' and 'relational' one.

'Constitutive' means that for Christians, the paschal mystery has a universal significance; it is the 'privileged channel' through which God saves his people. 'Relational' means that there is a reciprocal relationship between the way of Jesus Christ and those of other religious traditions. Consequently, the universal saving power of Jesus Christ does not contradict or deny the saving significance of other religious traditions. In other words, members of other religions are saved through their own traditions and not in spite of them.[85] God makes use of other religious beliefs as channels or paths of salvation. If Jesus Christ is the sole mediator between God and man, then other religions have 'participated forms of mediation'. However, *Redemptoris Missio* (no. 5) states that other religious traditions only have 'participated forms of mediation' in relation to Christ's own mediation.[86]

Dupuis claims that the action of the Word of God is not confined to the historic event of Christ's birth; nor is the activity of the Spirit constrained by the existence of the risen Christ. The mediation of God consists of different elements that need to be harmonized.[87] It is necessary to admit that God's presence is evident in other religions – their own religious practices are a means of salvation for their members. Dupuis insists that we cannot separate the 'personal, subjective religious life and objective religious tradition – made up of words, rites and sacraments' – in which the religious tradition of others is expressed. The mystery of salvation is present in all human beings beyond the confines of Christianity. It is explicitly present in the church, but in other religious traditions it is present implicitly, in a 'concealed manner, in virtue of an incomplete mode of mediation constituted by these traditions'.[88]

In the same way, the coming of Christ 'must not be allowed to obscure the abiding presence and action of the divine Word'. The 'saving power of the Logos is not circumscribed by the particularity of the historical event'. It goes beyond the limits of time and space. Dupuis writes: 'Through the transcendent power of the Logos, Trinitarian Christology is able to account for the mediatory function of religious traditions in the order of salvation, thus laying the foundation for the recognition of a pluralism in God's way of dealing with humankind.'[89]

Dupuis calling Christ the 'universal' and 'constitutive' but not the 'absolute' saviour troubled some theologians, especially Joseph Ratzinger. Dupuis speaks of the coming of Christ as 'decisive' rather than 'definitive'. Defending him, Gerald O'Collins argues that Dupuis has never wanted to reduce Christ to one saviour among others, but he is aware of the limits involved in the historical Christ-event. The incarnation was 'a free act of God's love and not unconditionally necessary'. O'Collins also cautions us against speaking about

God's work of salvation, culminating in the resurrection of Jesus Christ as the 'fullness' of revelation, because this ignores 'the glorious manifestation of our Lord' that will take place in the future. He argues that our knowledge of God as revealed in Jesus Christ is 'limited' and is 'neither "absolute" nor "definitive"'.[90]

In *Fides et Ratio*, O'Collins reminds us that John Paul II wrote, 'that every truth attained is but a step towards that fullness of truth which will appear with the final Revelation of God'.[91] As such, O'Collins thinks it is more accurate to speak of revelation culminating in Jesus Christ as 'decisive' rather than 'definitive', a term which implies that there is nothing more to expect.[92]

THE REIGN OF GOD AND THE CHURCH

In the Second Vatican Council document, *Lumen Gentium*, the church is identified with the reign of God both in its historical realization and its eschatological fulfilment. However, Dupuis notes that the reign of God in its historical reality extends beyond the church, to all people. This is of great significance for the theology of religions. He stresses that the encyclical letter *Redemptoris Missio* is the first official church document to distinguish between the church and the reign of God, although they are related and united with each other.[93]

Dupuis argues that Jesus did not identify the reign with the 'movement' he created and which later became the church. He was actually 'putting the Church at the service of the Reign when he commissioned the "twelve" … to proclaim the coming of the Kingdom' (Matthew 10:5–7). Thus the church is called to proclaim the reign of God and not itself.[94] This implies that the Kingdom of Christ is more comprehensive than the church; Christ's rule extends beyond the church to the world in general.[95] Hence, the theology of religions must teach Christians to be open to the actions of the Spirit in 'others' who also participate in the reality of the Kingdom of God in history. It is through this sharing that others are also subjected to the saving action of God, through Jesus Christ. Dupuis argues that the reignocentric and Christocentric perspectives are necessarily interconnected.[96]

The reign of God to which members of other religions belong is the Kingdom of God as preached by Jesus Christ. These members follow the call of God within their own traditions and are also 'active members of the Kingdom'. As such, a theology of religions that follows the kingdom-centred model cannot avoid the Christocentric approach. Dupuis claims that the personal life of the followers of other religions cannot be separated from their own traditions that give concrete expression to their religiosity.[97] He believes that their own sacred books and sacramental practices contain 'supernatural, grace-filled elements'. Their beliefs and traditions contribute to the building of God's Kingdom.[98]

According to Dupuis, this idea affects the way we view interreligious dialogue. He argues that interreligious dialogue 'makes explicit this already existing communion in the reality of salvation, which is the Reign of God that has come for all in Jesus'.[99] In spite of differences, members of different religious traditions are co-members of the reign of God throughout history, journeying together towards the fullness of God's Kingdom. Dupuis also makes it clear that the 'Church has no monopoly on the Reign of God'. While the church is in the world as the 'universal sacrament' of mediation, other religions also 'exercise a certain mediation of the Reign, different ... but no less real'.[100] Thus, we see Dupuis attempting to minimize the ecclesial context in the economy of salvation.

Karl Rahner argues that the church has only a 'provisional status' as it advances in history towards the promised future. Followers of other religious traditions also belong to the Kingdom of God. Though they are not members of the church, they share in the fullness of the Kingdom. Quoting the biblical scholar, Rudolf Schnackenburg, Dupuis writes that 'Christ's rule extends beyond the Church ... and one day the Church will have completed her earthly task and will be absorbed in the eschatological Kingdom of Christ and of God'.[101] Therefore, in Dupuis' opinion, it is better for a Christian theology of interreligious dialogue to adopt a kingdom-centred approach. He recognizes the reign of God as the decisive point of reference and that the church exists for the Kingdom, not vice versa.

In contrast, Ratzinger thinks this is misleading because regnocentricity will render ecclesiocentricity, Christocentricity and Theocentricity 'obsolete'. This kingdom-centred theology implies that all religions will move towards the reign of God and, therefore, there will be no need to move them closer to one another in their moral and religious teaching since they now 'serve as instruments for the construction of the future'. Ratzinger believes that such a theology will deprive religions of their 'content of any object' and also their 'point of reference'.[102]

INTERFAITH DIALOGUE

Jacques Dupuis teaches that dialogue, as an element of evangelization, is different from proclamation – it does not aim at conversion of others to

Christianity. It can take several forms: dialogue of life that is open to all; dialogue of commitment to justice and peace; intellectual dialogue; prayer and contemplation. In *Redemptoris Missio*, dialogue is part of the church's evangelizing mission. Dupuis thinks this is a fallback on a narrow view of evangelization which it identifies with proclamation. He acknowledges that there is an intimate link between dialogue and proclamation. Dialogue is understood to be 'a method and means of mutual knowledge and enrichment'; it 'leads to inner purification and conversion'.[103] It is not a question of converting others to Christianity, but of the conversion of all towards God.

In the document, 'Dialogue and Proclamation', other religious traditions are given a positive role in the salvation of their adherents. Members of other religions are saved by Christ, not in spite of, but in and through their own traditions. The aim of interreligious dialogue is 'a deeper conversion of all towards God' and, thus, dialogue has its own validity. Sincere dialogue implies 'mutual acceptance of differences' and 'even contradictions' as well as respect for the free decisions of others, taken in accordance with their consciences.[104]

Dupuis asserts that the principal agent of dialogue is the Spirit of God who guides the participants from both camps. The Christian partners in dialogue must give and receive; they must listen because they do not have a monopoly on truth, in spite of the fact that the 'fullness' of revelation is found in Jesus Christ. They must allow themselves to 'be possessed' by the truth. Christians can gain a lot from this kind of dialogue, such as 'enrichment of their own faith', deepening of those aspects of their understanding of the divine mystery, which have been 'communicated less clearly by Christian tradition', 'purification of their own faith' and of their own prejudices.[105] I would also like to add that Christianity has been too much identified with Western culture, and interreligious dialogue can help Christians discover the hidden divine mystery obscured by Western contextualization.

O'Leary also believes that while the church claims to be universal, it needs to be aware that it is bounded by the cultural and historical 'limitations of Christian discourse'. Only at the end of time will we know the full realization of the universality of Christ, but for now it is only, 'a projected perspective of faith, a regulative idea guiding the dialogue' between Christian and non-Christian religions. Although O'Leary believes that the fullness of truth dwells in Christ, he thinks that the churches themselves 'do not exhaust the totality of truth'. Christians can learn from other religions, such as Judaism, Islam, Buddhism and Hinduism, how to be better Christians. The truth of Christianity is not primarily a set of doctrines, but a 'living memory' of the death and resurrection of Jesus Christ. O' Leary is of the opinion that Western philosophy, as well as Buddhism, is of great value in helping to interpret Christianity. From a historical perspective, Christianity should be regarded as an ongoing project and, therefore, it 'cannot grasp its own significance completely'; much less can it fully grasp the significance of other religions. He asserts that the 'normativeness' of Christianity is an 'open-ended' project that can be enriched by communicating with other religious traditions.[106]

Dialogue also has a value in itself. The encounter and experience are an end in themselves because they enable the participants to be open to each other and to God and so, finally, to a deeper conversion of each to God. According to Dupuis, 'the common conversion of Christians and the members of other religious traditions to the same ... God of Jesus Christ' is the main aim of inter-religious dialogue.[107] He believes that harmony among religious communities can be achieved, not by a 'universal theology' which removes all differences, but by the development of different theological traditions that take religious pluralism, mutual differences and dialogue seriously.[108]

In presenting the declaration, *Dominus Iesus*, Joseph Ratzinger claims that dialogue has taken on a new meaning, different from the 'understanding through dialogue' promoted by the Second Vatican Council. He believes this new understanding has become an 'ideology' that seeks to abolish mission and the call to conversion. 'Dialogue is no longer understood as a way to discover the truth' that is 'purified through the encounter with the ... complete revelation of Jesus Christ.'[109] Ratzinger thinks this new understanding of dialogue is aimed at 'relativizing dogmas' and does not encourage mission to convert.[110] This means that it is merely an exchange of opinions that are fundamentally relative and equal in value, with the aim of promoting co-operation and harmony. Ratzinger has a lingering suspicion that Catholic theologians who do not promote the Catholic faith zealously in their encounters with non-Christians, in interreligious dialogue, are relativizing their own religion.

Dominus Iesus indicates a change in direction: moving us from dialogue *to* evangelization as opposed to the understanding of 'dialogue *as* evangelization' adopted by Dupuis. The document connects pluralism with the threat of religious relativism. At a press conference to mark the release of the document, Ratzinger stated clearly that he wanted to challenge a 'false concept of tolerance' in the theology of religious pluralism.[111] Although Ratzinger was not the author of *Dominus Iesus*, Gerard Mannion points out that this document contains 'familiar sentiments' of Ratzinger's. Mannion also remarks that in this case the dividing line between a private theological opinion and official church teaching needs further clarification.[112] No wonder that Ratzinger, based on his own understanding of evangelization as part of dialogue, initiated an investigation by the CDF of Dupuis' writing. In light of this, it would seem that any theologians working in the field of religious pluralism have to walk a tightrope.

THE NOTIFICATION[113]

Jacques Dupuis became a celebrity when the CDF published a Notification concerning his book, *Toward a Christian Theology of Religious Pluralism*. The Notification states that Dupuis' work contains 'notable ambiguities and difficulties on important doctrinal points, which could lead a reader to erroneous or harmful opinions'.[114] According to the church's teaching, it is wrong to believe that non-Christian religions are considered to be a means of salvation. The magisterium does not view the sacred texts of other religions 'as complementary to the Old Testament, which is the immediate preparation for the Christ event'.[115] In spite of the Notification, Dupuis' theology of religions actually coincides with the official teaching of the late John Paul II.

Gerald O'Collins has drawn attention to the way Dupuis developed these theological themes that came from Pope John Paul II in *Fides et Ratio*. For example, Dupuis stressed the need for interreligious dialogue, which is different from a 'falsely tolerant pluralism' and also emphasized 'God as the only One who is truly absolute' as well as 'the divine self-revelation whose definitive fullness will appear only at the end'. In addition, Dupuis made clear that we must have a deep respect for all 'the treasures of human wisdom and religion' (*Fides et Ratio*, 31) and 'a special interest in "Indian religious and philosophical tradition"'. O'Collins argues that, like John Paul II, Dupuis recognizes the goodness of non-Christian religions through which their members find salvation. He concludes that, 'to condemn Dupuis's book would ... be to condemn the Pope himself'.[116]

Ilaria Morali insists that there is no censure of Dupuis' work in the Notification. In fact, she says that the CDF recognized Dupuis' 'intellectual honesty' and that the Notification merely aimed to emphasize the doctrine of the church and correct erroneous interpretations of some of the issues raised by Dupuis' book.[117] This was confirmed in 2001 by Father Hans-Peter Kolvenback, superior general of the Jesuits, who wrote:

With the Notification just published by the Congregation for the Doctrine of the Faith, a long and important inquiry has ended. The book of Father Jacques Dupuis ... which has been justly recognized for the seriousness of its methodological research, the richness of its scientific documentation, and the originality of its exploration, dares to venture into a dogmatically fundamental area for the future of the interreligious dialogue. The Notification itself recognizes the intent and the efforts of Father Jacques Dupuis to remain within the teaching of the Catholic Faith as enunciated by the Magisterium. In line with the orientations of the document, *Dominus Iesus*, the Notification establishes the limits of this teaching to which the author has tried to adhere, even if he has not always succeeded. Thus, the Notification helps the reader to interpret the book according to the doctrine of the Church. On this solidly established dogmatic basis we hope that Father Jacques Dupuis can continue his pioneer research in the field of interreligious dialogue which in his recent Apostolic Letter *Novo Millennio Ineunte*, John Paul II encourages as a challenge for the evangelization in the third Millenium.[118]

In light of the above, William Burrows calls Jacques Dupuis a 'conservative revisionist'.[119] As a conservative, Dupuis believed that the church's teaching was guided by the Holy Spirit. As a revisionist, he attempted to interpret traditional doctrines in the light of the realities of the time.[120] Burrows argues that Dupuis attempted to 'keep in dialectic tension Scripture and tradition, on the one hand, and the valid insights of both the pluralists and "secular" historians and philosophers of religion, on the other hand'.[121] Dupuis had to walk a tightrope between adhering to magisterium teaching and responding to actual religious realities.

It is generally accepted that Dupuis appears to have been treated unjustly by church authorities. In investigating Dupuis' work, Franz Cardinal König says that the CDF did not show the same openness towards interreligious dialogue and religious pluralism as taught by *Dominu Iesus*. König asserts that a theological advisor was able to prove that *Toward a Christian Theology of Religious Pluralism* does not contain the serious errors that the CDF speaks about in the Notification. Furthermore, the CDF did not point out which passages in the book contained errors. A second version of the Notification was drafted that referred only to 'ambiguities' on matters of faith. Finally, on 27 February 2001, a third version of the Notification was officially presented to the public. It is obvious, according to König, that the CDF had difficulties with its 'procedural mechanism'.[122]

König criticizes the CDF for its 'undeserved harshness', and the 'discourteous and negative tone' it used towards a priest who is a distinguished theologian and a faithful servant of the church. The most serious shortcoming of the CDF was that it neglected the 'human aspect'. It forgot, it seems, that it deals not only with books, but with human beings who need to be treated with courtesy and understanding. A different approach would have avoided the deep hurt it caused Dupuis. With reference to such high-handedness, König also adds that 'no one loses authority just because they are courteous.'[123]

On the CDF side, Joseph Ratzinger equates the theology of religious pluralism to liberation theology and relativism. That is why Catholic theologians working in the field of religious pluralism are scrutinized closely. As prefect of the CDF, Ratzinger did not hesitate to discipline theologians whom he believed had deviated from the magisterium's teaching. All this is understandable as his intention was to safeguard the integrity of Catholic doctrine and to protect the church from the liberal and relativizing spirit of the age.

Jacques Dupuis had attempted to interpret the church's teaching on non-Christian religions in the light of the Second Vatican Council's call for more openness and dialogue. Consequently, it would seem that Dupuis' conflict with the CDF has more to do with Ratzinger's understanding of religious pluralism as a threat than with Dupuis' trespassing on traditional Catholic teachings. In fact, Dupuis retorted, 'If I had said, meant, or believed what they say, I would indeed be a heretic. But I don't.'[124] As we have seen, Ratzinger demanded no change in Dupuis' book except that his critique of it, in the Notification, should be included in subsequent editions.

In relation to the Notification and other church documents, in principle, it is important to distinguish between official statements signed by Cardinal Ratzinger as prefect of the CDF and his own writings as a private theologian. Statements issued by the CDF are part of the teaching of the magisterium, but Ratzinger's own writings as a scholar carry a different weight, based on the strength of his argument.[125] Instructions and Notifications, issued by the CDF and signed by the prefect, should not be considered to be Ratzinger's own theology but to be official church teaching. In practice, however, one cannot ignore the fact that Ratzinger's theological reflections on the topic will be taken into consideration when a particular document is being drafted by the CDF. For example, in Ratzinger's response to Dominus Iesus, his personal opinions definitely influenced his reflections on official documents.[126] This brings us finally to the role of theologians in the church.

THE ECCLESIAL VOCATION OF THE THEOLOGIAN

Freedom of expression and debate among theologians and church scholars are essential to the life of the church. Vincent Twomey asserts that what is of lasting value in theological research will be adopted by the church. The role of the theologians, therefore, is to communicate their insights into church doctrine to the public, using appropriate language and images. On behalf of the church, they assist in teaching 'truths to illuminate the human condition' and also offer a critique of postmodern culture. Twomey is critical of theologians who make use of the media to present their ideas as authoritative teachings of the church. This would probably result in confusion among the ordinary faithful, which greatly concerns Ratzinger.[127]

The CDF, therefore, has an important task to perform on behalf of the church. It is reasonable to accept that one of the main tasks of the magisterium is to protect the ordinary faithful who may not be able to appreciate the intricacies and nuances of theological arguments put forward by specialists. Ratzinger claims that 'the Magisterium has something like a democratic character: it defends the common faith, which recognizes no distinction of rank between the learned and the simple.'[128] Emphasizing the ecclesial character of theology, he insists that, if theology is the result of scientific reflection on the faith, it can only be so by conforming to the faith of the church: 'theology is never simply the private idea of one theologian. If it were, it could count for little, for as a private idea it would sink rapidly into insignificance. On the contrary, the Church, as a living subject which endures amid the changes of history, is the vital milieu of the theologian: the Church preserves faith's experience with God.'[129] This means that the theologian is bound to the faith of the church for he or she pursues theology not as an individual scholar, but as a member of the entire Christian community.[130]

Theologians such as Jacques Dupuis and Peter Phan, however, who were investigated by the CDF, remained within the bounds of orthodoxy in their writings. They were loyal servants of the church: Dupuis was a consultant for the Pontifical Council for Interreligious Dialogue and Phan worked closely with the Federation of Asian Bishops' Conferences (FABC). It is generally agreed that the CDF procedure for investigating theologians who are suspected of having deviated from official church teaching needs to be revised to become more open and transparent. In short, the CDF needs to be more human in its dealings with theologians.

In *Toward a Christian Theology of Religious Pluralism*, Jacques Dupuis has attempted to give us a more comprehensive and deeper understanding of the varieties of religions flourishing in the world, especially in Asia. Unfortunately, Dupuis had to deal with the prefect of the CDF who saw religious pluralism as a problem to be overcome rather than as a blessing to be welcomed. As we shall see in the next chapter, Peter Phan, a Vietnamese theologian influenced by Dupuis, was also investigated by church authorities with reference to some of his ideas on religious pluralism in his book *Being Religious Interreligiously*.

Chapter 10

Peter C. Phan

Like Dupuis, Peter C. Phan attempted to develop a broader interpretation of ecclesial dialogue with other religions and was subsequently investigated by church authorities for his pluralistic outlook. In view of this, critics have accused Joseph Ratzinger of promoting a 'restorationist agenda'.[1] As prefect of the Congregation for the Doctrine of the Faith, he was empowered to deal with these issues and it was thought, in light of his actions, that Ratzinger's private theological vision might have been translated into official church teaching.[2] It is obvious that Ratzinger initiated many of the investigations against those theologians who were open to pluralism and who were writing about the topic of interreligious dialogue. Consequently, the dividing line between Ratzinger's theological opinion and the teaching of the magisterium is worth reflecting on. As we have seen, Ratzinger believes Catholic theologians must serve the church because their vocation is an ecclesial one. He is afraid that theologians like Peter Phan would confuse the faithful and lead them astray by encouraging a pick and mix attitude towards church teachings.[3]

I will examine Peter Phan's understanding of religious pluralism in the light of the Vatican's Notification. Phan claims that his critical reflection on religious pluralism aimed to enhance interfaith dialogue, to correct the mistakes of the past regarding Christian mission and to establish an authentically Asian church. Hence, I argue that the tension that exists between the Vatican and Phan is due to different emphases on doctrine and practice in a church in which Ratzinger's theological view prevails.

THE INVESTIGATION

As mentioned earlier, Joseph Ratzinger perceives religious pluralism as a form of relativism. In the Asian context, Ratzinger believes the theology of religious pluralism teaches that Jesus Christ is just another spiritual genius like Buddha or Confucius and therefore that Christianity is just one valid path to salvation among others. Given his concern over religious relativism, it is not surprising that in 2007 Peter Phan was investigated by the United States Bishops' Doctrine Committee, which represents the United States Conference of Catholic Bishops (USCCB), because of several aspects of his book, *Being Religious Interreligiously: Asian Perspectives on Interfaith Dialogue*. The committee reported that Phan's book used 'certain terms in an equivocal manner' that opened the text up to 'significant ambiguity'. Although the committee emphasized the importance of understanding religious pluralism, it believed that Phan's book raised 'serious concerns' in the following three areas:

i. Jesus Christ as the unique, universal Saviour of all humankind.
ii. The salvific significance of non-Christian religions.
iii. The Church as the unique, universal instrument of salvation.[4]

Phan's *Being Religious Interreligiously* was considered by the CDF to be contradictory to the teachings of the declaration *Dominus Iesus* (2000), which states that non-Christians are 'in a gravely deficient situation in comparison with those who, in the church, have the fullness of the means of salvation'.[5] The CDF found in Phan's book the following errors that needed to be rectified:

i. Non-Christian religions have a positive role in salvation history and they are not just merely a preparation for the Christian Gospel.
ii. It makes little sense to try to convert non-Christians to Christianity.
iii. It would be better to avoid terms such as 'unique', 'absolute' and 'universal' with reference to the saving role of Christ.
iv. The Holy Spirit operates in a saving way, in non-Christian religions independently of the *Logos*.
v. The Catholic Church cannot be identified with the Church of Christ.
vi. God's covenant with the Jewish people does not find its culmination in Jesus Christ.[6]

The CDF also claimed that there was a 'gnostic tenor running through the book'. Phan said that some of the observations regarding his book were 'preposterous'.[7]

A distinguished theologian with three doctorates, Peter Phan is a prominent writer on the theology of religions whose works have been translated into many European and Asian languages.

A LEADING ASIAN THEOLOGIAN

Born in Vietnam in 1946, Peter Phan and his family went, as war refugees, to the United States in 1975. Phan has close ties to the Federation of Asian Bishops' Conferences(FABC). As one of the leading Asian theologians, he has convincingly argued that non-Christian religions have a positive role to play in God's plan of salvation. John Allen says Phan 'incarnates precisely the intersection of East and West to which the future Pope Benedict XVI referred'.[8] He points out that the protocol number for Peter Phan's case given by the CDF was 537/2004-21114, which shows that the investigation started in 2004 while Joseph Ratzinger was still the Congregation's prefect.[9]

Phan's theology of religious pluralism calls for a less Eurocentric church. He theologizes from an Asian perspective and his concern is pastoral rather than doctrinal. A committed theologian seeking a contemporary understanding of the faith within the Catholic tradition, Phan's understanding of that tradition goes beyond doctrines and takes into consideration the living experience of the faithful. He asserts that there are doctrines and practices found in Asian cultures and religions that are superior to Christianity. Therefore, Christians must learn about the reality of the divine in Asia, especially from the poor, before they can preach the gospel. Christian missionaries can be inspired and enlightened if they are humble and respectful towards the religious and cultural values of the local people in Asia. John Paul II adopted this positive and open attitude when he wrote:

> The people of Asia take pride in their religious and cultural values, such as love of silence and contemplation, simplicity, harmony, detachment, non-violence, the spirit of hard work, discipline, frugal living, the thirst for learning and philosophical enquiry. They hold dear the values of respect for life, compassion for all beings, closeness to nature, filial piety towards parents, elders and ancestors, and a highly developed sense of community. In particular, they hold the family to be a vital source of strength, a closely knit community with a powerful sense of solidarity. Asian peoples are known for their spirit of religious tolerance and peaceful co-existence.[10]

This is a far cry from the colonial days of old when Western Christian missionaries denounced adherents of other religious beliefs as heathens and condemned their rituals and practices. This leads Joseph O'Leary to write:

> Hasty insistence on stamping Christ and the church on every phenom-enon of creation and history leads to a counter-intuitive vision of real-ity and leaves no breathing space for the diversity of humanity and the transcendence of the divine. That is why missioners are mistrusted; they are too quick to stamp Christ on local cultures or to stamp out these cultures to make room for Christ. In Asia, the church is perhaps beginning to define itself as 'defender of faiths' as well as propagator of the faith. Interreligious dialogue is not to be used as an instrument of mission, but rather it is out of dialogue that authentic mission may emerge.[11]

Nonetheless, in spite of John Paul II's goodwill towards non-Christian reli-gions, tensions and conflicts between scholars working in the field of the theology of religions and ecclesiastical authorities occur as a result of different interpretations of religious pluralism.

BEYOND PLURALITY

Religious pluralism implies that we do not possess the entire truth about divine reality. It does not imply relativism or indifferentism to the truth, but it simply means that we cannot impose our beliefs on others. Religious plural-ism can also mean accepting the beliefs of other religions as valid but not necessarily true. Pluralists claim that the truth of each religion is valid within its own cultural context. Thus, pluralism is 'an affirmation of the validity of every religion and the refusal to choose between them'.[12] In this sense, religious pluralism teaches that all religions are equally valid paths to God. Pluralists believe that differences among religions are accidental rather than inevitable, and the different faiths lead to the same goal. The stress here is on tolerance and relativism because religious truths are relative. In this case, pluralists hold that truth is a 'social construction' created out of 'consensus and tradition' and that it does not exist independently of religious beliefs.[13] This is the point about which Ratzinger is critical.

   According to John Hick, religious pluralism is the 'belief that no one religion has a monopoly of the truth or of the life that leads to salvation'.

By salvation, he means 'a process of human transformation in this life from natural self-centeredness to a new orientation centred on the transcendent divine reality, God, and leading to its fulfilment beyond this life'. Hick believes that different religions, for all their differences and 'incompatibilities of belief', can be paths of salvation for their believers. He insists that religious plural- ism is not a form of relativism and also not, as some believe, a product of post-Enlightenment Western liberalism. Citing Nicholas of Cusa who, in the fifteenth century, wrote that 'there is only one religion in the variety of rites', Hick maintains that it is wrong to think of religious pluralism as a Western invention.[14]

Paul Knitter also reminds us that plurality is a significant fact of religious life and it is no longer possible for Christians to be completely sure that only they possess the truth and that others are mistaken.[15] The philosophical perspective that Knitter is exploring reckons plurality to be a force for greater unity. Many are called to be one, but it is a one that does not destroy the many; 'the many become one precisely by remaining the many' and each of the many makes a 'distinct contribution to the others and thus to the whole'. According to Knitter, 'whereas individualization is weakened, personalization is inten- sified; the individual finds its true self as part of other selves. So there is a movement not toward absolute or monistic oneness but toward what might be called "unitive pluralism": plurality constituting unity'. It simply means a movement toward a 'dialogical community' in which members live and interact with one another.[16]

The various religious traditions in the world are 'experiencing a new sense of identity' as they confront one another; they are awakened to a 'more dynamic and dialogical way of understanding themselves'. Adherents of different reli- gions are challenged to develop their identities within a wider community of other traditions. Like Peter Phan, Paul Knitter believes that one must be 'reli- gious interreligiously'.[17] This is particularly applicable in Asian societies where traditional religions such as Hinduism, Buddhism, Taoism and Islam flourish.

Edward Schillebeeckx teaches that 'the multiplicity of religions is not an evil which needs to be removed, but rather a wealth which is to be welcomed and enjoyed by all ... There is more religious truth in all religions together than in one particular religion ... This also applies to Christianity'.[18] It is in this sense that Peter Phan approaches the reality of religious pluralism and speaks of the necessity and opportunity of being Christian interreligiously in the context of Asia. Phan is an inclusive pluralist who adheres to the teaching of the Declaration on the Relation of the Church to non-Christian Religions – *Nostra Aetate*.

INCLUSIVE PLURALISM

Religious inclusivists believe Christ is always present in the saving action of God and regard the Christian faith as the fulfilment of other religions. This approach has been adopted by the Second Vatican Council in its document on non-Christian religions, *Nostra Aetate* (1965), which marked a new attitude on the part of the Roman Catholic Church towards other faiths and a willingness to recognize their positive contribution to humanity. Major non-Christian religions are seen as expressions of genuine human longing to answer the most fundamental question of how to live a good life. The Council teaches that salvific grace can operate in the hearts of those outside the church, even in those who do not believe in God. Peter Phan, influenced by Jacques Dupuis, has developed this new appreciation of non-Christian religions into a comprehensive Christian theology of religions and has sought to portray Christ as the source of saving grace in all religions.

While Peter Phan takes up an inclusive pluralist position, he rejects 'as incompatible with the Christian faith the kind of New Age syncretism' such as 'believing without belonging', 'nebulous esoteric mysticism' and 'Nietzschean neopaganism'.[19] He stresses the importance of dialogue as a means for the church to engage with other religions. Although it seems that the church has updated itself, as the title of the document of the Second Vatican Council, *Gaudium et Spes* implies, Phan believes that it has now fallen behind in its effort to scrutinize the 'signs of the times' as the world advances into postmodernity. He questions whether the church will repeat its mistakes, being seen to be resting on its laurels by promoting a 'restorationist agenda' or, in time, be carried away by postmodernity.[20] In other words, the church could retreat back into the past, becoming obsolete in the process, or it could, alternatively, be so caught up with the world that it loses its identity and mission. Phan is clearly searching for a middle path where the church can stay relevant and meaningful in the face of globalization and religious pluralism.

The theological basis for welcoming religious plurality and diversity is the fact that the Christian God is not a 'solitary monad', according to Phan, but a 'koinonia of three divine persons'. The Father generates the Son and breathes forth the Spirit through the Son; the Son breathes forth the Spirit by the power of the Father; and the Spirit proceeds from the Father through the Son, uniting them in love. It is because of divine diversity and plurality that God is one, not in spite of it, Phan asserts. The Trinity shows us that 'divine unity is constituted by the harmony of diverse eternal relations'. Ironically, if there were many gods, there would not be divine plurality. In fact, they would all be 'uniformly divine'; 'the more God is one, the more plural God is'. Thus 'God's oneness and plurality are in direct, not inverse proportion with each other'. The Father, the Son and the Holy Spirit 'are related in mutual *perichoresis* or *circumincessio*', which means it allows the persons to maintain their individuality while sharing in the life of each other. Thus, the oneness of God assures us of its plurality and divine unity does not mean one *nature or substance*, but 'the unity of the eternal threefold relations'.[21]

Another important foundation for religious pluralism, according to Phan, is creation, which reflects and embodies divine plurality in the variety and multiplicity of our world. The theology of the incarnation also shows the importance of religious plurality because when God became man, as the Council of Chalcedon teaches, 'the distinction between the natures was never abolished by their union but rather the character proper to each of the two natures was preserved as they came together in one person (*prosopon*) and one hypostasis'.[22] Finally, 'union with the divine is not an ontological dissolution of the human self', but rather, the 'deification of the human person' in which a real difference exists between the individual and God.[23]

All of this seems to indicate that there exists in Christianity, an inherent tendency to lean towards plurality and diversity. However, as Phan has pointed out, the church, in the last two thousand years, has always maintained that it neither universally accepted nor encouraged this movement. St Paul spoke about the variety of gifts for building the body of Christ (1 Corinthians 14), but there has always been a strong tendency, in any big organization with clearly defined structures and laws, such as the Roman Catholic Church, to support centralization and uniformity. Thus, the institutional church today feels threatened by the movement towards plurality and diversity.[24] It is a question of power and control. In the face of growing pluralism, the ecclesiastical authorities may find it hard to maintain the one holy, catholic and apostolic church.

As a result of this threat of religious pluralism and relativism, as understood by the church hierarchy, the Second Vatican Council has refrained from affirming that other religious traditions may function as a means of salvation comparable to Christianity. However, a new theology of religions has surfaced to reassess the role of Jesus Christ as the unique, universal saviour and the role of non-Christian religions in the economy of salvation.[25] Gavin D'Costa, after examining various church documents, agrees with Phan that the church has refused to acknowledge other religions per se as salvific structures. D'Costa concludes that this refusal shows that pluralism and inclusivism are considered by the Catholic Church to be inappropriate ways to view other faiths.[26]

Peter Phan argues that these religions may be a means of salvation because religious pluralism is part of God's providential plan. Such a viewpoint has far-reaching consequences for Christian mission and the questions of conversion and baptism as aims of evangelization. If we agree with Phan that religious pluralism is not the result of human sinfulness but, rather, evidence of God's abundance and generosity, then there is no need to convert others to Christianity. This is one of the issues that the CDF has brought up regarding Phan's work. Before we examine the legitimacy or feasibility of converting people to Christianity, it is important to understand the pluralistic and ambiguous nature of the Christian tradition. This will assist us in reflecting on the command to proclaim the gospel, as was done in the past.

THE AMBIGUITY OF CHRISTIAN TRADITION

Werner G. Jeanrond has observed that the 'originating event of Christian faith' is transmitted to us through a particular tradition. Christians encounter Jesus Christ and 'his particular theological initiatives through the various biblical witnesses and through the pluriform witness within the ongoing Christian movement'. Jeanrond says that these encounters are 'pluralistic and ambiguous by nature'. For example, the various accounts of the life of Christ in the four gospels lead to different interpretations. Each gospel provides a particular and limited aspect of Jesus' teachings. Therefore, it is the task of theology to articulate, validate and challenge the focus of these limited interpretations of the Christian message. Jeanrond asserts that the earliest witnesses of Christianity warned followers of Christ to be aware of 'ideological appropriation', by which they meant the 'distortions – of the significance of Jesus Christ'. For example, the portrayal of the disciples in Mark's Gospel 'is full of dramatic corrections of false interpretations and anticipations of Christ's identity'. We are warned against succumbing to the temptation to interpret the gospel solely from our limited and biased perspective. Therefore, it is crucial that Christians be open to the interpretation of the apostolic tradition in new and critical ways.[27] Jeanrond writes: 'As Mark's gospel emphasizes, the apostolic tradition itself is burdened by inauthentic acts of discipleship. The self-critical dimension of Markan and other New Testament texts has added to their "classic" character ... they have successfully resisted efforts of automatization, domestication, and manipulation by their hearers and readers.'[28]

Therefore, according to Jeanrond, the pluralistic and ambiguous nature of the Christian tradition requires the church to continue to evaluate all its doctrinal and symbolic expressions. This process may also require the church to rethink its criteria for ecclesiastical authenticity and to search for more adequate responses to Jesus Christ's call to participate in God's redemptive work in the church.[29] This leads Peter Phan to question the path followed by Christian mission tied to colonialism.

THE LEGITIMACY OF CHRISTIAN MISSION

While Peter Phan rejects relativism and scepticism, he takes criticism of modernity and the Enlightenment seriously. Religious pluralism is a product of postmodernism that affirms the reality of religious diversity and, thus, allows no particular religion to claim to have the monopoly of truth and universality. If such is the case, Phan says, religious pluralism 'calls into question the very legitimacy of Christian mission as understood and practiced in the past'. He questions whether missionaries can still proclaim the gospel effectively in a pluralistic society where Christianity is one, among many, legitimate religions.[30] In other words, if religious pluralism is a blessing to be accepted gratefully, then effort should be made to promote mutual enrichment among various religious traditions. Hence, according to Phan, 'to be religious is ... to be interreligious, and ... a theology of religions as an interreligious theology is a "universal imperative"'.[31]

Since religious pluralism is a threat to certain traditional Christian doctrines, Phan was not surprised that the CDF should take a negative view of it in *Dominus Iesus*. However, Phan says that if religious pluralism is regarded 'as forming part of God's plan of salvation for humanity', then we need to reinterpret three fundamental Christian beliefs. The first is 'the unity of God's plan of salvation'.[32] There is 'a plurality in the unity of God's single plan'. This means that God carried out his plan in several ways. According to St Irenaeus, there are four covenants, 'distinct but related, not parallel but complementary'. This refers to the four biblical covenants: 'with Adam before the flood, with Noah after the flood, with Moses in the Law, and in Jesus'.[33]

The second is 'the salvific significance of the Christ-event'. With reference to this, Phan asks if it is also possible to regard Buddha and other founders of religions as 'salvation figures'. The third concerns 'the Church as a necessary instrument of salvation'. Phan insists that the church as 'a necessary instrument of salvation does not exclude but rather includes the possibility that non-Christians and non-believers may be saved'. He believes that these individuals are saved by believing in the truths contained in their own religious traditions.[34] This means that if we accept religious pluralism, then we must also accept that other religions can be means of salvation for their followers. This brings us to the question of Christianity's alleged superiority.

UNIQUENESS AND UNIVERSALITY

Peter Phan makes an important distinction between 'claiming uniqueness and universality for one's religious founder and claiming them for one's religion.'[35] According to him, it is fine for Christians to claim uniqueness and universality for Jesus Christ, but not for the church, which is a human institution. Phan acknowledges that Christ and the church have, at times, been spoken of as one, but they have never been identified with each other. According to *Lumen Gentium*, the church is Christ's sacrament, a sign and instrument of communion with God and of unity among human beings. However, the church should not be identified with the Kingdom of God, much less with Christ himself.' Phan even goes to the extent of saying that identifying the church with Jesus is idolatry.[36]

The difference between Jesus and the church lies in the fact that Christians believe Jesus is divine and human, whereas the church is only human. Jesus is a historical person, but not a social institution called the church, which still exists as an organization with its own structures, dogmas and liturgy.[37] Phan argues that from a historical point of view, 'it is the claim of uniqueness and universality of the Christian church that is most problematic, and not the claim of uniqueness and universality of Jesus'. This is because the church has made mistakes and even committed atrocities as well as performed good works.[38] Phan thinks it is reasonable for Christians to assert that Jesus is God and unique saviour in the form of faith statements, affirming something that is true about Christ and expressing their love and devotion to him. Knitter calls this 'confessional' or 'love language'.[39]

In view of the above, I think that it is not really justifiable for the United States Bishops' Committee on Doctrine to accuse Peter Phan of not upholding the uniqueness of Jesus Christ and the universality of his salvific mission on the basis of Phan's more nuanced and subtle understanding of these concepts. Phan also claims that non-Christian religions are part of God's providence and they have a specific role to play in the economy of salvation. They are not just 'seeds' of Christianity, but each offers a proper and autonomous means of salvation to their followers. Thus, when we proclaim Jesus Christ as the 'unique', 'absolute', and 'universal' saviour, we must be mindful of the social, political and cultural contexts from which these adjectives spring. These contexts, Phan warns, are influenced by colonialism, economic exploitation and religious marginalization. Such proclamation may sound offensive and is unacceptable to non-Christians who have been victims of Western arrogance and exploitation.[40]

In keeping with Jacques Dupuis, Phan believes that there is a 'reciprocal relationship' between Jesus and other religions. Jesus' role is not absolute but definitive and relational as well. The saving mission of Jesus is complemented by other 'saving figures'.[41] There is a possibility that the Holy Spirit could lead the church to the full truth, by means of her encounter with other religions.[42] This implies that Phan acknowledges the salvific significance of non-Christian religions. He believes that Christians should be permitted to follow the teachings of other religious figures as long as these teachings are not contrary to the core beliefs of the Christian faith. However, Phan makes it clear that there is no need to abandon the claim of the uniqueness of Jesus Christ in order to engage in interreligious dialogue, provided we make a distinction between Jesus and Christianity. Phan maintains that Christians believe in Jesus Christ, not in the church.[43] This is the point that the CDF finds difficult to accept.

Aloysius Pieris teaches that the claim that Jesus is the absolute saviour is a 'kerygmatic affirmation'.[44] It is on the basis of their personal relationship with Christ that Christians proclaim Jesus as Lord and saviour. John Henry Newman speaks about the 'illative sense' when Christians, through inference and assent, affirm the lordship of Jesus. This claims that Jesus is the saviour and God is essentially an 'affirmation of faith'.[45] Phan argues that such a claim is not irrational nor unreasonable, although it cannot be proven by empirical evidence. In theological understanding, the person is being moved by divine grace and the Holy Spirit in order to make such a claim.[46]

If one does not suspend one's own belief when engaging in interreligious dialogue, then it is only natural that Christians will claim that Jesus is unique and that the other participants will also claim uniqueness for their own religious founders. Confirming Raimundo Panikkar's view, Phan writes that the aim of interfaith encounter is 'understanding and communication in order to bridge the gulfs of mutual ignorance and misunderstanding between the different cultures of the world, and not to win over or convert the other, or to come to a total agreement, or to found a universal religion'. He believes this should be the aim of interreligious dialogue. This does not exclude the possibility of any of the partners being converted as a result of the dialogue, but it should not be the condition for dialogue.[47]

Phan reminds us that people such as Francis of Assisi, Martin Luther, Mother Teresa and many others who defended the poor and oppressed against secular and ecclesiastical powers never felt the need to give up their belief in the uniqueness of Jesus. In fact, they found inspiration and strength in their faith in Jesus as Lord and saviour.[48] Thus, Phan believes that interreligious dialogue is not best served by Christians abandoning the claim that Jesus is the only saviour. At the same time, Teotonio R. de Souza warns us that:

> Christ cannot be anyone's proud possession. He is an unbound Christ who has broken all the bonds and represents a God-experience beyond all the names, a God-experience that many old spiritualists and religions of Asia and the world have aspired to, and not always in vain. God-experience should need no guises or disguises. Those who claim the power to bind in heaven what they bind on earth are probably also the ones of whom Jesus on the cross said that they do not know what they are doing and prayed for their forgiveness.[49]

Phan also recognizes that proclaiming Jesus as the only saviour is 'fraught with philosophical, cultural and theological difficulties, especially in light of the beliefs of Asia's great religions, deeply intertwined with cultural values and specific world views'.[50] Christ is perceived as a Western figure in Asia. Phan believes it is better to proclaim Jesus as a 'personal saviour', as the Pentecostal Christians do, than to proclaim Jesus as the only saviour. The stress here is on the 'personal and total commitment' to Jesus while not denying alternative ways in which God can reach other people. For Phan, the fundamental issue is not 'how *other* people can be saved, but rather how *I* can fully enter a personal relationship with God'.[51] Phan believes that adopting this disposition would allow us to recognize the saving presence of God in other religions.

CHRIST AND THE CHURCH

In the context of interreligious dialogue, Phan insists that making claims about the uniqueness and universality of the church should be abandoned altogether. The church is not only holy but sinful as well. In the past, the church has been linked to 'colonialism and religious imperialism'. Phan claims that it is 'the triumphalistic claim for Christianity as a social organization, and not the claim of the uniqueness and universality of Jesus as the crucified Christ, that produced in Christians self-righteousness, contempt for other religions, and lust for domination.'[52] Thus, he asserts that the fundamental article of faith of one's religion can be retained. By this, he means that we can retain the uniqueness and universality of our saviour, but we must abandon the claim to uniqueness and universality of our religious institution, namely the Christian church. Phan's position is contrary to the teaching found in *Dominus Iesus*, published in 2000, when Ratzinger was the prefect of the CDF:

> it is clear that it would be contrary to the faith to consider the Church as *one way* of salvation alongside those constituted by the other religions .... This truth of faith does not lessen the sincere respect which the Church has for the religions of the world, but at the same time, it rules out, in a radical way, that mentality of indifferentism characterized by a religious relativism which leads to the belief that 'one religion is as good as another'. If it is true that the followers of other religions can receive divine grace, it is also certain that *objectively speaking* they are in a gravely deficient situation in comparison with those who, in the Church, have the fullness of the means of salvation.[53]

It follows, therefore, that the questioning of Phan's understanding of the uniqueness of the church as the universal instrument of salvation by the United States Bishops' Committee on Doctrine was justified only in so far as it relates to the document *Dominus Iesus*.

It is easy to sympathize and agree with Peter Phan's concern for the church in Asia because, in our postmodern age, Asians do not need a church associated with imperialism and colonialism, exporting Western culture to the natives. It must be a church in solidarity with the poor and the oppressed; a church willing 'to empty itself of its own cultural tradition' in order to learn the richness of the more ancient cultures of these people so that its own understanding of the gospel can be enhanced.[54]

Furthermore, Phan argues that we do not need a church that proclaims itself to be the sole channel of God's grace and asserts its superiority over the religious traditions of the native people. What we do need is a church that journeys humbly with all those who seek God with a sincere heart. It must be a church that is willing to demonstrate to these people its faith in Jesus Christ as a manifestation of God's inclusive love for everyone, recognize in them the presence of the Spirit and learn from them ways to become more faithful to God's call. Phan believes that the future of the church lies not in trying to discover 'new fangled tricks from the world' in order to 'make disciples of all nations' (Matthew 28:19) but simply to find out how Jesus and God act in history or, in theological language, how the 'three divine persons relate among themselves in their inner trinitarian life'.[55] Peter Phan's teaching contradicts *Dominus Iesus*, but it is supported by other church documents.

CONTRASTING DOCUMENTS

Dominus Iesus is regarded as the most controversial document to emerge during Joseph Ratzinger's tenure as prefect of the CDF. The text signifies a shift in focus – from dialogue back to evangelization. *Dominus Iesus* sought to challenge a 'false concept of tolerance' regarding religious pluralism and asserted the church's missionary endeavour, which was perceived to be under threat from theories of religious pluralism.[56] However, *Dominus Iesus* is in stark contrast to the Second Vatican Council's explicit recognition of the presence of positive values in non-Christian religions and to the attribution of these values to the Logos and the Spirit. Such a positive evaluation of non-Christian religions by the Second Vatican Council raises 'the question of whether evangelization has not been replaced by interreligious dialogue'.[57]

Phan says this question has been answered by John Paul II in *Redemptoris missio*: 'Inter-religious dialogue is a part of the Church's evangelizing mission. Understood as a method and means of mutual knowledge and enrichment, dialogue is not in opposition to the mission *ad gentes*; indeed, it has special links with that mission and is one of its expressions.'[58] This position of John Paul II was also reiterated in *Dialogue and Proclamation*: 'Interreligious dialogue and proclamation, though not on the same level, are both authentic elements of the Church's evangelizing mission. Both are legitimate and necessary.'[59] This leads us to Phan's understanding of interreligious dialogue as a form of evangelization.

INTERRELIGIOUS DIALOGUE AS A FORM OF EVANGELIZATION

Peter Phan also adopts an inclusivistic position in interreligious dialogue that 'holds in fruitful tension two basic truths of the Christian faith, namely, the universal salvific will of God and the necessary mediation of Jesus Christ in the salvation of every individual'.[60] In such a position, interreligious dialogue can take place because the participants remain faithful to their religious tradition while, at the same time, recognizing that truth and goodness may be present in other traditions. In other words, interreligious dialogue takes differences seriously, trying to understand or overcome them. Phan insists that the inclusivist position makes a 'clear distinction between the claim for the universality and uniqueness of Jesus and that for the necessary instrumental role of the church'; it distinguishes between Jesus as the universal and unique Saviour and Christianity as a historical religion. Phan finds a need to combine a 'high' Christology and a 'low' ecclesiology.[61]

Influenced by Jacques Dupuis, Phan believes that interreligious dialogue is a form of evangelization. In some cases, it is the only way to proclaim Jesus Christ. We do not know the outcome of interreligious dialogue and, thus, we must trust in the guidance of the Holy Spirit. Interreligious dialogue can also be 'a moment of mutual evangelization' when participants on both sides 'purify and correct their own beliefs and values'. This means that Christians and non-Christians can learn from each other and be enriched.[62] In this regard, O'Leary has observed how Christianity could be tempered by Buddhist wisdom:

> The Christian perspective has its distinctive themes which no other religion offers, but there is in the other religions no pressing need to tune in to these themes. The Buddhist perspective has perhaps a more universal pertinence today, and all other religions may need to be tempered by Buddhist wisdom. Biblical faith, so often a destructive principle, may have lost its way, and the Gospel may need to be tempered by Buddhist wisdom so as to become good-tempered, recovering from a sorry history of theological acrimony; even-tempered, freed from the extremes of dogmatic 'eternalism' and sceptical 'nihilism' denounced by the Buddha.[63]

This affirms what I mentioned in Chapter 2, namely that Christianity could learn from the traditions of other faiths and could accept the fact that other religions can teach truths that are not yet understood by the church. Christianity could learn from Buddhism how to shed the violence of old Christendom in order to return to peaceful living, as dictated by the beatitudes.

ASIAN REALITIES

Aloysius Pieris states that any discussion about Asian theology must take into consideration the extreme poverty of the continent and the presence of many major religions. These two realities constitute the Asian context.[64] Emphasis on the suffering of the poor is not new, but set within the Asian context, this suffering has a certain immediacy and urgency. Pieris laments that Asian people are subjected to poverty because of the organized greed of a few Asians, as well as Westerners, who used them as 'pawns'. Foreigners manipulate international trade in their favour, ruthlessly exploit human and natural resources and indulge in 'cultural aggression by thrusting a dangerous kind of technocracy into the Asian ethos'.[65] Thus, the matrix of true Asian theology must deal with profound religiosity, which is a great asset, as well as with overwhelming poverty, which is disheartening.

Interreligious dialogue is important in Asia because of the presence of several major world religions. However, Michael Amaladoss says that interreligious dialogue is meaningless if it does not lead to a 'holistic liberation of the human person-in-community'. This alludes to the promotion of human and spiritual values. He suggests that the focus of evangelization and mission, in Asia, should be the Kingdom of God rather than the local church. For Amaladoss, this is not just a mere changing of terminology: it affects the way we preach the gospel.[66]

Through the power of the Spirit, God can establish his reign in ways unknown to Christians. The church, however, has to proclaim not only the reign of God, but also the death and resurrection of Jesus Christ, which is part of its mission. Thus, baptism is not just for our own salvation, but a call to mission. Otherwise, Amaladoss argues, it would not be true evangelization, just 'mere proselytism'. We need to see the church within the context of God's reign. In other words, we cannot ignore the wider perspective of the reign which Jesus proclaimed, but, at the same time, we must also have a passionate commitment to the 'memory' of Jesus.[67]

Amaladoss also insists that establishing the reign of God is a 'wider cosmic reality' and the Spirit calls us to this task in many and diverse ways which, in their entirety, are known to God alone. This means that establishing the Kingdom of God extends beyond the confines of the church. However, the demand for dialogue to collaborate in establishing the Kingdom does not require us to reduce our commitment to our faith. Authentic dialogue dictates that we can and should mutually enrich and respect each other's freedom in response to God's grace. The pluralistic nature of our society demands that we respect the identity and freedom of the other while, at the same time, not forgetting to affirm and to be faithful to our own identity. Otherwise any dialogue would be insincere.[68]

The Federation of Asian Bishops Conferences has also affirmed a Kingdom-centred understanding of the church which indicates that the church should serve the reign of God. Hence, conversion is not the top priority. In fact, dialogue which aims to convert others to one's faith, is 'dishonest and unethical' and certainly not the way to harmonious relationships. The dialogue envisioned by the Asian bishops can take place in 'basic human communities' where faith includes both Christians and non-Christians who want to work for the welfare of everyone.[69]

Finding the correct way in which to proclaim Jesus as the unique saviour presents a problem in the Asian context because of Asia's religious plurality. The Asian bishops, in general, suggest searching for a 'creative harmony rather than distinctions' because 'Truth is much more a matter of "both-and" rather than "either-or".' Therefore, the truth of Jesus must relate to and include the truths of other religious founders. In fact, Jesus, who emptied himself, did not dominate others, and so is an example other religions can accept.[70] Asian bishops promote Jesus as the servant of the poor, in a 'dialogue of liberation and of action'. They believe that mutual concern for the poor and the marginalized can be a topic for dialogue. Such a dialogue would encourage each religion to be creative and redemptive. Knitter also thinks along the lines of the Asian bishops who prefer to speak of Jesus not as the only saviour, but as a Liberator and Compassionate Friend of the Poor. These special titles of Jesus will not negate the uniqueness of other religious founders. In fact, Knitter believes that they can enhance cooperation between Christianity and other religions.[71]

Christians in Asia could gain new insights into the reign of God through dialogue with other religions in which they recognize the presence and activity of God's Word and Spirit. Non-Christian religions, in their continent, have traditions older than ones which come from elsewhere. According to Michael Amaladoss, the Buddhist vision of reality as 'inter-being' could help Christians to be in solidarity not only with people, but with the entire cosmos. The ecological movement could learn a lot from Buddhism. The relationship between *yin* and *yang*, male and female, could provide a new way of looking at gender relationships, without the masculine dominating the feminine. The preferential option for the poor, common to all religions in Asia, tells us that a humane life does not depend on 'having' but on 'being' and 'sharing'.[72] The stress here is on sharing and community living.

Christians in Asia are realizing that establishing the Kingdom of God is too big a job for one religion. Knitter stresses that to help people to become members of this Kingdom is more important than to make them members of the Christian church. Thus, mission does not equate to church expansion but, rather, to 'bringing the power of the Word to bear on any human situation to which it has a relevant message'.[73] Peter Phan believes that this power of the Logos is also present in other religions, especially in Asia, the home of ancient and venerable faiths, where belonging to more than one religion is acceptable.

SIMULTANEOUS MEMBERSHIP OF MULTIPLE RELIGIONS

The practice of belonging to several religions simultaneously is more of a challenge to Christian theology than a threat.[74] It occurs as a result of trying to focus on the ultimate spiritual experience that forms the core of all religious traditions rather than on a given religion itself. It also means remaining faithful to the 'symbolic framework' of one's own religious belief while adopting the 'hermeneutical framework' of another faith. For example, the Mahayana Buddhist tradition has been used to reinterpret Christian theology.[75] Increased awareness of religious pluralism in today's world has given people the ability to choose which religions they want to belong to and how many. This practice of belonging to more than one religious tradition appears to be a recent phenomenon in the West. However, in Asia, belonging to more than one religion is very much part of the religious history of China, Japan, India and Nepal. In the East and elsewhere in the ancient past, belonging to multiple religions may have been the rule rather than the exception.[76] Catherine Cornille has observed that 'the more encompassing a religion's claim to efficacy and truth, the more problematic the possibility of multi- religious belonging.'[77] Perhaps it is because of this axiom that Phan's understanding of this concept of belonging to more than one religion caught the attention of Catholic ecclesiastical authorities.

Membership of several religions simultaneously does not simply relate closely to inculturation and interreligious dialogue, it transcends them. According to Phan, it accepts the theory and practice of other religions and incorporates them into Christianity, in a modified form. It involves adopting and living out the beliefs, moral rules and rituals of various religious traditions in the midst of the community of the faithful of yet another religion. While supporting this practice, Phan is clearly critical of any 'postmodern form of syncretism' in which a person selects from a religion whatever doctrine or ethical practice of ritual he likes, without considering its value, in relation to truth.[78] As mentioned earlier, Phan rejects this kind of syncretism because it is often related to the New Age movement which he considers to be 'a symptom of unbridled consumerism' and 'excessive individualism.'[79]

In Asian countries such as China, Japan, Vietnam and India, member-ship of several religions simultaneously, which is different from syncretism or 'supermarket style belief', is a common practice, according to Phan. In contrast to the Western context where belonging to more than one religion implies membership of two or more religious belief systems, in Asia, religions have specialized functions which each respond to different needs and circumstances in a person's life.[80] Asians go to temples, churches, shrines and pagodas to pray and worship, and the basis for their choice, at any given time, depends on their needs and on what a particular deity or spirit is reputed to be able to grant. It would appear, therefore that Asian religions are not by nature exclusive, but that they only become exclusive when they come into contact with Christian-ity which claims to be superior to them – it is a reaction to the Christian claim of supremacy. Phan gives an example of Buddhism in Sri Lanka, in the nine-teenth century, when Christianity's claim to superiority led to competition between the two religions rather than tolerance.[81] I think the claim to superi-ority does not in itself make something exclusive. It only implies that the other thing is inferior. I believe this would lead even to rivalries and hatred. Hence, distrust and resentment still exist among non-Christians towards Christians in many parts of the world.

Phan thinks that belonging to multiple religions is not only desirable, but is also acceptable to many people. The rationale he gives is that if non-Christian religions contain 'elements of truth and of grace', then they can be considered means of salvation from whose traditions and practices Christians can learn and benefit, through dialogue. Hence, there should not be any objec-tion or censure if a Christian wishes to follow some doctrinal teachings and religious practices of Buddhism, Confucianism or Hinduism as long as they are not contrary to or incompatible with Christian faith and morals. Phan looks to the scriptures for evidence of people belonging to two religions at once and he finds it in Acts 3:46: 'They went to the temple area together every day, while in their homes they broke bread.' Here we find some early Christian converts still holding fast to their inherited Jewish beliefs.[82] The close rela-tionship between Judaism and Christianity makes membership of two reli-gions feasible. However, the idea of combining, for example, the practices of the Hindus with Christian faith may be problematic because, fundamentally, the two religions are very different, one being, arguably, polytheistic and the other being monotheistic. Phan, however, believes that such abstract consid-eration is not fruitful. One should focus on the actual experiences of believers who attempt to combine, in their spiritual lives, their Christian faith and the religious practices of other traditions.[83]

THEOLOGICAL EDUCATION AND THE ASIAN EXPERIENCE

In his approach to the practice of belonging to several religions simultaneously, Phan places importance on theological education. Theological reflections on religious pluralism should include multi-faith worship and prayer where non-Christian scriptures, prayers and rituals are used to complement the Christian liturgy. Phan also suggests the adoption of monastic practices and meditation techniques found in non-Christian religions in order to enhance our spiritual life. Another important aspect of this theological education is to work for the poor and marginalized and to share and collaborate with people of non-Christian faiths. Phan writes:

> Nothing can change a person's negative view about the possibility of salvation outside Christianity and about the positive values of non-Christian religions more quickly and effectively than an actual and prolonged encounter with non-Christians who are prayerful and holy, not rarely more so than Christians themselves. Interreligious dialogue is never carried out with religions as such but with flesh-and-blood believers and practitioners of other faiths.[84]

This implies that friendship with non-Christians can go a long way in fostering interreligious dialogue.

Monotheistic religions, such as Judaism, Christianity and Islam, naturally have difficulty accepting the concept of belonging to several religions at once. However, the religious landscape in the West has changed, with the influx of immigrants leading to heightened awareness of religious diversity. Hence, the Christian faith in a pluralistic society experiences the tension between claims to absolute truth and the uniqueness of one's saviour and the openness of more independent believers. Catherine Cornille characterized this phenomenon as a 'modern shift from a conception of truth and meaning framed in cosmology to one rooted in subjectivity'.[85] This sense of freedom and autonomy is now causing tension in Christian tradition and identity, at least in the West. However, the situation in the East is quite different. Phan's view of religious pluralism and multiple religious belonging originated from his experience in Asia.[86]

Phan argues that any discussion of God or the divine must be pluralistic given the cultural and religious diversities of Asia. If we stick to our own image of God on grounds of orthodoxy, it will lead to failure and irrelevance in relation to our efforts to establish interreligious dialogue. Before Christianity was established in Asia, there was not a 'religious void where God was dead or absent'.[87] The Asian bishops in the Asian Synod remind us that the Holy Spirit continues to sow seeds of truth among people, cultures and religions, and these cultures and religions are capable of helping people to lead a good life. We must acknowledge that God's Spirit was at work in Asian cultures, long before Christianity arrived on the scene. Hence, our attitude should be one of respect and humility: we must first be silent in order to learn and understand.[88]

I mentioned earlier that Peter Phan believes there are doctrines and practices found in Asian cultures and religions worth cultivating by Christians. Therefore, Christians must be taught about God by Asians before they can preach the gospel. Phan is not saying that Asian religions are identical with Christianity, nor does he acknowledge that there is a core religious experience. While not advocating religious pluralism like John Hick or Paul Knitter, he believes that some religions are better than others, and that there are fundamental and irreconcilable differences among different faiths. Precisely because of these differences, Phan argues that if Christianity and Asian religions try to learn from each other, it can only be advantageous for all concerned.[89]

CRITICAL REFLECTION

The CDF and USCCB regard Phan's understanding of religious pluralism, the salvific significance of the coming of Christ, and the church as a necessary instrument of salvation, as both ambiguous and contrary to official church teaching. The USCCB in particular reported that Phan's *Being Religious Interreligiously* was based on the idea that religious pluralism is part of God's plan of salvation and thus there is some kind of moral obligation for the church to refrain from converting people to Christianity and to membership of the church. This implies that evangelization of non-Christians is contrary to God's purpose in history, which is the offering of salvation for all peoples in many and diverse ways. The church, of course, believes that preaching the gospel to non-believers is not an imposition of power, but an expression of love. Since it is unfair to deny technological progress and the spread of modern civilization to other people, it would also not be right to deny the gospel to others. This is Ratzinger's rationale for mission, but he admits that we must proceed in our mission with more sensitivity to others' traditions.[90] Since the church does not believe that other religions possess the fullness of truth as revealed in

Jesus Christ, it follows that to offer the gift of Jesus Christ is to offer them the greatest of all gifts. The church believes there is no conflict between showing respect for other religions and proclaiming the gospel to all nations.

All these assertions are true within their own context. A Eurocentric church, zealous in protecting its own turf, feeling threatened by the 'negative theology' of Asia and giving precedence to the Western mode of thinking is compelled to draw the boundary lines as to where Roman Catholicism begins and ends. Joseph Fessio asks, 'How long would someone working for GM who was actually selling Fords last?'[91]

If Christianity was quick to appropriate Hellenistic and Roman ideas in its early years for its own survival and success, why is it so slow or even unwilling to inculturate itself to Asian realities now? In reference to this question, Peter Phan is acutely aware of the failure of the church in Asia and has highlighted the fact that for Asians, Christianity is still a Western religion. It will probably remain that way for a long time. This is because Western Christianity is too entrenched within its own Western mindset to allow itself to be enriched by the wealth of knowledge and understanding of other religious traditions and cultures in the world. Virgil Elizondo puts it this way:

> we had often kept the refreshing newness of the gospel from coming through because we had insisted so much on our linguistic / philo-sophical / theological presentations based on our Western cosmovision rather than trusting the dynamism of the gospel stories and imagery which would have easily entered into dialogue with the life-stories of any cosmovision in the world.[92]

Elizondo also makes this cutting remark on the successful blending of power, wealth and Christianity found in Christendom:

> 1492 marked the birth of colonial Christianity on a world-wide scale. The great Western expansion was characterized by the unquestioned syncretistic mixture of gods of Mammon and the Christian God of eternal life. Since Constantine inversion, this syncretism has been devel-oping in Western Christianity . . . This European religious syncretism produced a mixture of imagery which interwove (rather than opposed, as the Gospels did) the Roman Empire and all its power, might, pomp and grandeur with the Kingdom of God and its renunciation of power and call to poverty . . . these two contradictory notions of life became the basis of the syncretistic Christianity of the West which would allow

it to destroy and defend, wound and seek to heal, exterminate and seek to offer life, but in the end enslave, exploit, abuse and kill – all for the greater honour and glory of God.[93]

Thus, Timothy Light rightly argues that, 'all religion is syncretic and that orthodoxy is a matter of time, not permanence ... today's orthodoxy is the result of yesterday's mixing, and it has never been otherwise.'[94] This brings us to the issue of syncretism in the Western church.

SYNCRETISM AND EUROCENTRISM

Christianity, in its early expansionary phase could be characterized by its willingness to adapt to social and political situations, to the extent of being syncretistic, as mentioned by Elizondo. However, once it established itself as the dominant religion, it turned against syncretism. The desire to avoid syncretism was reasonable because it posed a genuine threat to the Christian religion and its integrity. The threat occurs when two religions are mixed in such a way that the core belief of one or the other or both is radically transformed into a 'theologically untenable amalgam'. Thus, it was understandable that the church was constantly fighting to keep the gospel message pure and untainted. Yet, as Jerald Gort has observed, the problem arose when syncretism 'came to be so broadly defined that the possibility of any positive relationship between Christianity and other traditions was *a priori* precluded'. The root cause of this problem lay in a Eurocentric church with its sense of superiority. European culture and its expression of the Christian faith became directly 'identified with the truth of the gospel and thus accorded universal normativity'.[95] This is what I mean when I say that there is a tendency in Joseph Ratzinger's theological writings to give precedence to Western thought in the sense of accepting Hellenistic philosophy as a norm for interpreting Christianity. As we have seen in Chapter 2, Ratzinger believes the move to the West was providential for the Christian faith.

This superiority complex led the 'self-consecrated' Western church to see its faith as being exclusive and to seek the abolition of other religions and cultures as a means of evangelization. This happened quite often in the missionary endeavours of the church, throughout its history. The Western church viewed the displacement of other religions as an acceptable way of proclaiming the gospel and considered 'any other outcome' as 'ipso facto syncretistic'. Thus, 'it was not the rejection of syncretism narrowly defined but rather exaggerated self-esteem that led, via an ever widening application of the concept of syncretism, to European Christianity's traditionally preponderating antipathy toward the views and ways of life of other peoples.'[96] In other words, Western Christianity's fear of excessive syncretism had to do with power and its sense of superiority.

Furthermore, Anton Wessels has acknowledged that, in the last forty years or so, Christian theologians from the Asian, African and Latin American continents have contributed greatly to the practice of theology by taking into consideration their own political, cultural and religious contexts. However, some Western theologians thought that this approach might have sacrificed the unique quality of the gospel. In fact, some wondered if contextual theology could really be called Christian. Consciously or unconsciously, these Western scholars believed that they represented a universal Christian theology. They set themselves up as the norm and standard against which to judge others and, thus, they tended to dismiss non-Western theology as 'syncretistic'.[97] Western theologians also found it difficult to accept the relevance and positive values of Asian, African and Latin American theology because they were not conscious of their own contextualization. They had not given enough thought to the issue of cultural adaptation of the gospel in Europe in the past or how the faith entered the continent in the first place.[98]

ORTHODOXY VERSUS ORTHOPRAXIS

Each time the CDF investigates a theologian, it is always on the basis of doctrinal (Christocentrism) issues. However, Phan, as well as the Asian bishops, see the problem of evangelization in Asia arising not from Jesus, the Christ, who is widely accepted and loved in Asia, but from the presence of a foreign church aligned with its colonial past and having little respect for the local culture. John Mansford Prior claims that 'the Latin Churches of Asia are a foreign presence. They are ... alien in that Christians have had to uproot themselves from their own cultural identity in order to claim a "hybrid" Christian one.'[99] Prior says the key missiological problem is not Christ, but the Western church's method of proclaiming the gospel.[100] If such is the case, the problem lies with the emphasis of the Western church on orthodoxy, while Phan's understanding of religious pluralism is based on orthopraxis.

The investigation of Peter Phan, a Catholic theologian, by church authorities had to do with the question of fidelity to the Catholic tradition. Francis Sullivan says that a Catholic theologian is one who is 'committed to seeking a contemporary understanding of the faith within the Catholic tradition'. This means that a Catholic theologian attempts to reinterpret religious tradition by thinking inside the boundaries of that tradition. In keeping with David Tracy, Sullivan writes:'only those who are fully committed to a religious tradition can grasp the meaning of that tradition in such a way as to achieve a reliable rein- terpretation of it'. If this is the case, then Catholic theologians must strive to understand the Catholic tradition of faith and then translate it into concepts and terms that will be meaningful and relevant to the faithful.[101] But how do we define Catholic tradition?

In reference to this question, Phan argues that the new trend seems to reject the traditional belief that Catholic identity is defined by an explicit adherence to certain doctrines. This is because Catholic identity or tradition cannot be easily standardized. Phan claims that the distinctive characteristics of Roman Catholicism are not uniformly understood and evaluated in the same way as in the West.[102] According to him, the Catholic identity is shaped, not by doctrines alone, but by worship and prayer, which he describes as the 'deep structures' of symbols and institutions. These structures have been identified as 'sacramentality, mediation, communion, and the "analogical imagination"'.[103]

Finally, the Vatican's Notification on Peter Phan's work highlights the importance of religious pluralism and its significance in our contemporary society. Joseph Ratzinger equates the religious pluralism of John Hick and Paul Knitter with relativism, which he thinks is damaging. However, he supports a pluralism which, in 'the interplay of Church, politics and society is a fundamental value for Christianity' and he also understands 'the relative value of all political and social achievements'.[104] Phan, too, rejects relativ- ism and would certainly agree with Ratzinger that pluralism is fundamental for Christianity to flourish. It could, therefore, be concluded that the clash between Phan's understanding of religious pluralism and the magisterium's teaching, influenced by Ratzinger's ecclesiology, ultimately has to do with the primacy of doctrine and discipline (orthodoxy) over practice and performance (orthopraxis).

Regarding orthopraxis, in the next chapter, we will look at the ethical vision offered by Hans Küng and Paul Knitter. Both theologians had clashes with Ratzinger and were censured by him. Küng once compared the then Cardinal Joseph Ratzinger with the head of the KGB in his capacity as the prefect of the CDF. Küng's licence to teach Catholic theology was revoked by Pope John Paul II and Ratzinger played a crucial role in this decision as a member of the German bishops' conference. Since then, Küng has been a leading critic of the doctrinal positions of Ratzinger and his method of investigating dissident theologians. Ratzinger also criticized the pluralist theology of Paul Knitter in his book *Truth and Tolerance*.

Chapter 11

Ethical Vision

As we have seen, the question of truth is fundamental in Joseph Ratzinger's theological discourse. For him, truth is what God revealed in Jesus Christ as taught by scripture, the teaching of the fathers and the church. Joseph Ratzinger thus insists on Christianity as the true religion. Hans Küng, however, proposes the concept of *humanum* as the basic norm for an ecumenical theology and for judging the authenticity of a religion.[1] He defines *humanum* as 'what is given and what it is given to do: it is both the *essence* and *the task* of humanity'.[2] This stress on the human element is also part of the transformation of Catholicism in the second half of the twentieth century.

For centuries, the Catholic Church had opposed the notion of human rights: Pope Pius VI considered the Declaration of the Rights of Man in the French National Assembly a direct attack against the Catholic Church. In his 1791 papal document, *Caritas*, he condemned the declarations on the rights to freedom of religion and freedom of the press as well as the declaration on the equality of all men as contrary to the divine principles of the church. The principle of religious freedom was a threat to the church because it considers all religions equal and insists on the separation of church and state.[3]

It was only in the 1960s that the church accepted human rights doctrines when John XXIII's encyclical *Pacem in Terris* (1963) adopted modern discourse on human rights, which has now become part and parcel of papal teachings and bishops' pastoral letters. Now the church consistently stresses the protection of human rights of every person as the moral foundation for a just and peaceful society; it calls for dialogue and peaceful negotiation as a means of resolving conflicts and promotes universal solidarity as the basis for the construction of a legitimate world order.

The inalienable rights of every individual to freedom of conscience based on the sacred dignity of the human person is recognized in the Second Vatican Council document, *Dignitatis Humanae*. This is a significant theological development: the transformation of the principle of *libertas ecclesiae* to *libertas personae*.[4] It is in this context that we can situate Küng's concept of *humanum* as a paradigm shift in theology.

Küng states that in the fight for *humanum*, Christianity and religions in general can provide reasons as to why morality and ethics are more than just a matter of private judgement or social norm. Religion can show that morality and ethical values are binding and applicable to all persons: 'it has proved that only the Unconditioned can itself impose an unconditional obligation, and only the Absolute can be absolutely binding.'[5] And in times of human atrophy and widespread permissiveness, Christianity can establish for the conscience of the individual the importance of morality which is more than a question of personal preference. A society without norms of behaviour or moral values, a minimum of binding values, cannot survive. Not only do people need basic norms of behaviour, they also cannot live in a spiritual void.[6]

The first part of this chapter attempts to critique Küng's *humanum* as a criterion for determining the truth and goodness of a religion. In addition, the thought of Ratzinger, who understands Christianity as the true religion, is presented to shed light on their different approaches. The second part focuses on the problems that all authentic religions must face – the sufferings of humanity – as understood by Paul Knitter in his emphasis on crossing the ethical–practical bridge as an approach to engage interreligious dialogue.

BEING HUMAN AND BEING CHRISTIAN

Hans Küng in *On Being a Christian* hits out at official representatives of churches who lack genuine humanity and thus give the idea that being a Christian cannot be an 'authentically human possibility'. He argues that the humanization of the whole person ought to be complementary to being a Christian: 'The Christian factor must be made not at the expense of the human, but for the benefit of the latter.' Another important point he makes is that human nature is not static and immutable, but dynamic and constantly changing, to be seen as a social reality. At the same time, he cautions that the person's freedom cannot be obtained solely by changing social conditions because the human being needs a basic spiritual bond and truth. In the light of this, Küng argues that if a person believes Jesus Christ as the concrete guiding principle and model, he can live a different, more authentic human life.[7]

Thus, through belief in Jesus Christ, human beings can develop new insights and tendencies: the disposition to commit oneself to one's fellow men and women, to identify with the disabled and to fight against unjust social and economic structures. Imitating Christ leads to new projects and actions, not only universal programmes to transform society, but 'concrete signs, testimonies, evidence of humanity and of humanizing both the individual and human society'. The realization of the Kingdom of God can come about only through the positive and negative aspects of human life as mirrored in the paschal mystery of Christ his suffering, death and resurrection.[8]

Being a Christian is not an addition to one's humanity, Küng argues; thus being a Christian, one does not cease to be human and vice versa. The Christian feature is neither a 'superstructure nor a substructure of the human'. Christian faith elevates the human person, preserving and surpassing the human; to be a Christian means other humanisms are transfigured and are affirmed as the human reality with all its positive and negative aspects. Christians see humanity, freedom, justice and so on in the light of Jesus who is the Christ.[9]

Küng calls for a radical humanism that affirms not only the good and beautiful, but integrates and copes with what is not good, untrue and inhuman. This means true humanism embraces sin, suffering and death. Only the crucified Christ can give meaning to suffering and death in our human existence. And even when reason breaks down, in pointless misery, we can still find meaning in life if we are sustained by God. Faith in Jesus gives us peace, but does not get rid of our problems; it makes us truly human when we respond to the needs of our neighbour.[10]

CHRISTIAN TRADITION AND HUMAN EXPERIENCE

Küng believes that academic theology must draw from two sources: Jewish–Christian tradition and contemporary human experiences of both Christians and non-Christians.[11] God's revelation can be perceived only through and in human experiences. This means that God's revelation encompasses human projects, events and interpretations, and so on. Küng says, 'human experiences do not account for God's revelation, rather God's revelation accounts for the human response in faith'.[12] Although revelation is not directly God's word, it remains a human word and bears witness to the word of God that people experience. Thus, there is no revelation outside human experience; and it is the specific experience of Jesus Christ who gives meaning to our lives without which there is no Christianity. The interpretative experience is a fundamental aspect of revelation. Metaphorically speaking, revelation comes from God 'above', but is experienced and interpreted from 'below' by men and women.

Another point that Küng makes is that the human experience of revelation is 'always given in advance only through human interpretation'.[13] This means that every experience of revelation, salvation and grace is never given purely but interpreted and identified in advance. In short, every experience is an interpretative process by itself and is finally enriched by expressing it in language. There is no experience or faith-statement in the Bible or by the church without this interpretative framework.

Therefore, the experience of Jesus was already interpreted in advance by the biblical authors; the message of salvation was given to us coloured by the experience of the synoptic gospel writers, by Paul and John. They came from a cultural milieu totally different from ours and thus the same gospel message has to be 'mediated afresh today'.[14] The criterion for the Christian faith is the 'living Jesus of history' and not the 'historical image of Jesus'. Küng believes a historical–critical approach to biblical study 'can clarify for us how the concrete contents of early Christian faith were "fulfilled" through the Jesus of faith'.[15]

Küng believes that historical–critical research can give us confirmation that the Christ of faith is also the Jesus of history. It is easy to distort the image of Christ through superstitions. Theologians have the responsibility to take seriously the religious difficulties and doubts of contemporary men and women; it is their task to defend the Christian faith against 'distortions and false conclusions on the part of the church'. Thus, we have 'a faith seeking historical understanding' and also 'a historical understanding seeking faith'.[16] This means our belief in Jesus must be historically rooted and verified. Küng insists that the findings of historical–critical exegesis cannot be ignored, evaded or domesticated by neo-scholastic conservatism.

The second source of theology is our human experience: 'the vital consciousness of men and women in the world, with their deepest problems with meaning, life and society'.[17] It is in the secular world that people experience alienation and crises of faith. Thus, theology must respond to these human experiences and give them a meaningful Christian interpretation. According to Schillebeeckx, 'The modern person reflects on specific experiences and interprets them, often groping carefully along, in a religious sense. The ambivalent experiences that he has are both positive (in the direction of infinity) and negative (in the direction of finity). They confront the contemporary person with a decision, that is, they are a summons to and an experience with these experiences.'[18]

In view of the above, Küng argues that the Christian message must be translated into our world of experience; the word of God can only be meaningful when it is experienced as a liberating answer to our problems in life. Theology must establish a 'critical correlation' between the Christian tradition of experience and today's experiences, if it is to serve preaching. This requires theologians and preachers to analyse the present-day world of experience, trace the constant structures of Christian experience based on the New Testament and relate the two sources critically. Thus, our daily experience must be present in theology in the form of a 'presence' of our modern existence, the 'feeling of life and contemporary impulses'. A good example is what Edward Schillebeeckx identifies as critical remembering of human suffering, the question of redemption and emancipation.[19]

THE TRUE RELIGION

Küng asks this question, 'Is there one true religion? From the outside (*i.e.*, objectively) there are many true religions; from the inside (subjectively) there is only one. Christians over the centuries have fallen into *untrue* religion. Prophets have had to arise in the Church and "enlightened ones" outside the Church to call the faithful back to this truth, among whom the prophet Muhammad and the Buddha should no doubt be included *par excellence*.'[20] Küng says a genuine religion must have an orientation to the human element, but that does not mean that it must be reduced to 'merely human'. Religion is convincing when it succeeds in bringing out the 'human element against the background of the Absolute'.[21]

Churches reacted against freedom of religion and conscience. Thus, humanism called upon the often rather unchristian churches to translate into reality what were truly Christian values such as freedom, equality, fraternity and human dignity. Küng argues: 'For it was precisely by being religiously and ecclesiastically emancipated in modern autonomy that the *human* element could once again find a home in the domain of Christianity – before all other religions.'[22]

Thus, according to Küng, insofar as a religion serves the virtue of humanity, supports human beings in their dignity and allows them to gain meaningful and fruitful existence, it is a true and good religion. But if religion spreads inhumanity and hinders human beings in their human identity and meaningfulness, preventing them from achieving a meaningful and fruitful existence, it is a false and bad religion.[23]

In view of this, all religions reflect again the demands of human nature; this human element is given to all men and women; it is a general criterion that holds for all religious beliefs. And all religions will continually remind themselves of their 'primal, peculiar essence' as found in their sacred writings and saints. Time and again, their prophets and reformers will remind them if they have been untrue or violating their own essence. The original essence unique to every religion is a general criterion by which each can be measured.[24]

Thus, in Küng's view, a religion is true when it promotes human flourishing – when it creates social solidarity and tolerance, when it replaces ecclesiocentrism with philanthropy, when it relativizes religious constitutions for human good: this means that the more humane Christianity is, the more it appears to the outside as a true religion. It is a pragmatic assessment and not an existential one.

Küng asserts that in the Christian faith, the specifically Christian criterion coincides with the general ethical criterion of humanity. The Sermon on the Mount is a proclamation of a 'true humanity'. This new humanity implies a 'more radical way of being human' as demonstrated by solidarity with one another and also with one's opponents. This also implies that Christians enter into fellowship with members of other religions as well. Küng says that the more humane Christianity is, the more Christian it is. Thus, 'true humanity is the prerequisite for true religion'; and 'true religion is the perfecting of true humanity'.[25]

Küng also makes it clear that the truth in Christianity does not exclude the truth in other religions. They are all conditionally true religions as long as they do not contradict the essential Christian message; in fact other religions can 'complete, correct and enrich the Christian religion'.[26] In the end no religion will be left standing, not even Christianity, Küng asserts, but the one 'Inexpressible' to whom all religions are oriented. Even Jesus Christ will no longer stand as a separate figure: Paul says, 'When everything is subjected to him, then the Son himself will [also] be subjected to the one who subjected everything to him, so that God may be all in all' (1 Corinthians 15:28).

THE GOLDEN RULE

Küng believes that humanity is entering a new phase in history and its very survival requires a radical paradigm shift – a world ethic for humankind to survive in the recent economic, social, political and ecological crisis. There must be a minimum consensus, he insists, for societies to survive; this minimum consensus provides the foundation of moral obligation to do good and not evil.

This choice to do good 'is the one unconditional in all that is conditioned that can provide a basis for the absoluteness and universality of ethical demands, that primal ground, primal support, primal goal of human beings and the world that we call God'.[27] This basic consensus can be found in the golden rule which is shared by all major world religions. Küng views Kant's categorical imperative as the modernization and secularization of this golden rule, and thus can be shared by non-believers as well.[28]

CRITICAL REFLECTION

Küng's main thesis regarding the authentic religion is that only a religion that promotes true humanity can be true and good. This can lead to misunderstanding and opposition because members of other religions stress that religion is about the relationship between the individual person and the divine; Küng's anthropocentric thesis undermines this relationship. On the one hand, representatives of Eastern religions may see Küng's *humanum* as merely a product of Christian liberal thinking. On the other hand, there are people who want to renew the Christian faith which has been weakened by the liberal influence on the church; they see Küng's affirmation of the *humanum* as another idea from the Enlightenment. Perhaps Küng sees this resistance as a retreat from public responsibility; but for these theologians, Christians can only make an impact on society by the 'particularities of their distinctive heritage'.[29] Thus, the effort to find common ground with the secular world or other religions belongs to the legacy of the Enlightenment or modernity, which is disappearing.

Küng did not elaborate on the idea of *humanum* as it applies to biblical studies, ethics and politics, nor did he give concrete suggestions as to how it can be implemented in real life. Leonard Swidler, however, sees human life in three connected aspects: practical, cognitive and spiritual. In the cognitive aspect, we seek to understand and express in various ways our perception of the world and life experiences; in the practical area, we seek to 'affect and effect' the world; and in the spiritual aspect, we discern the deeper meanings of our experiences and of the world. This spiritual or in-depth dimension of our life, our imagination and feelings, plays an important role; it brings into consciousness the images and emotions of our daily experience. The three areas of our life must be well integrated so that we can live a holistic life.[30]

John Cobb questions whether Küng's *humanum* is an adequate basis for the needed ethos because it does not go beyond anthropocentricism. He argues that the discussion of *humanum* reveals that Küng is a child of the Enlightenment. It is important for Cobb to affirm human dignity without the anthropocentricism and individualism of the Enlightenment. He is right to suggest that Hinduism and Buddhism can help to do just that.[31] An alternative model to Küng's *Humanum* is Cobb's 'person-in-community' which embraces both humans and other creatures. This would counteract the individualistic tendency of *humanum*.[32]

Cobb also argues that the weakness of Küng's *humanum* comes from its close link with 'Enlightenment individualism and dualism', and other religious traditions are resistant to it. He claims that his idea of 'persons-in-community-with-one-another-and-with-other-creatures' is more acceptable to other religious and secular communities because of its 'communitarian character of personal life and its embeddedness in the natural context'.[33] Cobb is concerned that an ethos that originates from an individualistic and dualistic philosophical tradition is destroying the developing countries; he believes that the strengthening of human communities is more relevant than Küng's *humanum* for improving the lives of people, especially in the Third World.

Having discussed Küng's understanding of *humanum* as the criterion for a true religion and its shortcomings, we now turn to Joseph Ratzinger who presents a different philosophical-theological approach and supports the claim of Christianity as the *religio vera*.

THE HISTORICAL CHARACTER OF CHRISTIANITY

Ratzinger stresses the historical character of Christianity. He points to the character of Christianity as a monotheistic religion and the unhistorical nature of mysticism which expresses itself in symbols. In mysticism, the experience is all that counts – this experience or content transcends everything temporal. Christianity, on the other hand, is a divine calling, a relationship that is historically dated; it is a 'faith in an event' according to Jean Danielou. Mysticism and some non-Christian religions have the trait of being unhistorical in that 'they revolt against concrete time' and they long 'for a periodic return to the mystic time of origin'. Christianity is a historical faith, 'a path whose direction we call progress and whose attitude we call hope'.[34]

In spite of his stress on the historical character of Christianity, Ratzinger recognizes that the attempt to establish Christology firmly on the historical foundation has created a dilemma in modern theology. The push to make Christology 'accurate' and 'demonstrable' cannot succeed because it limits the phenomenon of Christianity: to confine Jesus in history is to limit our faith in him and his influence on our life. Faith in Jesus is a personal experience of the apostles and thus cannot be reduced to the 'demonstrable'. To escape from the dilemma of the historical altogether, as Hegel and Bultmann did, is also a futile attempt, according to Ratzinger.[35]

We are thus given two courses in this historical dilemma: the first is to reduce Christology to history, and the second is to escape history entirely, abandon it as irrelevant to faith. Ratzinger summarizes it as: Jesus or Christ? He remarks that modern theology starts by turning away from Christ and moving towards Jesus as a historically comprehensible figure. Later, Bultmann took the opposite direction by returning to Christ.[36]

So it is a question of Jesus versus Christ – we turn to Jesus who is love and move away from Christ who represents dogma. According to Harnack, the decisive break occurred when the preaching of Jesus was transformed into the preached Christ who demanded faith and became dogma. Jesus proclaimed the message of love and displaced Pharisaical orthodoxy with the simple trust in the Father and the brotherhood of man. But later this had been substituted with the doctrine of the God-man; and so brotherly love, which is salvation, was replaced by a doctrine of salvation, and thus the conflict began. The battle cry now is back past the preached Christ to the preaching of Jesus; back to the 'unifying power of love under the one Father with all our brothers.'[37]

Ratzinger recognizes that many people are now attracted to the humanity of Jesus – the most human of all human beings – whose 'humanity seems to them in a secularized world like the last shimmer of the divine left after the "death of God"'. Jesus remains a symbol of hope and trust which gives us courage to go on, but nothing more. Thus, believing only in the humanity of Jesus is part of the theology of the 'death of God'. Ratzinger is astonished to find that those who had been critical are now willing to accept uncritically a theology without God so as to appear to be progressive. He thinks that the attempt to pursue theology without God is a manifestation of an uncritical attitude.[38] Perhaps this is a criticism of liberal theologians such as Küng and others.

The attempt to construct a pure Jesus is intrinsically absurd in Ratzinger's view. At the same time, 'mere history creates no present', it only confirms what happened in the past. The romantic approach to Jesus is just as futile as the flight to the kerygma. For Ratzinger, 'Jesus only subsists as the Christ and the Christ only subsists in the shape of Jesus'. And we should put more trust in the presence of the faith which has endured for centuries, a faith which aims only to understand who and what this Jesus really was.[39]

FAITH AND CULTURE

Ratzinger prefers to talk about 'interculturality' instead of 'inculturation' because this term presupposes a culturally naked faith can easily be transferred into another culture even if they are alien to each other. This, according to him, is artificial and unreal because faith is never culture-free, and at the same time there is no such thing as a religion-free culture. Only when cultures are potentially universal and are open to others can interculturality take place and lead to fruitful forms. The openness of all people to others is hidden in our souls and touched by truth. We cannot see all religions as superstitions and at the same time it is also wrong to think that all religions are good, one and the same.[40]

In *Dialectics of Secularization*, Ratzinger states that to discuss human existence, it is absolutely necessary to take into account the intercultural dimension. Such discussion cannot take place exclusively within the Christian framework or Western rational tradition although they claim to be universal. But, in fact, they are only accepted by a small proportion of humanity. Küng believes there is a common universal principle that binds people, *humanum*; Ratzinger thinks there is no uniformity within the individual cultural spheres, only 'profound tensions within their own cultural tradition' which is obvious in Western countries. Secularism and Christianity continue to exert influence on people; at times they are willing to learn from each other, at other times, they reject each other.[41]

Ratzinger insists that we cannot simply allow religions to remain as they are; religions have to move with history and cannot be confined to a museum, as it were. Such a view is unrealistic because 'the meeting of cultures and the gradual growing together of the separate geographical areas of history into one common history of mankind are grounded in the nature of man himself'.[42] It would be unfair to deny technological progress and the spread of modern civilization to other people. Hence, it would also not be right to deny the gospel to others. This is Ratzinger's rationale for mission, but he admits that we must proceed in our mission with more sensitivity to the others' traditions.

THE PRIMACY OF THE PARTICULAR

Joseph Ratzinger admits that Christian belief is not just concerned with the eternal and 'other worldly' but 'with God in history, with God as man'. Revelation bridges the gulf between the temporal and the eternal, between the visible and invisible.[43] Jesus is that person in whom God comes to meet us (John 1:18). Ratzinger points out that what seems to be the most radical revelation, the disclosure of God in Jesus, is also the most extreme of obscurity and concealment. What he means is that God has come so close to us that we can kill him: the 'death of God' is now part of our human history and he ceases to be God for us. Perhaps many would think it might be easier to believe in the 'Mysterious Eternal' as in some Eastern religions than to 'give oneself up to the positivism of belief in one single figure and to set up the salvation of man and of the world on the pin-point … of this one chance moment in history'.[44] But Christianity is fundamentally a belief in a person.

Thus, according to Ratzinger, the most fundamental feature of Christian faith is its personal character, 'I believe in Thee'; 'it is the encounter with the human being Jesus, and in this encounter it experiences the meaning of the world as a person'.[45] The Christian belief in God is first of all a belief in the pre-existing Logos which is not a neutral consciousness but a person. Thus, the Christian option for belief in the Logos is an option for the 'primacy of the particular as against the universal'. The Christian faith is above all an option for man as the 'irreducible, infinity-related being'.[46]

Ratzinger stresses that the particular is more than the universal; thus the unique person is not just an individual but the ultimate and highest thing. The Christian sees in man and woman not an individual but a person and it is here that we see the primacy of particular over the universal. This means also that the Christian faith is more than just monotheism, it is the belief in the triune God.[47]

DISCOVERING THE TRUTH

In *Truth and Tolerance*, Ratzinger acknowledges that Christianity's recognition of other religions as a preparation for the gospel is perceived as a sign of arrogance. The dominant attitude of most people today is that all religions with their multiplicity of forms can actually lead us to the divine.[48] This attitude, known as relativism, is an ideology that he relentlessly seeks to discredit. Ratzinger's theology of religions is in stark contrast to Küng's, who insists that a religion is true when it promotes human flourishing. It is a fact that there are varieties of religions and the question of truth seems illusory, Ratzinger recognizes. However, there is this commonly shared religious experience; the various religious traditions are also related spiritually with one another. Regarding this, Küng speaks about the golden rule that exists in all major religious traditions, as we have seen.

In *Many Religions – One Covenant*, Ratzinger also argues that interreligious dialogue is possible only if we enter deeply into discovering the truth; scepticism and pragmatism do not unite people. We need to respect the beliefs of others and be ready to search for the truth in the other; for such truth can correct and lead us. Ratzinger admits that we do not possess the whole truth about the divine, and thus we need the help of others in our earthly pilgrimage.[49]

Ratzinger makes the interesting point that giving an absolute value to a religion is not peculiar to monotheism alone; it also applies to mysticism and enlightenment. Everyone makes an absolute claim for what they believe to be true, not just Christians. There are those who follow someone like Radhakrishnan who teaches the relativity of all religions and at the same time gives this experience of mysticism an absolute value. This is no less arrogant than the Christian claim to be the one true religion. Enlightenment, too, gives rational knowledge an absolute value – scientific knowledge becomes the only valid knowledge and it denies the absolute value of religious belief, which is actually a different kind of reality.[50]

People now substitute practice for truth and that is why the whole axis of religion is displaced. To lay claim to truth for one religious belief appears to be presumptuous today, Ratzinger laments. The focus is now on the 'kingdom' or 'regnocentricity' which all religions must move towards. Hence, it is not necessary for all religions to move closer to one another, but towards the centre which is the kingdom. He believes this movement towards the kingdom will deprive religions of their content of 'any object or point of reference.'[51]

Religions cannot stand still, Ratzinger insists, in a world that is moving with history. The Christian faith carries within itself the heritage of other great religions and opens it to the Logos, to true reason, which can make possible a real synthesis of technological rationality and religion. Christian mission must understand other religions more deeply and accept them at a more profound level, and other religions must recognize that their best elements can flourish when they are pointed towards Christ. In this way we can proceed on an intercultural search for the common truth.[52]

Following the teaching of St Augustine, Ratzinger states that Christianity is not based on myths or justified by political exigency but it is related to that divine presence that can be perceived by reason. Christianity is *religio vera* in the sense that it is not based on poetry and politics as the pagan religions, but on knowledge. For Küng, as we have seen, it is the human element that is the decisive factor concerning the truth of religion. Ratzinger argues that Christianity is the worship of the 'true God', and enlightenment is part of this religion; it embodies 'the victory of demythologization, the victory of knowledge ... and the victory of truth'.[53] It appears to be intolerant because it refuses to accept relativism and the interchangeability of gods or to be used for political purposes. But for Ratzinger, Christianity is not just one religion among others, but it represents the victory of perception and truth.

Ratzinger asserts that the Christian faith is convincing and its success in the early years of its foundation was due to its connection of faith with reason. Charity is the foundation of its belief – loving care for the suffering, poor and the weak. This is its inner power – love. The synthesis of reason, faith, and life makes Christianity a *religio vera*. He believes the only way to resolve the crisis of faith in Christianity in modern times is for love and reason to come together as the two pillars of life: 'the true reason is love, and love is the true reason.'[54]

This is obviously very different from Küng's approach, which regards religion as true as long as it promotes human welfare. He believes that insofar as a religion promotes the dignity of human beings, helps people to live a meaningful and dignified life, it is a true and good religion. It seems that Küng has substituted practice for truth.

THE CHURCH

According to Ratzinger, there is a dynamic impulse inherent in Christianity – it is not simply a network of institutions and ideas, but a living faith that develops again and again within the church. The dynamic of the conscience and the silent presence of God in our religion guide us along towards salvation. We have to continue searching for God's will, which is not fossilized in dogmas and institutions.[55]

Ratzinger reminds us that theology has an essentially ecclesiastical identity and it is not simply the private opinion of one person. The church as a living organism endures amid changes in history, but the idea of one theologian fades rapidly into insignificance.

Thus, theologians must work in the 'vital milieu' of the ecclesiastical community, and theology can remain historically relevant only if it acknowledges and participates in this environment. Ratzinger claims that the church transcends the narrowness of individuals and thus it can provide the condition that makes theological activity possible. He acknowledges that historical research and human sciences are privileged partners of the theologians, and he also calls for inner participation in the 'organic structure of the Church'.[56]

Küng, however, thinks of himself as a modern Erasmus when he calls for a revival of biblical thinking without biblicism, a renewal of tradition without traditionalism, and a restoration of Christian authority without authoritarianism. Erasmus was 'the first conscious European, the first militant friend of peace, the most eloquent advocate of a humanistic ideal warmly disposed toward the world and mind'. He was 'the irresolute Anti-Luther, the rationalistic early Enlightenment figure, the classical humanist'; he believed that we can be 'authentically human by being a Christian, and be a Christian by being human'.[57]

A year before he died, Erasmus wrote to Luther: 'Thus I put up with this Church, until I see a better one; and she is forced to put up with me, until I myself become better'.[58] Perhaps Küng thinks of himself as a loyal critic whom the Catholic Church must learn to accommodate. He says he has always understood his theological work as a service to the Roman Catholic Church.

In sum, the emphasis on *humanum* in theological investigation can be seen as part of the *Nouvelle Théologie* which ascribes an important role to history that had earlier been relegated to take second place to theological abstractions and speculations. Thus the 'old theology' or neo-scholasticism took dogmas as its point of departure and through deduction arrived at new insights compatible with the tenets of faith.[59]

Hans Küng, the *avant-garde* theologian, was keen to abandon such closed thinking and to resist this 'unworldly notional system'. He appeals to a positive theology which has its sources in the Bible and the concrete life of faith, and believes that a valid contribution to Catholic theology can only be carried out through critical source analysis.[60]

Joseph Ratzinger is able to embrace the difficult challenge of meeting diverse understandings of spiritual truth while defending the Catholic faith. He offers a more comprehensive and profound outlook regarding the theology of religions than does Küng's stress on the human element.

Nonetheless, examining the thought of Ratzinger, one finds that many of his theological insights are not contrary to Küng's more liberal outlook, although their approaches are different. Ratzinger stresses the particularity and primacy of the Christian religion, whereas Küng highlights the universal dimension of *humanum* as the criterion for true religion. Thus, their theological approaches can be summarized as particularity versus universality. The theologies of Ratzinger and Küng can complement each other and enable us to grasp more deeply the nature of the Christian belief and its relation to other religions.

THE ETHICAL–PRACTICAL BRIDGE

In his survey of various models, Paul Knitter, in his *Introducing Theologies of Religions*, reveals his preferential option for the ethical-practical bridge – concern for the sufferings of humanity and the earth – which is one of the bridges that Christians must cross in the mutuality model.[61] This ethical–practical bridge focuses on the common problems that world religions face: poverty, victimization, violence and patriarchy. Concerns of poverty and justice have become the topic of interreligious dialogue as most religious traditions seek to improve the well-being of their adherents. Besides human sufferings, there is also this urgent concern for the environment, the destruction of our planet and all the creatures on it.

Postmodern thinking may doubt the reality of common faith or common mystical experience, and postmodern societies are characterized by that lack of shared premises that Knitter acknowledged.[62] But he insists that it cannot deny the reality of human sufferings and the destruction of the environment due to industrialization and relentless consumption. Knitter rightly believes that if a religion has nothing to say about the reality of suffering in the world, it has lost its relevance. He stresses that there are many religions but only one earth, which is constantly being threatened by our hedonistic and consumeristic lifestyle. Thus the common ground of a threatened earth provides all religions with a common purpose.

Knitter states that a shared ethical dialogue will open doors and lead to effective sharing of religious experiences. This ethical approach also helps to avoid the danger of relativism as it decides whether a particular religious practice is able to bring about greater justice and peace to the people. In this kind of dialogue, the cries of the poor and the victims are a 'privileged voice' which can inform religious leaders of the realities of our broken world. For Knitter, just as the Kingdom is the focus of Jesus' preaching, so it must also be for the church. This Kingdom-centred or regnocentric approach will also help the church to understand itself in relation to other religious communities.

In spite of the many criticisms of his writings, from no less a person than Joseph Ratzinger, this chapter attempts to show that many of Knitter's theological ideas converge with the main thrust of Asian theology.[63] It seeks to demonstrate that his regnocentric approach is a sincere attempt to remedy the failure of the church to be relevant and prophetic.[64] Although there are limitations and shortcomings in his theological model, I will attempt to show how Knitter's approach is relevant and acceptable in Asian communities characterized by poverty and religious pluralism. Many theologians of religions try to justify their positions by criticizing Knitter, but I believe his writings have influenced Asian theological reflection more than have been acknowledged. First of all, I would like to set Knitter's theological crossing within a wider theological framework.

EXTRA MUNDUM NULLA SALUS

Knitter's ethical–practical approach in his theologies of religions can be seen as an affirmation of Edward Schillebeeckx's transformation of the official church axiom from *extra ecclesiam nulla salus* to *extra mundum nulla salus*.[65] Schillebeeckx describes a worldly process in which everyone on this planet experiences pain and suffering which are basic to human existence. These are the first stirrings of religious experience which he calls 'pre-religious experience'. Believers and agnostics possess this experience and it is the basis for solidarity between all people and a common commitment to create 'a better world with a human face'.[66] He also teaches that the human experience of suffering and evil is 'the basis and source of the fundamental "no" that men and women say to their actual situation of being-in-this-world'. It is an experience that no one can deny and 'indignation' is our basic experience of human existence. The goodness and beauty of life seems to be crushed by evil, hatred and abuse of power. But in spite of our wretchedness, we believe that the world can be improved and we are open to the unknown. Christians believe that God saves us through human beings and the secular event becomes the 'material of the "word of God"'.[67]

Thus, worldly processes have religious and human significance: 'Revelation presupposes a process meaningful to men and women, an event that already has relevance for them and liberates them, without direct reference to God.'[68] What is important is that good action, which liberates people, and only in secular history in which people are liberated for true humanity can God reveal himself. Schillebeeckx argues that God cannot reveal himself in the sufferings of humanity except as judgement of them. We see the face of God in the history of our liberation. It is not important whether you affirm or deny the existence of God but, 'Which side do you choose in the struggle between good and evil, between the oppressors and the oppressed?'[69]

The basis for Schillebeeckx's affirmation of history as liberating men and women for the good of humanity is God's saving history found in the structure of the Jewish–Christian revelation (Deuteronomy 25:5–9). Here the secular event of history is reread by those who believe in Yahweh and interpreted as salvation; believers in God have the insight that the Lord God saved the people from Egypt. They believed that God saved them in the particular human activity in the world and in history. He says, 'without Jesus' human career the whole of christology becomes an ideological superstructure'.[70] This means that only the human meaning of our historical process can become the basis of divine revelation.

Hence salvation history cannot be reduced to the history of Judaism and Christianity or the history of religions. It has to include the whole secular history which is already under the guidance of the liberating God. In other words, salvation comes from our secular history of which God is the liberator as well as the judge. Schillebeeckx asserts: 'The world and human history in which God wills to bring about salvation are the basis of the whole reality of faith; it is there that salvation is achieved in the first instance ... or salvation is rejected and disaster is brought about'.[71] Thus *extra mundum nulla salus* means that our world and history are the sphere of God's saving action in and through human mediation; salvation from God comes first of all in the worldly reality of our human existence and not primarily in the consciousness of the believers. An examination of some of Knitter's writings will reveal how closely he follows the axiom of Schillebeeckx's *extra mundum nulla salus*.

FROM ECCLESIOCENTRISM TO REGNOCENTRISM

In *Jesus and the Other Names*, Knitter tells us that since the Second Vatican Council, there has been a shift from an eccelsiocentric or church-centred understanding of mission to what Asian bishops call a regnocentric or Kingdom-centred view.[72] Today we no longer identify the church with the Kingdom of God: they are related but are not the same thing.[73] Thus we are being sent into the world not to build the church but the Kingdom of God: the church is to serve the Kingdom and not the other way round. Therefore the church lives out its true nature when it is Kingdom-centred and not self-centred. This also implies that the primary purpose of missionary endeavour is not to plant the church, but to establish the reign of God. Planting the church is important, but it is only a means to establish the Kingdom of God.[74] Knitter argues that the church is to witness to the Kingdom, to proclaim Jesus and to form disciples. In doing this, the church discovers that the mystery of God is actually everywhere, in various ways, and it does not have an exclusive claim. Therefore, the church must collaborate and dialogue with the various religious traditions, and thus makes 'specific contribution to the integral wholeness of the Kingdom'.[75]

In this Kingdom-centred mission theology, the church does not place itself at the centre but is at the service of the people. For only the Kingdom has the fullness of God's manifestation and therefore only the Kingdom is absolute. Knitter goes so far as to say that putting the Kingdom at the service of the church is a kind of idolatry. Hence, all our missionary activities such as planting the church, proclaiming the Word, dialoguing with other religions and so on must be subordinated to the Kingdom. As such, Knitter warns us that we have to be careful of traditional theological language about the Kingdom being fulfilled in the church.[76] We must avoid turning the 'fulfilling' role of the church into an idol; the church is only a 'fulfilling means for realizing God's Reign on Earth', but 'the church is not *the* means'. This is because there are other different fulfilling ways of appropriating the activity of the Spirit and realizing the Kingdom.[77]

THE SPIRIT

According to Knitter, our understanding of the church and its mission has traditionally been based almost exclusively on the mission of the Word, Jesus, the second person of the Trinity, but now we need to take into consideration the mission of the third person, the Spirit, in order to balance and expand our understanding of mission and the church. Our ecclesiology and missiology have placed too much emphasis on Christology and there is an urgent need to develop a comprehensive pneumatology. Knitter argues that we can only understand the church fully if we take into consideration the role of Jesus Christ as well as the Spirit.[78]

Knitter insists that the Spirit is not confined to 'the Spirit of Christ' and we must recognize the Spirit as really different from the Word: it is the Spirit who 'fills and renews the Earth' and who works beyond the confines of the church. The Kingdom of God is alive and active in the world through Jesus (the Word) and the Spirit filling the earth: these are two different ways in which it can be experienced by people. This means that Jesus and the Spirit are related but distinct. In other words, while the Spirit can never be understood and experienced without relating it to the Word, neither can the Spirit be reduced or subordinated to the Word: there is a 'hypostatic independence', which means there is real effective difference. Thus 'the economy of the Spirit is a consequence of the incarnation, originating from it (*Filoque*) but living out its own identity (its own *hypostasis*)'. At the same time, such independence is qualified in the sense that the economy of the Word and the Spirit are also bonded to each other in a relationship that is complete within the Godhead but still in a process of realizing itself.[79]

In view of the above Trinitarian theology, Knitter argues that we must acknowledge the working of the Spirit beyond the boundary of the church and in other religious traditions, which is different from the incarnate Word that is revealed in the church. The reign of God realized under the breadth of the Spirit can be seen as 'an all-comprehensive phenomenon of grace' which is an economy of grace distinct from the Word incarnate in Jesus.[80] This means that the Kingdom of God, which is independent, cannot be subordinated to the church just as the Spirit cannot be subordinated to the Word. Knitter also points out that the Kingdom of God has this worldly quality about it: to seek the Kingdom of God is to seek the welfare of others in the concrete sense, for God intends that all peoples and creatures have life abundantly. Thus mission is connected to the question of justice and peace, the distribution of material and spiritual goods. This implies that the spiritual and political conversion must be distinguished but not separated.

A Kingdom-centred ecclesiology must affirm other religious traditions as possible agents of saving grace and their members as co-workers for the Kingdom. Knitter claims that God's grace is also operative within the beliefs and practices of other religions and this grace must transform not only the human heart but society as well. This grace must enable us to create a new world of love and justice out of all the brokenness that we experience in our world today. Knitter writes: 'Like the Christian church, the religions of the world can be *simul justus et peccator*, both sinful and justified, both impediment to and instrument of the Kingdom.'[81] Knitter also claims that to hold up the Kingdom of God for interreligious dialogue is to call for a level playing field where members of different religious traditions can participate as equal partners.

If Christians believe in universal revelation, that 'God, after He spoke long ago to the fathers in the prophets in many portions and in many ways' (Hebrew

1:1), then what is made known to other religions must be respected by Christians. They must also converse with these 'other Words' because the Christian Word is incomplete without the other Words. This means respecting the religious texts of Hindus, Buddhists, Muslims and so on, while upholding the Bible as the Word of God.[82]

SOTERIOCENTRISM

In *One Earth Many Religions*, Knitter attempts to demonstrate that the widespread sufferings of humanity and environmental problems that threaten our planet must be the common concern of all religions. This confirms the 'global ethic' that has been proposed in many international and interreligious dialogues. Knitter insists that dialogue must be rooted in 'liberative praxis' and must provide a preferential option for the poor and thus proposes a 'globally responsible or liberative' model of theology of religions.[83]

According to Knitter, a genuine dialogue of religions seeks to find opportunity that arises out of the necessity for Christians to respond to the overwhelming suffering that is afflicting humankind. There is an urgency and moral obligation to help other Christians and non-Christians who are suffering. This means that a concern for *soteria* (salvation) in terms of economic well-being and justice can be a common platform for interfaith dialogue. Concern for people and the earth can be a theological key to 'understand the gospel in a more dialogical openness to other religions' and also provide a hermeneutical key to understand the differences in other religions with respect. He considers this approach a move towards a 'soteriocentric or salvation-centered focus'.[84]

Knitter reminds us that there is 'a common *context* that contains a common complex of *problems*' which is the sufferings of people and the planet.[85] He believes global responsibility for suffering and environmental problems can provide a motivation outside one's tradition to engage interreligious dialogue. People from various religious traditions can see the crisis we are facing and each tradition can look beyond itself, recognize the problem and respond to it.

LIBERATIVE PRAXIS

Praxis plays a crucial role in Knitter's call for a soteriocentric interreligious dialogue. This means the truth that matters to us is practical: it concerns our struggles to live a meaningful and dignified life. It is related to the practical wisdom or prudence to know the true and the good that is rooted in our moral life. Knitter believes that there is a common praxis for practical thinking available to all religious traditions when they search for the truth and this common content is the suffering of the poor and the abuse of the planet. The confrontation with these crises facing us can be the starting point for reflection and action on the part of all religious people committed to dialogue and conversation; they can be engaged in the 'shared project of transforming structures of injustice and ecological exploitation'.[86] Here Knitter is suggesting that praxis can be the hermeneutical key to open up interreligious dialogue which he admits is part of Western and Christian tradition.

PEDAGOGY OF THE POOR

Related to this liberative praxis, Knitter insists that we must give priority to listening to the voice of the victims who have to play a central role in our dialogue. The victims and those suffering from injustice, including those who fight for their cause, have a 'hermeneutical privilege'.[87] They must be given a privileged voice because of the overwhelming sufferings that they experience: it is a question of predominance and not an 'ontological priority of suffering'. Knitter also says that when those of us who come from the First World take seriously the reality of the poor and suffering, we are transformed and see the world differently: we become enlightened to the reality of domination and injustice.[88]

Knitter is aware of the fact that countless poor people are excluded from participating in dialogue, conversations and deliberating place in universities, parliaments and even in churches. He suggests that these excluded people must be included for they have a special voice in the conversation, their experience and testimony have a 'hermeneutical privilege' in our search for the truth and good.[89] Recognizing the privilege of the oppressed voices is not an option, but a crucial condition in interreligious dialogue.

Poor people are excluded from interreligious dialogue and even in forums where social justice and peace are being discussed. Aloysius Pieris says this is a real dilemma in the Asian church because theologians are not yet poor and the poor are not yet theologians. But this dilemma can be resolved at the grass-roots level in the local church where theologians and the poor are reconciled through mutual evangelization: the theologians 'are awakened into the liberative dimension of poverty and the poor are conscientized into the liberative potentialities of their religiousness.'[90] The appropriate model for the Asian church would be communities where the positive aspects of religion and poverty converged.

Thus the voices of the oppressed must play a privileged role in dialogue because without them we cannot detect the 'worm of ideology' in our language and 'to carry out a hermeneutical suspicion of our own tradition'.[91] Knitter insists that in our interfaith encounters, the poor and suffering and those who are concerned for the environment must be given a privileged place in our dialogue; those in power must listen and act with and for them.[92]

APPROACHES TO THE PROBLEM OF THE POOR

Yvon Ambroise presents three different approaches in which the church in India has tried to respond to the plight of the poor, which he describes as an evolutionary move from charity to people's organization. This development was influenced by the new awareness of the oppression of the poor within the church and social consciousness in society, and this response had a qualitative effect on the faith.[93]

The first approach is charity driven: the ideology behind this is that poverty cannot be eradicated, but can be lessened when the rich share with the poor. Thus almsgiving and charitable donation are encouraged as part of the corporal works of mercy. The second approach is the institutional based: this method tries to remove poverty by using its human and national resources fully through education and training people, the setting up of schools and hospitals.[94]

The third approach, consonant with Knitter's soteriocentrism, is the organization and participation of people. This response consists in organizing people at grass-roots level, among the poor and oppressed, in order to make them aware of their unjust situation so that they can be responsible for making a change for the better. Training programmes can be conducted to help people to fight against injustice. Christians and non-Christians can participate in this programme under the umbrella of social action group. The theological ideology behind this approach is that poverty is maintained by unjust socio-economic structures perpetuated by the rich and powerful. These structures can be changed if poor people organize themselves and are empowered to struggle for a more equitable society.[95]

THE ENLIGHTENMENT TRADITION

Kingdom-centred theology has been criticized on two grounds in the 1990 papal document, *Redemptoris Missio* (RM). First, to place human welfare as the main purpose of missionary activity is to reduce the role of the church to performing a social service: it becomes anthropocentric. In making human needs the focus of mission, the Kingdom becomes completely secularized. Thus only programmes and struggles for socioeconomic and political liberation matter and the transcendent aspect of mission is forgotten. This becomes an 'ideology of purely earthly progress'.[96]

Second, the Kingdom-centred missiology is so concerned in reducing the role of the church that it has also neglected Christ; there is a fear that Christians may lose their centring in Christ. The discussion on the mystery of creation and the need to protect our environment led to downgrading the importance of our salvation: 'they keep silent about the mystery of redemption'.[97] This encyclical teaches that 'the Kingdom cannot be detached either from Christ or from the Church'.[98] Therefore, although the Kingdom and the church can be distinguished, they cannot be separated.

Joseph Ratzinger characterized Knitter's model as the pragmatic approach to faith. He admits that working for peace, justice and the protection of the environment play an important role in our Christian life. But religions cannot tell us exactly what serves peace here and now, or how justice is to be implemented, or how our environment should be protected. These things must be worked out individually and rationally. And if we say that only one path is the correct one, 'religion is perverted into an ideological dictatorship, with a totalitarian passion that does not build peace but destroys it'.[99] Ratzinger insists that religion cannot be used as a practical-political tool where man tries to manipulate God. This would degrade God and man himself as well. Of course, this does not mean that we should not be educating people for peace, justice and love of our planet. It means that we do not turn our religion into a political moralism. He also asserts that in such an approach, truth is produced by praxis and this so-called 'practical theology' became fashionable when suddenly theologians became representatives of the neo-Marxist movement. There is a curious paradox here in which theologians and Marxists became strange bedfellows.[100]

Knitter is aware of these criticisms, but he assures us that even though the missionary and the social worker may share the same goal of working for the betterment of people, the Christian missionary possesses the vision and values of the gospel. It is a humanism infused with the Spirit that makes the work spiritual.[101] When the spirit is explicitly acknowledged, the charitable work will be more meaningful.

It would be naive to think that Knitter's theology of religions conforms squarely with the teachings of Asian bishops. There are a number of divergences that concern the role of Jesus Christ between both of them. First of all there is a significant difference between Knitter's and FABC's theology in terms of origin and development. Although Knitter and FABC's theologies are both regnocentric, Knitter's approach is characterized as reactionary liberal pluralism; his soteriocentrism and his theology must be seen within a larger Western context.

Gavin D'Costa's critique of Knitter aptly captures this context in which he is located. He argues that Knitter's theology of religions represents a form of pluralism that stems from the Enlightenment tradition begun by Kant. Although the stress on the poor is laudable, in D'Costa's view, ultimately this kind of pluralism hinders Knitter's political intentions. Kantian philosophy is attractive because it appeals to common universals, moving beyond petty religious interests. Jesus Christ then becomes a mere representative of truths.[102]

In contrast to Knitter, the FABC's Kingdom-centred approach emerges out of the Asian church's encounter with other religious traditions and experiences with the overwhelming poor population.[103] Unlike in the West, where the interests and awareness of other religions have occurred only recently, Christians in Asia have always been living side by side with Buddhists, Muslims and Hindus. Religious pluralism is a fact of daily life. Thus the point of departure of Asian theology of religions starts from its concrete experience with people of other faiths. Asian theologians have to reinterpret their faith and redefine their identity as they enter into dialogue with non-Christians.

Both FABC and Knitter agree that dialogue is crucial in the Asian context, but they disagree on the uniqueness of Christ. Knitter is against using absolutist language to depict the Saviour in dialogue; the Asian bishops do not consider the church's claim with regard to the centrality of Jesus Christ an obstacle to interfaith encounter. Naturally, as custodian of the faith, the Asian bishops would consider the uniqueness of Jesus Christ as a non-negotiable tenet of the faith. Knitter writes much about the problems connected to proclaiming the uniqueness of Jesus in interreligious dialogue. But Asian theologians are more interested in how the gospel is to be proclaimed and how the faith is to be reinterpreted in a way faithful to the Christian tradition and also meaningful to Asians. In response to this issue, the bishops have stressed the need to proclaim Jesus using symbols and images that are consonant with Asian sensibilities.

Knitter, on the other hand, writes about the relational understanding of the uniqueness of Jesus: the Saviour is to be understood in relation with other saviours.[104] Although Jesus is truly the Word of God, Knitter thinks that he is not the only word; he is 'God's universal, decisive and indispensable manifestation of saving truth and grace.'[105] According to Knitter, the creed and the other Christian dogmas about Jesus are to be interpreted symbolically as expressions of the church's experience of Christ. Here, Knitter's insight is contrary to the traditional church's teaching about Jesus as having an ontological foundation. Naturally, Knitter's teaching about the relational uniqueness of Jesus is not acceptable to Asian bishops because it alters the way in which the faith is proclaimed and it also deviates from what is central to Christianity.[106]

THE FAILURE OF THE CHURCH

In spite of the above shortcomings and limitations of his theological approach, I believe Knitter's crossing the ethical–practical bridge might find a home that is welcoming in Asia. This movement with its emphasis on dialogue is a step in the right direction when applied to the Asian context because of the presence of religious diversity and the immense poverty of the masses. The failure of the church in the past to adapt itself to the local culture and to respond to the struggles of the people prompts us to rethink evangelization and this is where Knitter's regnocentrism and soteriocentrism may prove to be relevant and acceptable.

Christianity has always been perceived as a foreign religion in Asia. Many mistakes were made in the past when missionaries quarrelled among themselves over methods of evangelization. In China, the unique claims of the Christian faith and the cultural superiority maintained by the Chinese made the clash between Christianity and the other religions unavoidable. Julia Ching rightly asserts that the worst mistakes were made when missionaries depended on gunboat diplomacy of the colonial government for their protection. These mistakes made them opportunists and even imperialists.[107] It is no wonder that when the communists took over China, Christianity had remained a Western missionary religion while Buddhism had thoroughly accommodated itself to the local culture.

In China, the church seems foreign because it is part of a well-structured international organization and is suspected of being controlled from abroad, dependent on foreign funds and personnel. In India, the church is linked to the colonial past, its educational institutions appear to be bearers of modernity, and there is thus a tension between tradition and modernity. These institutions are admired for the material values that they represent and not for the gospel they witness.[108]

Felix Wilfred makes the same point when he says that 'foreignness' characterized all the local churches in Asia. This is not because Christianity was introduced into the region from outside; Buddhism entered China, Japan and Thailand and so on and yet it is not considered alien. He says the main reason why Christianity has been perceived as a foreign religion is because local churches kept themselves aloof from the struggles of the common people.[109]

Throughout history, the Asian continent has been characterized by the search for the divine and for its lofty spiritual values. Wilfred reminds us that all the great religions in the world were born and nurtured in Asia and, thus, the Asian worldview, life and institutions are infused with remarkable religious sensitivity. This positive appreciation of other religions comes not from comparing doctrine or theological studies, but from direct experience with the encounter with people from different faiths. Our dialogue with them must be a 'dialogue of life'.[110]

About eighty percent of the people in Asia live in poverty and therefore the church cannot evangelize effectively without getting involved with the living reality of the poor, and such involvement has to be Christian without being ecclesiastical, as over the centuries the church expressed its concern for the poor through charitable works and later in development projects. Now the FABC wants to go beyond these approaches to become the church of the poor in its proclamation and lifestyle. This preferential option for the poor carried out as an act of faith is similar to Knitter crossing the ethical-practical bridge.

Asian churches should understand themselves as being on a mission in the world to build the Kingdom of God and not primarily to build itself, and the church would free itself from temptation to power that comes from numbers. Pieris asserts that every Asian culture has a 'soteriological nucleus' waiting to be discovered and assimilated into Christian consciousness.[111] An Asian theology of liberation is waiting to be discovered, and perhaps it is here that Knitter's ethical-practical approach in his theology of religions is the bridge that would lead to a recovery of the ancient revelation.

Conclusion

The Federation of Asian Bishops' Conferences[1]

T here is no theologian today who better represents the mainstream of
Western, European and contemporary theology than Joseph Ratzinger. He brings to his writings a formidable intellect that is at home
with the many theological currents that represent a normative Catholic position today. Having worked as a theologian in Europe both before and after
the Second Vatican Council, and having attended the Council as a *peritus*, he
has navigated all the currents that flowed into and sprang from the Council's
work. In his more recent works (writing in his private capacity), such as the
second volume of *Jesus of Nazareth*, he has shown a willingness to engage in
controversies and adopt new ideas. I conclude this book by examining how
and to what extent the understanding of the Federation of Asian Bishops'
Conferences (FABC) regarding religious pluralism differs from and converges
with Joseph Ratzinger's theological position.

The FABC recognizes the significant and positive elements in other religious traditions, especially their profound spiritual and ethical values. Asian
bishops have asserted that over the centuries, traditional non-Christian religions have been a source of strength and light for their communities. These
religions have been the authentic expression of the deepest spiritual longings
of the heart and have played an important role in the histories and cultures of
Asian societies. Like Ratzinger, the Asian bishops do not subscribe to a multiplicity of divine mediations that consider all religions to be equally valid. They
are convinced that 'the Spirit is leading them not to some nebulous syncretism
but to an organic integration of all that is good, true and beautiful in the traditions and cultures of their nations, into the vast treasures of the Christian
heritage.'[2]

The FABC has acknowledged the teaching of the Second Vatican Council concerning the presence of the Spirit beyond the confines of the visible church. It admits that the same Spirit who was active in the life, death and resurrection of Jesus and in the church, was also active among the peoples of Asia before the incarnation of Christ and is still active among them today. The understanding of the Spirit, as the 'author of plurality', fits well with the experience of the Asian churches. This experience of the Spirit as the agent of diversity and plurality enables us to overcome the temptation to move towards uniformity or of 'steamrolling all differences and forcing them into pre-conceived moulds and standardized patterns'.[3] At the same time, the Spirit of God also guides all nations, cultures and languages towards wholeness and harmony.

More importantly for our study of religious pluralism is the stress placed by the FABC on the existence of the presence of the Spirit in other religions in Asia, in the faith of the people, in their sacred books, creeds and cults, and in their commitment to the religious truths found in their traditions. Above all, it is the moral and religious values embodied in Asian religions that allow us to discover the presence of God through the Spirit. In concrete terms, we discover in these non-Christian religions, the 'fruits of the Spirit', such as goodwill, generosity, openness, compassion and a profound sense of God's presence in all things (Galations 5:22–23). A clear sign of the presence of the Spirit in the living faiths of Asia is the 'living out of the moral code' and the common desire to work for the alleviation of hunger and poverty, as well as for the promotion of justice and peace.[4]

The major religions of Asia, with their respective traditions, reveal to us the diverse ways of responding to God whose Spirit is active in all peoples. In the context of God's saving action through the Spirit, it follows that 'every religion is a historically and culturally conditioned response to the action of the Spirit, and therefore limited and partial'. Thus, religions must relate to and hold dialogue with one another in order to have a better grasp of the truth. In this regard, the Asian bishops have asserted that all the religions have an 'intrinsically *relative* character' to the extent that they are open to meaningful communication with other religions.[5] Thus the FABC proposes a model of the theology of religions called *receptive pluralism*: 'The presence of the Holy Spirit in and beyond the church in Asia may be perceived in a variety of ways. This is due, in part, to the fact that people encounter the Spirit in their context, which is pluralistic in terms of religions, culture and worldviews. In this light, we affirm a stance of *receptive pluralism*.'[6] This kind of pluralism is close to the approach of Joseph O'Leary when he writes: 'The pluralism I am advocating is not a pluralism erected into a system, wherein a conceptual relativism on the empirical level would issue in a flattening out of differences at the transcendental level. Rather it is a contextual pluralism emphasizing the finite and historical character of every religious discourse.'[7]

Asian bishops acknowledged that no community's religious experience is complete in itself and that they must all be open to the experiences of other faiths. Therefore, the FABC affirms receptive pluralism as a way to respond to the promptings of the Holy Spirit. This means there is a complementarity among the various religions, consistent with the plurality and unity of God's saving plan. This idea suits the Asian psyche well, with its stress on harmony as a way of coping with the tension between unity and diversity.[8] Thus, beyond the extremes of exclusivism and inclusivism, the FABC proposes a pluralism that resonates well with the reality of constitutive plurality in the continent.

Receptive pluralism is an effort by the FABC to express a theology of religion rooted in the Asian reality. In such a vision, nothing is absolute in itself, but everything, even opposites such as *yin–yang*, is related to everything else.[9] Though differences among religions exist, they are not irreconcilable and have their 'true value in the profound interrelation and harmony that unites all aspects of reality'.[10] Wary of the danger of 'dubious syncretism', the FABC stresses an integration that is 'profound and organic in character'. It teaches that the religions of Asia have a crucial role to play in God's economy of salvation by promoting 'peace, communion and a more humane way of life to all peoples in Asia'. Asian bishops believe the religious traditions of Asia have been endowed with 'creative and redemptive forces' which can change the world according to God's plan.[11]

With reference to the relationship between Christianity and other faiths, Joseph Ratzinger writes:

> Christianity stands at one and the same time in both a positive and a negative relation to the religions of the world: it recognizes itself as being linked with them in the unity of the concept of a covenant relationship and lives out of the conviction that the cosmos and its myth, just like history and its mystery, speak of God and can lead men to God; but it is equally aware of a decided No to other religions and sees in them a means by which man seeks to shield himself from God instead of leaving himself open to his demands.[12]

It is obvious Ratzinger favours the Abrahamic religions – Christianity, Islam and Judaism – which are related to one another through one ancestral covenant.

Ratzinger's main concern is that religious pluralism dilutes the essential message of Christianity and the unique role of Jesus Christ as the Saviour of the world. Instead of pluralism, he emphasizes unity and harmony. Although he accepts pluralism in the secular world, he fears pluralism in the church would lead to a relativism which treats all religious beliefs as equally valid. Ratzinger sees religious pluralism as a problem and a challenge to the church to continue to proclaim the gospel. The situation is even more urgent in the face of aggressive secularism in the West. The publication of *Dominus Iesus* (2000) by the CDF during Cardinal Ratzinger's tenure as prefect, was meant to correct what he perceived as dangerous pluralistic theologies that he classified as 'ideologies'.

Relativism maintains that there are many versions of truth that vary according to whoever holds them and their particular view of reality. A pluralism that regards every view of reality to be of equal value leads to relativism. This kind of relativism will only destroy the richness of pluralism.[13] The FABC teaches that pluralism need not always involve a 'radical subjectivism and relativism' in the sense of levelling all points of view. At the same time, the Asian bishops are also aware that pluralistic and democratic societies have resulted in the development of 'excessive individualism and subjectivism, and a consequential relativizing of all reality'.[14] Asian bishops, thus, reject a relativism that claims all points of view of reality are equal.

The FABC promotes a pluralism that supports the 'human search for an underlying unity that enables us to understand plurality better'. Asian philosophies and theologies have focused on the 'unity and harmony behind pluralism'.[15] In tandem, both Joseph Ratzinger and the Asian bishops favour unity and harmony in our pluralistic societies. However, Ratzinger, as a critic of Western Enlightenment, fears that religious pluralism could lead to the relativism that seeks to level all the differences between the various religions. Asian bishops, on the other hand, because of their experience in this continent in which many ancient religions flourished and gave meaning to the lives of millions, affirm pluralism as a gift from God. The concern of Ratzinger may be relevant in Europe due to the influence of post-Enlightenment ideas. However, Christianity has flourished in Asia without the influence of this liberal atmosphere.

The theology of receptive pluralism suggested by the FABC means the Asian bishops look upon non-Christians not only as fellow pilgrims on the road to the Kingdom of God, but also as co-builders of that same kingdom in history. Hence, the ancient religious traditions in Asia are active partners in the realization of God's plan of salvation. This, in effect, calls upon the church to abandon its ghetto mentality. Receptive pluralism does not view the church as the only means to realize the Kingdom of God, and so it encourages other religions to join forces to build a better world, making the reign of God a concrete reality in Asia. The Kingdom of God is a gift entrusted to all humanity and, thus, every religion, every people and culture must be responsible for it. Therefore, the church has no monopoly on the Kingdom but is co-partner with members of other religions to realize it on earth.[16]

From the start, the FABC documents described the pilgrimage towards the Kingdom as a journey that involved all humankind, with particular focus on Asia, its peoples and the pluralism that characterizes them. This pilgrimage is, thus, an inter-religious project.[17] The Asian bishops point out that God's reign has a communitarian and social dimension because the Kingdom of God is about relationships and 'the Christian travels not alone, but in community'.[18] Diversity and plurality in Asian, multicultural, religious societies are not opposed to the building of the Kingdom of God, but are actually necessary for its realization.

The FABC is keenly aware that the struggle for human liberation is not confined to the Christian community alone, much less to the church. The bishops acknowledge the many great religious traditions in Asia that have formed the basis of the establishment and growth of cultures and nations in this vast continent. In solidarity with them, they seek the flourishing of the human person and the transformation of Asia.[19] Thus, it is clear that the FABC adopts an open attitude towards other religions because of its understanding of the reign of God as a universal reality, extending beyond the confines of the church. The Kingdom of God unites us all in spite of differences in our religious beliefs.

Joseph Ratzinger admits that the church can learn from the 'historically evolving currents of theology'. He writes: 'Every new situation of humanity also opens new sides of the human spirit and new points of access to reality. Thus, in her encounter with the historical experience of humanity, the Church can be led ever more deeply into the truth and perceive new dimensions of it that could not have been understood without these experiences.'[20] However, Ratzinger is not open to the idea that other religions can be co-builders of the Kingdom of God. Critical of politicized theologians, he is afraid that such an interpretation would imply that 'the Kingdom of God becomes the product of the human act of liberation'.[21] He believes that a way of interpreting the church must be compatible with its 'base memory' and the text of scripture, otherwise it will just be an ideology originating from a particular period.[22] Ratzinger associates the Kingdom of God with Jesus himself: 'the Kingdom was promised, what came was Jesus'. However, Jesus is never alone; for he came to gather the new people, an assembly we recognize as the church.[23]

Ratzinger's ecclesiology maintains that the Kingdom of God is identified with the person of Jesus Christ and was realized in his life, death and resurrection. Jesus did not merely proclaim the Kingdom of God – he *is* the Kingdom of God.[24] The invitation to believe in this good news – the gospel – implies believing in Jesus Christ. Since Jesus also founded the church to continue his work of redemption, Ratzinger argues, the church thus becomes the visible realization of the Kingdom. This means that proclaiming the church and establishing the church are the means of building the Kingdom of God on earth. Ratzinger is critical of the Kingdom-centered approach in the theology of religions. This approach teaches that all religions will move towards realizing the Kingdom of God. According to him, this is close to relativism and will deprive religion of its message and identity. Ratzinger also has the fear that such regnocentric theology will weaken the church's missionary imperative because it implies that people can reach the divine through their own religious traditions, without the need to convert to Christianity.[25]

Critical of those who separate the Kingdom of God from the church, Ratzinger insists it was Jesus who proclaimed the Kingdom of God, a proclamation that gave birth to the church. However, in the Asian context, with its plurality of religions and cultures and massive poverty, some believe it is more appropriate to stress the reign of God rather than the church, since the church is foreign to most people.

The ecclesiology of the FABC characterizes the church as the 'Church of the Poor' and the 'Servant Church'. The Asian bishops insist that if the church wants to become part of the life of the continent, it should ally itself with the multitude of Asian poor. The church cannot isolate itself by being seen to be an affluent institution surrounded by people who lack the basic necessities of life. It should bear witness to 'evangelical simplicity' and reach out to the poor. The church should also speak out for the rights of the disadvantaged and the powerless against all forms of injustice. The FABC teaches that the church cannot compromise itself by consorting with the wealthy and powerful in our own countries.[26]

Not only must the church in Asia be the church *of* the poor, it must also be *with* the poor, sharing their lives, aspirations and struggles to the extent of becoming a 'poor Church'. One document of the FABC calls for achieving the goal of becoming a poor church through 'inculturation', in form of the local church living in 'solidarity with the poor, their traditions, customs and ways of life'.[27] It calls upon the local church to conform to the 'pattern of the

Suffering Servant of Yahweh' so that it can successfully bring the living Christ to Asia.[28] Just as Christ wished to be identified with the naked, the hungry, the thirsty and the imprisoned, the church in Asia must also bear witness to Christ through its commitment to the poor.

This idea of being the church of the poor and the church with the poor also means we must get rid of an 'ecclesiocentric attitude' that places institutional interests above the needs of people. An Asian church that is more interested in the preservation of its structures, schools, hospitals and bureaucracy than in serving the poor cannot be a credible witness to the gospel.[29] Thus, Asian bishops have come to realize that the church has projected images that go against the values of the gospel. Now is the time we must renew the church, so that it is a true servant of the cause of justice and peace.

A servant church has no fear of becoming a minority for it is a pilgrim church journeying towards the Kingdom. As a community of faith, the church is not centred on itself but on Christ. The servant church, in its teachings, clearly makes a distinction between the gospel and its own doctrinal interpretation of the gospel. In its daily existence, the church 'puts doing the truth before formulations of doctrine'. It reflects the values of the Kingdom of God and not of those in power. There is no dichotomy between public role and personal faith, no social segregation between the ordained hierarchy and the laity.[30]

The definition of the local church embraced by the Asian bishops suggests an 'ecclesiology from below', in contrast to Ratzinger's 'ecclesiology from above'. Ratzinger insists that the church is not a human construct but a sacramental gift from God. Suspicious that the image of the church as the 'church of the poor' and the 'servant church' smacks of Marxist influence, his preference is for an ecclesiology of communion that avoids dividing the church into rich and poor. Fearful that expressions such as 'people of God' and 'church of the poor' might turn into political slogans, Ratzinger emphasizes the vertical dimension of ecclesiology. He is critical of those who reduce the ecclesiology of communion to a preoccupation with the relations between the local churches and the universal church.

The primary focus of the Asian bishops, in their task of evangelization, is the building of a truly local church. But Ratzinger cautions against the horizontal idea of communion with its focus on self-determination and autonomy that he believes is dominating the church. While he recognizes the need to correct the excesses of Roman centralization, he insists on the ontological and temporal priority of the universal church over particular churches. Ratzinger regards local churches in different places as distinctive expressions of the universal church of Christ. This means we cannot fashion or construct a church according to our own ideas because the local church has its ecclesiality in and from the universal church. Ultimately, he argues that the relationship between the universal church and the particular churches is a mystery, so we cannot compare the church to any human organization.

As a high-ranking prelate with enormous responsibilities towards the entire church, it is natural for Joseph Ratzinger to emphasize the universality of the church. Asian bishops, however, need to establish, in cooperation with other members of their communities, local churches that are involved in the struggles of the people. In the vision of the FABC, the church in the pluralistic context of Asia should acknowledge that the reign of God is at work in the socio-political, cultural and religious situations in Asia, and should enter into dialogue with people working in these situations.[31] This is due to the fact that the church is not the only instrument of the Kingdom. It serves and promotes the Kingdom together with other members of the reign of God. The church must help to realize the values of the Kingdom so that these values can be inscribed deeply into the fabric of Asian society. Conscious that it does not have a monopoly on the Spirit of Christ, for the Spirit blows where it will, the church must collaborate with other religious communities for the sake of human development and, eventually, the salvation of all.

Asian bishops, together with other Christians, members of other religions and all people of goodwill hope the church will be a 'catalyst' for justice and peace and, so, make the Kingdom of God a reality in Asia. This involves facilitating dialogue among different socio-political forces, religions and cultures.[32] Dialogues among different faiths should lead to a 'better articulation and expression of the unifying and liberative potential of each religion', and should be conducted for the realization of justice, peace and protection of the environment as well. To perform this task well, the church needs to undergo a deep transformation in order to become a 'truly participative Church' which works with believers of other religions for a 'communion of all life'.[33] It also calls for a new style of leadership that encourages people to have initiative and to develop their potential. In order to do this, the laity must be empowered to have an active role in the church. The marginalized and the poor must also be heard in the church.[34]

The call for a participative church worries Joseph Ratzinger because he thinks it promotes a kind of Marxist interpretation of the Bible with its emphasis on equality: the Kingdom of God now becomes no more than a classless society. The church as envisioned by the Asian bishops appears to Ratzinger to be the establishment of a popular church, in the service of the

Kingdom of God, siding with the poor, against the rich and powerful. As we have seen, Ratzinger regards this kind of reading of scripture and signs of the times not as theology, but as an ideology arising from a specific time and place. The reform of the church that Ratzinger advocates is not in the form of structural change, but a renewal of faith in each individual that involves a personal admission of sin. What the church needs, he believes, is not managers but martyrs. Reform of the church implies the conversion of sinners and not the transformation of churches.[35]

Further, as we have seen, Ratzinger's view of the church-world relationship is dualistic and Manichean in outlook. This pessimistic outlook on the world, conditioned by his reading of Augustine and Bonaventure, results in his preference for an authoritarian, hierarchical model of leadership within the church, which he believes would lead our society back to God. In contrast to this traditional Western dualistic view of the church versus the world, in the East we have an organic approach to reality. According to the FABC, 'wherein the whole, the unity, is the sum-total of the web of relationships, and interaction of the various parts with each other ... The parts are understood in terms of their mutual dependence.'[36] Some prefer the term 'organic pluralism' to 'receptive pluralism' because it implies diversity as well as the acceptance of opposition.

It is important to emphasize that, in spite of his negative attitude towards religious pluralism and his insistence on the superiority of the Catholic faith, Joseph Ratzinger is not blind to truths found in other religious traditions. In fact, he has supported an inclusivist position that does not lead to the absorption of one religion by another or syncretism. It is an inclusivism that advocates the transformation of a pluralism, where all religions are deemed to be equally valid, to a plurality, where different religions coexist together in harmony, each striving towards the truth. Ratzinger recognizes that we must look for what is positive in other religious traditions because they can also contain the precious pearl of wisdom. At the same time, he admits that religions can be perverted and destructive.[37] Agreeing with Karl Barth, Ratzinger warns that a 'Christian can succumb to sickness and become superstitious' and, thus, personal faith must always be 'purified on the basis of truth'.[38] This constant search for the truth lies at the heart of Joseph Ratzinger's theology.

The relentless quest for the truth leads Ratzinger to adopt an open inclusivism that acknowledges that there are truths that Christianity can discover in other religious traditions. Critical of the tired faith of Europe, he admits that the religious commitment of non-Christians puts Christians to shame. These non-Christians have something to offer to Christians and, thus, it was wrong to destroy the religious culture of the people, as the early missionaries sought to do. This has great implications for our understanding of mission, especially when Asian churches face immense challenges in proclaiming the gospel in a continent that is the most populous and pluralistic and least Christian in the world. Asian churches need to establish a new relationship with the great religions and traditions existing in the continent. In fact, Ratzinger recognizes that we must undertake our mission with greater sensitivity to the cultural traditions of people. In this way Christians, non-Christians and even people with no religious beliefs can proceed together to search for the common truth that unites us all.

In spite of his inclusivism, Joseph Ratzinger has generally been resistant to many of the new theological ideas coming from Asia and has opposed some important Asian theologians as we have discussed in earlier chapters. However, his willingness to move the Catholic tradition forward based on solid scholarship – even when it goes against accepted former norms – makes him a significant figure whom we should try to understand. Where he has set up barriers, particularly in areas that directly affect issues of great relevance to the Asian churches, it is important to determine his reasoning in each case. It is critical that Catholic theologians seek to understand where the open and closed doors are. Even though Ratzinger is no longer the reigning pope, his position on religious pluralism will continue to be dominant in the church.

Finally, Asian theologians could work better, in collaboration with Western theologians, to deepen their insights in proclaiming the good news. We need to transform what has largely been an antagonistic relationship between Asian theologians and the Vatican into a productive dialogue. This can be achieved by understanding the theological fault lines between the East and the West – fault lines that can be plainly seen by studying the thought of this bastion of Western theology, the Bavarian theologian, Pope Emeritus Benedict XVI.

Notes

INTRODUCTION

1. D. Vincent Twomey SVD, *Pope Benedict XVI: The Conscience of Our Age* (San Francisco: Ignatius Press, 2007), 70.

2. Ibid. 65.

3. Ibid. 67–8. See also Joseph Ratzinger, *Truth and Tolerance* (San Francisco: Ignatius Press, 2004), 62–3.

4. Joseph Ratzinger, *A Turning Point For Europe* (San Francisco: Ignatius Press, 1994), 43.

5. See Jacques Dupuis SJ, *Toward a Christian Theology of Religious Pluralism* (Maryknoll, NY: Orbis Books, 1997), 84–109.

6. Paul Hedges, *Controversies in Interreligious Dialogue and the Theology of Religions* (London: SCM Press, 2010), 38–9.

7. Ibid. 42.

8. Ibid. 45.

9. Ibid. 48. See also Kathryn Tanner, *Theories of Cultures* (Minneapolis: Fortress Press, 1997), 66.

10. Robert J. Schreiter, *The New Catholicity: Theology between the Global and the Local* (Maryknoll, NY: Orbis Books, 1997), 2. See also Peter C. Phan, 'Doing Theology in the Context of Cultural and Religious Pluralism: An Asian Perspective', *Louvain Studies* 27 (2002), 534.

11. Quoted in Peter C. Phan, 'Doing Theology in the Context of Cultural and Religious Pluralism: An Asian Perspective', *Louvain Studies* 27 (2002), footnote 42.

12. Robert J. Schreiter, *The New Catholicity: Theology between the Global and the Local* (Maryknoll, NY: Orbis Books, 1997), 49.

CHAPTER 1: FOUNDATIONS

1. Joseph Ratzinger, *Pilgrim Fellowship of Faith* (San Francisco: Ignatius Press, 2005), 209.

2. Ibid. 210.

3. Ibid. 210–11.

4. Ibid. 211–12.

5. Ibid. 212–13.

6. Ibid. 213–14.

7. Ibid. 215.

8. Joseph Ratzinger, *Milestones: Memoirs, 1927–1977* (San Francisco: Ignatius Press, 1998), 9.

9. Ibid. Though an intellectual, Ratzinger always expresses great admiration for the 'simple faithful' like his parents, who were the bearers of the true faith. As prefect of the CDF, Ratzinger stresses the magisterium's role in defending orthodoxy so as to protect the simple faithful.

10. Aidan Nichols OP, *The Thought of Pope Benedict XVI* (London: Burns & Oates, 2007), 1.

11. John L. Allen, *Pope Benedict XVI* (New York: Continuum, 2000), 4. Perhaps this explains why Ratzinger is uncomfortable with the pluralist theology of religion. He has the tendency to generalize all Asian religions, lumping them together under the category of 'mysticism'.

12. Ibid. 10.

13. Joseph Ratzinger, *Milestones: Memoirs, 1927–1977* (San Francisco: Ignatius Press, 1998), 23.

14. Ibid. 33.

15. John L. Allen, *Pope Benedict XVI* (New York: Continuum, 2000), 23.

16. Joseph Ratzinger, *The Ratzinger Report* (San Francisco: Ignatius Press, 1998), 166.

17. Joseph Ratzinger, *Milestones: Memoirs, 1927–1977* (San Francisco: Ignatius Press, 1998), 27.

18. John L. Allen, *Pope Benedict XVI* (New York: Continuum, 2000), 24.

19. Joseph Ratzinger, *Milestones: Memoirs, 1927–1977* (San Francisco: Ignatius Press, 1986), 42.

20. Joseph Ratzinger, *The Ratzinger Report* (San Francisco: Ignatius Press, 1998), 168.

21. John L. Allen, *Pope Benedict XVI* (New York: Continuum, 2000), 3. However, Vincent Twomey, a former student of Ratzinger, disagrees with Allen's analysis, classifying it as 'appealing as a sound bite' but it 'does not stand up to scrutiny'. He argues that according to Ratzinger himself, 'the best antidote to totalitarianism is the upright conscience typically associated with the poor and the weak'. D. Vincent Twomey SVD, *Pope Benedict XVI: The Conscience of Our Age* (San Francisco: Ignatius Press, 2007), 166–7.

22. Ibid. 17. Concerning Allen's claims that 'Hitler came to power on the back of Catholic support', ibid. 27, Twomey says it is a 'serious misinterpretation of events' for which Allen gives no evidence. He accuses Allen of trying to cast a shadow over Ratzinger's youth by following some 'very biased reading of the historical events'. Twomey, *Pope Benedict XVI: The Conscience of Our Age* (San Francisco: Ignatius Press, 2007), 168.

23. Joseph Ratzinger, *Milestones: Memoirs, 1927–1977* (San Francisco: Ignatius Press, 1998), 15.

24. Joseph Ratzinger, *The Ratzinger Report* (San Francisco: Ignatius Press, 1998), 168.

25. Joseph Ratzinger, *The Nature and Mission of Theology* (San Francisco: Ignatius Press, 1995), 45.

26. Ibid. 46.

27. Ibid. 48.

28. Quoted in Anton Wessels, *Europe: Was it Ever Really Christian?* (London: SCM Press, 1994), 163.

29. Anton Wessels, *Europe: Was it Ever Really Christian?* (London: SCM Press, 1994), 163–4.

30. David Gibson, *The Rule of Benedict* (New York: HarperCollins, 2006), 147.

31. Joseph Ratzinger, *Milestones: Memoirs, 1927–1977* (San Francisco: Ignatius Press, 1998), 42.

32. Ibid. 43.

33. Ibid.

34. Ibid. 44.
35. Ibid. 45.
36. Ibid. 48.
37. Ibid. 50.
38. Ibid. 51.
39. Ibid. 52.
40. Ibid.
41. Ibid. 52–3.
42. Ibid. 53.
43. Ibid. 53–4.
44. Quoted in Joseph Ratzinger, *Many Religions – One Covenant* (San Francisco: Ignatius Press, 1999), 25.
45. Ibid. 36.
46. See John L. Allen, *Pope Benedict XVI* (New York: Continuum, 2000), 251.
47. Joseph Ratzinger, *Jesus of Nazareth: Holy Week: From the Entrance into Jerusalem to the Resurrection* (San Francisco: Ignatius Press, 2011), 44.
48. Quoted in Joseph Ratzinger, *Jesus of Nazareth: Holy Week: From the Entrance into Jerusalem to the Resurrection* (San Francisco: Ignatius Press, 2011), 44.
49. Ibid. 45. According to James Roberts, there has been improvement and success in Jewish–Catholic relations. Benedict's papacy 'has been characterised by the "best relations ever between Church and Rabbinate", according to Israel's Chief Rabbi Yona Metzger. Israel's Chief Sephardic Rabbi Shlomo Amar called the Pope a "justice warrior" and said he should be commended for his "steadfast fight against any expression of anti-Semitism and Holocaust denial, inside and outside the Church". 'Viewpoints: Successes and failures of Benedict XVI', *BBC News*, www.bbc.co.uk/news/world-europe-21429808.
50. Lieven Boeve and Gerard Mannion, eds, *The Ratzinger Reader* (London: T & T Clark, 2010), 2.
51. Ibid. 2–3.
52. Ibid. 3. In many of Ratzinger's writings, his main concern is to defend the integrity of the faith against modern adaptation. He thinks that there are 'thoughtless people who always uncritically accept what is new as necessarily better' and thus, exchange the 'lump of gold' (faith) for a 'whetstone' (new interpretation of the faith) which they think will give them complete freedom. Joseph Ratzinger, *Introduction to Christianity* (San Francisco: Ignatius Press, 2004), 31.
53. Ibid.
54. Ibid. 4.
55. Ibid. 6.
56. 'It goes without saying that this book is in no way an exercise of the magisterium, but is solely an expression of my personal search "for the face of the Lord"' (cf. Psalm 27:8). Joseph Ratzinger, *Jesus of Nazareth* (London: Bloomsbury, 2007), xxiii.
57. Joseph Ratzinger, *Salt of the Earth* (San Francisco: Ignatius Press, 1997), 33.
58. Ibid. 61.
59. Quoted in Tracey Rowland, *Ratzinger's Faith* (New York: Oxford University Press, 2008), 3.
60. Quoted in Aidan Nichols OP, *The Thought of Pope Benedict XVI* (London: Burns & Oates, 2007), 17.
61. Ibid. 27.
62. Joseph Ratzinger, *Salt of the Earth* (San Francisco: Ignatius Press, 1997), 80.
63. Joseph Ratzinger, *The Ratzinger Report* (San Francisco: Ignatius Press, 1998), 45.

64. Ibid. 46.

65. Aidan Nichols OP, *The Thought of Pope Benedict XVI* (London: Burns & Oates, 2007), 21.

66. Ibid. 20.

67. Ibid. 21.

68. Quoted in Aidan Nichols OP, *The Thought of Pope Benedict XVI* (London: Burns & Oates, 2007), 22.

69. Aidan Nichols OP, *The Thought of Pope Benedict XVI* (London: Burns & Oates, 2007), 23.

70. Ibid. 28.

71. Quoted in Aidan Nichols OP, *The Thought of Pope Benedict XVI* (London: Burns & Oates, 2007), 28.

72. Aidan Nichols OP, *The Thought of Pope Benedict XVI* (London: Burns & Oates, 2007), 29.

73. Ibid. 31.

74. Joseph Ratzinger, *The Ratzinger Report* (San Francisco: Ignatius Press, 1998), 79.

75. Joseph Ratzinger, *Salt of the Earth* (San Francisco: Ignatius Press, 1997), 66.

76. Vincent Twomey SVD, *Pope Benedict XVI: The Conscience of Our Age* (San Francisco: Ignatius Press, 2007), 47.

77. Aidan Nichols OP, *The Thought of Pope Benedict XVI* (London: Burns & Oates, 2007), 34.

78. Joseph Ratzinger, *Milestones: Memoirs, 1927–1977* (San Francisco: Ignatius Press, 1998), 104.

79. See Joseph Ratzinger, *Milestones: Memoirs, 1927–1977* (San Francisco: Ignatius Press, 1998), 107–9.

80. Ibid. 108.

81. Ibid.109.

82. D. Vincent Twomey SVD, *Pope Benedict XVI: The Conscience of Our Age* (San Francisco: Ignatius Press, 2007), 52.

83. Ibid.

84. Ibid. 53.

85. Ibid. 52.

86. Joseph Ratzinger, *Milestones: Memoirs, 1927-1977* (San Francisco: Ignatius Press, 1998), 110.

87. Aidan Nichols OP, *The Thought of Pope Benedict XVI* (London: Burns & Oates, 2007), 36.

88. Gediminas T. Jankunas, *The Dictatorship of Relativism* (New York: St Pauls, 2011), 52–3.

89. He made this remark in reference to the threat of liberation theology. See Joseph Ratzinger, *The Ratzinger Report* (San Francisco: Ignatius Press, 1998), 175.

90. Quoted in Aidan Nichols OP, *The Thought of Pope Benedict XVI* (London: Burns & Oates, 2007), 44.

91. Aidan Nichols OP, *The Thought of Pope Benedict XVI* (London: Burns & Oates, 2007), 43.

92. D. Vincent Twomey SVD, *Pope Benedict XVI: The Conscience of Our Age* (San Francisco: Ignatius Press, 2007), 157.

93. Ibid.157–8.

94. Ibid. 158.

95. Joseph Ratzinger, *Principles of Catholic Theology: Building Stones for a Fundamental Theology* (San Francisco: Ignatius Press, 1987), 60.

96. D. Vincent Twomey SVD, *Pope Benedict XVI: The Conscience of Our Age* (San Francisco: Ignatius Press, 2007), 48.

97. Ibid. 50.

98. Lieven Boeve and Gerard Mannion, eds, *The Ratzinger Reader* (London: T & T Clark, 2010), 7.

99. Ibid. 8.

100. Ibid. I, however, agree with Keith Ward, who through his own pastoral experience suggests that the issue of truth is not a major concern in the lives of most believers. One may join a religion for many other reasons: social relations, aesthetic satisfaction, moral and psychological support. Keith Ward, 'The Truth and Diversity of Religion', in Philip L. Quinn, Kevin Meeker, eds, *The Philosophical Challenge of Religious Diversity* (Oxford: Oxford University Press, 2000), 111.

101. Ibid.

102. Joseph Ratzinger, *Principles of Catholic Theology: Building Stones for a Fundamental Theology* (San Francisco: Ignatius Press, 1987), 16.

103. Ibid.

104. Ibid.17.

105. Joseph Ratzinger, *Milestones: Memoirs, 1927–1977* (San Francisco: Ignatius Press, 1998), 54.

106. Ibid. 57.

107. John L. Allen, *Pope Benedict XVI* (New York: Continuum, 2000), 235.

108. Ibid.

109. Ibid. 236.

110. Joseph Ratzinger, 'Christ, Faith and the Challenge of Cultures', given in Hong Kong to the presidents of the Asian bishops' conferences and the chairmen of their doctrinal commissions during a 2–5 March 1993 meeting, www.ewtn.com/library/curia/ratzhong.htm

111. Joseph Ratzinger, *The Ratzinger Report* (San Francisco: Ignatius Press, 1998), 29.

112. Ibid. 30.

113. Ibid.

114. 'Pope resignation: Full text', *BBC News*, www.bbc.co.uk/news/world-europe-21412609

CHAPTER 2: RELIGIOUS PLURALISM

1. Joseph Ratzinger, *Theological Highlights of Vatican II* (New York: Paulist Press, 1966), 246. Ilaria Morali is also of the opinion that in the last three centuries of Catholic theology, there is no evidence to lead one to think that non-Christian religions have salvific value. Ilaria Morali, 'The Travail of Ideas in the Three Centuries Preceding Vatican II (1650–1964)', in Karl J. Becker and Ilaria Morali, eds, *Catholic Engagement with World Religions* (Maryknoll, NY: Orbis Books, 2010), 120–1.

2. Ibid.

3. Ibid. 247.

4. Ratzinger prefers the term 'interculturality' and thinks that the idea of inculturation seems to imply that a 'culturally naked faith' could be transplanted into a religiously indifferent culture in such a way that the two agents, unknown to each other before, meet and fuse. Ratzinger says just as there is no such thing as a 'culture-free faith', there is also no such thing as a 'religion-free culture'. His idea of interculturality suggests that the meeting of two cultures can take place in such a way that they do not absorb, but enrich each other. Joseph Ratzinger, *Truth and Tolerance* (San Francisco: Ignatius Press, 2004), 64. Aylward Shorter is more critical when he writes that Ratzinger 'went on to imply that the Christian faith is communicated through Western culture and to say that this culture is "fused" with the evangelized culture'. Ratzinger's dislike of the term 'inculturation' is apparently based on his opposition to an authentic re-expression of the faith in terms of the evangelized culture. Shorter thus calls Ratzinger an 'exponent of Western monoculturalism'. Aylward Shorter, *Evangelization and Culture* (London: Geoffrey Chapman, 1994), 90.

5. Lieven Boeve and Gerard Mannion, eds, *The Ratzinger Reader* (London: T & T Clark, 2010), 174. Actually, when we speak of religious pluralism corresponding to the will of God, we are in accord with the teaching of scripture regarding the universal salvific will of God, the intuitions of the Second Vatican Council and the church fathers. Claude Geffré, 'Double Belonging and the Originality of Christianity as a Religion', in Catherine Cornille, ed., *Many Mansions?* (Maryknoll, NY: Orbis Books, 2002), 100.

6. Harold Coward, *Pluralism in the World Religions* (Oxford: Oneworld Publications, 2000), 58. Stephen Bevans argues that the Christian message 'originally so adaptable soon became captive of Greek categories, but every true theology must liberate that message from those categories and restore it to its original flexibility'. Stephen B. Bevans, *Models of Contextual Theology* (Maryknoll, NY: Orbis Books 2002), 37.

7. Joseph Ratzinger, *Introduction to Christianity* (San Francisco: Ignatius Press, 2004), 142.

8. Harold Coward, *Pluralism in the World Religions* (Oxford: Oneworld Publications, 2000), 58. Tom F. Driver offers another perspective. He asserts that from the very beginning, most of Christianity's expansion in the world was done through the colonizing efforts of the nations. Thus, its attitude towards other religions has been influenced by the 'colonial mentality'. This means that non-Christian religions must be 'subdued and brought into conformity with Christian ideas and practice'. This was evident in Europe. See Tom F. Driver, 'The Case for Pluralism', in John Hick and Paul F. Knitter, eds, *The Myth of Christian Uniqueness* (London: SCM Press, 1987), 207–8. Paul Tillich asserts that 'Jews and Christians were both influenced religiously by the religions of the conquered and conquering nations.' Frequently these religions almost suppressed Judaism and Christianity and caused violent reactions in both of them. Paul Tillich, *The Future of Religions*, ed. Jerald C. Brauer (New York: Harper & Row, 1966), 84.

9. Harold Coward, *Pluralism in the World Religions* (Oxford: Oneworld Publications, 2000), 58.

10. Ibid. 59.

11. Ibid. Bernard Lonergan discusses the ways in which the unity of the faith may be conceived. He writes: 'On classicist assumptions there is just one culture ...Within this set-up the unity of faith is a matter of everyone subscribing to the correct formulae. Such classicism, however, was never more than the shabby shell of Catholicism.' Bernard J. F. Lonergan, *Method in Theology* (London: Darton, Longman & Todd, 1975), 326–7.

12. Edward Schillebeeckx, *Church: The Human Story of God* (New York: Crossroad, 1990), xvii.

13. Dogmatic Constitution on the Church, *Lumen Gentium*, www.vatican.va/ archive/hist_councils/ii_vatican_council/documents/vat-ii_const_19641121_lumen-gentium_en.html, no.16

14. Edward Schillebeeckx, *Church: The Human Story of God* (New York: Crossroad, 1990), xvii.

15. Ibid. 43.

16. See Jacques Dupuis, *Toward a Christian Theology of Religious Pluralism* (Maryknoll, NY: Orbis Books, 1997), 386–7.

17. Paul Tillich, *The Future of Religions*, ed. Jerald C. Brauer (New York: Harper & Row, 1966), 91. See also Alan Race, *Christians and Religious Pluralism* (Maryknoll, NY: Orbis Books, 1982), 4.

18. Joseph Ratzinger, 'Are non-Christians Saved?' www.beliefnet.com/Faiths/Catholic/2007/01/Are-Non-Christians-Saved.asp

19. Letter of Cardinal Ratzinger regarding *Dominus Iesus*, www.catholicculture. org/culture/library/view.cfm?recnum=3133. Jacques Dupuis, however, claimed that the Declaration, *Dominus Iesus,* 'contains half truth, in the sense that, while one aspect of the truth is one-sidedly stressed, the complementary aspect is often overlooked altogether. The positive statements of Vatican Council II on other religions have practically been pushed to the wayside.' Jacques Dupuis, 'The Declaration *Dominus Iesus* and My Perspective on it', in William R. Burrows, ed., *Jacques Dupuis Faces the Inquisition: Two Essays by Jacques Dupuis on* Dominus Iesus *and the Roman Investigation of His Work* (Eugene, OR: Pickwick Publications, 2012), 71.

20. Joseph Ratzinger, *Truth and Tolerance* (San Francisco: Ignatius Press, 2004), 9.

21. Dogmatic Constitution on the Church, *Lumen Gentium*, solemnly promulgated by His Holiness Pope Paul VI on 21 November 1964. www.vatican.va/archive/hist_councils/ii_vatican_council/documents/vat-ii_const_19641121_lumen-gentium_en.html, no. 13

22. Ibid. no. 16.

23. Ibid.

24. Ibid.

25. Gerald O'Collins, SJ, *The Second Vatican Council on Other Religions* (Oxford: Oxford University Press, 2013), 78.

26. Dogmatic Constitution on the Church, *Lumen Gentium*, solemnly promulgated by His Holiness Pope Paul VI on November 21, 1964. www.vatican.va/archive/hist_councils/ii_vatican_council/documents/vat-ii_const_19641121_lumen-gentium_en.html, no. 17

27. Gerald O'Collins, SJ, *The Second Vatican Council on Other Religions* (Oxford: Oxford University Press, 2013), 81.

28. Declaration on the Relation of the Church to Non-Christian Religions *Nostra Aetate* proclaimed by His Holiness Pope Paul VI on October 28, 1965. www.vatican.va/archive/hist_councils/ii_vatican_council/documents/vat-ii_decl_19651028_nostra-aetate_en.html, no. 2.

29. Ibid. no. 3.

30. Apostolic Exhortation, *Evangelii Gaudium* of The Holy Father Francis to the Bishops, Clergy, Consecrated persons and the lay faithful on the Proclamation of the Gospel in Today's Word. http://w2.vatican.va/content/francesco/en/apost_exhortations/documents/papa-francesco_esortazione-ap_20131124_evangelii-gaudium.html, no. 252

31. Joseph Ratzinger, *Truth and Tolerance* (San Francisco: Ignatius Press, 2004), 21. Karl Barth presents a theory which represents the most extreme form of exclusivism. Barth believes that only the Christian faith can save people. Other religions do not lead to salvation and nor does Christianity, as a religion. He distinguishes religion and revelation. Barth believes that religion is contrary to faith; religion consists of human attitudes constructed to reach God. His guiding principle is the revelation of God in Jesus Christ as given in the scripture. The most important representative of the inclusivist position is Karl Rahner, who is always associated with the theory of 'Anonymous Christianity.' Rahner believes there is such a thing as an 'anonymous Christian' in the sense that someone who has no concrete, historical contact with the explicit Christian message can nevertheless be justified and live in the grace of Christ. This person possesses God's gift of supernatural self-communication in grace, accepts it and in reality, really accepts the essentials of Christianity.

John Hick is the most prominent theologian to promote the pluralist paradigm in the Christian theology of religions. According to Hick, pluralism 'is the view that the transformation of human existence from self-centredness to Reality-centredness is taking place in different

ways within the contexts of all great religious traditions.' Thus there is a plurality of divine revelation, making possible diverse forms of human response to salvation. Philosophically, religious
pluralism, Hick asserts, is the view that the great world religious traditions embody different
perceptions and responses to the Real. Thus the great religious traditions are to be regarded as
different ways in which human beings can find salvation, liberation, enlightenment or fulfilment

32. Ibid. 44.

33. Ibid. 81–2.

34. Gavin D'Costa, *Christianity and World Religions* (Oxford: Wiley-Blackwell, 2009), 23–4.

35. Joseph Ratzinger, *Truth and Tolerance* (San Francisco: Ignatius Press, 2004), 54. Regarding
Pope Benedict XVI's particular interest in the theme of Christianity's relations with other faiths,
Ilaria Morali says that three affirmations can be found in his remarks to the Italian Bishops'
Conference on 24 May 2007. First, he acknowledges that the presence of the seeds of the word
in other religions serves as preparation for the gospel. Second, this presence does not lessen
the uniqueness of Christ's revelation. Third, the 'necessity of rooting faith in Christ' and hence,
it is necessary to oppose relativism. This danger of relativism, according to him, is found not
only in Western culture but has serious impact in Asia as well. Time and again, Benedict XVI
stresses the uniqueness of Christianity as a religion of love. Ilaria Morali, 'Salvation, Religions,
and Dialogue in the Roman Magisterium', in Karl J. Becker and Ilaria Morali, eds, *Catholic
Engagement with World Religions* (Maryknoll, NY: Orbis Books, 2010), 140.

36. Ibid. 81. Regarding the influence of Greek thought on Christianity, see Joseph Ratzinger,
Introduction to Christianity (San Francisco: Ignatius Press, 2004), 137–48.

37. Joseph Cardinal Ratzinger, *Many Religions – One Covenant* (San Francisco: Ignatius Press,
1998), 92.

38. Paul J. Griffiths, *Problems of Religious Diversity* (Oxford: Blackwell, 2001), 63.

39. Claude Geffré, 'From the Theology of Religious Pluralism to an Interreligious Theology', in
Daniel Kendall and Gerald O'Collins, eds, *In Many and Diverse Ways* (New York: Orbis Books,
Maryknoll, 2003), 49.

40. Ibid. 50. See also Michael Amaladoss, *Making All Things New: Dialogue, Pluralism &
Evangelization in Asia* (New York: Orbis Books, Maryknoll, 1990), 72–82.

41. Joseph Cardinal Ratzinger, *The Nature and Mission of Theology* (San Francisco: Ignatius
Press, 1993), 81. At the Synod of Bishops in 1977, Pedor Arrupe, superior general of the
Jesuits, said, ' pluralism is thought to be a danger for the Church when in fact the crisis of unity
often results from an insufficient pluralism that makes it difficult for some to express and live
their faith within their own culture'. Quoted in Aylward Shorter, *Evangelization and Culture*
(London: Geoffrey Chapman, 1994), 86.

42. Ibid. 82.

43. Ibid. 96.

44. Ibid. 97.

45. Ibid. 83.

46. Ibid. 84.

47. Ibid. 85.

48. Ibid. 95.

49. Ibid.

50. Ibid. 97.

51. Ibid.

52. Ibid. 98.

53. John Paul II, *Redemptoris Missio*, www.vatican.va/holy_father/john_paul_ii/ encycli-
cals/documents/hf_jp-ii_enc_07121990_redemptoris-missio_en.html.no.28. Due to the

inseparable link between religion and culture, Claude Geffré asserts that the inculturation of the Christian message, especially in South and East Asia, must involve dialogue with the other great religious traditions. Claude Geffré, 'Double Belonging and the Originality of Christianity as a Religion', in Catherine Cornille, ed., *Many Mansions?* (Maryknoll, NY: Orbis Books, 2002), 97.

54. Congregation for the Doctrine of the Faith, Declaration *Dominus Iesus* on the Unicity and Salvific Universality of Jesus Christ and the Church, www.vatican.va/roman_curia/congregations/cfaith/documents/rc_con_cfaith_doc_20000806_dominus-iesus_en.html. no.22

55. Jacques Dupuis, 'The Declaration *Dominus Iesus* and My Perspective on it', in William R. Burrows, ed., *Jacques Dupuis Faces the Inquisition: Two Essays by Jacques Dupuis on* Dominus Iesus *and the Roman Investigation of His Work* (Eugene, OR: Pickwick Publications, 2012), 67.

56. Ibid. 65.

57. See Joseph Ratzinger, *Truth and Tolerance* (San Francisco: Ignatius Press, 2004), 106–9. See also Stratford Caldecott, 'Benedict XVI and inter-religious dialogue', *Transformation*, 23/4 October 2006, 201.

58. Thomas P. Rausch, *Pope Benedict XVI: An Introduction to His Theological Vision* (New York: Paulist Press, 2009), 62.

59. John L. Allen, *Pope Benedict XVI* (New York: Continuum, 2000), 236.

60. Francis Xavier Clooney, 'Dialogue Not Monologue: Benedict XVI & Religious Pluralism', *Commonweal*, 21 October 2005, 14. Perry Schmidt-Leukel rightly states: 'If through interfaith encounter religions become fully aware of their respective claims, they have the moral and intellectual obligation to reply to each other's claims and consider whether these might be true or not. This is the central task of any theology of religions. The price of refraining from the challenge is simply to deafen one's ears and harden one's heart against the witness of one's neighbour.' Perry Schmidt-Leukel, 'Pluralism: How to Appreciate Religious Diversity Theologically', in Alan Race and Paul M. Hedges, eds, *Christian Approaches to Other Faiths* (London: SCM Press, 2008), 86.

61. Ibid.

62. Ibid.

63. Joseph Ratzinger, *Many Religions – One Covenant* (San Francisco: Ignatius Press, 1998), 107. John Cobb believes that since Christians have been influenced by Greek philosophy and modern science, they can also learn much from Judaism, Islam, Hinduism and Buddhism. This suggests that Christians need to appropriate the wisdom and practice of Asian religions and the other monotheistic faiths. John B. Cobb Jr, 'Multiple Religious Belonging and Reconciliation', in Catherine Cornille, ed., *Many Mansions?* (Maryknoll, NY: Orbis Books, 2002), 27.

64. Ibid. 108.

65. Ibid. 109.

66. Ibid. 110. This line of thinking is close to Joseph O'Leary who writes: 'all religions have their mighty finds and their ongoing quests. The incompleteness of their understanding does not mean that they have not found what they seek; and the fact that Christians securely possess the fullness of divine truth does not mean that they are not seeking still for what they have found. The attempt to view this universal process of human religious seeking and finding as the medium and mode of even biblical revelation, and conversely to find a divine revelatory activity at work in the non-biblical trajectories of religious experience and questioning, seems to me an irreversible path of theological reflection, imposed on us by the facts of religious pluralism themselves.' Joseph S. O'Leary, 'Toward a Buddhist Interpretation of Christian Truth', in Catherine Cornille, ed., *Many Mansions?* (Maryknoll, NY: Orbis Books, 2002), 36.

67. Ibid.

68. Ibid. 111.

69. Joseph O'Leary, *Religious Pluralism and Christian Truth* (Edinburgh: Edinburgh University Press, 1996), 3.

70. Joseph Ratzinger, *Many Religions – One Covenant* (San Francisco: Ignatius Press, 1998), 112.

71. Ibid. 113.

72. Paul J. Griffiths, *Problems of Religious Diversity* (Oxford: Blackwell, 2001), 63.

73. Joseph Ratzinger, *Truth and Tolerance* (San Francisco: Ignatius Press, 2004), 169. We will discuss this in more detail in Chapter 11.

74. Ibid. 170.

75. Joseph Ratzinger, *Truth and Tolerance* (San Francisco: Ignatius Press, 2004), 183.

76. Ibid. 85–6.

77. Pope Benedict XVI, 'Meeting with the Representatives of Science' (Regensburg Lecture), www.vatican.va/holy_father/benedict_xvi/speeches/2006/september/documents/hf_ben-xvi_spe_20060912_university-regensburg_en.html. David Burrell argues that the professorial address at Regensburg is poorly constructed with the lecturer quoting Khoury, who in turn quotes the Byzantine emperor Paleologus, regarding Islam's indifference to reason. Burrell writes: 'so many citations within citations that the lecturer's view of the matters in question was utterly obfuscated. Careless rhetorical construction could not but lead to utter distraction, yet when an intelligent theologian who is also pope distracts us, industrious speculators try to tell us what he meant by doing something so inept. It is difficult to ascertain what the lecturer himself actually stated regarding the matter. Therefore the most charitable comment would be that the pope has made an unintentional blunter, which he must admit.' David Burrell CSC, 'Dialogue between Muslims and Christians as Mutually Transformative Speech', in Catherine Cornille, ed., *Criteria of Discernment in Interreligious Dialogue* (Eugene, OR: Cascade Books, 2009), 87–8.

78. James V. Schall, 'The Regensburg Lecture: Thinking Rightly about God and Man', www.ignatiusinsight.com/features2006/schall_regensburg_sept06.asp.

79. Pope Benedict XVI, 'Meeting with the Representatives of Science (Regensburg Lecture), www.vatican.va/holy_father/benedict_xvi/speeches/2006/september/documents/hf_ben-xvi_spe_20060912_university-regensburg_en.html. Ernst Troeltsch puts it this way: 'Christianity is the religion of Western culture: Western culture has been decisively shaped by Christianity even as Christianity has been decisively shaped by it.' Kathryn Tanner, *Theories of Cultures* (Minneapolis: Fortress Press, 1997), 62.

80. Ibid.

81. James V. Schall, *The Regensburg Lecture* (South Bend, IN: St Augustine Press, 2007), 110.

82. Pope Benedict XVI, 'Meeting with the Representatives of Science' (Regensburg Lecture), www.vatican.va/holy_father/benedict_xvi/speeches/2006/september/documents/hf_ben-xvi_spe_20060912_university-regensburg_en.html.

83. Joseph Ratzinger, *The Ratzinger Report* (San Francisco: Ignatius Press, 1985), 194.

84. Thomas P. Rausch, *Pope Benedict XVI: An Introduction to his Theological Vision* (New York: Paulist Press, 2009), 59.

85. Claude Geffré, 'Double Belonging and the Originality of Christianity as a Religion', in Catherine Cornille, ed., *Many Mansions?* (Maryknoll, NY: Orbis Books, 2002), 95–6.

86. Pope Benedict XVI, 'Meeting with the Representatives of Science' (Regensburg Lecture), www.vatican.va/holy_father/benedict_xvi/speeches/2006/september/documents/hf_ben-xvi_spe_20060912_university-regensburg_en.html.

87. Quoted in James V. Schall, *The Regensburg Lecture* (South Bend, IN: St Augustine Press, 2007), 90.

88. Joseph Ratzinger, *The Ratzinger Report* (San Francisco: Ignatius Press, 1985), 193.

89. James V. Schall, *The Regensburg Lecture* (South Bend, IN: St Augustine Press, 2007), 87.

90. Joseph Ratzinger, *The Ratzinger Report* (San Francisco: Ignatius Press, 1985), 193. Looking at the pluralistic nature of Christianity, Joseph O'Leary wonders what the faith would be like if it had been planted in another culture. In fact, he presents another picture of Christianity when he writes: 'A reading of history starting from the current pluralist awareness reveals the surprising fact that Christianity has existed as a series of strategic constructions born of always unforeseeable cultural circumstances, to such an extent that all attempts to formulate its essential and invariable form find themselves contaminated by references proper to a certain period, which contradict this claim to permanence. Even its origins betray this contamination. The new religion was not a self-sufficient monad or a flawless crystallisation of the whole previous tradition. Its dependence, for its initial formulation, on the Greek language and the Hellenised culture of Palestine … the transfusion of the institutions and ideologies of the Empire carried out by Constantine; everything in this genealogy invites us to dream of what the Christian movement might have been (if it could have been) within another culture.' Joseph O'Leary, *Religious Pluralism and Christian Truth* (Edinburgh: Edinburgh University Press, 1996), 14.

91. Aloysius Pieris, *Love Meets Wisdom* (Maryknoll, NY: Orbis Books, 1990), 21. According to John Cobb, our Christian history is filled with persecution of Jews and heretics, 'we have sanctioned and sanctified conquest and slavery. We have undergirded patriarchy in extreme and horrific forms … used political and economic power to force our beliefs on others.' Thus, we must confess and admit that Christianity sanctioned imperialism and used this power 'to implement its proselytizing project.' John B. Cobb Jr, 'Multiple Religious Belonging and Reconciliation', in Catherine Cornille, ed., *Many Mansions?* (Maryknoll, NY: Orbis Books, 2002), 25.

92. Ibid. 22.

93. Aloysius Pieris, *An Asian Theology of Liberation* (Edinburg: T & T Clark, 1988), 52.

94. Ibid.

95. Ibid. 53.

96. Ibid.

97. Ibid.

98. Ibid.

99. Jaroslav Pelikan, *The Vindication of Tradition* (New Haven: Yale University Press, 1984), 55. For a more detailed study see also Jaroslav Pelikan, *Christianity and Classical Culture* (New Haven: Yale University Press, 1993).

100. Ibid. 56.

101. Ibid. 65.

CHAPTER 3: ECCLESIOLOGY

1. See Lieven Boeve and Gerard Mannion, eds, *The Ratzinger Reader* (London: T & T Clark, 2010), 81–2. Maximilian Heim claims that Ratzinger had exerted influence on the Second Vatican Council's ecclesiology and, at the same time, the Council had also influenced his theology. The reciprocal effect is still undeniable. Maximilian Heinrich Heim, *Joseph Ratzinger: Life in the Church and Living Theology* (San Francisco: Ignatius Press, 2007), 11.

2. For a detailed study of these two terms, see Roger Haight, *Christian Community in History* (New York: Continuum, 2004), 1: 18–25, 56–66. Haight does not identify particular ecclesiological models regarding these two expressions. I will attempt to show that Haight's 'ecclesiology from above' is an accurate description of Ratzinger's understanding of the church. Concerning ecclesiology from below, see also Edward Schillebeeckx, *Church: The Human Story of God* (New York: Crossroad, 1990), 5–15.

3. Lieven Boeve and Gerard Mannion, eds, *The Ratzinger Reader* (London: T & T Clark, 2010), 114. Murphy argues that Ratzinger's ecclesiology is as ecumenical as it is papal. For a sympathetic account of Ratzinger's ecclesiology, see Francesca Aran Murphy, 'Papal Ecclesiology', in John C. Cavadini, ed., *Explorations in the Theology of Benedict XVI* (Notre Dame, IN: University of Notre Dame Press, 2012), 215–35.

4. Ibid. 85. Michael Fahey, however, says Ratzinger has championed collegiality, liturgical reforms and has also been concerned about the negative influence of Archbishop Lebefvre. Ratzinger's ecclesiology shows 'an amazing consistency': he is always concerned about protecting the simple faithful against 'the power of intellectuals', against the emphasis on orthopraxis, and against an erroneous interpretation of the Second Vatican Council, especially *Gaudium et spes*. For a succinct account of Ratzinger's ecclesiological concerns, see Michael Fahey, 'Joseph Ratzinger as Ecclesiologist and Pastor', *Concilium*, ed., Gregory Baum (Edinburgh: T & T Clark, 1981), 76–83.

5. Joseph Ratzinger, *The Ratzinger Report* (San Francisco: Ignatius Press, 1998), 53.

6. Maximilian Heinrich Heim, *Joseph Ratzinger: Life in the Church and Living Theology* (San Francisco: Ignatius Press, 2007), 197.

7. Joseph Ratzinger, *The Ratzinger Report* (San Francisco: Ignatius Press, 1998), 37.

8. Aidan Nichols OP, *The Thought of Pope Benedict XVI* (London: Burns & Oates, 2007), 173. While Ratzinger favours *Lumen Gentium* as being 'the fundamental document, ecclesiologically-speaking', he finds *Gaudium et Spes* 'more problematic'. See Lieven Boeve and Gerard Mannion, eds, *The Ratzinger Reader* (London: T & T Clark, 2010), 85. When the Second Vatican Council was formulating its teaching on the church, Ratzinger says it was not to outline a new theory on ecclesiology, nor was it a question of the church reflecting on herself. He writes: 'The essence of the Church is that it counts for nothing in itself, in that the thing about it that counts is what it is not, in that it exists only to be dispossessed, in that it possesses a light that it is not and because of which alone it nonetheless is. The Church is the moon – the *mysterium lunae* – and thus exists for the faithful, for thus it is the place of an enduring spiritual decision.' Quoted in Maximilian Heinrich Heim, *Joseph Ratzinger: Life in the Church and Living Theology* (San Francisco: Ignatius Press, 2007), 233.

9. Joseph Cardinal Ratzinger, *Called to Communion* (San Francisco: Ignatius Press, 1996), 18.

10. Ibid. 19. Connected to this is Ratzinger's critique of liberation theology. See CDF, *Instruction on Certain Aspects of the 'Liberation Theology'*, 6 August 1984, www. vatican.va/roman_curia/congregations/cfaith/documents/rc_con_cfaith_doc_19840806_theology-liberation_en.html. See also Joseph Ratzinger, *A Turning Point for Europe* (San Francisco: Ignatius Press, 1994), 75, 77, 83.

11. Ibid. 23.

12. Ibid. 19.

13. Ibid. 20.

14. Ibid. 23.

15. Ibid. 24.

16. Ibid.

17. Ibid. 30. Commenting on the Munich Statement, Aidan Nichols writes: 'The origin of the Church in a given place is not interpreted sociologically but as the novel presence of the "Jerusalem from on high ... coming down from God", the Trinitarian *koinônia* itself, which makes of the Church, compared to the world, "a new creation". Aidan Nichols OP, *Rome and the Eastern Churches* (San Francisco: Ignatius Press, 2010), 361.

18. Ibid. 31.

19. Ibid. 36.

20. Ibid. 37.

21. Ibid. 43.

22. Ibid.

23. Ibid. 44. Commenting on the 'universalist' model of the church, Nichols writes: 'Because the universal Church precedes the particular churches in the divine plan and gives them whatever they have, so Jesus Christ, in sending the apostles to the entire world, made them doctors of the whole Church before they had even begun to form particular churches.' Aidan Nichols OP, *Rome and the Eastern Churches* (San Francisco: Ignatius Press, 2010), 372

24. Ibid. 45.

25. Lieven Boeve and Gerard Mannion, eds, *The Ratzinger Reader* (London: T & T Clark, 2010), 94.

26. Ibid. 97.

27. Ibid. Way back in 1965, Ratzinger said that: 'The Church cannot be manipulated at will. The Church cannot become up to date according to the wishes of the times; Christ and his Church cannot be accommodated to the times and their fashions; it is the different times that must be measured by the norm of Christ. Here lies the difference between genuine and false reformation and renewal which, at first sight, may look so much alike that they are apt to be confused.' Joseph Ratzinger, 'The Pastoral Implications of Episcopal Collegiality', *Concilium*, 1965, vol. 1, 31.

28. Ibid. 98.

29. Ibid. 99.

30. Ibid.100.

31. Ibid. 94.

32. Joseph Ratzinger, *Church, Ecumenism & Politics* (San Francisco: Ignatius Press, 2008), 25.

33. Ibid. 26.

34. Ibid. 27.

35. Ibid. 25.

36. Joseph Ratzinger, prefect of the CDF, 'The Ecclesiology of Vatican II', Conference of Cardinal Ratzinger at the opening of the Pastoral Congress of the Diocese of Aversa (Italy), www.ewtn. com/library/curia/cdfeccv2.htm.

37. Ibid. In this regard, Ratzinger thinks that the crisis of faith in Western society is before all else a crisis of the understanding of the church: 'My impression is that the authentically Catholic meaning of the reality "Church" is tacitly disappearing, without being expressly rejected. Many no longer believe that what is at issue is a reality willed by the Lord himself. Even with some theologians, the Church appears to be a human construction, an instrument created by us and one which we ourselves can freely reorganize according to the requirements of the moment.' He also adds that 'without a view of the mystery of the Church that is also *supernatural* and not only *sociological*, christology itself loses its reference to the divine in favour of a purely human structure, and ultimately it amounts to a purely human project: the Gospel becomes the *Jesus project*, the social-liberation project or other merely historical, immanent projects that can still seem religious in appearance, but which are atheistic in substance.' Joseph Ratzinger, *The Ratzinger Report* (San Francisco: Ignatius Press, 1998), 45–6.

38. Joseph Ratzinger, 'The Pastoral Implications of Episcopal Collegiality', *Concilium*, 1965, vol. 1, 28. From an Orthodox point of view, see Nicolas Afanasiev, 'Una sancta', in Michael

Plekon, ed., *Tradition Alive: On the Church and the Christian Life in Our Time/ Readings from the Eastern Church* (Lanham: Rowman & Littlefield Publishers, 2003), 14–30.

39. Joseph Ratzinger, *Called to Communion: Understanding the Church Today* (San Francisco: Ignatius Press, 1996), 28.

40. Ibid. 29.

41. Joseph Ratzinger, *Church, Ecumenism & Politics* (San Francisco: Ignatius Press, 2008), 17–18. Claude Geffré is more radical when he writes: 'the visible belonging to the church guaranteed by the confession of the same creed and the communion in the eucharistic body of Christ can be a sacrament of an invisible belonging to Christ, who transcends the borders of the visible church and who may coincide with belonging to the other great non-Christian traditions'. Claude Geffré, 'Double Belonging and the Originality of Christianity as a Religion', in Catherine Cornille, ed., *Many Mansions?* (Maryknoll, NY: Orbis Books, 2002), 104.

42. Ibid, 18.

43. Aidan Nichols OP, *Rome and the Eastern Churches* (San Francisco: Ignatius Press, 2010), 359–60.

44. Joseph Ratzinger, *Church, Ecumenism & Politics* (San Francisco: Ignatius Press, 2008), ibid. 20.

45. In the period between 1980–90, a range of ecclesiological issues received special attention from the CDF whose chief was Joseph Ratzinger. These include topics regarding the exercise of power and authority in the church and liberation theology. Bradford Hinze writes: 'In these investigations ecclesiological writings were evaluated in light of the final report from The Extraordinary Synod of Bishops in 1985, which identified communion as the central motif in the ecclesiology of Vatican II. Significantly, communion was the defining theological rubric for the new Code of Canon Law in 1983 and also an organizing doctrine for the Universal Catechism of the Catholic Church in 1992. This provides the broader context for the "Letter on Some Aspects of the Church understood as Communion" (1992).' Bradford E. Hinze, 'A Decade of Disciplining Theologians', *Horizons* 37, no.1 (Spring 2010), 96–7.

46. Joseph Ratzinger, Congregation for the Doctrine of the Faith, 'Letter to the Bishops of the Catholic Church on some aspects of the Church understood as Communion', www.vatican.va/roman_curia/congregations/cfaith/documents/rc_con_cfaith_doc_28051992_communionis-notio_en.html.

47. Joseph Ratzinger, prefect of the CDF, 'The Ecclesiology of Vatican II', Conference of Cardinal Ratzinger at the opening of the Pastoral Congress of the Diocese of Aversa (Italy), www.ewtn. com/library/curia/cdfeccv2.htm. See also Francesca Aran Murphy, 'Papal Ecclesiology', in John C. Cavadini, ed., *Explorations in the Theology of Benedict XVI* (Notre Dame, IN: University of Notre Dame Press, 2012), 222–4.

48. Ibid.

49. Joseph Ratzinger, CDF, 'Letter to the Bishops of the Catholic Church on some aspects of the Church understood as Communion', www.vatican.va/roman_curia/congregations/cfaith/documents/rc_con_cfaith_doc_28051992_communionis-notio_en.html, nos. 3–4.

50. Ibid. no. 6.

51. Lecture by Cardinal Ratzinger at the Bishops' Conference of the Region of Campania in Benevento (Italy) on the topic: 'Eucharist, Communion and Solidarity', www.vatican.va/roman_curia/congregations/cfaith/documents/rc_con_cfaith_doc_20020602_ratzinger-eucharistic-congress_en.html.

52. Ibid.

53. Cardinal Joseph Ratzinger, prefect of the CDF, 'The Ecclesiology of Vatican II', Conference of Cardinal Ratzinger at the opening of the Pastoral Congress of the Diocese of Aversa (Italy), www.ewtn. com/library/curia/cdfeccv2.htm.

54. Lieven Boeve and Gerard Mannion, eds, *The Ratzinger Reader* (London: T & T Clark, 2010), 83.

55. Joseph Ratzinger, prefect of the CDF, 'The Ecclesiology of Vatican II', Conference of Cardinal Ratzinger at the opening of the Pastoral Congress of the Diocese of Aversa (Italy), www.ewtn. com/library/curia/cdfeccv2.htm.

56. Ibid.

57. Joseph Ratzinger, CDF, 'Letter to the Bishops of the Catholic Church on some aspects of the Church understood as Communion', www.vatican.va/roman_curia/congregations/cfaith/ documents/rc_con_ cfaith_doc_28051992_communionis-notio_en.html, no.9.

58. Ibid.

59. Ibid.

60. Ibid. no.10.

61. Walter Kasper, 'On the Church', *America*, 23 April 2001; 184(14), 9.

62. Kilian McDonnell, 'The Ratzinger/Kasper debate: the universal church and local churches', *Theological Studies*,1 June 2002; 63(2), 230.

63. Walter Kasper, 'On the Church', *America*, 23 April 2001; 184(14), 10.

64. Kilian McDonnell, 'The Ratzinger/Kasper debate: the universal church and local churches', *Theological Studies*, 1 June 2002; 63(2), 231.

65. Walter Kasper, 'On the Church', *America*, 23 April 2001; 184(14), 10–11.

66. Ibid. 11.

67. Ibid.

68. Ibid. 13.

69. Ibid.

70. Ibid.

71. Ibid.

72. Ibid.14.

73. Joseph Ratzinger, 'The local church and the universal Church : a response to Walter Kasper', *America*, 19 November 2001; 185(16), 10. Thus, Ratzinger continues, 'the inner precedence of God's idea of one Church over all its empirical realizations in particular churches is basically unrelated to the problem of centralism'. Kilian McDonnell, 'The Ratzinger/Kasper debate: the universal church and local churches', *Theological Studies*, 1 June 2002; 63(2), 243. Christopher Ruddy says that there was an effort to decentralize the church at the early stage of Pope Benedict XVI's papacy. The pope seemed more willing to allow local bishops a greater role in the church's government and reduce 'papal maximalization' that has gained momentum in recent years. Christopher Ruddy, *The Local Church: Tillard and the future of Catholic Ecclesiology* (New York: Crossroad, 2006), 154.

74. Walter Kasper, 'From the President of the Council for Promoting Christian Unity', *America*, 26 November 2001; 185 (17), 29. See under 'Letters'.

75. 'The Church in and formed out of the Churches (Ecclesia in et ex Ecclesiis), is inseparable from this other formula: The Churches in and formed out of the Church (Ecclesia in et ex Ecclesiis)', Joseph Ratzinger, CDF, 'Letter to the Bishops of the Catholic Church on some aspects of the Church understood as Communion', www.vatican.va/roman_curia/congregations/cfaith/documents/rc_con_ cfaith_ doc_28051992_communionis-notio_en.html.

76. Kilian McDonnell, 'The Ratzinger/Kasper debate: the universal church and local churches', *Theological Studies*,1 June 2002; 63(2), 248. Richard Gaillardetz has also criticized the official version of communion ecclesiology. He argues that to give priority to the universal church is to conceive the church as an international corporation divided into many branch offices. To give priority to the local church would suggest that the universal church is a confederation of independent local churches. He insists that we must accept the radical relational character of

the one church understood as communion. Gaillardetz also claims that prioritizing either the universal church or local churches would go against the trinitarian understanding of God as a community of co-equals. He writes: 'A theology of communion cannot be properly Trinitarian if it gives priority to either the universal or the local; this would violate the perichoretic relationship of the particular Churches as the manifestation of the universal Church. This is the principal shortcoming of the CDF instruction "Some aspects of the Church Understood as Communion"'. See Richard Gaillardetz, *Teaching with Authority: A Theology of the Magisterium in the Church* (Collegeville, MN: Liturgical Press, 1997), 16–17 and 16, n. 25.

77. According to the CDF, Leonardo Boff writes that Jesus in his lifetime did not have a church in mind, much less founded one. The church came about only after the resurrection as part of the 'process of de-eschatologization' and as a result of the inevitable sociological needs of institutionalization. It also states, 'this relativizing concept of the church stands at the basis of the radical criticisms directed at the hierarchic structure of the Catholic Church'. Congregation for the Doctrine of the Faith, 'Notification to Father Leonardo Boff', 11 March 1985, www. ewtn.com/library/curia/cdfboff. htm. In his book referred to by CDF, Boff asks, 'Was Jesus thinking of founding a Church organized with ecclesial structures? Or was the complicated structure of the Church born as the historical result of the encounter of many factors, for example, Jesus' message about the kingdom, certain eschatological structures (the Twelve) present in his actions, his death and resurrection, the delay of the parousia, the coming of the Gentiles to the faith, and so on?' See Leonardo Boff, *Church: Charism and Power* (London: SCM Press, 1985), 73–4.

78. Kilian McDonnell, 'The Ratzinger/Kasper debate: the universal church and local churches', *Theological Studies*, 1 June 2002; 63(2), 249.

79. Lieven Boeve and Gerard Mannion, eds, *The Ratzinger Reader* (London: T & T Clark, 2010), 87.

80. Eamon Duffy, 'Urbi, but not Orbi ...The Cardinal, the Church and the Word', *New Blackfriars*, vol. 66, no.780, June 1985, 273.

81. Ibid. 274. According to Charles Curran, Ratzinger, influenced by St Augustine, 'equates the heavenly city with the church, and the earthly city with the world'. Hence, his theological writings reveal a 'strong opposition between the church and the world'. Curran, a theological Thomist, however, 'accepts the basic goodness of humanity' while acknowledging the devastating effect of sin. The church has learned from the world as shown by the fact that it has changed its view on 'religious freedom, human rights, the condemnation of slavery, and the equal role of women in society'. See Charles Curran, 'A Place for Dissent: My Argument with Joseph Ratzinger', *Commonweal* 132, no.9, 6 May 2005, 18–20. O'Regan, however, argues that we must not use '"Augustinian" as a trope for a dialectical or negative view with regard to the saeculum'. Cyril O'Regan, 'Benedict the Augustinian', in John C. Cavadini, ed., *Explorations in the Theology of Benedict XVI* (Notre Dame, IN: University of Notre Dame Press, 2012), 21.

82. Ibid. 273.

83. Ibid. 277. Charles Curran insists that the Catholic Church is not a monarchy and we urgently need to 're-emphasize the importance of the local and national churches, the collegiality of all bishops together with the bishop of Rome', and the role of the laity. The papacy is above all, a 'sign of unity'. Today we encounter a very difficult challenge of how to preserve unity in the midst of diversity and pluralism in our world. The Catholic Church has stressed uniformity rather than a unity that gives space for 'legitimate diversity'. Charles Curran, 'A Place for Dissent: My Argument with Joseph Ratzinger', *Commonweal* 132, no. 9, 6 May 2005, 19.

84. Ibid. 278.

85. Roger Haight, *Christian Community in History* (New York: Continuum, 2004), 1:19. This is close to the universal ecclesiology formulated by Cyprian of Carthage. See Nicolas Afanassieff, 'The Church which Presides in Love', in John Meyendorff, ed., *The Primacy of Peter: Essays in Ecclesiology and the Early Church* (New York: St Vladimir's Seminary Press, 1992), 91–143.

86. Ibid. 1:20.

87. Ibid. 1:21.

88. Ibid. On the relationship between the Spirit and the church, Tom Greggs writes, 'Ecclesiology is always a subset of pneumatology: the Spirit creates the church at Pentecost, and the creed lists the church's existence under the third article. Put formally one might say that the presence of the Spirit is the *sine qua non* of the church, but the church is not the *sine qua non* of the presence of the Spirit, who in His freedom blows wherever He wills.' Tom Greggs, *Theology Against Religion* (London: T & T Clark International, 2011), 127. See also John McIntyre, *The Shape of Pneumatology: Studies in the Doctrine of the Holy Spirit* (Edinburgh: T & T Clark, 1997).

89. Ibid. 1:23. Besides this danger of ecclesiocentrism, there is also the danger of Eurocentrism. In this regard, Shorter writes, 'there are many obvious ways in which local Churches can develop their own spontaneous expressions of faith, worship, ministry and Christian life independently of centralized authority, especially at the grass-roots. The tragedy is that Eurocentrism and over-centralization often make it difficult for bishops to provide leadership and to recognize local initiative, and there is a danger that grass-roots Catholicism may grow in a different direction.' And this poses a threat to Catholic unity. Aylward Shorter, *Evangelization and Culture* (London: Geoffrey Chapman, 1994), 117–18.

90. Ibid.

91. Nicholas M. Healy, *Church, World and the Christian Life* (Cambridge: Cambridge University Press, 2000), 38.

92. Joseph Ratzinger, *The Ratzinger Report* (San Francisco: Ignatius Press, 1998), 30.

93. Alberto Melloni, 'Passionate prophet of the conciliar Church,"' *The Tablet*, 8 September 2012, 7.

94. In this interview, Cardinal Carlo Martini, an influential voice in the hierarchy who passed away on 31 August 2012, also said, 'The Church is tired in affluent Europe and in America. Our culture has grown old, our Churches are big, our religious houses are empty, the bureaucracy of our Churches is growing out of proportion, our liturgies and our vestments are pompous. Yet maybe these things express what we've become today? The Pope and the bishops should find 12 unconventional people to take on leadership roles', *The Tablet*, 8 September 2012, – 9.

95. Roger Haight, *Christian Community in History* (New York: Continuum, 2004), 1:4.

96. Ibid. 1:5.

97. Ibid.

98. Ibid. 1:27–35.

99. Ibid. 1:38.

100. Ibid. 1:63.

101. Dupuis writes: 'Christian faith has it that the action of the Spirit and that of Jesus Christ, though distinct, are nevertheless complementary and inseparable'. This issue of pneumatocentrism and Christocentrism will be discussed in greater detail in Chapter 9. See Jacques Dupuis SJ, *Toward a Christian Theology of Religious Pluralism* (Maryknoll, NY: Orbis Books, 1997), 196–7.

102. Aloysius Pieris, *An Asian Theology of Liberation* (Edinburgh: T&T Clark, 1988), 36. The churches in Asia are trying to be 'more Roman than Rome', Vietnamese theologian, Peter

Phan laments, perhaps due to the lack of the necessary resources to be independent. Now that the Asian churches have matured, they should be able to be 'self-governing, self-supporting and self-propagating'. This is the only way for the 'churches *in* Asia to become truly churches *of* Asia', as suggested by Aloysius Pieris. Peter C. Phan, *Christianity with an Asian Face* (Maryknoll, NY: Orbis Books, 2003), 175.

103. Ibid.

104. Ibid. 45. Earlier Pieris says, 'when the church faces established Marxism, it sees, as in a mirror, its own authoritarianism and dogmatism, its own reluctance to give autonomy to local communities on the periphery, and its own maneuvers to centralize power'. Aloysius Pieris, *An Asian Theology of Liberation* (Edinburgh: T&T Clark, 1988), 45.

105. Ibid. 47. Peter Phan insists that Asian theological categories should not be determined beforehand, but must be shaped by the concrete situations of each Asian country. To determine how best to proclaim the gospel of Jesus Christ, Asian churches must 'exercise the God-given right, based on the mystery of divine incarnation' This means that the right to proclaim the good news is not a privilege granted by some higher church authorities. Unlike Joseph Ratzinger, Peter Phan insists on the primacy of the local churches. Peter C. Phan, *Christianity with an Asian Face* (Maryknoll, NY: Orbis Books, 2003), 175–6

106. Gerard Mannion, *Ecclesiology and Postmodernity* (Collegeville, Minnesota: Liturgical Press, 2007), 44.

107. Quoted in Gerard Mannion, *Ecclesiology and Postmodernity* (Collegeville, Minnesota: Liturgical Press, 2007), 45.

108. Gerard Mannion, *Ecclesiology and Postmodernity* (Collegeville, Minnesota: Liturgical Press, 2007), 37.

CHAPTER 4: ECUMENISM

1. Lieven Boeve and Gerard Mannion, eds, *The Ratzinger Reader* (London: T & T Clark, 2010), 139.

2. Ibid. 140. In taking a cautious and critical approach to ecumenism, Joseph Ratzinger is actually following the precedent of previous popes. Pius XI's encyclical of 1928, *Mortalium animos*, criticized the ecumenical movement and accused it of 'seeking to reach unity by too easy compromise and by focussing too exclusively on service'. In 1896, Leo XIII also 'expressed similar sentiments' in *Satis Cognitum*. It was taken for granted that the ecumenical movement was a 'Protestant affair'. There was no need for Catholics to search for Christian unity because unity was already established in the Chair of Peter in Rome in the Mystical Body of Christ. There was also a fear that the ecumenical movement could 'threaten the doctrine of the identity and nature of the Catholic Church'. It was only in 1939 that Pius XII's encyclical, *Summi Pontificatus*, expressed 'friendliness toward Protestants, acknowledging their goodwill'. However, the 'return' of 'separated brethren' remained the aim of dialogue. Jeffrey Gros FSC, Eamon McManus, Ann Riggs, *Introduction to Ecumenism* (New York: Paulist Press, 1998), 29.

3. Joseph Ratzinger, *Church, Ecumenism and Politics* (San Francisco: Ignatius Press, 2008), 133.

4. Ibid.

5. Ibid.

6. Ibid.

7. Joseph Ratzinger, *Principles of Catholic Theology: Building Stones for a Fundamental Theology* (San Francisco: Ignatius Press, 1987), 303.

8. Thomas P. Rausch, *Pope Benedict XVI: An Introduction to His Theological Vision* (New York: Paulist Press, 2009), 45.

9. Joseph Ratzinger, *Church, Ecumenism and Politics* (San Francisco: Ignatius Press, 2008), 134. According to Aidan Nichols, 'Such ecumenism from above is a caricature of the Catholic view of the ministerial priesthood, just as ecumenism from below is a caricature of the Protestant view of the priesthood of the laity.' Aidan Nichols OP, *The Thought of Pope Benedict XVI* (London: Burns & Oates, 2007), 192.

10. Ibid. 108.

11. Ibid. 123.

12. Quoted in Maximilian Heinrich Heim, *Joseph Ratzinger: Life in the Church and Living Theology* (San Francisco: Ignatius Press, 2007), 202.

13. Ibid.

14. Joseph Ratzinger, *Pilgrim Fellowship of Faith* (San Francisco: Ignatius Press, 2005), 260. Edward Schillebeeckx, however, believes that dogma should be understood as 'a proclamation of the historical realization of the salvific promise, and essentially includes an openness to *new* future historical realization'. This means that our act of interpretation should lead us to action, 'that orthodoxy becomes orthopraxis: the future is not an object of contemplation but a task, an engagement of life to be undertaken in the spirit of *hope*'. Pavel Rebernik, 'Reflections on the Philosophical Presuppositions of the Pluralist Theology of Religions', in Karl J. Becker and Ilaria Morali, eds, *Catholic Engagement with World Religions* (Maryknoll, NY: Orbis Books, 2010), 354.

15. Ibid.

16. Ibid. 261. Defending *Dominus Iesus*, the Declaration of the Congregation for the Doctrine of the Faith, Ratzinger says that its teaching is 'intended to transform the indifference with which all churches are regarded as different but equally valid'. If all churches are equally valid, the validity of the faith 'disappears into scepticism'. This means that when everything is regarded as valid, then nothing is important. Here we see Ratzinger criticizing relativism and pluralism. It is not about tolerance, he argues, but it is about the truth that we must suffer for it. See Joseph Ratzinger, *Pilgrim Fellowship of Faith* (San Francisco: Ignatius Press, 2005), 241.

17. Ibid. 262.

18. Ibid. 263.

19. Ibid.

20. Ibid. 264.

21. Ibid. 265.

22. Ibid. 266.

23. Ibid. 269.

24. Joseph Ratzinger, *Church, Ecumenism and Politics* (San Francisco: Ignatius Press, 2008), 134.

25. Quoted in Maximilian Heinrich Heim, *Joseph Ratzinger: Life in the Church and Living Theology* (San Francisco: Ignatius Press, 2007), 440.

26. Joseph Ratzinger, *Theological Highlights of Vatican II* (New York: Paulist Press, 1966), 45.

27. Ibid. 46.

28. Joseph Ratzinger, *Pilgrim Fellowship of Faith* (San Francisco: Ignatius Press, 2005), 255. Aidan Nichols defines schism as 'the crystallization of orthodox dissent'. For a detailed account of the concept of schism, see Aidan Nichols OP, *Rome and the Eastern Churches* (San Francisco: Ignatius Press, 2010), 27–51.

29. Ibid.

30. Ibid. 256.

31. Ibid. 257.

32. John Macquarrie, *Christian Unity and Christian Diversity* (London: SCM Press, 1975), 34.

33. Joseph Ratzinger, *Church, Ecumenism and Politics* (San Francisco: Ignatius Press, 2008), 72.

34. Ibid. 75.

35. Ibid.

36. Ibid.76.

37. Quoted in Joseph Ratzinger, *Church, Ecumenism and Politics* (San Francisco: Ignatius Press, 2008), 77.

38. Joseph Ratzinger, *Church, Ecumenism and Politics* (San Francisco: Ignatius Press, 2008), 78.

39. Aidan Nichols, English Dominican, formerly an Anglican, says that only the English can understand Anglicanism. Irish, Italians or people of Slavonic descent, even if born and raised in England, struggle to comprehend it. Aidan Nichols OP, *The Thought of Pope Benedict XVI* (London: Burns & Oates, 2007), 193.

40. Joseph Ratzinger, *Church, Ecumenism and Politics* (San Francisco: Ignatius Press, 2008), 79, no. 18.

41. Ibid. 79–80.

42. Joseph Ratzinger, *Principle of Catholic Theology* (San Francisco: Ignatius Press, 1987), 197–8.

43. Joseph Ratzinger, *Church, Ecumenism and Politics* (San Francisco: Ignatius Press, 2008), 92.

44. Ibid.

45. Ibid. 93. See also Lieven Boeve and Gerard Mannion, eds, *The Ratzinger Reader* (London: T & T Clark, 2010), 102.

46. Joseph Ratzinger, *Church, Ecumenism and Politics* (San Francisco: Ignatius Press, 2008), 80.

47. Ibid. 81.

48. Ibid. 93.

49. Ibid. 81.

50. Ibid. 82. Joseph Ratzinger writes that the Catholic principle of tradition is the 'apostolic traditions' that arose out of 'divine right'. These unwritten traditions were based on revelation. Although 'human traditions' ought to be acknowledged, they cannot be brought to the level of divine revelation. The crisis of exegesis led scholars to rely on traditions that are more reliable. Ratzinger laments that now it no longer matters much whether the tradition originated in the tenth, sixteenth or twentieth century. All traditions are supposed to be equally valid. Ibid. 97.

51. Ibid. 96.

52. Ibid. 97.

53. Joseph Ratzinger, *Principle of Catholic Theology* (San Francisco: Ignatius Press, 1987), 246.

54. Ibid.

55. Joseph Ratzinger, *Church, Ecumenism and Politics* (San Francisco: Ignatius Press, 2008), 82.

56. John L. Allen, *Pope Benedict XVI* (New York: Continuum, 2000), 230.

57. David Murphy, 'The Ordinariates and Ecumenism', http://ordinariateexpats. /2012/03/14/the-ordinariates-and-ecumenism/.

58. Joseph Ratzinger, *Pilgrim Fellowship of Faith* (San Francisco: Ignatius Press, 2005), 229.

59. Ibid. 232.

60. Ibid.

61. Ibid. 233. See also Radu Bordeianu, 'Orthodox–Catholic dialogue: retrieving Eucharistic ecclesiology', *Journal of Ecumenical Studies* 44, no. 2 (1 March 2009), 239–65.

62. Ibid. 235.

63. Ibid. 236.

64. Ibid. 237.

65. Ibid. 239. Here Ratzinger is following the teaching of the Second Vatican Council which attempted to depict the one Church of Christ as united in *koinonia*. Before the Council, the Catholic Church identified itself with the one true Church implying that other Christians are living outside the Church. The Council fathers applying the theology of *koinonia* used the term 'subsist in' rather than 'is' to depict the relationship of the Church of Christ to the Catholic Church. This means that instead of saying the Church of Christ *is* the Catholic Church, the Second Vatican Council teaches that the Church of Christ *subsists in* the Catholic Church. The aim of this new understanding of the church is 'to avoid sociological identification of the Church with the present structure and formulations of the Roman Catholic institutions'. It also avoids implying that the Eastern Churches that are not in communion with Rome are not real churches. The Decree on Ecumenism also states that other Christian communities contain elements of the true Church. Thus, members of these ecclesial communities are saved 'through the mediation of their communities, and not in spite of them'. This change in language from *est* to *subsistit* allows the possibility of expressing the reality of the 'Church as transcendent' and not merely a sociological structure. Other Christian communities are also recognized as having elements of the church, its 'spiritual and mystical reality'. Jeffrey Gros FSC, Eamon McManus, Ann Riggs, *Introduction to Ecumenism* (New York: Paulist Press, 1998), 68–9.

66. Ibid.

67. Ibid.

68. Joseph Ratzinger, *Principle of Catholic Theology* (San Francisco: Ignatius Press, 1987), 199.

69. Ibid. 194.

70. Ibid. 245.

71. Ibid. 194.

72. Ibid.

73. Ibid. 195.

74. Theologians such as Afanasieff and others who opposed the juridical concept of the church in the West are now developing a Eucharistic ecclesiology that is at the same time an ecclesiology of the local church. This means that the Eucharist forms the church. Where the Eucharist is celebrated, Christ and the whole church are present with the whole mystery of the sacrament. According to Ratzinger, for such view, 'the unity of the universal Church is a pleromatic enhancement but not a complement, not an augmentation of ecclesiality'. Put simply, it is the nature of the church to be one and, thus, unity is not something extra to be added. Joseph Ratzinger, *Principle of Catholic Theology* (San Francisco: Ignatius Press, 1987), 292.

75. Richard Gaillardetz, *Teaching with Authority: A Theology of the Magisterium in the Church* (Collegeville, MN: Liturgical Press, 1997), 47. Russian Orthodox theologians stress the notion of *sobornost*, 'the organic unity of the whole Church'. This unity applies particularly to the 'relationship between bishops and the whole Church'. The bishop is the presider of the local Eucharistic community in relation to the church he serves. This authority is always 'exercised *within* rather than *above* the Church'. See ibid. 33.

76. Ibid.

77. Ibid. 48.

78. This refers to the mutual lifting of excommunications in a joint Catholic–Orthodox declaration, approved by Pope Paul VI and Ecumenical Patriarch Athenagoras I of Constantinople, read simultaneously on 7 December 1965, at a public meeting of the ecumenical council in Rome and at a special ceremony in Istanbul.

79. Joseph Ratzinger, *Principle of Catholic Theology* (San Francisco: Ignatius Press, 1987), 209.

80. Ibid. 210.

81. Ibid. 211.

82. Joseph Ratzinger, *Church, Ecumenism and Politics* (San Francisco: Ignatius Press, 2008), 135.

83. Ibid. 136.

84. Joseph Ratzinger, *Theological Highlights of Vatican II* (New York: Paulist Press, 1966), 111.

85. Ibid. 112.

86. Ibid.,113.

87. Ibid. 113–14.

88. Ibid. 114.

89. Ibid. 11415.

90. Ibid. 115.

91. Joseph Ratzinger, *Pilgrim Fellowship of Faith* (San Francisco: Ignatius Press, 2005), 258. See also Joseph Ratzinger, 'What Unites and Divides Denominations? Ecumenical Reflections, in Pope Benedict XVI, *Joseph Ratzinger in Communio: Volume 1, The Unity of the Church* (Grand Rapids, MI: William B. Eerdmans, 2010), 1–9.

92. Joseph Ratzinger, *Theological Highlights of Vatican II* (New York: Paulist Press, 1966), 114–15.

93. See Decree on the Catholic Churches of the Eastern Rite, *Orientalium Ecclesiarium*, solemnly promulgated by His Holiness Paul IV on 21 November 1964, www.vatican.va/archive/hist_councils/ii_vatican_council/documents/vat-ii_decree_19641121_orientalium-ecclesiarum_en.html.

94. Edward P. Echlin, 'Unity Without Absorption', *Journal Of Ecumenical Studies* 9, no. 1 (1 December 1972), 51–2.

95. Paul Tillich, *Systematic Theology*, Volume III (Chicago: University of Chicago Press, 1963), 169–70.

96. Joseph Ratzinger, *Church, Ecumenism and Politics* (San Francisco: Ignatius Press, 2008), 137.

97. Ibid. 138.

98. John Macquarrie, *Christian Unity and Christian Diversity* (London: SCM Press, 1975), 23. According to Kathryn Tanner, theology is often identified with the writings of scholars and clergy 'in which conceptual precision and logical coherence are at a premium'. But Christian theology has to do 'with the meaning dimension of Christian practices, the theological aspect of all socially significant Christian action'. See Kathryn Tanner, *Theories of Cultures* (Minneapolis: Fortress Press, 1997), 69–70

99. Joseph Ratzinger, *Church, Ecumenism and Politics* (San Francisco: Ignatius Press, 2008), 119.

100. John Macquarrie, *Christian Unity and Christian Diversity* (London: SCM Press, 1975), 24.

101. Ibid. 25.

102. Ibid.

103. Augustine Cardinal Bea, *Unity in Freedom* (New York: Harper & Row, 1964), 214. K. H. Ting claims that, 'The Christ who rose and now sits at the right hand of God is not only the Lord of the churches but also the Lord of the secular World. The secular movements of the people have an important significance. What man achieves in history is not finally to be negated or destroyed but, in the new heaven and new earth, will be received in Christ and transfigured.' Kim Yong Bock, 'Human Rights and the Structures of Injustice', in Ninan Koshy, ed., *A History of the Ecumenical Movement in Asia*, vol. II (Hong Kong: World Student Christian Federation, Asia-Pacific Region, Asia and Pacific Alliance of YMCA, Christian Conference of Asia, 2004), 296.

104. Christopher Ruddy, *The Local Church: Tillard and the future of Catholic Ecclesiology* (New York: Crossroad, 2006), 155. Konrad Raiser writes: 'a Christian congregation can only become a parable of shared life to the extent that it shares the goodness of God's creation with all human beings. In the course of the discussions in recent years there have been many stormy disputes as to whether sharing proves itself principally in fellowship and solidarity between Christians and churches or in solidarity with the poor in the struggle for justice and human dignity.' Quoted in Ans Van der Bent, *Commitment to God's World: A Concise Critical Survey of Ecumenical Social Thought* (Geneva: WCC, 1995), 153. See also Konrad Raiser, *Ecumenism in Transition: A Paradigm Shift in the Ecumenical Movement?* (Geneva: WCC, 1991).

105. Gerard Mannion, *Ecclesiology and Postmodernity* (Collegeville, Minnesota: Liturgical Press, 2007), 135.

106. Ans Van der Bent, *Commitment to God's World: A Concise Critical Survey of Ecumenical Social Thought* (Geneva: WCC, 1995), 171.

107. Ibid. 172.

108. Ibid. 173. See also Ambrose Mong Ih-Ren, 'Crossing the Ethical–Practical Bridge: Paul Knitter's Regnocentrism in Asian Perspective', *The Ecumenical Review*, vol. 63, no. 2, July 2011, 187–8.

109. Ibid. 174.

110. Ibid. 175.

111. Ibid. 176.

112. Ibid.

113. Lieven Boeve and Gerard Mannion, eds, *The Ratzinger Reader* (London: T & T Clark, 2010), 144.

114. Joseph Ratzinger, *Principles of Catholic Theology: Building Stones for a Fundamental Theology* (San Francisco: Ignatius Press, 1987), 180–1.

115. Joseph Ratzinger, *Church, Ecumenism and Politics* (San Francisco: Ignatius Press, 2008), 216.

116. K. M. George, 'Ecumenism in Asia: Some Theological Consideration', in *Windows into Ecumenism: Essays in Honour of Ahn Jae Woong* (Hong Kong: Christian Conference of Asia, 2005), 123.

117. Ibid. 124.

CHAPTER 5: SECULARISM

1. See José Casanova, 'The Secular and Secularisms', *Social Research* 76.4 (Winter 2009), 1049–66.

2. Pope Benedict XVI, 'The Church and the challenge of secularization', *Christ to the World* 53, no. 5 (September 2008), 390. Gary D. Glenn says that the 'natural consequence for Europe's abandoning Christianity for liberal secularism is that it is to become Moslem. Perhaps

Heidegger was right when he said, "Only a god can save us." Gary D. Glenn, 'Is secularism the end of liberalism?: Reflections on Europe's demographic decline drawing on Pope Benedict, Habermas, Nietzsche and Strauss', *Catholic Social Science Review* 13 (2008), 92.

3. Ibid. Contrary to Ratzinger's understanding, Vinoth Ramachandra has observed that just where secularism is widespread, like in the West, there is a renewed interest in the 'transcendence'. Vinoth Ramachandra, *Faith in Conflicts?* (Downers Grove, Illinois: InterVarsity Press, 1999), 141.

4. *DailyTelegraph*, www.telegraph.co.uk/news/newstopics/religion/the-pope/8006272/Pope-Benedict-XVI-warns-against-aggressive-secularism-in-Britain.html. See also Benedict XVI, 'The Church and the challenge of secularization', *Christ to the World* 53, no. 5 (September 2008), 389–92. Ratzinger believed that truth, which should have re-energized Europe, was denied. This was in reference to the European constitutional treaty signed in October 2004. According to George Weigel, 'the drafters of Europe's new constitution were determined ... to declare secularism – and the scepticism and relativism that inform secularism – as the official creed ... of the newly expanded European Union'. To mention the historical and cultural contributions of Christianity to a Europe committed to freedom, human rights and democracy in the preamble would be to acknowledge that freedom and the spiritual dimension of the human experience were related. This is what the drafters of Europe's constitution were determined to avoid. George Weigel, *God's Choice* (New York: HarperCollins, 2005), 221.

5. *Christian Science Monitor*, www.csmonitor.com/World/Europe/2010/1107/In-Spain-Pope-Benedict-XVI-lambasts-aggressive-secularism. Ratzinger as pope has noticed that the most 'religious arid' parts of the world, the places most influenced by modernization, which produced secularization, were in 'Catholicism's historic homeland, Europe'. George Weigel, *God's Choice* (New York: HarperCollins, 2005), 218.

6. See Martin Rhonheimer, 'Christian secularity, political ethics and the culture of human rights', *Josephinum Journal of Theology* 16, no. 2 (Summer–Fall 2009), 321.

7. See Ambrose Mong Ih-Ren, 'Challenges and Opportunities for the Church in Secular Societies', *Asia Journal of Theology*, vol. 25, no.1, April 2011, 148–51.

8. Nancy A. Dallavalle, 'Cosmos and ecclesia: a response to Richard Lennan', *Philosophy & Theology* 17, no. 1–2 (1 January 2005), 285.

9. Owen Chadwick, *The Secularization of the European Mind in the Nineteenth Century* (Cambridge: Cambridge University Press, 1975), 8. For a concise account of the Christian origin of secularism, see Craig Calhoun, Mark Juergensmeyer and Jonathan VanAntwerpen, eds, *Rethinking Secularism* (Oxford: Oxford University Press, 2011), 6–14, 55–60.

10. Ibid. 138.

11. Hastings writes that it is hard to prove that in the past society was ever very religious. Furthermore, society evolves and religious beliefs find ways and means to express and adapt themselves to different times and places. Adrian Hastings, *A History of English Christianity 1920–1990* (London: SCM Press, 1991), 669.

12. Quoted in Vinoth Ramachandra, 'Learning from modern European secularism: A view from the Third World church', *European Journal of Theology* 12, no. 1 (1 January 2003), 37.

13. Owen Chadwick, *The Secularization of the European Mind in the Nineteenth Century* (Cambridge: Cambridge University Press, 1975), 2. See also Charles Taylor, *A Secular Age* (Cambridge, Massachusetts: Belknap Press, 2007), 1–22.

14. Joseph Ratzinger, *Christianity and the Crisis of Cultures* (San Francisco: Ignatius Press, 2005), 13.

15. Ibid. 14.

16. Ibid. 30.

17. Martin Rhonheimer, 'Christian secularity, political ethics and the culture of human rights', *Josephinum Journal of Theology* 16, no. 2 (Summer–Fall 2009), 329.

18. Joseph Ratzinger, *Christianity and the Crisis of Cultures* (San Francisco: Ignatius Press, 2005), 40.

19. Ibid. 42.

20. Joseph Ratzinger, *Handing on the Faith in an Age of Disbelief* (San Francisco: Ignatius Press, 2006), 13–14.

21. Joseph Ratzinger, *The Nature and Mission of Theology* (San Francisco: Ignatius Press, 1993), 77.

22. Ibid. In *The Transparent Society* (1992), Gianni Vattimo discusses the negative side of technological and scientific civilization in terms of 'counter-utopia' or the emergence of the 'counter-finality of reason'. Vattimo argues that it is not only certain negative experiences like the two world wars and massive exploitation of the earth that have led us to a realization that scientific–technological progress can lead to disastrous results. Such a possibility is always acknowledged: 'technical advances have always brought with them the possibility of their wrongful application, or have given rise to risks that were previously unknown'. Gianni Vattimo, *The Transparent Society* (Cambridge: Polity Press, 1992), 77–8.

23. Joseph. Ratzinger, *The Nature and Mission of Theology* (San Francisco: Ignatius Press, 1993), 22.

24. Ibid. 23. According to Martin Heidegger, 'Western metaphysics ... since its beginning with the Greeks has eminently been both ontology and theology'. Quoted in Richard Rorty, *An Ethics for Today* (New York: Columbia University Press, 2011), 37. On the other hand, Harnack claims that 'the original teaching of Jesus on the merciful love of the Father for every soul, and the consequent love commandment laid on humanity, was lost to view in the metaphysical speculations of patristic thought'. Aidan Nichols OP, *The Shape of Catholic Theology* (Edinburgh: T&T Clark, 1991), 275.

25. Ibid.

26. Ibid. 24.

27. Ibid.

28. Ibid.

29. Ibid. 25.

30. Ibid. 102. John Milbank believes that a 'neutral, secular, political space free from religious commitments does not exist. He argues that any theory of human life must define the 'telos of human beings', and the vision of human *telos* cannot be grounded on reason alone. All theories depend on 'mythical narratives or the wagers of faith'. Milbank thus argues that the modern 'distinction between the religious and the secular is itself theological'. Tyler T. Roberts, 'Toward secular diaspora: relocating religion and politics', in *Secularisms* (Durham, NC: Duke University Press, 2008), 289–90.

31. Ibid. 102–3.

32. Ibid.

33. Gianni Vattimo, *After Christianity* (New York: Columbia, 2002), 4.

34. Ibid. 5.

35. Ibid. 6. Calvinist philosopher, Alvin Plantinga, rejects classical foundationalism as well as Richard Rorty's relativism, which we will discuss in Chapter 6. Explicating John Calvin, Plantinga believes that 'God has created us in such a way that under the right conditions we naturally form such beliefs as that he has created us and that we owe him allegiance. The disposition to form these beliefs, then, is really a capacity for grasping certain truths about God'. See Alvin C. Plantinga, 'On Reformed Epistemology', *Reformed Journal* 32, no. 1 (1 January 1982), 16–17.

36. Ibid. 98.

37. Gianni Vattimo, *Belief* (Stanford, California: Stanford University Press, 1999), 47.

38. Ibid. 48.

39. Gianni Vattimo, *After Christianity* (New York: Columbia, 2002), 99.

40. Ibid.100.

41. Ibid.

42. Ibid.101.

43. 'Pope Benedict XVI: Marxist ideology no longer corresponds to reality', www.telegraph.co.uk/news/religion/the-pope/9164373/Pope-Benedict-XVI-Marxist-ideology-no-longer-corresponds-to-reality.html.

44. Owen Chadwick, *The Secularization of the European Mind in the Nineteenth Century* (Cambridge: Cambridge University Press, 1975), 48.

45. Ibid. 49.

46. Ibid. 59.

47. Ibid. 64.

48. Ibid. 65.

49. Alasdair MacIntyre, *Marxism & Christianity* (London: Duckworth, 1995), vi.

50. Owen Chadwick, *The Secularization of the European Mind in the Nineteenth Century* (Cambridge: Cambridge University Press, 1975), 68.

51. Ibid. 69.

52. Joseph Ratzinger, *The Nature and Mission of Theology* (San Francisco: Ignatius Press, 1993), 79.

53. John F. Thornton and Susan B. Varenne, eds, *The Essential Pope Benedict XVI* (New York: HarperCollins, 2007), 78.

54. Vincent Twomey, 'When God is denied …', *Inside the Vatican* 17, no. 8 (October 2009), 37. According to Vattimo, the term utopia 'concerns the realization of an optimal reality by way of rational design, whether it be oriented metaphysically or technologically'. Gianni Vattimo, *The Transparent Society* (Cambridge: Polity Press, 1992), 79.

55. Jürgen Habermas and Joseph Ratzinger, *The Dialectics of Secularization* (San Francisco: Ignatius Press, 2006), 64.

56. Ibid.11.

57. Ibid. 32.

58. Ibid. 29.

59. Ibid. 32.

60. Ibid. 29.

61. Ibid. 38.

62. Ibid. 42. In *The Dialectic of Enlightenment*, Horkheimer and Adorno claim that reason has gone astray, 'giving rise to a totally administered world' and 'to the manipulation of consciousness'. Gianni Vattimo, *The Transparent Society* (Cambridge: Polity Press, 1992), 82.

63. Ibid. 43.

64. Ibid. 45.

65. Gary D. Glenn, 'Is secularism the end of liberalism?: Reflections on Europe's demographic decline drawing on Pope Benedict, Habermas, Nietzsche and Strauss', *Catholic Social Science Review* 13 (2008), 93.

66. Quoted in Gary D. Glenn, 'Is secularism the end of liberalism?: Reflections on Europe's demographic decline drawing on Pope Benedict, Habermas, Nietzsche and Strauss', *Catholic Social Science Review* 13 (2008), 94.

67. Ibid. 94.

68. Gianni, Vattimo, *The Transparent Society* (Cambridge: Polity Press, 1992), 40.

69. Gary D. Glenn, 'Is secularism the end of liberalism?: Reflections on Europe's demographic decline drawing on Pope Benedict, Habermas, Nietzsche and Strauss', *Catholic Social Science Review* 13 (2008), 94.

70. Quoted in Gary D. Glenn, 'Is secularism the end of liberalism?: Reflections on Europe's demographic decline drawing on Pope Benedict, Habermas, Nietzsche and Strauss', *Catholic Social Science Review* 13 (2008), 94–5.

71. Ibid. 95.

72. Ibid. 96.

73. Ibid.

74. Leo Strauss, *Natural Right and History* (Chicago: University of Chicago, 1953), 6.

75. Joseph Ratzinger and Marcello Pera, *Without Roots* (New York: Basic Books, 2007), 128.

76. Jürgen Habermas and Joseph Ratzinger, *The Dialectics of Secularization* (San Francisco: Ignatius Press, 2006), 58.

77. Ibid.

78. Ibid. 59. Following Jacques Derrida, Tracy claims that, 'Our "democracies" are more accurately described as oligarchies with democratic ideals and pretensions functioning now well, now poorly, by means of the ideals of full equality and personal liberty.' David Tracy, 'Western Hermeneutics and Interreligious Dialogue', in Catherine Cornille and Christopher Conway, eds, *Interreligious Hermeneutics* (Eugene, OR: Cascade Books, 2010), 42.

79. Ibid. 59–60.

80. Ibid. 65.

81. Ibid. 66.

82. Ibid. 75.

83. Ibid. 77.

84. Ibid. 30.

85. Ibid. 35.

86. Ibid. 45.

87. Jonathan Bowman, 'Extending Habermas and Ratzinger's *Dialectics of Secularization*: Eastern Discursive Influences on Faith and Reason in Postsecular Age', *Forum Philosophicum* 14 (2009), 40. Charles Taylor refers to this as a 'post-secular' Europe where we see not the reversal of the decline of religion of the last century, but 'the hegemony of the mainstream master narrative of secularization will be more and more challenged'. Charles Taylor, *A Secular Age* (Cambridge, Massachusetts: Belknap Press, 2007), 534.

88. Jürgen Habermas and Joseph Ratzinger, *The Dialectics of Secularization* (San Francisco: Ignatius Press, 2006), 79.

89. Jonathan Bowman, 'Extending Habermas and Ratzinger's *Dialectics of Secularization*: Eastern Discursive Influences on Faith and Reason in Postsecular Age', *Forum Philosophicum* 14 (2009), 41.

90. Ibid. 42.

91. Jürgen Habermas and Joseph Ratzinger, *The Dialectics of Secularization* (San Francisco: Ignatius Press, 2006), 79–80.

92. Virgil Nemoianu, 'The Church and the secular establishment: A philosophical dialog between Joseph Ratzinger and Jürgen Habermas', *Logos* 9, no. 2 (Spring 2006), 22.

93. Ibid. 23.

94. Ibid. 25–6.

95. Jürgen Habermas and Joseph Ratzinger, *The Dialectics of Secularization* (San Francisco: Ignatius Press, 2006), 37.

96. Ibid. 38.

97. Ibid. 43.
98. Ibid. 44.
99. Ibid. 46.
100. Virgil Nemoianu, 'The Church and the secular establishment: A philosophical dialog between Joseph Ratzinger and Jürgen Habermas', *Logos* 9, no. 2 (Spring 2006), 27–8.
101. Ibid. 29.
102. Jürgen Habermas and Joseph Ratzinger, *The Dialectics of Secularization* (San Francisco: Ignatius Press, 2006), 77.
103. Virgil Nemoianu, 'The Church and the secular establishment: A philosophical dialog between Joseph Ratzinger and Jürgen Habermas', *Logos* 9, no. 2 (Spring 2006), 30.
104. Ibid. 31.
105. Ibid. 32.
106. 'Church in the World', *The Tablet*, https://thetablet.co.uk/article/1866.
107. Quoted in Donal Murray, 'The secular versus religion?' *Origins* 37, no. 26 (6 December 2007), 412.
108. Ibid. 413.
109. 'Healthy secularism for a peaceful coexistence', *L'Osservatore Romano*, Wednesday 19 November 2008, 6.
110. See *Foreword* by Charles Taylor in Geoffrey Brahm Levey and Tariq Modood, *Secularism, Religion and Multicultural Citizenship* (Cambridge: Cambridge University Press, 2009), xi – xii.
111. José Casanova, 'The Secular, Secularizations, Secularisms', in Craig Calhoun, Mark Juergensmeyer and Jonathan VanAntwerpen, eds, *Rethinking Secularism* (Oxford: Oxford University Press, 2011), 72.
112. Ibid. 61.
113. Ibid. 64.
114. Ibid. 72.
115. Ibid. 73.
116. Richard Madsen, 'Secularism, Religious Change, and Social Conflict in Asia', in Craig Calhoun, Mark Juergensmeyer and Jonathan VanAntwerpen, eds, *Rethinking Secularism* (Oxford: Oxford University Press, 2011), 268, note 6. According to Madsen, unlike in the West, the practice of religion in Asia has not been relegated to the private domain. In fact, religious practice in Asian societies is more in the form of ritual and myth than belief. It forms part of the public life of the local communities. Ibid. 266.

CHAPTER 6: RELATIVISM

1. Ratzinger's theological presuppositions are based on the readings of Augustine and Bonaventure which he employs to understand the perniciousness of relativism. According to Gediminas Jankunas, 'the respected tradition of the Munich School of Theology have taught him to appreciate and understand history, not as a chain of accidental events, but as a process of human and divine exchange. Real truth is beyond the makings of history, but at the same time history becomes meaningful only if truth realizes itself in history.' Gediminas T. Jankunas, *The Dictatorship of Relativism* (New York: St Pauls, 2011), 262.
2. *Address of His Holiness Benedict XVI to the Roman Curia offering them his Christmas Greetings.* www.vatican.va/holy_father/benedict_xvi/speeches/2005/december/documents/hf_ben_xvi_spe_20051222_roman-curia_en.html
3. Ibid.

4. 'Cardinal Ratzinger's Homily', *Vatican Radio*, http://storico.radiovaticana.org/en1/storico/2005-04/33987.html

5. According to Weigel, St Benedict of Nursia foresaw the coming of the Dark Ages with the collapse of the Roman Empire and Pope Benedict XVI with the rise of relativism in all spheres of modern life. He believes this present Benedict is prepared to fight the darkness being brought about by relativism and its adherents. Benedict XVI is 'a man thoroughly convinced that ideas have real–world consequences and that decent human societies cannot be built upon a foundation of falsehood'. See George Weigel, *God's Choice: Pope Benedict XVI and the Future of the Catholic Church* (New York: Harper Perennial, 2006), 140, 217.

6. See D. Vincent Twomey, *Pope Benedict XVI: The Conscience of Our Age* (San Francisco: Ignatius Press, 2007), 63, 107, 121, 123, 134.

7. J. Christopher Paskewich, 'Liberalism Ex Nihilo: Joseph Ratzinger on Modern Secular Politics', *Politics* 28, no. 3 (2008), 170.

8. Joseph Ratzinger, *Christianity and the Crisis of Cultures* (San Francisco: Ignatius Press, 2005), 27.

9. Joseph Ratzinger, *Truth and Tolerance* (San Francisco: Ignatius Press, 2003), 116.

10. J. Christopher Paskewich, 'Liberalism Ex Nihilo: Joseph Ratzinger on Modern Secular Politics', *Politics* 28, no. 3 (2008), 171. See also Joseph Ratzinger, *Introduction to Christianity* (San Francisco: Ignatius Press, 2004), 14–15.

11. Terry Eagleton, *The Illusions of Postmodernism* (Oxford: Blackwell, 1996), vii. Frederic Jameson in his foreword to François Lyotard, *The Postmodern Condition* (Manchester: Manchester University Press, 1984) states that postmodernism is understood as involving 'a radical break, both with a dominant culture and aesthetic'. It has been variously called media society, 'the society of the spectacle', consumer society, the 'bureaucratic society of controlled consumption', or 'postindustrial society' (vii). See also Joseph Natoli and Johannes Willem Bertens, eds, *Postmodernism: The Key Figures* (Malden, Mass.: Blackwell, 2002), Johannes Willem Bertens, *The Idea of the Postmodern: A History* (New York: Routledge, 1995), Christopher Butler, *Postmodernism: A Very Short Introduction* (Oxford: Oxford University Press, 2002) and Gianni Vattimo, *The Transparent Society* (Baltimore: Johns Hopkins University Press, 1992).

12. Ibid. 133.

13. Ibid. 134.

14. Ernest Gellner, *Postmodernism, Reason and Religion* (London: Routledge, 1992), 23–4.

15. Ibid. 82–3. Relativism adopts Kant's sense of reason which means denying any metaphysical knowledge. Ratzinger believes that if metaphysical knowledge is not accepted, faith will be weakened because human beings will be limited by their perception set by Kant. See Gediminas T. Jankunas, *The Dictatorship of Relativism* (New York: St Pauls, 2011), 210.

16. Ibid. 84–5.

17. Ibid. Regarding faith, Ernest Gellner speaks of three basic approaches: fundamentalism, a position which believes in a unique truth which it possesses; relativism, a position which discards the idea of a unique truth, but attempts to treat each particular belief as more or less true; enlightenment rationalism, a position which retains the faith in its uniqueness, but does not believe that anyone possesses it fully. Underlying fundamentalism is the idea that faith is upheld firmly in the full and literal form and that doctrine which is fixed forms its basic core. Fundamentalism rejects the modern idea that religion must be adaptable to changing situations; it repudiates tolerance and acceptance of other religious and non-religious traditions as equal in validity. See Ernest Gellner, *Postmodernism, Reason and Religion* (London: Routledge, 1992), vii, 3.

18. Michael Luntley, *Reason, Truth and Self* (London: Routledge, 1995), 2–3.

19. See François Lyotard, *The Postmodern Condition* (Manchester: Manchester University Press, 1984), xxiv, 34, 37. See also Claudia Moscovici, *Double Dialectics* (Oxford: Rowman & Littlefield , 2002), 2.

20. See Virgil Nemoianu, *Postmodern & Cultural Identities* (Washington, DC: The Catholic University of America Press, 2010), 14–15.

21. Ibid. 16–17.

22. Ibid. 18.

23. Aidan Nichols OP, *The Thought of Pope Benedict XVI* (London: Burns & Oates, 2007), 223.

24. Quoted in Aidan Nichols OP, *The Thought of Pope Benedict XVI* (London: Burns & Oates, 2007), 223.

25. Joseph Ratzinger, 'Relativism: The Central Problem for Faith Today', in *The Essential Pope Benedict XVI*, John F. Thornton and Susan B. Varenne, eds (New York: HarperSanFrancisco, 2007), 227–8.

26. Joseph Ratzinger, *The Ratzinger Report* (San Francisco: Ignatius Press, 1998), 174, 177.

27. Ibid. 175.

28. Joseph Ratzinger, 'Relativism: The Central Problem for Faith Today', in *The Essential Pope Benedict XVI*, John F. Thornton and Susan B. Varenne, eds (New York: HarperSanFrancisco, 2007), 235.

29. John L. Allen, *Pope Benedict XVI* (New York: Continuum, 2000), 99.

30. Ibid. 264.

31. Joseph Ratzinger, *Truth and Tolerance* (San Francisco: Ignatius Press, 2003), 117.

32. Quoted in Maximilian Heinrich Heim, *Joseph Ratzinger: Life in the Church and Living Theology* (San Francisco: Ignatius Press, 2007), 390.

33. Quoted in Jeffrey Stout, 'A House Founded on the Sea: Is Democracy a Dictatorship of Relativism?' *Common Knowledge* 13: 2–3 (Spring–Fall 2007), 385.

34. Joseph Ratzinger, *Truth and Tolerance* (San Francisco: Ignatius Press, 2003), 117.

35. *Address of His Holiness Benedict XVI to H.E. Mr. Anton Morell Mora, Ambassador of the Principality of Andorra to the Holy See.* www.vatican.va/holy_father/benedict_xvi/speeches/2005/december/documents/hf_ben_xvi_spe_20051201_ambassador-andorra_en.html

36. Quoted in Maximilian Heinrich Heim, *Joseph Ratzinger: Life in the Church and Living Theology* (San Francisco: Ignatius Press, 2007), 391. Weigel believes the illness that affects Western society is its 'deliberate willful forgetting of the truth that the human person does not himself *invent* morality on the basis of calculations of expediency but rather *finds* it already present in the essence of things'. George Weigel, *God's Choice: Pope Benedict XVI and the Future of the Catholic Church* (New York: Harper Perennial, 2006), 219.

37. Jeffrey Stout, 'A House Founded on the Sea: Is Democracy a Dictatorship of Relativism?' *Common Knowledge* 13: 2–3 (Spring–Fall 2007), 395.

38. Ibid. 395–6.

39. Joseph Ratzinger, *Truth and Tolerance* (San Francisco: Ignatius Press, 2003), 117–18.

40. Declaration 'Dominus Iesus' on the Unicity and Salvific Universality of Jesus Christ and the Church, www.vatican.va/roman_curia/congregations/cfaith/documents/rc_con_cfaith_doc_20000806_dominus-iesus_en.html, 4.

41. Joseph Ratzinger, *Truth and Tolerance* (San Francisco: Ignatius Press, 2003), 73.

42. Joseph Ratzinger, 'Relativism: The Central Problem for Faith Today', in *The Essential Pope Benedict XVI*, John F. Thornton and Susan B. Varenne, eds (New York: HarperSanFrancisco, 2007), 230.

43. Ibid. 231.

44. Quoted in Gediminas T. Jankunas, *The Dictatorship of Relativism* (New York: St Pauls, 2011), 262.

45. Joseph Ratzinger, *Truth and Tolerance* (San Francisco: Ignatius Press, 2003),73.

46. Ibid. 120.

47. Joseph Ratzinger, 'Relativism: The Central Problem for Faith Today', in *The Essential Pope Benedict XVI*, John F. Thornton and Susan B. Varenne, eds (New York: HarperSanFrancisco, 2007), 230.

48. Joseph Ratzinger and Marcello Pera, *Without Roots* (New York: Basic Books, 2007), 128. In line with this, Vattimo says, 'Liberals are in tune with the pope's anti-relativism in that they hold, as he does, that to initiate dialogue with another religion or society or culture, one needs a clear and definite identity of one's own. Without that strong identity on both sides, what follows is the dissolution of one or both into a well-intentioned mess. But the relativist, or even a devil's advocate, may ask: does not a dialogue of any sort presuppose that the other might be right and that "our side" might be wrong?' Gianni Vattimo, 'A 'Dictatorship of Relativism"? Symposium in Response to Cardinal Ratzinger's Last Homily', *Common Knowledge* 13: 2–3 (Spring–Fall 2007), 217.

49. 'Dominus Iesus', On the Unicity and Salvific Universality of Jesus Christ and the Church, www.vatican.va/roman_curia/congregations/cfaith/documents/rc_con_cfaith_doc_20000806_dominus-iesus_en.html.

50. Ibid.

51. Joseph Ratzinger, *Truth and Tolerance* (San Francisco: Ignatius Press, 2003), 122. In the Western world, relativism has manifested itself in diverse forms, such as the 'New Age' movement, and pragmatism in the life of the church. For the supporters of New Age, Ratzinger tells us, the solution to the problem of relativism is sought not in a new encounter of the self with another, but 'in overcoming subjective consciousness, in a re-entry into the dance of the cosmos through ecstasy'. Ratzinger also believes that New Age, pastoral pragmatism and democratization in church government are interconnected. For unless faith and the apostolic ministry come to us through the incarnate Word and the church, they possess no absolute value. When relativism sets into the church, the content of faith can be determined by the majority rather than by appeal to the church of all ages. Joseph Ratzinger, *Truth and Tolerance* (San Francisco: Ignatius Press, 2003), 127. See also Aidan Nichols OP, *The Thought of Pope Benedict XVI* (London: Burns & Oates, 2007), 225.

52. Ibid. 128–9.

53. Joseph Ratzinger, 'Relativism: The Central Problem for Faith Today', in *The Essential Pope Benedict XVI*, John F. Thornton and Susan B. Varenne, eds (New York: HarperSanFrancisco, 2007), 231–2.

54. Joseph Ratzinger, *Many Religions – One Covenant* (San Francisco: Ignatius Press, 1999), 96.

55. Joseph Ratzinger, *Introduction to Christianity* (San Francisco: Ignatius Press, 2004), 20.

56. Ibid. 21.

57. Ibid. 24.

58. Ibid. 25.

59. Joseph Ratzinger, *Many Religions – One Covenant* (San Francisco: Ignatius Press, 1999), 107.

60. David Bloor, 'Epistemic Grace Antirelativism as Theology in Disguise', *Common Knowledge* 13: 2–3 (Spring–Fall 2007), 256.

61. Ibid. 279.

62. Gianni Vattimo, 'A "Dictatorship of Relativism"? Symposium in Response to Cardinal Ratzinger's Last Homily', *Common Knowledge* 13: 2–3 (Spring–Fall 2007), 218.

63. Ibid.

64. Jeffrey Stout, 'A House Founded on the Sea: Is Democracy a Dictatorship of Relativism?' *Common Knowledge* 13: 2–3 (Spring–Fall 2007), 388.

65. Barbara Herrnstein Smith, 'Relativism, Today and Yesterday', *Common Knowledge* 13: 2–3 (Spring–Fall 2007), 232.

66. Richard Rorty, *An Ethics for Today: Finding Common Ground Between Philosophy and Religion* (New York: Columbia University Press, 2011), xix.

67. Ibid.10.

68. Ibid.11.

69. Ibid.13.

70. Ibid.15.

71. Ibid.14.

72. Joseph Ratzinger, *The Ratzinger Report* (San Francisco: Ignatius Press, 1998), 80.

73. Richard Rorty, *An Ethics for Today: Finding Common Ground Between Philosophy and Religion* (New York: Columbia University Press, 2011), 17.

74. Joseph Ratzinger, *Truth and Tolerance* (San Francisco: Ignatius Press, 2003), 117.

75. J. Christopher Paskewich, 'Liberalism Ex Nihilo: Joseph Ratzinger on Modern Secular Politics', *Politics* 28, no. 3 (2008), 170.

76. Tissa Balasuriya, 'Some Asian questions on dictatorship of relativism,'" *Voices from the Third World* 29, no. 1 (1 June 2006), 23–4.

77. Ibid. 24.

78. Ibid. 26–7.

79. Ibid. 27.

80. Ibid. 28.

81. Ibid. 28–9.

82. Ibid. 29–30.

83. Ibid. 30.

84. Maximilian Heinrich Heim, *Joseph Ratzinger: Life in the Church and Living Theology* (San Francisco: Ignatius Press, 2007), 327.

85. Joseph Ratzinger, *The Nature and Mission of Theology* (San Francisco: Ignatius Press, 1993), 81.

CHAPTER 7: EUROPE

1. James V. Schall SJ, Foreword to the second edition in Joseph Cardinal Ratzinger, *A Turning Point For Europe* (San Francisco: Ignatius Press, 1994), 12. Assessing his role as pontiff after he announced his resignation on 11 February 2013, *The New York Times* reported, 'Benedict himself had a mixed record in dealing with cultures outside his own, triggering fury among Muslims with a speech critical of Islam in 2006 and angering many in Africa by opposing the use of condoms to combat the scourge of AIDS', www.nytimes.com/reuters/2013/02/11/world/europe/11reuters-pope-resignation.html?src=un&feedurl=http%3A%2F%2Fjson8.nytimes.com%2Fpages%2Fworld%2Feurope%2Findex.jsonp.

2. Lieven Boeve, 'Europe in Crisis: A Question of Belief or Unbelief? Perspectives from the Vatican', *Modern Theology* 23, no. 2 (1 April 2007), 205–6.

3. James V. Schall, SJ, Foreword to the second edition in Joseph Cardinal Ratzinger, *A Turning Point For Europe* (San Francisco: Ignatius Press, 1994), 12.

4. Ibid. 13.

5. Ibid. 14–15. It was no surprise that in choosing a pope in April 2005, the cardinals had turned to Joseph Ratzinger because he seemed to be the best person to deal with the crisis of faith in Europe. Pope Benedict XVI launched his 'Take Back Europe' in 2006, visiting Spain and Poland, in order to build momentum and reawake the Christian roots of the Old Continent. John L. Allen writes that 'symbolically, Poland represents Benedict's hope for a European future rooted in Christian values; Spain illustrates instead a runaway version of the "dictatorship of relativism"'.John L. Allen Jr, 'Benedict travels Europe to revitalize Christian roots', *National Catholic Reporter* 42, no. 31, 2 June 2006, 8. 'On 18 February 2012, Pope Benedict created 22 new cardinals, including Bishop John Tong of Hong Kong. Nearly three quarters of those receiving a red hat are from Europe, including seven from Italy. Clearly Pope Benedict intends to keep the papacy in European hands.' Robert Mickens, 'The Church's new princes', *The Tablet*, 14 January 2012, 4–6.

6. Joseph Ratzinger and Marcello Pera, *Without Roots* (New York: Basic Books, 2007), 52. Besides Ratzinger's cultural identity of Europe, Pablo Jiménez Lobeira also discusses the concept of European identity given by Jacques Derrida, Anthony Giddens, etc. See Pablo C. Jiménez Lobeira, 'Normative Conceptions of European Identity – A Synthetic Approach'. *Australian Journal of Professional and Applied Ethics*, vol. 12, nos 1 and 2, 2010, 159–70.

7. Jeffrey Morris, 'Pope Benedict XVI on faith and reason in Western Europe', *Pro Ecclesia*, vol.17, no. 3 (1 June 2008), 330.

8. Joseph Ratzinger, 'Europe in the Crisis of Cultures', *Communio* 32, Summer 2005, 347.

9. Quoted in Joseph Ratzinger, *A Turning Point For Europe* (San Francisco: Ignatius Press, 1994), 146.

10. James Corkery SJ, *Joseph Ratzinger's Theological Ideas: Wise Cautions & Legitimate Hopes* (New York: Paulist Press, 2009), 113.

11. Joseph Ratzinger, 'Europe in the Crisis of Cultures', *Communio* 32, Summer 2005, 347.

12. James Corkery SJ, *Joseph Ratzinger's Theological Ideas: Wise Cautions & Legitimate Hopes* (New York: Paulist Press, 2009), 113.

13. Joseph Ratzinger, 'Europe in the Crisis of Cultures', *Communio* 32, Summer 2005, 348.

14. Ibid. 349.

15. Joseph Ratzinger and Marcello Pera, *Without Roots* (New York: Basic Books, 2007), 128.

16. James Corkery SJ, *Joseph Ratzinger's Theological Ideas: Wise Cautions & Legitimate Hopes* (New York: Paulist Press, 2009), 116.

17. Werner Ustorf, 'A Missiological Postscript', in Hugh McLeod and Werner Ustorf, *The Decline of Christendom in Western Europe, 1750–2000* (Cambridge: University of Cambridge Press, 2003), 224.

18. Ibid. 224.

19. Joseph Ratzinger, 'Europe in the Crisis of Cultures', *Communio* 32, Summer 2005, 348–9.

20. *The Tablet* interview, 'Slaying the secular dragon', *The Tablet*, 18 February 2012, 4.

21. Joseph Ratzinger, 'Europe in the Crisis of Cultures', *Communio* 32, Summer 2005, 349.

22. Ibid. 352.

23. Ibid. 353.

24. Ibid.

25. Louis Dupré, 'The ties that bind us', *The Tablet*, 24 April 2004, www. thetablet.co. uk/article/2521.

26. Ibid.

27. Ibid.

28. Ibid.

29. Max Horkheimer and Theodor W. Adorno, *Dialectic of Enlightenment*, trans. John Cumming (London: Allen Lane, 1972), 3.

30. Ibid. 6.

31. Ibid. 7.

32. Ibid. 121.

33. Joseph Ratzinger, *A Turning Point For Europe* (San Francisco: Ignatius Press, 1994), 175.

34. Ibid. 176.

35. Ibid. 174.

36. Henri de Lubac, SJ, *The Drama of Atheist Humanism* (Cleveland and New York: World Publishing Co., 1963), 18.

37. Ibid. 19.

38. Ibid. 20.

39. Ibid.

40. Ibid. 22.

41. Ibid. 34.

42. Ibid. 35.

43. Ibid. 33.

44. Joseph Ratzinger, *A Turning Point For Europe* (San Francisco: Ignatius Press, 1994), 121.

45. Ibid. 125.

46. Ibid. 127.

47. Ibid. 144.

48. Ibid. 153.

49. Gerald J. Russello, ed., *Christianity and European Culture: Selections from the Work of Christopher Dawson* (Washington, DC: The Catholic University of America Press, 1998), x–xi.

50. Joseph Ratzinger, *A Turning Point For Europe* (San Francisco: Ignatius Press, 1994), 129.

51. Joseph Ratzinger, *Values in a Time of Upheaval* (San Francisco: Ignatius Press, 2006), 139–40. Earlier, Ratzinger writes: 'The great religious traditions of Asia, above all Buddhism, which gives expression to its mystical component, are rising up as intellectual forces against a Europe that denies its religious and ethical foundations.' The resurgence of Islam should be understood as a particular response to the crisis of Europe. Ibid. 139.

52. Ibid. 158. Ratzinger argues that 'technology and physics had, as it were, absorbed ethics'. Joseph Ratzinger, 'Technological Security as a Problem of Social Ethics', in Pope Benedict XVI, *Joseph Ratzinger in Communio: Volume 2, Anthropology and Culture*, eds David L. Schindler and Nicholas J. Healy (Grand Rapids, MI: William B. Eerdmans, 2013), 43.

53. Ibid. 159.

54. Joseph Ratzinger, *A Turning Point For Europe* (San Francisco: Ignatius Press, 1994), 163–164.

55. Joseph Ratzinger, *Values in a Time of Upheaval* (San Francisco: Ignatius Press, 2006), 158.

56. See Michel Lagrée, 'The Impact of Technology on Catholicism in France (1850–1950)', in Hugh McLeod and Werner Ustorf, *The Decline of Christendom in Western Europe, 1750–2000* (Cambridge: University of Cambridge Press, 2003), 177.

57. Joseph Ratzinger, *A Turning Point For Europe* (San Francisco: Ignatius Press, 1994), 94.

58. Ibid. 95.

59. Ibid. 140.

60. Ibid. 140.

61. Ibid. 141.

62. Quoted in Joseph Ratzinger, *A Turning Point For Europe* (San Francisco: Ignatius Press, 1994), 143.

63. Joseph Ratzinger, *A Turning Point For Europe* (San Francisco: Ignatius Press, 1994), 129.

64. Ibid. 130.

65. Ibid. 89.

66. Joseph Ratzinger, *Values in a Time of Upheaval* (San Francisco: Ignatius Press, 2006), 144–5.

67. Ibid. 145.

68. Ibid. 165.

69. Lieven Boeve, 'Europe in Crisis: a Question of Belief or Unbelief? Perspectives from the Vatican', *Modern Theology* 23, no. 2 (1 April 2007), 208.

70. Ibid. 209 .

71. Joseph Ratzinger, *A Turning Point For Europe* (San Francisco: Ignatius Press, 1994), 34.

72. Joseph Ratzinger, 'Europe in the Crisis of Cultures', *Communio* 32, Summer 2005, 347–8.

73. Ibid. 346.

74. Joseph Ratzinger and Marcello Pera, *Without Roots* (New York: Basic Books, 2007), 66.

75. Joseph Ratzinger, *Values in a Time of Upheaval* (San Francisco: Ignatius Press, 2006), 148.

76. Ibid.

77. Ibid.149.

78. Ibid.149–50.

79. James Corkery SJ, *Joseph Ratzinger's Theological Ideas: Wise Cautions & Legitimate Hopes* (New York: Paulist Press, 2009), 117.

80. Ibid. 117–18.

81. Joseph Ratzinger, *Values in a Time of Upheaval* (San Francisco: Ignatius Press, 2006), 41.

82. Ibid. 43.

83. Ibid.

84. Ibid. 44.

85. Ibid. 65.

86. Ibid. 66.

87. Tracey Rowland, *Ratzinger's Faith* (New York: Oxford University Press, 2008), 122.

88. Joseph Ratzinger, *Values in a Time of Upheaval* (San Francisco: Ignatius Press, 2006), 69. Claude Geffré also asserts that 'the gospel become the good news of every man and woman beyond his or her race, language, culture, and even religious belonging'. Claude Geffré, 'Double Belonging and the Originality of Christianity as a Religion', in Catherine Cornille, ed., *Many Mansions?* (Maryknoll, NY: Orbis Books, 2002), 103.

89. Ibid. 111.

90. Ibid. 112.

91. Ibid. 125.

92. Ibid. 125–6.

93. Ibid. 126.

94. Ibid.

95. Ibid. 145.

96. Ibid. 147–8.

97. Joseph Ratzinger, *A Turning Point For Europe* (San Francisco: Ignatius Press, 1994), 146.

98. Joseph Ratzinger, *Values in a Time of Upheaval* (San Francisco: Ignatius Press, 2006), 150.

99. Ibid. 115.

100. Joseph Ratzinger, 'Europe in the Crisis of Cultures', *Communio* 32 (Summer 2005), 354.

101. Ibid. 355.

102. Lieven Boeve, 'Europe in Crisis: A Question of Belief or Unbelief? Perspectives from the Vatican', *Modern Theology* 23, no. 2 (1 April 2007), 214.

103. Joseph Ratzinger, *Values in a Time of Upheaval* (San Francisco: Ignatius Press, 2006), 67–8.

104. Joseph A. Komonchak, 'The Church in crisis: Pope Benedict's theological vision', *Commonweal*, vol. 132, no. 11 (3 June 2005), 13.

105. Ibid.

106. Ibid. 12.

107. Ibid. 13.

108. Ibid.

109. Ibid. 14.

110. Philip Jenkins, 'Godless Europe?' *International Bulletin Of Missionary Research*, vol. 31, no. 3, July 1, 2007, 115.

111. Ibid. 118.

112. Anton Wessels, *Europe: Was it Ever Really Christian?* (London: SCM Press, 1994), 3.

113. Quoted in Anton Wessels, *Europe: Was it Ever Really Christian?* (London: SCM Press, 1994), 5.

114. Quoted in Sandro Magister, 'The Church Is Under Siege. But Habermas, the Atheist, Is Coming to its Defense', http://chiesa.espresso.repubblica.it/articolo/20037?eng=y.

115. Richard King, *Orientalism and Religion: Postcolonial Theory, India and 'The Mystic East'* (London: Routledge, 1999), 10.

116. Ibid. 170. According to O'Leary, there is no need to conceive our religious tradition in an essentialist manner so that it would not be contaminated by other traditions. This is because religious identity 'is made to be reborn, modified but recognisable, in diverse situations and relationships in which it has to construct itself'. Joseph Stephen O'Leary, *Religious Pluralism and Christian Truth* (Edinburgh: Edinburgh University Press, 1996), 2–3.

117. Ibid. 4.

118. Patrik Fridlund, *Mobile Performances: Linguistic Undecidability as Possibility and Problem in the Theology of Religions* (Leuven: Peeters, 2011), 117.

119. See Edward W. Said, *Orientalism* (London: Penguin, 2003), 1–28.

120. Werner G. Jeanrond, 'The Future of Christianity in Europe', in Werner G. Jeanrond and Andrew D. H. Mayes, eds, *Recognising the Margins: Developments in Biblical and Theological Studies* (Dublin: The Columba Press, 2006), 184.

121. Ibid. 185.

122. Ibid.

123. Aylward Shorter, *Evangelization and Culture* (London: Geoffrey Chapman, 1994), 93.

124. Werner G. Jeanrond, 'The Future of Christianity in Europe', in Werner G. Jeanrond and Andrew D. H. Mayes, eds, *Recognising the Margins: Developments in Biblical and Theological Studies* (Dublin: The Columba Press, 2006), 185.

125. Ibid. 185–6. Regarding the disappearance of religious homogeneity in Europe in recent times, Jeanrond argues that 'The political–religious program of *cuius regio eius religio*, promoted both by the Augsburg Peace of 1555 and the Westphalian settlement of 1648 as a means for overcoming interconfessional warfare, followed the old Roman conviction that a state could survive in the long run only if it was built on a unitary religious formula. The breakdown of this conviction and resulting political projects has given rise to new anxieties. In Christian churches, in debates on the future of European integration ... critical voices ask how to deal with religious pluralism, religious identity, and religious otherness.' Werner G. Jeanrond, 'Toward an Interreligious hermeneutics of Love', in Catherine Cornille and Christopher Conway, eds, *Interreligious Hermeneutics* (Eugene, OR: Cascade Books, 2010), 44.

126. Ibid. 188.

127. Ibid.

128. Ibid.

129. Ibid. 189.

130. Ibid. 192.

131. Ibid. 193.

132. Hugh McLeod and Werner Ustorf, *The Decline of Christendom in Western Europe, 1750–2000* (Cambridge: Cambridge University Press, 2003), 1.

133. Ibid.

134. Ibid. 2.

135. Ibid.

136. Yves Lambert, 'New Christianity, Indifference and Diffused Spirituality', in Hugh McLeod and Werner Ustorf, *The Decline of Christendom in Western Europe, 1750–2000* (Cambridge: Cambridge University Press, 2003), 76. Christopher Dawson believes that 'Christianity maintains within itself the seeds of its own renewal', thus it can 'remain independent of secular culture and can draw on its own internal resources when challenged'. In other words, Christianity has the capacity to resist those who wish to make the religion a tool of the state or to abolish it altogether. Gerald J. Russello, ed., *Christianity and European Culture: Selections from the Work of Christopher Dawson* (Washington, DC: The Catholic University of America Press, 1998), xi.

137. Quoted in Yves Lambert, 'New Christianity, Indifference and Diffused Spirituality', in Hugh McLeod and Werner Ustorf, *The Decline of Christendom in Western Europe, 1750–2000* (Cambridge: Cambridge University Press, 2003), 66.

138. Yves Lambert, 'New Christianity, Indifference and Diffused Spirituality', in Hugh McLeod and Werner Ustorf, *The Decline of Christendom in Western Europe, 1750–2000* (Cambridge: Cambridge University Press, 2003), 67.

139. Ibid. 77.

140. Jonathan J. Bonk, 'Europe: Christendom graveyard or Christian laboratory?', *International Bulletin Of Missionary Research* vol. 31, no. 3 (1 July 2007), 113.

141. This refers to the decisive battle at the Milvian Bridge in Rome on 28 October 312. Anton Wessels, *Europe: Was it Ever Really Christian?* (London: SCM Press, 1994), 51.

142. Jonathan J. Bonk, 'Europe: Christendom graveyard or Christian laboratory?', *International Bulletin Of Missionary Research* vol. 31, no. 3 (1 July 2007), 114.

143. Lamin Sanneh, 'Can Europe be saved? A Review Essay', *International Bulletin Of Missionary Research*, vol. 31, no. 3 (1 July 2007), 121.

144. Ibid.

145. Lieven Boeve, 'Europe in Crisis: A Question of Belief or Unbelief? Perspectives from the Vatican', *Modern Theology* 23, no. 2 (1 April 2007), 222. Tom Greggs puts it this way: 'Added to the fact that de-Christianization has taken place simultaneous to the growth of religious plurality, it is not simply the case that now less people are going to church: more people are now attending mosques, temples and gurdwaras in societies once divided only by which form of Christian denomination one chose to worship on a Sunday.' Thus we ask, 'what do a church, a community, a sermon, a liturgy, a Christian life mean in a simultaneously de-Christianized *and religiously pluralist society?*' Tom Greggs, *Theology Against Religion* (London: T & T Clark, 2011), 124–5. O'Leary is more positive in his observation when he writes: 'The great world religions lose their appearance of permanence when one treats them as human institutions born of function of the needs of an epoch ... and now, to a sceptical observer, nearing the exhaustion of their resources. Yet as they broach a new millennial threshold the religions seem in better shape than had been foretold, their mighty engines purring, their rich traditions relucent, despite – or rather because of – critical contestation and pluralist dispersion. Perhaps the greatest challenge they face is that of assessing, rationally and responsibly, their status and function, so that in addition to arousing faith and devotion they will also continue to illuminate human minds questing for what is not only meaningful but true.' Joseph Stephen O'Leary, *Religious Pluralism and Christian Truth* (Edinburgh: Edinburgh University Press, 1996), 10.

146. Ibid. 223.

CHAPTER 8: TISSA BALASURIYA OMI

1. Paul Collins, ed., *From Inquisition to Freedom* (London: Continuum, 2001), 82.

2. *AsianNews.it*, www.asianews.it/news-en/Fr-Tissa-Balasuriya,-controversial-Sri-Lankan-theologian,-laid-to-rest-26925.html. See also *The Guardian*, www.theguardian.com/world/2013/mar/06/father-tissa-balasuriya and Basil Fernando, *Power versus Conscience* (Hong Kong: Asian Human Rights Commission and Asian Legal Resource Centre Ltd, 1997), 1–15.

3. Tissa Balasuriya, *Mary and Human Liberation: the Story and the Text* (Harrisburg, Pennsylvania: Trinity Press International, 1997), 26–7.

4. Ibid. 29.

5. Ibid. 30.

6. Ibid. 33.

7. Ibid. 43.

8. Ibid. 161.

9. Ibid. 165.

10. Ibid. 57.

11. Ibid. 58.

12. Ibid.

13. Ibid. 59–60.

14. Ibid. 66.

15. Ibid. 68.

16. Ibid. 74.

17. Ibid. 70.

18. Ibid. 78.

19. Ibid. 89–90.

20. Ibid. 132–3.

21. Ibid. 133–4.

22. Ibid. 139.

23. Ibid.

24. Ibid. 140–2.

25. Ibid. 142.

26. Ibid. 143.

27. Ibid.

28. Ibid. 144.

29. Ibid.

30. Ibid.

31. Tissa Balasuriya, 'An Asian Perspective', in K. C. Abraham, ed., *Third World Theologies* (Maryknoll, NY: Orbis Books, 2002), 114.

32. Ibid. 117.

33. Ibid.

34. Ibid. 118.

35. Tissa Balasuriya, *Mary and Human Liberation: the Story and the Text* (Harrisburg, Pennsylvania: Trinity Press International, 1997), 48.

36. Ibid.

37. Ibid. 49.

38. Ibid. 105.

39. Tissa Balasuriya, 'An Asian Perspective', in K. C. Abraham, ed., *Third World Theologies* (Maryknoll, NY: Orbis Books, 2002), 115.

40. Ibid. 115–16.

41. Tissa Balasuriya, *Mary and Human Liberation: the Story and the Text* (Harrisburg, Pennsylvania: Trinity Press International, 1997), 109.

42. Ibid. 110.

43. Ibid. 111.

44. Ibid. 112.

45. Ibid.

46. Ibid.

47. Ibid. 113.

48. Ibid. 114.

49. Ibid. 128–9.

50. Ibid. 129.

51. Ibid. 129–30.

52. Ibid. 157.

53. Ibid. 160.

54. Ibid.

55. Ibid. 160–1.

56. See Tissa Balasuriya, *Planetary Theology* (Maryknoll, NY: Orbis Books, 1984), 2–16.

57. Notification concerning the Text *Mary and Human Liberation* by Father Tissa Balasuriya, OMI, Congregation for the Doctrine of the Faith, www.vatican.va/roman_curia/congregations/cfaith/documents/rc_con_cfaith_doc_19970102_tissa-balasuriya_en.html.

58. Tissa Balasuriya, 'Communication and Liberation', in Paul Collins, ed., *From Inquisition to Freedom* (London: Continuum, 2001), 98.

59. Celestine Bohlen, *New York Times*, 7 January 1997, 'Sri Lankan Priest Excommunicated for "Relativism"', www.erowid.org/spirit/traditions/ christianity/catholicism/catholicism_media1.shtml.

60. *National Catholic Reporter*, 'Curran welcomes Balasuriya to theological outcast status', http://natcath.org/NCR_Online/archives2/1997a/020797/020797d.htm.

61. *The Tablet*, 25 January 1997, 'The Balasuriya File', http://archive.thetablet.co.uk/article/25th-january-1997/13/the-balasuriya-file.

62. Ibid.

63. *The Tablet*, 1 February 1997, 'The Heart of the Matter', http://archive.thetablet.co.uk/article/1st-february-1997/3/the-heart-of-the-matter.

64. Joseph Ratzinger, 'Relativism: The Central Problem for Faith Today', www.ewtn.com/library/curia/ratzrela.htm.

65. *The Tablet*, 1 February 1997, 'The Heart of the Matter', http://archive.thetablet.co.uk/article/1st-february-1997/3/the-heart-of-the-matter.

66. Ibid.

67. Bradford E. Hinze, 'A Decade of Disciplining Theologians', *Horizons* 37, no. 1 (Spring 2010), 119–20.

68. Ibid. 120–22.

69. Thomas J. Reese, *Inside the Vatican: The Politics and Organization of the Catholic Church* (Cambridge, MA: Harvard University Press, 1996), 254.

70. Quoted in Thomas J. Reese, *Inside the Vatican: The Politics and Organization of the Catholic Church* (Cambridge, MA: Harvard University Press, 1996), 252–3.

71. Tissa Balasuriya, 'Communication and Liberation', in Paul Collins, ed., *From Inquisition to Freedom* (London: Continuum, 2001), 106.

72. *The Tablet*, 11 October 1997, 'The Burden on Balasuriya', http://archive.thetablet.co.uk/article/11th-october-1997/3/the-burden-on-balasuriya.

73. See Tissa Balasuriya, 'On the Observation of the SCDF on my book *Mary and Human Liberation*', in Tissa Balasuriya, *Mary and Human Liberation: the Story and the Text* (Harrisburg, Pennsylvania: Trinity Press International, 1997), 201–23.

74. Bradford E. Hinze, 'A Decade of Disciplining Theologians', *Horizons* 37, no. 1 (Spring 2010), 121.

75. Quoted in Philip Kennedy, *Twentieth-century Theologians: A New Introduction to Modern Christian Thought* (London and New York: I. B. Tauris, 2010), 269.

76. Tissa Balasuriya, 'Communication and Liberation', in Paul Collins, ed., *From Inquisition to Freedom* (London: Continuum, 2001), 98.

77. Ibid. 102.

78. Quoted in Thomas J. Reese, *Inside the Vatican: The Politics and Organization of the Catholic Church* (Cambridge, MA: Harvard University Press, 1996), 252. The Cologne Declaration, issued on 6 January 1989, was signed by 163 theologians from Germany, Austria, Switzerland and the Netherlands, criticizing certain church policies such as John Paul's appointments of bishops, the Vatican's refusal to grant certain theologians licence to teach, etc. 'Remembering the Cologne Declaration', http://natcath.org/NCR_Online/archives2/1999a/011599/011599s.htm.

79. Thomas J. Reese, *Inside the Vatican: The Politics and Organization of the Catholic Church* (Cambridge, MA: Harvard University Press, 1996), 250–1.

80. Quoted in Thomas J. Reese, *Inside the Vatican: The Politics and Organization of the Catholic Church* (Cambridge, MA: Harvard University Press, 1996), 251.

81. Ibid. 254.

82. Quoted in Thomas J. Reese, *Inside the Vatican: The Politics and Organization of the Catholic Church* (Cambridge, MA: Harvard University Press, 1996), 254–5.

83. Thomas J. Reese, *Inside the Vatican: The Politics and Organization of the Catholic Church* (Cambridge, MA: Harvard University Press, 1996), 260.

84. *The Tablet*, 24 January 1998, 'Holy See lifts the excommunication of Tissa Balasuriya', http://archive.thetablet.co.uk/article/24th-january-1998/20/holy-see-lifts-the-excommunication-of-tissa-balasu.

85. Tissa Balasuriya, *Mary and Human Liberation: the Story and the Text* (Harrisburg, Pennsylvania: Trinity Press International, 1997), 22.

86. Tissa Balasuriya, 'Communication and Liberation', in Paul Collins, ed., *From Inquisition to Freedom* (London: Continuum, 2001), 98

CHAPTER 9: JACQUES DUPUIS SJ

1. See Joseph Ratzinger, 'Christ, Faith and the Challenge of Cultures', www.ewtn.com /library/curia/ratzhong.htm. He gave this speech to the Asian bishops' conferences and the chairmen of doctrinal committees in Hong Kong (2–5 March 1993).

2. John L. Allen, *Pope Benedict XVI* (New York: Continuum, 2000), 238. Ratzinger was referring to the views of Jacques Dupuis, 'The Kingdom of God and World Religions', in *Vidyajyoti, Journal of Theological Reflection* 51 (1987), 530–44.

3. Thomas P. Rausch, *Pope Benedict XVI: An Introduction to his Theological Vision* (New York: Paulist Press, 2009), 29. It was a Jesuit who reported Dupuis to the CDF. Robert Blair Kaiser, the writer for *Newsweek*, asked the man's academic specialization, Dupuis growled, 'Any damn thing.' Robert Blair Kaiser, 'Dupuis Profile', in Daniel Kendall and Gerald O'Collins, eds, *In Many and Diverse Ways: In Honor of Jacques Dupuis* (Maryknoll, NY: Orbis Books, 2003), 228. By condemning Dupuis, Burrows claims that the CDF was trying to protect church authorities that 'have lost the ability to speak effectively' to the contemporary world of 'practical agnosticism' and secularism. Being open to the goodness and grace in other religions, Dupuis was in agreement with those who are critical of Western secularism and religious exclusivism. William R. Burrows, 'The Man, the Message, the Controversy', in William R. Burrows, ed., *Jacques Dupuis Faces the Inquisition: Two Essays by Jacques Dupuis on Dominus Iesus and the Roman Investigation of His Work* (Eugene, OR: Pickwick Publications, 2012), 17.

4. Congregation for the Doctrine of the Faith, *Notification* on the book *Toward a Christian Theology of Religious Pluralism* (Orbis Books: Maryknoll, NY, 1997) by Father Jacques Dupuis, SJ, www.vatican.va/roman_curia/congregations/cfaith/documents/rc_con_cfaith_doc_20010124_dupuis_en.html. Regarding theologians being called to Rome for a colloquium with representatives of the CDF, Hinze claims that what transpires is an interrogation in which the theologian is placed in the position of defending his or her position before a group of people who have already reached certain conclusions about what is required of the theologian, what positions must be repudiated, what innovations are deemed unacceptable. There is no possibility of mutual listening and learning to take place in this environment.' Bradford E. Hinze, 'A Decade of Disciplining Theologians', *Horizons* 37, no. 1 (Spring 2010), 122.

5. Declaration on the Relations of the Church to Non-Christian Religion, *Nostra Aetate*, proclaimed by His Holiness Pope Paul VI on 28 October 1965, no. 2, www.vatican.va /archive/hist_ councils/ii_vatican_council/documents/vat-ii_decl_19651028_nostra-aetate_en.html.

6. See Joseph Ratzinger, *Many Religions – One Covenant* (San Francisco: Ignatius Press, 1999), 27–8.

7. Robert Blair Kaiser, 'Dupuis Profile', in Daniel Kendall and Gerald O'Collins, eds, *In Many and Diverse Ways: In Honor of Jacques Dupuis* (Maryknoll, NY: Orbis Books, 2003), 223.

8. Ibid.

9. Jacques Dupuis SJ, *Christianity and the Religions: From Confrontation to Dialogue* (Maryknoll, NY: Orbis Books, 2002), 90.

10. Ibid. 135.

11. Ibid. 136.

12. *Verbum incarnandum* is the Word before the incarnation; *Verbum incarnatum* is 'the state of kenosis during his human life or after the resurrection in the glorified state'. Ibid. 140.

13. Ibid. 263.

14. 'Father Jacques Dupuis', *The Times*, 12 January 2005, www.timesonline.co.uk/tol/comment/obituaries/article411125.ece.

15. Quoted in 'Father Jacques Dupuis', *The Times*, 12 January 2005, www.timesonline.co.uk/tol/comment/obituaries/article411125.ece. Perhaps Dupuis' experience in India leads him to ask: 'Has not Christian dogma been unduly absolutized, whereas in reality, when all is said and done, it is only relative?' Jacques Dupuis, SJ, 'Christianity and Religions: Complementarity and Convergence', in Catherine Cornille, ed., *Many Mansions?* (Maryknoll, NY: Orbis Books, 2002), 71

16. Joseph Ratzinger, *The Nature and Mission of Theology* (San Francisco: Ignatius Press, 1995), 105.

17. Jacques Dupuis SJ., *Toward a Christian Theology of Religious Pluralism* (Maryknoll, NY: Orbis Books, 1997), 3.

18. Ibid. 5.

19. Ibid. 6.

20. Ibid. 7. O'Leary insists that our religious identity must be seen in relation to the other beliefs to avoid the confusion of pluralism. This leads him to assert that 'a religion that has become dialogical is better able to distinguish between the deep and the shallow levels of its own heritage, or between its tribal conditioning and its universal spiritual reach, and thus acquires a critical relation to its own truth ... the meaning of a religion is never given once for all, but takes the form of a mobile history, marked at each epoch by exchanges with the surrounding culture.' Joseph O'Leary, *Religious Pluralism and Christian Truth* (Edinburgh: Edinburgh University Press, 1996), 2.

21. Joseph Ratzinger, *Truth and Tolerance* (San Francisco: Ignatius Press, 2004), 64.

22. Ibid. 65.

23. Ibid. 65–6.

24. Jacques Dupuis, SJ, *Toward a Christian Theology of Religious Pluralism* (Maryknoll, NY: Orbis Books, 1997), 198.

25. Ibid. 386.

26. Ibid. For a comprehensive theology of mission, see David J. Bosch, *Transforming Mission: Paradigm Shifts in Theology of Mission* (Maryknoll, NY: Orbis Books, 1991).

27. Ibid. 387.

28. Ibid.

29. Ibid.

30. Ibid. 388. Alvin Plantinga believes that 'knowledge of the facts of pluralism could initially serve as a defeater, but in the long run have precisely the opposite effect'. See Alvin Plantinga, 'Pluralism: A Defense of Religious Exclusivism', in Philip L. Quinn, Kevin Meeker, eds, *The Philosophical Challenge of Religious Diversity* (Oxford: Oxford University Press, 2000), 172–92.

31. Ibid.

32. Ibid. 390. Influenced by Pierre Teilhard de Chardin, Dupuis writes: 'A general convergence of religions upon a universal Christ who fundamentally satisfies them all: that seems to me the only possible conversion of the world, and the only form in which a religion of the future can be conceived.' Quoted in Jacques Dupuis SJ, 'Christianity and Religions: Complementarity and Convergence', in Catherine Cornille, ed., *Many Mansions?* (Maryknoll, NY: Orbis Books, 2002), 69.

33. Ilaria Morali says that it would be a mistake to associate Dupuis' theology with that of Knitter and Hick. Dupuis sought 'to remain firmly anchored in the faith' and thus 'set him light years apart from the pluralists, who are much less concerned than he about keeping their thought within the confines of orthodoxy'. Dupuis was convinced that the pluralism proposed by Hick and Knitter would dilute the mystery of Jesus Christ in the Christian faith. Hence, Dupuis proposed an 'inclusive Christocentrism' which means that Christocentrism and Theocentrism 'together constitute the very character of Christian theology'. Ilaria Morali, 'Overview of Some Francophone and Italian Trends', in Karl J. Becker and Ilaria Morali, eds, *Catholic Engagement with World Religions* (Maryknoll, NY: Orbis Books, 2010), 325–6.

34. Gerald O'Collins, 'Jacques Dupuis: His Person and Work', in Daniel Kendall and Gerald O'Collins, eds, *In Many and Diverse Ways: In Honor of Jacques Dupuis* (Maryknoll, NY: Orbis Books, 2003), 25.

35. William R. Burrows, 'The Man, the Message, the Controversy', in William R. Burrows, ed., *Jacques Dupuis Faces the Inquisition: Two Essays by Jacques Dupuis on Dominus Iesus and the Roman Investigation of His Work* (Eugene, OR: Pickwick Publications, 2012), 10.

36. David Tracy, 'Western Hermeneutics and Interreligious Dialogue', in Catherine Cornille and Christopher Conway, eds, *Interreligious Hermeneutics* (Eugene, OR: Cascade Books, 2010), 4.

37. Declaration 'Dominus Iesus' on the Unicity and Salvific Universality of Jesus Christ and the Church, www.vatican.va/roman_curia/congregations/cfaith/documents/rc_con_cfaith_doc_20000806_dominus-iesus_en.html, no.4.

38. Bradford E. Hinze, 'A Decade of Disciplining Theologians', *Horizons* 37, no. 1 (Spring 2010), 96. Regarding the title of the Declaration, *Dominus Iesus, On the Unicity and Salvific Universality of Jesus Christ and the Church*, Dupuis criticizes it for placing the mystery of Jesus Christ and that of the church on the same level. The church, according to Dupuis, is secondary to the role of Jesus Christ in the economy of salvation. Jacques Dupuis, 'The Declaration *Dominus Iesus* and My Perspective on it', in William R. Burrows, ed., *Jacques Dupuis Faces the Inquisition: Two Essays by Jacques Dupuis on Dominus Iesus and the Roman Investigation of His Work* (Eugene, OR: Pickwick Publications, 2012), 32.

39. Declaration 'Dominus Iesus' on the Unicity and Salvific Universality of Jesus Christ and the Church, www.vatican.va/roman_curia/congregations/cfaith/documents/rc_con_cfaith_doc_20000806_dominus-iesus_en.html, no. 4.

40. Ibid. 15.

41. Jacques Dupuis, 'The Declaration *Dominus Iesus* and My Perspective on it', in William R. Burrows, ed., *Jacques Dupuis Faces the Inquisition: Two Essays by Jacques Dupuis on Dominus Iesus and the Roman Investigation of His Work* (Eugene, OR: Pickwick Publications, 2012), 31.

42. Declaration 'Dominus Iesus' on the Unicity and Salvific Universality of Jesus Christ and the Church, www.vatican.va/roman_curia/congregations/cfaith/documents/rc_con_cfaith_doc_20000806_dominus-iesus_en.html, no. 4.

43. Jacques Dupuis, SJ, *Toward a Christian Theology of Religious Pluralism* (Maryknoll, NY: Orbis Books, 1997), 181.

44. Ibid. 185. Burrows writes that what was wrong in Dupuis's work, according to the CDF and his critics, was perhaps his 'minimalist view of the church'. This means the church 'played a minimal role in the universal economy of salvation for him'. Thus, the CDF needed to discipline him. William R. Burrows, 'The Man, the Message, the Controversy', in William R. Burrows, ed., *Jacques Dupuis Faces the Inquisition: Two Essays by Jacques Dupuis on Dominus Iesus and the Roman Investigation of His Work* (Eugene, OR: Pickwick Publications, 2012), 21.

45. Ibid. 185–6.

46. Ibid. 186. The mission of the church is to witness to the reality of God's grace. The Protestant view emphasizes that the church cannot cause salvation. According to Karl Barth, 'the goal of missions is not to convert heathen in the sense of bringing them to a personal enjoyment of their salvation. Neither at home nor abroad can it be the work of the community to convert men. This is the work of God alone.' Quoted in Tom Greggs, *Theology Against Religion* (London: T & T Clark, 2011), 108.

47. Ibid. 190.

48. Joseph Ratzinger, *Truth and Tolerance* (San Francisco: Ignatius Press, 2004), 119.

49. Ibid. 120.

50. Hick says Ratzinger misrepresents his position, if it excluded the vertical dimension of transcendence and reduced it to a purely 'horizontal horizon'. John Hick, 'Ratzinger absolutely wrong on relativism', *National Catholic Reporter*, http://natcath.org/NCR_Online/

archives2/1997d/102497/102497i.htm. See also John Hick, *Dialogues in the Philosophy of Religion* (London: Palgrave Macmillan, 1993), 157 ff.

51. Jacques Dupuis, SJ, *Toward a Christian Theology of Religious Pluralism* (Maryknoll, NY: Orbis Books, 1997), 195.

52. Ibid. 196.

53. Ibid. In this regard, Amos Yong has argued 'that human life and experience is dependent only on the prevenient grace and activity of God through the Holy Spirit, and that this should put us on the alert for possible experiences of the Spirit and alternative specifications of the pneumatological imagination outside of explicitly Christian contexts'. Amos Yong, *Discerning the Spirit(s): A Pentecost–Charismatic Contribution to Christian Theology of Religions* (Sheffield: Sheffield Academic Press, 2000), 182.

54. Ibid. 197.

55. Ibid. 198.

56. Ibid. 203.

57. Ibid. 204. In the same way, O'Leary asserts: 'Each religion is in contact with an absolute reality; but none is itself absolute, or rather each religion claims a different type of absoluteness. The fragmentary character of sacred texts, the deep marks of historical contingency on the culture which produced them and on their very composition, betray the impossibility of giving an absolute status to the traditions they found.' Joseph O'Leary, *Religious Pluralism and Christian Truth* (Edinburgh: Edinburgh University Press, 1996), 26.

58. Ibid. 205.

59. Ibid. 205–6.

60. Gerald O'Collins, 'Jacques Dupuis: His Person and Work', in Daniel Kendall and Gerald O'Collins, eds, *In Many and Diverse Ways: In Honor of Jacques Dupuis* (Maryknoll, NY: Orbis Books, 2003), 26.

61. Ibid. 27.

62. Jacques Dupuis SJ, *Toward a Christian Theology of Religious Pluralism* (Maryknoll, NY: Orbis Books, 1997), 206.

63. Ibid. 207. Regarding the danger of Christomonism, O'Leary writes: 'The paschal mystery is universal because it touches the essence of human living and dying; this universality is not imposed from without, by preaching Christ, but discovered from within, in every human destiny, as a horizon of hope, given a certain definitiveness in the cross. Modesty is de rigueur in making such claims, since we are dealing with realities of faith, not of final vision. An eschatological proviso, a *docta ignorantia*, must qualify all our affirmations. We grasp only dimly and from within a human historical perspective what the Spirit is saying to the religions and to us through the religions.' Joseph S. O'Leary, 'Toward a Buddhist Interpretation of Christian Truth', in Catherine Cornille, ed., *Many Mansions?* (Maryknoll, NY: Orbis Books, 2002), 37.

64. Ibid.

65. Ibid. For a good discussion on the tension between the universal love of God and the particularity of salvation brought by Jesus Christ, see Amos Yong, *Discerning the Spirit(s): A Pentecost-Charismatic Contribution to Christian Theology of Religions* (Sheffield: Sheffield Academic Press, 2000), 35–58.

66. Ibid. 209.

67. Ibid. 217.

68. Ibid. 218.

69. Ibid. 219.

70. Ibid. 221.

71. Ibid. 222.

72. Ibid. 224.
73. Ibid. 225.
74. Ibid. 226.
75. Ibid. 228.
76. Ibid. 226.
77. Ibid. 227.
78. Ibid. 233.
79. Ibid. 235.
80. Ibid. 237.
81. Ibid. 303.
82. Ibid. 304.
83. Joseph Ratzinger, *Many Religions – One Covenant* (San Francisco: Ignatius Press, 1999), 27.
84. Ibid. 28.
85. Jacques Dupuis SJ, *Toward a Christian Theology of Religious Pluralism* (Maryknoll, NY: Orbis Books, 1997), 305.
86. Ibid. 307. In spite of positive elements found in other religions as taught by the Second Vatican Council in *Lumen Gentium* and *Nostra Aetate*, there is no clear affirmation from church teaching that these religions also contain salvific means. Karl Rahner and Jacques Dupuis teach that the Council is silent on this issue. Mikka Ruokanen and Paul Hacker argue that the Council would not accept other religions as legitimate paths to salvation. For them, these non-Christian religions have only 'anthropological achievements': 'the best the human spirit can achieve in moving towards the living God'. Paul Knitter, however, believes that the Council has affirmed other religions as ways to gain salvation for their members. Gavin D'Costa, 'Roman Catholic Reflections on Discerning God in Interreligious Dialogue: Challenges and Promising Avenues', in Catherine Cornille, ed., *Criteria of Discernment in Interreligious Dialogue* (Eugene, OR: Cascade Books, 2009), 73.
87. Ibid. 316.
88. Ibid. 319.
89. Ibid. 321. O'Leary has argued that the traditional Nicene and Chalcedonian Christology can be read in pluralistic and relativisitic terms because 'Jesus Christ himself is plural' and 'he has no identity except in relation to others'. O'Leary believes that Christ 'is disseminated across history, and that our construction of his identity is a contingent historical *upaya*, subject to profound alterations in the light of new encounters'. Joseph O' Leary, *Religious Pluralism and Christian Truth* (Edinburgh: Edinburgh University Press, 1996), 4.
90. Gerald O'Collins, 'Jacques Dupuis: His Person and Work', in Daniel Kendall and Gerald O'Collins, eds, *In Many and Diverse Ways: In Honor of Jacques Dupuis* (Maryknoll, NY: Orbis Books, 2003), 24.
91. *Fides et Ratio*, www.vatican.va/holy_father/john_paul_ii/encyclicals/documents/hf_jp-ii_enc_15101998_fides-et-ratio_en.html, no.2.
92. Gerald O'Collins, 'Jacques Dupuis: His Person and Work', in Daniel Kendall and Gerald O'Collins, eds, *In Many and Diverse Ways: In Honor of Jacques Dupuis* (Maryknoll, NY: Orbis Books, 2003), 24.
93. Jacques Dupuis, SJ , *Toward a Christian Theology of Religious Pluralism* (Maryknoll, NY: Orbis Books, 1997), 341.
94. Ibid. 343.
95. Ibid. 344.
96. Ibid. 345.
97. Ibid.

98. Ibid. 345–6.

99. Ibid. 346.

100. Ibid. 356.

101. Ibid. 357.

102. Joseph Ratzinger, *Truth and Tolerance* (San Francisco: Ignatius Press, 2004), 72–3.

103. Jacques Dupuis SJ, *Toward a Christian Theology of Religious Pluralism* (Maryknoll, NY: Orbis Books, 1997), 365. Tom Greggs argues that the role of the church engaging with people of other religions and those who have none is not to seek to convert them. Only God can do that. When a person does convert, it is not mainly for attaining 'personal salvation', but to witness together with the other Christians the 'reality of God's reconciliation of the world in Christ'. The church is not to exploit people with the fear of death and damnation, but must place God at the centre of its message. Nor can the church engage in trying to civilize non-Christians as in the days of colonialism. Tom Greggs, *Theology Against Religion* (London: T & T Clark, 2011), 108–9.

104. Ibid. 367. This is also the view of Michael L. Fitzgerald who asserts that the deeper aim of dialogue is conversion in the sense of returning to God in humble submission to his will. The focus is on God and not on one's religion. The possibility of converting to another religion is left open, but no one should be coerced to change religious allegiance. See Michael L. Fitzgerald, 'A Theological Reflection on Interreligious Dialogue', in Karl J. Becker and Ilaria Morali, eds, *Catholic Engagement with World Religions* (Maryknoll, NY: Orbis Books, 2010), 388–9.

105. Ibid. 382. O'Leary says 'dialogue … saves Christianity from turning in on itself in an incestuous rehash of its traditions, lets in some fresh air, and restores a human, natural complexion to religious language'. Joseph O'Leary, *Religious Pluralism and Christian Truth* (Edinburgh: Edinburgh University Press, 1996), x.

106. Joseph O'Leary, 'Toward a Buddhist Interpretation of Christian Truth', in Catherine Cornille, ed., *Many Mansions?* (Maryknoll, NY: Orbis Books, 2002), 38.

107. Jacques Dupuis SJ, *Toward a Christian Theology of Religious Pluralism* (Maryknoll, NY: Orbis Books, 1997), 383.

108. Ibid, 384. See also Stephen B. Bevans and Roger P. Schroeder, *Prophetic Dialogue: Reflections on Christian Mission Today* (Maryknoll, NY: Orbis Books, 2011), 19–39.

109. Joseph Ratzinger, *Pilgrim Fellowship of Faith* (San Francisco: Ignatius Press, 2005), 211.

110. Ibid, 212. David Tracy claims that 'successful dialogue are, in fact, very rare. Instead of full dialogue, religious authorities often prefer that interlocutors "exchange viewpoints" (a practice suspiciously like political negotiations between states); more positively, the interlocutors in official interreligious dialogues should clarify differences and sustain legitimate boundaries of each tradition. They may very well through dialogue find some similarities in ethical and even religious purposes (e.g., social justice) that allow for common ethical and political action.' David Tracy, 'Western Hermeneutics and Interreligious Dialogue', in Catherine Cornille and Christopher Conway, eds, *Interreligious Hermeneutics* (Eugene, OR: Cascade Books, 2010), 19.

111. Lieven Boeve and Gerard Mannion, eds, *The Ratzinger Reader* (London: T & T Clark, 2010), 142.

112. Ibid, 143. Mannion also points out that the author of *Dominus Iesus* later got a 'curial promotion' from Ratzinger. William Burrows is of the opinion that Tarcisio Bertone and Angelo Amato did a bad job in drafting *Dominus Iesus* and the Dupuis Notification and, therefore, did a disservice to Ratzinger. He also accuses Ratzinger of appointing subordinates who are merely 'yes men'. Preface in William R. Burrows, ed., *Jacques Dupuis Faces the Inquisition: Two Essays by Jacques Dupuis on* Dominus Iesus *and the Roman Investigation of His Work* (Eugene, OR: Pickwick Publications, 2012), xxi.

113. Regarding Dupuis' responses to the Vatican's criticism, which he was not permitted to publish when he was alive, see Jacques Dupuis, 'The CDF Process and Notification and My Perspectives on Them', in William R. Burrows, ed., *Jacques Dupuis Faces the Inquisition: Two Essays by Jacques Dupuis on* Dominus Iesus *and the Roman Investigation of His Work* (Eugene, OR: Pickwick Publications, 2012), 74–102.

114. Congregation for the Doctrine of the Faith, *Notification* on the book *Toward a Christian Theology of Religious Pluralism* (Orbis Books: Maryknoll, NY, 1997), by Father Jacques Dupuis SJ, www.vatican.va/roman_curia/congregations/cfaith/documents/rc_con_cfaith_doc_20010124_dupuis_en.html.

115. Ibid.

116. Quoted in Gerald O'Collins, 'Jacques Dupuis: His Person and Work', in Daniel Kendall and Gerald O'Collins, eds, *In Many and Diverse Ways: In Honor of Jacques Dupuis* (Maryknoll, NY: Orbis Books, 2003), 21.

117. Ilaria Morali, 'Salvation, Religions, and Dialogue in the Roman Magisterium', in Karl J. Becker and Ilaria Morali, eds, *Catholic Engagement with World Religions* (Maryknoll, NY: Orbis Books, 2010), 138.

118. Quoted in Jacques Dupuis, 'The CDF Process and Notification and My Perspectives on Them', in William R. Burrows, ed., *Jacques Dupuis Faces the Inquisition: Two Essays by Jacques Dupuis on* Dominus Iesus *and the Roman Investigation of His Work* (Eugene, OR: Pickwick Publications, 2012), 102.

119. *Preface* in William R. Burrows, ed., *Jacques Dupuis Faces the Inquisition: Two Essays by Jacques Dupuis on* Dominus Iesus *and the Roman Investigation of His Work* (Eugene, OR: Pickwick Publications, 2012), xi.

120. Ibid. xii.

121. Ibid. xiii.

122. Franz Cardinal König, 'Let the Spirit Breathe', in Daniel Kendall and Gerald O'Collins, eds, *In Many and Diverse Ways: In Honor of Jacques Dupuis* (Maryknoll, NY: Orbis Books, 2003), 16. Hinze argues for the need to 'interpret and discern the laments of the theologians' investigated by the CDF. These laments 'give voice to the frictions, frustrations, and failures' that occurred in the investigation procedures. They also express something that is happening in the local church communities as well as in the universal church in some cases. Hinze also claims that lamentations 'offer a source of wisdom, renewal, and reform in the church. They are a privileged site for hearing the Spirit of God who groans in the human heart and the suffering world when something is struggling into existence and when the Spirit is being stifled.' Bradford E. Hinze, 'A Decade of Disciplining Theologians', *Horizons* 37, no. 1 (Spring 2010), 119–20.

123. Ibid. 17.

124. Quoted in *Preface* in William R. Burrows, ed., *Jacques Dupuis Faces the Inquisition: Two Essays by Jacques Dupuis on* Dominus Iesus *and the Roman Investigation of His Work* (Eugene, OR: Pickwick Publications, 2012), xiv.

125. D. Vincent Twomey SVD, *Pope Benedict XVI: The Conscience of Our Age* (San Francisco: Ignatius Press, 2007), 34–5.

126. Ibid. 35.

127. Ibid. 62–3.

128. Joseph Cardinal Ratzinger, *The Nature and Mission of Theology* (San Francisco: Ignatius Press, 1993), 63.

129. Ibid. 105.

130. Joseph Cardinal Ratzinger, *The Ratzinger Report* (San Francisco: Ignatius Press, 1985), 71. Ratzinger is critical of Hans Küng who has emphasized that theologians stand 'equal and independent, side by side with what previously was exclusively known as the apostolic succession, i.e., the sequence of bishops and their office'. Joseph Ratzinger, 'What Unites and Divides Denominations? Ecumenical Reflections' in Pope Benedict XVI, *Joseph Ratzinger in Communio: Volume 1, The Unity of the Church* (Grand Rapids, MI: William B. Eerdmans, 2010), 2–3.

CHAPTER 10: PETER C. PHAN

1. Lieven Boeve and Gerard Mannion, *The Ratzinger Reader* (London: T & T Clark, 2010), 95. Regarding this issue, Hinze writes: 'One of the most ominous laments is that the CDF has relentlessly and effectively fostered the formation of the church not as a disciplined church of witness in a weary world, but as a disciplinary community that is stifling the critical and creative agency of the Spirit. How many times since Vatican II have we heard theologians cry out: "Do not extinguish the Spirit!"?' Bradford E. Hinze, 'A Decade of Disciplining Theologians', *Horizons* 37, no. 1 (Spring 2010), 123.

2. Ibid. 96.

3. Ibid. 181.

4. 'USCCB Doctrine Committee Faults Book by Father Peter Phan', www.usccb.org/comm/archives/2007/07-200.shtml.

5. *Dominus Iesus*, www.vatican.va/roman_curia/congregations/cfaith/documents/rc_con_cfaith_ doc_20000806_dominus-iesus_en.html, no. 22. See also John L. Allen, 'Why is Fr. Peter Phan under investigation?', *National Catholic Reporter*, http://ncronline. org/blogs/all-things-catholic/why-fr-peter-phan-under-investigation.

6. John L. Allen, 'Why is Fr. Peter Phan under investigation?' *National Catholic Reporter*, http://ncronline.org/blogs/all-things-catholic/why-fr-peter-phan-under-investigation.

7. Ibid. According to Hinze, 'Theologians who are working in the church at the frontiers of theology are being held to doctrinal definitions and standards that are treated as frozen in time by means of a-historical appeals to doctrinal positions. In areas where dramatic doctrinal developments are occurring, the CDF is judging people using a strict and often narrow propositional approach to doctrinal formulations. Dogmatic propositions are treated as rigid rules, rather than as a living tradition ... From this concern results the widespread charge of creeping infallibilism.' Bradford E. Hinze, 'A Decade of Disciplining Theologians', *Horizons* 37, no. 1 (Spring 2010), 121.

8. Ibid.

9. Ibid. Allen says no theologian working in ecumenical dialogue has been censured by Ratzinger when they deviate, but Ratzinger does not hesitate to discipline Catholic theologians working in interreligious dialogue who stray from official church teaching. John L. Allen, Jr, *Pope Benedict XVI* (New York: Continuum, 2000), 235.

10. John Paul II, 'Ecclesia in Asia', www.vatican.va/holy_father/john_paul_ii/apost_exhortations/ documents/hf_jp-ii_exh_06111999_ecclesia-in-asia_en.html, no. 6.

11. Joseph O'Leary, 'Toward a Buddhist Interpretation of Christian Truth', in Catherine Cornille, ed., *Many Mansions?* (Maryknoll, NY: Orbis Books, 2002), 37. Lamin Sanneth, a West African academic, however, is against the popular charge that Christian missions in Africa and Asia destroyed local cultures in the form of Western cultural hegemony. In fact, Sanneth believes that the translation of the Bible into vernacular has been instrumental in indigenous cultural renewal in many places and 'these languages received their first breath of life from Christian interest'. Hence it is ironic that such indigenous renewal has turned into 'anti-missionary stridency'. Vinoth Ramachandra, *Faith in Conflicts?* (Downers Grove, IL: InterVarsity Press, 1999), 137.

12. *Religious Tolerance.org. Ontario Consultants on Religious Tolerance*, 'The diversity of meanings of the term "religious pluralism"', www.religioustolerance.org/rel_plur1.htm. See also David Basinger, 'Religious Diversity (Pluralism)', *The Stanford Encyclopedia of Philosophy (Spring 2012 Edition)*, Edward N. Zalta, ed., http://plato.stanford. edu/archives/spr2012/entries/religious-pluralism/.

13. Ibid.

14. John Hick, 'Religious Pluralism and Islam', Lecture delivered to the Institute for Islamic Culture and Thought, Tehran, February 2005, www.johnhick.org.uk/article11.html. The most developed version of his understanding of religious pluralism is found in John Hick, *An Interpretation of Religion* (London: Macmillan, 1989), 233–96.

15. Paul F. Knitter, *Introducing Theologies of Religions* (Maryknoll, NY: Orbis Books, 2002), 7.

16. Ibid.10.

17. Ibid.

18. Edward Schillebeeckx, *The Church: The Human Story of God* (New York: Crossroad, 1990), 167 and 166.

19. Peter C. Phan, *Being Religious Interreligiously* (Maryknoll, NY: Orbis Books, 2004), 62. Catholicism implies an acceptance of heterogeneous elements and thus Catholicity is synonymous with universality. Claude Geffré sees the attraction towards syncretism as a symptom of postmodernism and increasing individualism in our globalized world. It also coincided with the loss of credibility of the Christian tradition taught by the official churches which seems too institutional and dogmatic. In addition, the failure of secular society characterized by 'anonymity', 'unbridled consumerism' and superficiality, encourage people to search for a 're-enchantment of the world' which they cannot find in the mainstream churches. Claude Geffré, 'Double Belonging and the Originality of Christianity as a Religion', in Catherine Cornille, ed., *Many Mansions?* (Maryknoll, NY: Orbis Books, 2002), 94–5. Boff , however, is in favour of syncretism, the Catholicity of Catholicism. See Leonardo Boff, *Church: Charism and Power* (London: SCM Press, 1985), 89–107.

20. Ibid. xxi.

21. Ibid.

22. Quoted in Peter C. Phan, *Being Religious Interreligiously* (Maryknoll, NY: Orbis Books, 2004), xxi.

23. Peter C. Phan, *Being Religious Interreligiously* (Maryknoll, NY: Orbis Books, 2004), xxii.

24. Ibid. For a critical analysis of power and control in the Roman Catholic Church, see Leonardo Boff, *Church: Charism and Power* (London: SCM Press, 1985), 47–88.

25. Ibid. xxiii.

26. Gavin D'Costa, *The Meeting of Religions and the Trinity* (Maryknoll, NY: Orbis Books, 2000), 109. John Hick too thinks that inclusivism is an inappropriate way to view other religions: 'This is a novel and somewhat astonishing doctrine. How are we to make sense of the idea that the salvific power of the dharma taught five hundred years earlier by the Buddha is a consequence of the death of Jesus in approximately 30 C.E.?' John Hick, 'Religious Pluralism and Salvation', in Philip L. Quinn, Kevin Meeker, eds, *The Philosophical Challenge of Religious Diversity* (Oxford: Oxford University Press, 2000), 65.

27. Werner G. Jeanrond, 'Belonging or Identity?', in Catherine Cornille, ed., *Many Mansions?* (Maryknoll, NY: Orbis Books, 2002),110.

28. Ibid.

29. Ibid. 111.
30. Peter C. Phan, *In Our Own Tongues* (Maryknoll, NY: Orbis Books, 2003), 135.
31. Ibid. 175–6.
32. Ibid. 176.
33. Ibid. 177.
34. Ibid. S. Mark Heim thinks that it makes more sense to speak of 'salvations', because the goals of various religions are varied. See S. Mark Heim, *Salvations* (Maryknoll, NY: Orbis Books, 1995).
35. Peter C. Phan, *Being Religious Interreligiously* (Maryknoll, NY: Orbis Books, 2004), 92.
36. Ibid. 93.
37. Ibid. 94.
38. Ibid. 95.
39. Ibid. 96.
40. Ibid. 143.
41. Ibid. 144.
42. Ibid. 145.
43. Peter C. Phan, 'Are there other "Saviors" for other People?', in Peter C. Phan, ed. *Christianity and the Wider Ecumenism* (New York: Paragon House, 1990), 168–9.
44. Ibid. 169.
45. Ibid. 172–3.
46. Ibid. 173.
47. Ibid. 176.
48. Ibid.
49. Teotonio R. de Souza, 'Some Guises of "Christ" in Asia', in Leonardo Boff and Virgil Elizondo, eds, *Any Room for Christ in Asia* (London: SCM Press, 1993), 8.
50. Quoted in Peter C. Phan, *Christianity with an Asian Face* (Maryknoll, NY: Orbis Books, 2003), 180.
51. Peter C. Phan, *Christianity with an Asian Face* (Maryknoll, NY: Orbis Books, 2003), 181.
52. Peter C. Phan, *Being Religious Interreligiously* (Maryknoll, NY: Orbis Books, 2004), 100.
53. *Dominus Iesus*, www.vatican.va/roman_curia/congregations/cfaith/documents/rc_con_cfaith_doc_20000806_dominus-iesus_en.html, nos. 20-21.
54. Peter C. Phan, *Being Religious Interreligiously* (Maryknoll, NY: Orbis Books, 2004), xxvii.
55. Ibid.
56. Lieven Boeve and Gerard Mannion, *The Ratzinger Reader* (London: T & T Clark, 2010), 142–3. Regarding negative responses to *Dominus Iesus*, see Leonardo Boff, 'Joseph Cardinal Ratzinger: The Executioner of the Future?, A Response to *Dominus Iesus*', www.servicioskoinonia. org/relat/233e.htm, and Gregory Baum, 'The Theology of Cardinal Ratzinger. A Response to *Dominus Iesus*', www.culture-et-foi.com/dossiers/dominus_jesus/gregory_baum.htm.
57. Peter C. Phan, *In Our Own Tongues* (Maryknoll, NY: Orbis Books, 2003), 29.
58. *Redemptoris missio*,www.vatican.va/holy_father/john_paul_ii/encyclicals/documents/hf_jp-ii_enc_07121990_redemptoris-missio_en.html, no. 55.
59. *Dialogue and Proclamation*, www.vatican.va/roman_curia/pontifical _councils/ interelg/ documents/ rc_pc_interelg_doc_19051991_dialogue-and-proclamatio_en.html.
60. Peter C. Phan, *In Our Own Tongues* (Maryknoll, NY: Orbis Books, 2003), 30.
61. Ibid. 31.
62. Ibid. For a more philosophical approach to interreligious dialogue see Catherine Cornille and Christopher Conway, eds, *Interreligious Hermeneutics* (Eugene, OR: Cascade Books, 2010).
63. Joseph O'Leary, *Religious Pluralism and Christian Truth* (Edinburgh: Edinburgh University Press, 1996), 12.

64. Aloysius Pieris, *An Asian Theology of Liberation* (Edinburgh: T & T Clark, 1988), 69.

65. Aloysius Pieris, *Love Meets Wisdom* (Maryknoll, NY: Orbis Books, 1990), 94.

66. Michael Amaladoss, *Making All Things New* (Maryknoll, NY: Orbis Books, 1990), 108.

67. Ibid. 110.

68. Ibid.

69. Paul F. Knitter, *Introducing Theologies of Religions* (Maryknoll, NY: Orbis Books, 2002), 96–7.

70. Ibid. 97.

71. Ibid. 98.

72. Michael Amaladoss, *Life in Freedom* (Maryknoll, NY: Orbis Books, 1997), 142.

73. Quoted in Paul F. Knitter, *Jesus and the Other Names* (Maryknoll, NY: Orbis Books, 1996), 121. See also Paul F. Knittter, 'Mission and dialogue', *Missiology* 33, no. 2 (1 April 2005), 200–10.

74. Catherine Cornille, 'Introduction', in Catherine Cornille, ed., *Many Mansions?* (Maryknoll, NY: Orbis Books, 2002), 4.

75. Ibid. 5. In his essay, 'Show Me Your Resurrection', David Eckel claims that there is a lot of borrowing between religions. Thus 'religious ideas are fluid and flow into different religions, at times consciously and at times unconsciously, rendering the notion of religious property almost vacuous … Since all religious borrowing presupposes a certain affinity to particular teachings or practices, it is often difficult to determine where one religion begins and the other ends'. Catherine Cornille, 'Introduction: On Hermeneutics in Dialogue', in Catherine Cornille and Christopher Conway, eds, *Interreligious Hermeneutics* (Eugene, OR: Cascade Books, 2010), xviii. See also David Eckel, '"Show Me Your Resurrection": Preaching on the Boundary of Buddhism and Christianity', Ibid. 149–62.

76. Ibid. 1.

77. Ibid. 2.

78. Peter C. Phan, 'Multiple religious belonging: Opportunities and challenges for theology and church', *Theological Studies* 64, no. 3 (1 September 2003), 497. According to Claude Geffré, multiple-religious belonging 'is the effect of an increasingly effective network of communication on a worldwide scale, and of a de-institutionalization that furthers the free circulation of beliefs detached from their tradition of origin'. It is related to changes in the Christian theological landscape which has come to take seriously the issue of religious pluralism. Geffré also makes the important distinction between *multiple belonging* and *double belonging*: the former expression is characteristic of Western modernity. The second expression refers to the encounter between Christianity with non-Western cultures and religions. Claude Geffré, 'Double Belonging and the Originality of Christianity as a Religion', in Catherine Cornille, ed., *Many Mansions?* (Maryknoll, NY: Orbis Books, 2002), 93.

79. Ibid. 498. André Droogers asserts that 'an almost decisive factor determining the reaction of a religion to syncretism (in the objective sense), is the concept of truth prevailing in the religion. In situations of contact, exclusivist claims will give rise to accusations of syncretism (in the negative subjective sense) as their necessary complement.' He writes: 'the exclusive claims are often maintained by a class of religious specialists who monopolize … the definition of truth, and spend a lot of time eliminating possible contradictions and oppositions'. André Droogers, 'Syncretism: The Problem of Definition, the Definition of the Problem', in Jerald D. Gort, Hendrik M. Vroom, Rein Fernhout and Anton Wessels, eds, *Dialogue and Syncretism: An Interdisciplinary Approach* (Grand Rapids, MI: William B. Eerdmans, 1989), 16.

80. Ibid. 498.

81. Ibid. 499.

82. Ibid. 504.

83. Ibid. 507.

84. Ibid. 518.

85. Catherine Cornille, 'Introduction', in Catherine Cornille, ed., *Many Mansions?* (Maryknoll, NY: Orbis Books, 2002), 3.

86. See Peter Phan, 'Praying to the Buddha: Living Amid Religious Pluralism', *Commonweal*, vol. CXXXIV, no. 2 (26 January 2007), 10–14.

87. Peter C. Phan, *Being Religious Interreligiously* (Maryknoll, NY: Orbis Books, 2004), 117.

88. Ibid. 117–18.

89. Ibid. 119–20.

90. Joseph Ratzinger, *Truth and Tolerance* (San Francisco: Ignatius Press, 2004), 76.

91. Quoted in John L. Allen, Jr, *Pope Benedict XVI* (New York: Continuum, 2000), 111.

92. Leonardo Boff and Virgil Elizondo, eds, *Any Room for Christ in Asia* (London: SCM, 1993), viii. In the same way, an Indian theologian insisted that 'Christianity, with its universal message, cannot grow as a religion today, unless it abandons its preference for western culture, with its rational, technically minded, masculine bias, and opens up to the feminine, intuitive understanding of reality in the east.' Quoted in Aylward Shorter, *Evangelization and Culture* (London: Geoffrey Chapman, 1994), 88.

93. Ibid.

94. Timothy Light, 'Orthosyncretism: an account of melding in religion', *Method and Theory in the Study of Religion* 12, 184–5. Likewise, historian Rebecca Lyman questions if there has ever been such a thing as orthodoxy. She writes: "'Christianity" defined as "orthodoxy" rests uncomfortably on a history of inner conflict and persistent multiplicity. This intractable problem of diversity together with the ideological claim of unity only reinforces the cultural uniqueness or ideological paradox of Christian exclusivity in late antiquity.' Quoted in Rosemary Radford Ruether and Marion Grau, eds, *Interpreting the Postmodern: Responses to "Radical Orthodoxy"* (London: T & T Clark, 2006), vii.

95. Jerald D. Gort, 'Syncretism and Dialogue: Christian Historical and Earlier Ecumenical Perceptions', in Jerald D. Gort, Hendrik M. Vroom, Rein Fernhout and Anton Wessels, eds, *Dialogue and Syncretism: An Interdisciplinary Approach* (Grand Rapids, MI: William B. Eerdmans, 1989), 38. See also 'In Defence of Syncretism', in Perry Schmidt-Leukel, *Transformation by Integration* (London: SCM Press, 2009), 67–89.

96. Ibid.

97. Anton Wessels, *Europe: Was it Ever Really Christian?* (London: SCM Press, 1994), 14.

98. Ibid. 15.

99. John Mansford Prior, 'Unfinished Encounter: A Note on the Voice and Tone of *Ecclesia in Asia*', in Peter C. Phan, ed., *The Asian Synod* (Maryknoll, NY: Orbis Books, 2002), 240.

100. Ibid. 241.

101. Francis Sullivan, SJ, *Creative Fidelity: Weighing and Interpreting Documents of the Magisterium* (Eugene, OR: Wipf and Stock, 2003), 8. Leonardo Boff characterizes Catholicism as 'a principle of the incarnation of Christianity', a 'historical concretization of the Gospel' and an 'objectification of Christian faith'. See Leonardo Boff, *Church: Charism and Power* (London: SCM Press, 1985), 77–9.

102. Peter C. Phan, *Being Religious Interreligiously* (Maryknoll, NY: Orbis Books, 2004), 45. Edward Schillebeeckx asserts that 'true orthodoxy can be realized only *in the context of* the modern interpretative understanding of the faith, one that has remained faithful to the interpretation of faith that the Bible itself offers us. In fact, we can never ignore the interpretation of an interpretation that has already been offered to us – of biblical origin – and that only in the reinterpretation of the scriptural passage can be grasped in the character of its true authenticity.'

Quoted in Pavel Rebernik, 'Reflections on the Philosophical Presuppositions of the Pluralist Theology of Religions', in Karl J. Becker and Ilaria Morali, eds, *Catholic Engagement with World Religions* (Maryknoll, NY: Orbis Books, 2010), 352.
103. Ibid. 55.
104. Joseph Cardinal Ratzinger, *The Nature and Mission of Theology* (San Francisco: Ignatius Press, 1993), 81.

CHAPTER 11: ETHICAL VISION

1. The concept of *humanum* is not new; it is related to the theology of deification found in the writings of St Irenaeus and St Athanasius in the second and third centuries: 'For this is why the Word became man, and the Son of God became the Son of man: so that man, by entering into communion with the Word and thus receiving divine sonship, might become a son of God.' 'For the Son of God became man so that we might become God' (*Catechism of the Catholic Church* www.vatican., va/archive/catechism/p122a3p1.htm). Deification is a 'process towards achieving authentic *humanum* in Christ'. To put it simply, becoming human is related to becoming divine. Humanization is also one of the main purposes of creation and one can attain salvation only through the world and human history. Human life and work is at the centre of the historical process towards humanization. See Nikos A. Nissiotis, 'Secular and Christian Images of Human Person', Theologia 33, Athens 1962, pp. 947–89; *Theologia* 34, Athens 1963, 90–122. www.myriobiblos.gr/texts/english/nissiotis_secular_15.html. Jaroslav Pelikan states that 'The coming of that man in the flesh could be called "the incarnation of the Logos and the deification of humanity"'. See *The Spirit of Eastern Christendom* 600–1700 (Chicago: The University of Chicago Press, 1977), 46.
2. Hans Küng and Julia Ching, *Christianity and Chinese Religions* (London: SCM Press, 1989), 114.
3. José Casanova, 'The Sacralization of the Humanum: A Theology for a Global Age', *International Journal of Politics, Culture, and Society*, vol. 13, no. 1 (Fall, 1999), 22.
4. This means moving from the freedom of the church to the freedom of the person. See José Casanova, 'The Sacralization of the Humanum: A Theology for a Global Age', *International Journal of Politics, Culture, and Society*, vol. 13, no. 1 (Fall, 1999), 22. Ratzinger stresses that the value and dignity of the human person can only be protected on the foundation of God who 'stands over against us, so that religion, being human, is in the last resort a relationship – love – that becomes a union'. See Joseph Ratzinger, *Truth and Tolerance* (San Francisco: Ignatius Press, 2003), 45.
5. Hans Küng, *Global Responsibility* (London: SCM Press, 1991), 87. Küng has said that modern science and technology have proved to be incapable of providing the foundation for universal values and human rights. See *Global Responsibility* 42.
6. Küng argues that human beings cannot tolerate a spiritual vacuum, something already foreseen by Nietzsche; it is thus being filled by substitute values: money for example, which now becomes the idol, in place of the true absolute. Everything is sacrificed voluntarily to satisfy personal vanity, integrity and solidarity. Küng writes about the 'modern pseudo-religion' expressed in the 'Singapore dream'. He continues, 'Instead of the age old five Cs of true religion, Creed, Cult, Code, Conduct, and Community, the mundane five Cs of pseudo-religion: Cash, Condominium, Country Club, Credit Card and Car. Will not such unconcealed materialism and egotism in time lead even in that Asian country which so far is most free from corruption

to an equally unfair, polarized, split society of the privileged and the unprivileged, despite tremendous election results for the ruling party? The most recent controversy in Singapore over certain privileges of those in power suggests this. See Hans Küng, *Global Ethic for Global Politics and Economics*, http://site.ebrary.com/lib/cuhk/274. Doc?id=10142361&ppg=293.

7. Hans Küng, *On Being A Christian* (London: Image Books, 1984), 530–1.

8. Ibid. 552–3.

9. Ibid. 602.

10. Ibid.

11. In *Theology for the Third Millennium*, Küng reviews favourably Edward Schillebeeckx's works, *Jesus: An Experiment in Christology* and *Christ: The Experience of Jesus as Lord*. Schillebeeckx's writings reinforce Küng's own theological presuppositions in his *On Being Christian* and *Does God Exist: An Answer for Today*. He believes there is a 'fundamental hermeneutical agreement' between him and Schillebeeckx. See *Theology for the Third Millennium*, 108.

12. Hans Küng, *Theology for the Third Millennium* (New York: Doubleday, 1988), 109.

13. Ibid.

14. Ibid. 110.

15. Quoted in Hans Küng, *Theology for the Third Millennium* (New York: Doubleday, 1988), 111.

16. Ibid. 112.

17. Quoted in Hans Küng, *Theology for the Third Millennium* (New York: Doubleday, 1988), 116.

18. Ibid. 117.

19. Ibid. 118, 120.

20. Ibid. 251.

21. Ibid. 241.

22. Ibid.

23. Ibid. 244.

24. Ibid. 245.

25. Ibid. 252–3.

26. Ibid. 254.

27. Hans Küng, *Global Responsibility* (London: SCM Press, 1991), 53.

28. Küng says, 'What I mean by this can be demonstrated relatively simply by means of that Golden Rule of humanity which we find in all the great religious and ethical tradition. Here are some of its formulations: - Confucius (c.551–489 BCE): "What you yourself do not want, do not do to another person" (Analects 15.23). - Rabbi Hillel (60 BCE–10 CE): "Do not do to others what you would not want them to do to you" (Shabbat 31a). - Jesus of Nazareth: "Whatever you want people to do to you, do also to them" (Matt.7.12; Luke 6.31). - Islam: "None of you is a believer as long as he does not wish his brother what he wishes himself." See Hans Küng, *Global Ethic for Global Politics and Economics* (Cary, NC: Oxford University Press, 1998), 98. http://site.ebrary.com/lib/cuhk/Doc?id=10142361&ppg=117.

29. John Cobb, 'Inter-religious Dialogue, World Ethics and the Problem of the Humanum', in *Hans Küng: New Horizons for Faith and Thought*, eds Karl-Josef Kuschel and Hermann Häring (London: SCM Press, 1993), 287.

30. Leonard Swidler, 'Interreligious and Interideological Dialogue: The Matrix for All Systematic Reflection Today', in Leonard Swidler, ed., *Towards a Universal Theology of Religion* (Maryknoll, NY: Orbis Books, 1988), 30.

31. John Cobb, "Inter-religious Dialogue, World Ethics and the Problem of the Humanum', in *Hans Küng: New Horizons for Faith and Thought*, eds Karl-Josef Kuschel and Hermann Häring (London: SCM Press, 1993), 291.

32. Chris Sugden believes that the challenge to the gospel is to discover the significance of the individual. He also asserts that the biblical understanding of humanity is of 'persons-in-community'. God's response to human problem was to establish a new community; his way of salvation was through starting a family, 'Abraham and his seed'. See Chris Sugden, 'Called to Full Humanity–A perspective from Western Europe'. *Transformation* 15 (1 January 1998), 28–9.

33. John Cobb, 'Inter-religious Dialogue, World Ethics and the Problem of the Humanum', in *Hans Küng: New Horizons for Faith and Thought*, eds Karl-Josef Kuschel and Hermann Häring (London: SCM Press, 1993), 292.

34. Joseph Ratzinger, *Truth and Tolerance* (San Francisco: Ignatius Press, 2003), 40, 44. See also Karl Rahner, *Foundation of Christian Faith* (New York: Crossroad, 2010), 138–75.

35. Joseph Ratzinger, *Introduction to Christianity* (New York: Herder and Herder, 1969), 144–5.

36. Ibid. 145.

37. Ibid. 146.

38. Ibid. 147.

39. Ibid. 148.

40. Joseph Ratzinger, *Truth and Tolerance* (San Francisco: Ignatius Press, 2003), 64–5.

41. Joseph Ratzinger and Jürgen Habermas, *Dialectics of Secularization* (San Francisco: Ignatius Press, 2005), 73–4. Ratzinger and Küng would agree that faith is a fundamental human attitude; it is indispensable in our life, otherwise nothing would function. Human life would be impossible if we cannot trust and rely on others' prior experience and knowledge. See Joseph Ratzinger, *Christianity and the Crisis of Cultures* (San Francisco: Ignatius Press, 2006), 81 and Hans Küng, *On Being A Christian* (London: Image Books, 1984), 514–17.

42. Joseph Ratzinger, *Truth and Tolerance* (San Francisco: Ignatius Press, 2003), 76.

43. Joseph Ratzinger, *Introduction to Christianity* (New York: Herder and Herder, 1969), 27.

44. Ibid. 28.

45. Ibid. 47.

46. Ibid. 111.

47. Ibid. 113.

48. Joseph Ratzinger, *Truth and Tolerance* (San Francisco: Ignatius Press, 2003), 22–3.

49. Joseph Ratzinger, *Many Religions – One Covenant* (San Francisco: Ignatius Press, 1999), 109–10.

50. Joseph Ratzinger, *Truth and Tolerance* (San Francisco: Ignatius Press, 2003), 30–1.

51. Ibid. 73.

52. Ibid. 78–9.

53. Ibid. 170.

54. Ibid. 183.

55. Ibid. 54.

56. Joseph Ratzinger, *The Nature and Mission of Theology* (San Francisco: Ignatius Press, 1995), 105.

57. Hans Küng, *Theology for the Third Millennium* (New York: Doubleday, 1988), 19–20.

58. Quoted in Hans Küng, *Theology for the Third Millennium* (New York: Doubleday, 1988), 46.

59. Jürgen Mettepenningen, 'Yves Congar and the "Monster" of Nouvelle Théologie', *Horizons*, vol. 27, no. 1 (Spring 2010), 54.

60. Ibid. 54–5.

61. The mutuality model stresses authentic dialogue and relationship with other religions; it also seeks to preserve the diversity and differences among the religions. Knitter describes the three different but complementary bridges that Christians must cross to reach the mutuality model: the philosophical–historical bridge, the religious–mystical bridge and the ethical–practical bridge. See Paul F. Knitter, *Introducing Theologies of Religions* (Maryknoll, NY: Orbis Books, 2002), 109–69.

62. Robert J. Schreiter, 'Religious pluralism from the postmodern perspective: A response to Paul F Knitter', *Anglican Theological Review* 74, no. 4 (1 September 1992), 446.

63. See Joseph Ratzinger in 'Relativism: The Central Problem for Faith Today', www.acu-adsum.org/ratzrel.pdf. See also Anne Hunt, 'No other name: A critique of religious pluralism', *Pacifica* 3, no. 1 (1 February 1990): 45–60.

64. Few people would doubt the sincerity and intuition of Paul Knitter; what concerns his critics is his curious admixture of modernist, postmodernist and post-liberal tenets that underpin his theological ideas. But this is a problem for Western theologians; Asian theologians are more concerned with praxis as this chapter will show. See Robert J. Schreiter, 'Religious pluralism from the postmodern perspective: A response to Paul F Knitter', *Anglican Theological Review* 74, no. 4 (1 September 1992), 444. See also Thor Hall, 'Paul Knitter's presuppositions for interfaith dialogue: A critique.' *Perspectives in Religious Studies* 17, no. 1 (1 March 1990): 43–52.

65. *Extra ecclesiam nulla salus* means outside the church there is no salvation and *Extra mundum nulla salus* means outside the world there is no salvation. The expression *extra ecclesiam nulla salus* is believed to have come from St Cyprian of Carthage, a bishop in the third century. In this context, Cyprian was referring to heretics who were outside the church and not non-Christians. Many church fathers have made reference to it, including St Ignatius of Antioch, who stressed the unity of the church. Irenaeus referred to this axiom in the context of the Gnostic heresy in which they claimed to have superior knowledge to which no ordinary Christians can have access. Irenaeus wanted the separatists to know that only in the true church can one share in the life of grace and, thus, by separating themselves from the church, the Gnostics are depriving themselves. It is 'guilty separation from the Church' which is the reason for not being saved. See Jacques Dupuis, SJ , *Toward a Christian Theology of Religious Pluralism* (Maryknoll, NY: Orbis Books, 1997), 86.

66. Edward Schillebeeckx, *Church: The Human Story of God* (New York: Crossroad, 1990), 6.

67. Ibid. 7.

68. Ibid.

69. Ibid.

70. Ibid. 8.

71. Ibid. 12.

72. Karl Rahner argues that the church has only a provisional status as it advances in history towards the promised future. The followers of other religious traditions also belong to the Kingdom of God. Though they are not members of the church, they share in the fullness of the Kingdom. This is because Christ's rule extends beyond the church and one day the church will also be absorbed into the Kingdom of God. Dupuis says it is better for a Christian theology of interreligious dialogue to adopt a regnocentric approach. See Jacques Dupuis, SJ, *Toward a Christian Theology of Religious Pluralism* (Maryknoll, NY: Orbis Books, 1997), 359.

73. Paul F. Knitter, *Jesus and the Other Names* (Maryknoll, NY: Orbis Books, 1996), 108.

74. Ibid. 109.

75. Quoted in Paul F. Knitter, *Jesus and the Other Names* (Maryknoll, NY: Orbis Books, 1996), 109.

76. Paul F. Knitter, *Jesus and the Other Names* (Maryknoll, NY: Orbis Books, 1996), 110.

77. Ibid. 111.

78. Ibid. 112.

79. Ibid. 113.

80. Ibid.

81. Ibid. 119.

82. Ibid. 158.

83. Paul F. Knitter, *One Earth Many Religions* (Maryknoll, NY: Orbis Books, 1995), 35. See also Paul F. Knitter, 'A common creation story? Interreligious Dialogue and Ecology', *Journal of Ecumenical Studies*, 37, no. 3–4 (1 June 2000), 296–8.

84. Ibid. 35–7.

85. Ibid. 57.

86. Ibid. 85.

87. Ibid. 87.

88. Ibid. 88.

89. Ibid. 91.

90. Aloysius Pieris, *An Asian Theology of Liberation* (Edinburgh: T & T Clark, 1988), 44.

91. Paul F. Knitter, *One Earth Many Religions* (Maryknoll, NY: Orbis Books, 1995), 94.

92. Ibid. 95.

93. Yvon Ambroise, 'Oppression and Liberation', in Felix Wifred, ed., *Leave the Temple* (Maryknoll, NY: Orbis Books, 1992), 41.

94. Ibid. 42–3.

95. Ibid. 43–4.

96. *Redemptoris Missio*, http://www.vatican.va/holy_father/john_paul_ii/encyclicals/documents/hf_jp-ii_enc_07121990_redemptoris-missio_en.html.

97. Ibid.

98. *Redemptoris Missio*, http://www.vatican.va/holy_father/john_paul_ii/encyclicals/documents/hf_jp-ii_enc_07121990_redemptoris-missio_en.html

99. Joseph Ratzinger, *Many Religions – One Covenant* (San Francisco: Ignatius Press, 1998), 101–2.

100. See Joseph Ratzinger, *The Nature and Mission of Theology* (San Francisco: Ignatius Press, 1993), 79–80.

101. Paul F. Knitter, *Jesus and the Other Names* (Maryknoll, NY: Orbis Books, 1996), 131.

102. Gavin D'Costa, *The Meeting of Religions and the Trinity* (Maryknoll, NY: Orbis Books, 2000), 35. In his response to Knitter's soteriocentric model, Paul Eddy also questions: does it work, is it Christian? See Paul R. Eddy, 'Paul Knitter's Theology of Religions : A Survey and Evangelical Response', *Evangelical Quarterly* 65 (1 July 1993): 241–5.

103. See Gaudencio B. Rosales DD and C. G. Arévalo SJ, eds, *For All Peoples of Asia* (Quezon City: Claretian Publications, 1992), 11–26.

104. Mahmut Adyin says that Knitter's portrayal of Jesus as unique only in a relational sense may encourage Christians and non-Christians to reread the Bible in order to understand the significance of Christ. This non-absolute stance may encourage people of other religions to evaluate scripture more positively. See Mahmut S. Aydin, 'Changing Roman Catholic christologies: The case of Hans Küng and Paul Knitter', *American Journal of Islamic Social Sciences* 18, no. 3 (1 June 2001), 41.

105. Paul F. Knitter, *Jesus and the Other Names* (Maryknoll, NY: Orbis Books, 1996), 76.

106. According to D'Costa, Knitter's Christology follows the Kantian model. Although Knitter views Jesus as the best personal response, he denies the uniqueness of Christ as the only way to salvation. For D'Costa, this Kantian notion of religion that Knitter uses, viewing religion as a product of particular culture, is a product of modernity. Knitter rejects constitutive Christologies because they are not *universal sites* for they prioritize the particular. This promotes sectarianism which Knitter rejects. Traditional Christian teaching about Jesus as the way,

the truth and the life, threatens dialogue and moral imperative. Hence, only modern liberals within religions can participate in interreligious dialogue in Knitter's model. Thus most people who embrace living faiths as they are practiced are automatically excluded. This, according to D'Costa, is a 'non-religious form of exclusivism'. See Gavin D'Costa, *The Meeting of Religions and the Trinity* (Maryknoll, NY: Orbis Books, 2000), 35–7.

107. Hans Küng and Julia Ching, *Christianity and Chinese Religions* (London: SCM Press, 1993), 222.

108. Michael Amaladoss, *Making All Things New* (Maryknoll, NY: Orbis Books, 1990), 115.

109. Felix Wilfred, 'The Federation of Asian Bishops' Conferences (FABC): Orientations, challenges and impact', *Pro Mundi Vita Studies* no. 7 (1 January 1989), 12.

110. Ibid.

111. Aloysius Pieris, *An Asian Theology of Liberation* (Edinburgh: T & T Clark, 1988), 71.

CONCLUSION

1. The Federation of Asian Bishops' Conferences (FABC), founded in 1970, has members from the following countries: Bangladesh, India (CBCI, Syro-Malabar; Syro-Malankara & Latin Rite), Indonesia, Japan, Kazakhstan, Korea, Laos-Cambodia, Malaysia-Singapore-Brunei, Myanmar, Pakistan, Philippines, Sri Lanka, Taiwan, Thailand and Vietnam. It also has associate members from Baucau, East Timor, Dili, East Timor, Hong Kong, Irkutsk, Siberia, Macau, Maliana, East Timor, Mongolia, Nepal, Novosibirsk, Siberia, Kyrgyzstan, Tajikistan and Turkmenistan.

2. Gaudencio B. Rosales and C. G. Arévalo, eds, *For All the Peoples of Asia* (Quezon City: Claretian Publications, 1992), 46. See also Kathryn Tanner, *Theories of Cultures* (Minneapolis: Fortress Press, 1997).

3. Franz-Joseph Eilers SVD, ed., *For All the Peoples of Asia, Federation of Asian Bishops' Conferences Documents from 1997–2001*, vol. 3 (Quezon City: Claretian Publications, 2002), 321.

4. Miguel Marcelo Quatra, *At the Sides of the Multitudes* (Quezon City: Claretian Publications, 2001), 41.

5. Ibid. 42.

6. Gaudencio B. Rosales and C. G. Arévalo, eds, *For All the Peoples of Asia* (Quezon City: Claretian Publications, 1992), 261.

7. Joseph Stephen O'Leary, *Religious Pluralism and Christian Truth* (Edinburgh: Edinburgh University Press, 1996), 24.

8. Franz-Joseph Eilers, SVD, ed., *For All the Peoples of Asia, Federation of Asian Bishops' Conferences Documents from 1997–2001*, vol. 3 (Quezon City, Claretian Publications, 2002), 127.

9. Ibid. 257, 321.

10. Miguel Marcelo Quatra, *At the Sides of the Multitudes* (Quezon City, Claretian Publications, 2001), 45.

11. Ibid. 46.

12. Joseph Ratzinger, *Truth and Tolerance* (San Francisco, Ignatius Press, 2004), 21.

13. Franz-Joseph Eilers SVD, ed., *For All the Peoples of Asia, Federation of Asian Bishops' Conferences Documents from 1997–2001*, vol. 3 (Quezon City: Claretian Publications. 2002), 333.

14. Ibid. 334.

15. Ibid.

16. Gaudencio B. Rosales and C. G. Arévalo, eds, *For All the Peoples of Asia* (Quezon City: Claretian Publications, 1992), 261.

17. Ibid. 304

18. Ibid. 184.

19. Ibid. 179.

20. Joseph Ratzinger, *Called to Communion* (San Francisco: Ignatius Press, 1996), 19–20.

21. Joseph Ratzinger, *A Turning Point for Europe* (San Francisco: Ignatius Press, 1994), 77.

22. Joseph Ratzinger, *Called to Communion* (San Francisco: Ignatius Press, 1996), 20.

23. Ibid. 23.

24. Ibid.

25. Joseph Ratzinger, *Truth and Tolerance* (San Francisco: Ignatius Press, 2004), 73, 120.

26. Gaudencio B. Rosales and C. G. Arévalo, eds, *For All the Peoples of Asia* (Quezon City: Claretian Publications, 1992), 5–6.

27. Miguel Marcelo Quatra, *At the Sides of the Multitudes* (Quezon City: Claretian Publications, 2001), 121.

28. Gaudencio B. Rosales and C. G. Arévalo, eds, *For All the Peoples of Asia* (Quezon City: Claretian Publications, 1992), 95.

29. Ibid. 146.

30. Ibid. 340.

31. Ibid. 344. See also Stephen B. Bevans and Roger P. Schroeder, *Prophetic Dialogue: Reflections on Christian Mission Today* (Maryknoll, NY: Orbis Books, 2011).

32. Ibid.

33. Miguel Marcelo Quatra, *At the Sides of the Multitudes* (Quezon City: Claretian Publications, 2001), 169.

34. Franz-Joseph Eilers SVD, ed., *For All the Peoples of Asia, Federation of Asian Bishops' Conferences Documents from 1997–2001*, vol. 3 (Quezon City: Claretian Publications, 2002), 158.

35. Joseph Ratzinger, *The Ratzinger Report* (San Francisco: Ignatious Press, 1998), 53.

36. Franz-Joseph Eilers, SVD, ed., *For All the Peoples of Asia, Federation of Asian Bishops' Conferences Documents from 1992–1996*, vol. 2 (Quezon City: Claretian Publications, 1997), 276–7.

37. Joseph Ratzinger, *Many Religions – One Covenant* (San Francisco: Ignatius Press, 1998), 110.

38. Ibid. 111.

Bibliography

THE WORKS OF JOSEPH RATZINGER

Ratzinger, Joseph. *Theological Highlights of Vatican II*. New York: Paulist Press, 1966.

——. *The Theology of History in Saint Bonaventure*. Trans. Zachary Hayes. Chicago: Franciscan Herald Press, 1971.

——. *Dogma and Preaching*. Trans. Matthew J. O'Connell. Chicago: Franciscan Herald Press, 1985.

——. *The Ratzinger Report*. Trans. Salvator Attanasio and Graham Harrison. San Francisco: Ignatius Press, 1985.

——. *Feast of Faith: Approaches to a Theology of the Liturgy*. Trans. Graham Harrison. San Francisco: Ignatius, 1986.

——. *Principles of Catholic Theology: Building Stones for a Fundamental Theology*. Trans. Sister Mary Frances McCarthy SND. San Francisco: Ignatius Press, 1987.

——. *Eschatology, Death, and Eternal Life*. Trans. Michael Waldstein. Washington, DC: Catholic University of America Press, 1988.

——. *Co-Workers of the Truth: Meditations for Every Day of the Year*. Ed. Irene Grassl. Trans. Mary Frances McCarthy and Lothar Krauth. San Francisco: Ignatius, 1992.

——. *A Turning Point For Europe?* Trans. Brian McNeil CRV. San Francisco: Ignatius Press, 1994.

——. *In the Beginning: A Catholic Understanding of the Story of Creation and the Fall*. Trans. Boniface Ramsey. Grand Rapids: Eerdmans, 1995.

——. *The Nature and Mission of Theology: Approaches to Understanding Its Role in the Light of Present Controversy*. Trans. Adrian Walker. San Francisco: Ignatius Press, 1995.

——. *Called to Communion*. Trans. Adrian Walker. San Francisco: Ignatius Press, 1996.

——. *A New Song for the Lord: Faith in Christ and Liturgy Today*. Trans. Martha M. Matesich. New York: Crossroad Publishing, 1997.

——. *Salt of the Earth*. Trans. Adrian Walker. San Francisco: Ignatius Press, 1997.

——. *Milestones: Memoirs, 1927–1977*. Trans. Erasmo Leiva-Merikakis. San Francisco: Ignatius Press, 1998.

——. *Many Religions – One Covenant*. Trans. Graham Harrison. San Francisco: Ignatius Press, 1999.

——. *The Spirit of the Liturgy*. Trans. John Saward. San Francisco: Ignatius Press, 2000.

——. *God and the World*. San Francisco: Ignatius Press, 2002.

——. *God is Near Us: The Eucharist, the Heart of Life*. Trans. Henry Taylor. San Francisco: Ignatius Press, 2003.

——. *Introduction to Christianity*. Trans. J. R. Foster. San Francisco: Ignatius Press, 2004.

——. *Truth and Tolerance*. Trans. Henry Taylor. San Francisco: Ignatius Press, 2004.

——. *Pilgrim Fellowship of Faith*. Trans. Henry Taylor. San Francisco: Ignatius Press, 2005.

——. *On the Way to Jesus Christ*. Trans. Michael Miller. San Francisco: Ignatius, 2005.

——. *Christianity and the Crisis of Cultures*. Trans. Brian McNeil. San Francisco: Ignatius Press, 2006.

——. *Handing on the Faith in an Age of Disbelief*. Trans. Michael J. Miller. San Francisco: Ignatius Press, 2006.

——. *Values in a Time of Upheaval*. Trans. Brian McNeil. San Francisco: Ignatius Press, 2006.

——. *Jesus of Nazareth: From the Baptism in the Jordan to the Transfiguration*. Trans. Adrian J. Walker. New York: Doubleday, 2007.

——. *The Apostles: The Origin of the Church and Their Co-Workers*. Huntington, IN: Our Sunday Visitor Publishing Division, 2007.

——. *Church, Ecumenism and Politics*. Trans. Michael J. Miller et al. San Francisco: Ignatius Press, 2008.

——. *Church Fathers: From Clement of Rome to Augustine*. English trans. *L'Osservatore Romano*. San Francisco: Ignatius Press, 2008.

——. *The God of Jesus Christ*. San Francisco: Ignatius Press, 2008.

——. *The Fathers*. Huntington, IN: Our Sunday Visitor Publishing Division, 2008.

——. *Credo for Today*. Trans. Michael J. Miller et al. San Francisco: Ignatius Press, 2009.

——. *Light of the World: The Pope, the Church, and the Signs of the Times*. A Conversation with Peter Seewald. Trans. Michael J. Miller and Adrian J. Walker. San Francisco: Ignatius Press, 2010.

——. *Jesus of Nazareth: Holy Week: From the Entrance into Jerusalem to the Resurrection*. English translation provided by the Vatican Secretariat of State. San Francisco: Ignatius Press, 2011.

Ratzinger, Joseph, Heinz Schürmann and Hans Urs von Balthazar. *Principles of Christian Morality*. Trans. Graham Harrison. San Francisco: Ignatius Press, 1986.

Ratzinger, Joseph and Christoph Schönborn. *Introduction to the Catechism of the Catholic Church*. San Francisco: Ignatius Press, 1994.

Ratzinger, Joseph and Jürgen Habermas. *The Dialectics of Secularization*. Trans. Brian McNeil, CRV. San Francisco: Ignatius Press, 2006.

Ratzinger, Joseph and Marcell Pera. *Without Roots*. Trans. Michael F. More. New York: Basic Books, 2007.

Ratzinger, Joseph. 'Relativism: The Central Problem for Faith Today.' In *The Essential Pope Benedict XVI*, eds John F. Thornton and Susan B. Varenne. New York: Harper, 2007.

Pope Benedict XVI. *Joseph Ratzinger in Communio: Volume 1, The Unity of the Church*. Introduction by David L. Schindler. Grand Rapids, MI: William B. Eerdmans, 2010.

Pope Benedict XVI. *Joseph Ratzinger in Communio: Volume 2, Anthropology and Culture*. Ed. David L. Schindler and Nicholas J. Healy. Grand Rapids, MI: William B. Eerdmans, 2013.

ESSAYS, INTERVIEWS AND LETTERS

Ratzinger, Joseph. 'The Pastoral Implications of Episcopal Collegiality.' *Concilium* 1 (1965) 20–33.

——. 'Letter to the Bishops of the Catholic Church on Some Aspects of the Church Understood as Communion.' (28 May 1992). www.vatican.va/roman_curia/congregations/cfaith/documents/rc_con_cfaith_doc_28051992_communionis-notio_en.html.

——. 'Christ, Faith and the Challenge of Cultures.' Given in Hong Kong to the Presidents of the Asian Bishops' Conferences and the chairmen of their doctrinal commissions during a meeting (2–5 March 1993). www.ewtn.com/library/curia/ratzhong.htm.

——. 'Letter of Cardinal Ratzinger Regarding *Dominus Iesus*.' (14 September 2000). www.catholicculture.org/culture/library/view.cfm?recnum=3133.

——. 'The Ecclesiology of Vatican II', Conference of Cardinal Ratzinger at the opening of the Pastoral Congress of the Diocese of Aversa (Italy). (15 September 2001). www.ewtn.com/library/curia/cdfeccv2.htm.

——. 'The Local Church and the Universal Church: A Response to Walter Kasper', *America* 185 (19 November 2001) 7–11.

——. 'Eucharist, Communion and Solidarity. (2 June 2002). www.vatican.va/roman_curia/congregations/cfaith/documents/rc_con_cfaith_doc_20020602_ratzinger-eucharistic-congress_en.html.

——. 'Cardinal Ratzinger's Homily', *Vatican Radio* (18 April 2005). http://storico.radiovaticana.org/en1/storico/2005-04/33987.html.

——. 'Europe in the Crisis of Cultures', *Communio* 32 (Summer 2005) 345–56.

——. 'Address of His Holiness Benedict XVI to HE Mr Anton Morell Mora, Ambassador of the Principality of Andorra to the Holy See.' (1 December 2005). www.vatican.va/holy_father/benedict_xvi/speeches/2005/december/documents/hf_ben_xvi_spe_20051201_ambassador-andorra_en.html.

——. 'Address of His Holiness Benedict XVI to the Roman Curia offering them his Christmas Greetings.' (22 December 2005). www.vatican.va/holy_father/benedict_xvi/speeches/2005/december/documents/hf_ben_xvi_spe_20051222_roman-curia_en.html.

——. 'Deus Caritas Est' (25 December 2005). www.vatican.va/holy_father/benedict_xvi/encyclicals/documents/hf_ben-xvi_enc_20051225_deus-caritas-est_en.html.

——. 'Meeting with the Representatives of Science' (Regensburg Lecture). (12 September 2006). www.vatican.va/holy_father/benedict_xvi/speeches/2006/september/documents/hf_ben-xvi_spe_20060912_university-regensburg_en.html.

——. 'Are Non-Christians Saved?' (January 2007). www.beliefnet.com/Faiths/Catholic/2007/01/Are-Non-Christians-Saved.asp.

——. 'The Church and the Challenge of Secularization.' *Christ to the World* 53 (September 2008) 389–92.

——.'Healthy Secularism for a Peaceful Coexistence.' *Osservatore Romano* 2070 (weekly edition in English), (19 November 2008) 6.

SECONDARY LITERATURE ON JOSEPH RATZINGER

Allen, John L. Jr, *Pope Benedict XVI*. New York: Continuum, 2000.

Baum, Gregory. 'The Theology of Cardinal Ratzinger. A Response to *Dominus Iesus.*' *The Ecumenist* 37 (Fall 2000). www.culture-et-foi.com/dossiers/dominus_jesus/gregory_baum.htm.

Boeve, Lieven and Gerard Mannion, eds. *The Ratzinger Reader*. London: T & T Clark, 2010.

Boff, Leonardo. 'Joseph Cardinal Ratzinger: The Executioner of the Future? A Response to *Dominus Iesus.*' www.servicioskoinonia.org/relat/233e.htm.

Corkery, James, SJ. *Joseph Ratzinger's Theological Ideas: Wise Cautions & Legitimate Hopes*. New York: Paulist Press, 2009.

Gibson, David. *The Rule of Benedict*. New York: HarperCollins, 2006.

Heim, Maximilian Heinrich. *Joseph Ratzinger: Life in the Church and Living Theology*. San Francisco: Ignatius Press, 2007.

Nichols, Aidan, OP. *The Thought of Pope Benedict XVI*. London: Burns & Oates, 2007.

Rausch, Thomas P. *Pope Benedict XVI: An Introduction to His Theological Vision*. New York: Paulist Press, 2009.

Rowland, Tracey. *Ratzinger's Faith*. New York: Oxford University Press, 2008.

Thornton, John F. and Susan B. Varenne, eds. *The Essential Pope Benedict XVI*. New York: Harper SanFrancisco, 2007.

Tracy, David. 'Western Hermeneutics and Interreligious Dialogue.' In Catherine Cornille and Christopher Conway, eds, *Interreligious Hermeneutics*. Eugene, OR: Cascade Books, 2010.

Twomey, D. Vincent. *Pope Benedict XVI: The Conscience of Our Age*. San Francisco: Ignatius Press, 2007.

Weigel, George. *God's Choice: Pope Benedict XVI and the Future of the Catholic Church*. New York: HarperCollins, 2005.

ADDITIONAL LITERATURE

Abraham, K. C., ed. *Third World Theologies*. Maryknoll, NY: Orbis Books, 2002.

Alfeyev, Hilarion. 'European Christianity and the Challenge of Militant Secularism.' *Ecumenical Review* 57 (1 January 2005) 82–91.

Allen, John L. 'Benedict travels Europe to revitalize Christian roots.' *National Catholic Reporter* 42 (2 June 2006) 8.

——. 'Why is Fr Peter Phan under investigation?' *National Catholic Reporter* (14 September 2007). http://ncronline.org/blogs/all-things-catholic/why-fr-peter-phan-under-investigation.

Amaladoss, Michael. *Making All Things New*. Maryknoll, NY: Orbis Books, 1990.

——. *Life in Freedom*. Maryknoll, NY: Orbis Books, 1997.

Ambroise, Yvon. 'Oppression and Liberation' in Felix Wilfred, ed. *Leave the Temple*. Maryknoll, NY: Orbis Books, 1992.

Arinze, Francis. 'Catholic Universities/Interreligious Dialogue.' *Origins* 27 (19 February 1998) 592–96.

——. *Meeting other Believers*. Huntington, IN: Our Sunday Visitor, 1998.

Aydin, Mahmut S. 'Changing Roman Catholic Christologies: The case of Hans Kung and Paul Knitter.' *American Journal of Islamic Social Sciences* 18, no. 3 (1 June 2001) 17–50.

Baghramian, Maria. *Relativism*. New York: Routledge, 2004.

Balasuriya, Tissa. *Planetary Theology*. Maryknoll, NY: Orbis Books, 1984.

——. *Mary and Human Liberation: the Story and the Text*. Harrisburg, PA: Trinity Press International, 1997.

——. 'Communication and Liberation', in *From Inquisition to Freedom*, ed. Paul Collins. London: Continuum, 2001.

——. 'An Asian Perspective', in *Third World Theologies*, ed. K. C. Abraham. Maryknoll, NY: Orbis Books, 2002.

——. 'Some Asian Questions on Dictatorship of Relativism.' *Voices from the Third World* 29 (1 June 2006) 14–31.

Balthasar, et al. *The Church and Women: A Compendium*. Ed. Helmut Moll. San Francisco: Ignatius Press, 1998.

Banchoff, Thomas, ed. *Religious Pluralism, Globalization and World Politics*. Oxford: Oxford University Press, 2008.

Basinger, David. 'Religious Diversity (Pluralism).' *The Stanford Encyclopedia of Philosophy* (Spring 2012 edition). Ed. Edward N. Zalta. http://plato.stanford.edu/archives/spr2012/entries/religious-pluralism/.

Bea, Augustine Cardinal. *Unity in Freedom*. New York: Harper & Row, 1964.

Becker, Karl J. and Ilaria Morali, eds. *Catholic Engagement with World Religions*. Maryknoll, NY: Orbis Books, 2010.

Bertens, Johannes Willem. *The Idea of the Postmodern: A History*. New York: Routledge, 1995.

Bevans, Stephen B. *Models of Contextual Theology*. Maryknoll, NY: Orbis Books 2002.

Bevans, Stephen B. and Roger P. Schroeder. *Prophetic Dialogue: Reflections on Christian Mission Today*. Maryknoll, NY: Orbis Books, 2011.

Bloor, David. 'Epistemic Grace: Antirelativism as Theology in Disguise.' *Common Knowledge* 13 (2007) 250–80.

Boeve, Lieven. 'Europe in crisis: A question of belief or unbelief? Perspectives from the Vatican.' *Modern Theology* 23 (1 April 2007) 205–27.

Boff, Leonardo. *Church: Charism and Power*. London: SCM Press, 1985.

Boff, Leonardo and Virgil Elizondo, eds. *Any Room for Christ in Asia*. London: SCM Press, 1993.

Bonk, Jonathan J. 'Europe: Christendom graveyard or Christian laboratory?' *International Bulletin Of Missionary Research* 31 (1 July 2007), 113–14.

Bordeianu, Radu. 'Orthodox-Catholic dialogue: retrieving Eucharistic ecclesiology.' *Journal of Ecumenical Studies* 44 (1 March 2009), 239–65.

Bosch, David J. *Transforming Mission: Paradigm Shifts in Theology of Mission*. Maryknoll, NY: Orbis Books, 1991.

Borelli, John. 'The Catholic Church and Interreligious Dialogue', In *Vatican II: The Continuing Agenda*, ed. Anthony J. Cernera. Fairfield, CT: Sacred Heart University Press, 1997.

——. 'The Virgin Mary in the Breadth and Scope of Interreligious Dialogue.' *Marian Studies: Marian Spirituality and Interreligious Dialogue* 47 (1996), 29–49.

Bowman, Jonathan. 'Extending Habermas and Ratzinger's *Dialectics of Secularization*: Eastern Discursive Influences on Faith and Reason, in Postsecular Age.' *Forum Philosophicum* 14 (2009) 39–55.

Brahm Levey, Geoffrey and Tariq Modood. *Secularism, Religion and Multicultural Citizenship.* Cambridge: Cambridge University Press, 2009.

Burrell, David. *Faith and Freedom: An Interfaith Perspective.* Malden, MA: Blackwell Publishing, 2004.

Burrows, William R., ed. *Jacques Dupuis Faces The Inquisition: Two Essays by Jacques Dupuis on Dominus Iesus and the Roman Investigation of His Work.* Eugene, OR: Pickwick Publications, 2012.

Burrows, William R. 'A Concluding Personal Postscript on a Conservationist Revisionist', in *Jacques Dupuis Faces the Inquisition: Two Essays by Jacques Dupuis on Dominus Iesus and the Roman Investigation of His Work*, ed. William R. Burrows, 110. Eugene, OR: Pickwick Publications, 2012.

Butler, Christopher. *Postmodernism: A Very Short Introduction.* Oxford: Oxford University Press, 2002.

Cahill, Lisa Sowle. 'Caritas in veritate: Benedict's global reorientation.' *Theological Studies* 71 (June 2010) 291–319.

Caldecott, Stratford. 'Benedict XVI and Inter-Religious Dialogue.' *Transformation* 23 (October 2006) 199–204.

Calhoun, Craig, et al., eds. *Rethinking Secularism.* Oxford: Oxford University Press, 2011.

Carson, D. A. *The Intolerance of Tolerance.* Grand Rapids, MI: William B. Eerdmans, 2012.

Casanova, José. 'The Sacralization of the Humanum: A Theology for a Global Age', *International Journal of Politics, Culture, and Society.* Vol. 13, no. 1 (Fall, 1999), 21–40.

——. 'The Secular and Secularisms.' *Social Research* 76 (Winter 2009), 1049–66.

——. 'The Secular, Secularizations, Secularisms', in *Rethinking Secularism*, ed. Craig Calhoun, et al. Oxford: Oxford University Press, 2011.

Cavadini, John C., ed. *Explorations in the Theology of Benedict XVI.* Notre Dame, IN: University of Notre Dame, Press, 2012.

Cerutti, Furio and Enno Rudolph, eds. *A Soul for Europe: On the Political and Cultural Identity of Europeans. Volume 1. An Essay Collection.* Sterling, VA: Peeters Leuven, 2001.

——. *A Soul for Europe: On the Political and Cultural Identity of Europeans. Volume 2. A Reader.* Sterling, VA: Peeters Leuven, 2001.

Chadwick, Owen. *The Secularization of the European Mind in the Nineteenth Century.* Cambridge: Cambridge University Press, 1975.

Chia, Edmund Kee-Fook. 'Of Fork and Spoon or Fingers and Chopsticks: Interreligious Dialogue in *Ecclesia in Asia*', in *The Asian Synod*, ed. Peter C. Phan. Maryknoll, NY: Orbis Books, 2002.

——. *Edward Schillebeeckx and Interreligious dialogue.* Eugene, OR: Pickwick Publications, 2012.

Cheetham, David. 'Inclusivisms: Honouring Faithfulness and Openness', in *Christian Approaches to Other Faiths*, ed. Alan Race and Paul M. Hedges. London: SCM Press, 2008.

Clooney, Francis Xavier. 'Dialogue Not Monologue: Benedict XVI & Religious Pluralism.' *Commonweal* (21 October 2005) 12–17.

Cobb, John. 'Inter-religious Dialogue, World Ethics and the Problem of the Humanum', in *Hans Küng: New Horizons for Faith and Thought*, ed. Karl-Josef Kuschel and Hermann Häring. London: SCM Press, 1993 283–93.

Coffey, David M. 'A Trinitarian Response to Issues Raised by Peter Phan.' *Theological Studies* 69 (December 2008), Vol. 69, vol. 4, 852–74.

Confessing Christian Faith in a Pluralistic Society. Collegeville, MN: Institute for Ecumenical and Cultural Research, 1995.

Collins, Paul, ed. *From Inquisition to Freedom*. London: Continuum, 2001.

Coppa, Frank. *The Modern Papacy since 1789*. London: Longman, 1998.

Cornille, Catherine, ed. *Many Mansions?* Maryknoll, NY: Orbis Books, 2002.

——'Introduction', in *Many Mansions?* Ed. Catherine Cornille, Maryknoll, NY: Orbis Books, 2002.

——, ed. *Criteria of Discernment in Interreligious Dialogue*. Eugene, OR: Cascade Books, 2009.

Cornille, Catherine and Christopher Conway, eds. *Interreligious Hermeneutics*. Eugene, OR: Cascade Books, 2010.

Coward, Harold. *Pluralism in the Word Religions*. Oxford: Oneworld Publications, 2000.

Cragg, G. R. *The Church and the Age of Reason 1648–1789*. Harmondsworth, Middlesex: Penguin Books, 1960.

Curran, Charles. 'A Place for Dissent: My Argument with Joseph Ratzinger.' *Commonweal* 132 (6 May 2005) 18–20.

Dallavalle, Nancy A. 'Cosmos and Ecclesia: A Response to Richard Lennan.' *Philosophy & Theology* 17 (1 January 2005) 279–91.

Daniel-Rops, H. *The Church in an Age of Revolution*. London: J.M. Dent & Sons Ltd., 1965.

Dawes Donald G. and John B. Carman, eds. *Christian Faith in a Religiously Plural World*. Maryknoll, NY: Orbis Books, 1978.

D'Costa, Gavin. *Theology and Religious Pluralism*. Oxford: Basil Blackwell, 1986.

——. Ed., *Christian Uniqueness Reconsidered*. Maryknoll, NY: Orbis Books, 1990.

——. *The Meeting of Religions and the Trinity*. Maryknoll, NY: Orbis Books, 2000.

——. *Christianity and World Religions*. Oxford: Wiley–Blackwell, 2009.

De Lubac, Henri. *The Drama of Atheist Humanism*. Trans. from French by Edith M. Riley. Cleveland: The World Publishing Company, 1963.

De Souza, Teotonio R. 'Some Guises of "Christ" in Asia', in *Any Room for Christ in Asia*, ed. Leonardo Boff and Virgil Elizondo. London: SCM, 1993.

Dinoia, J. A. *The Diversity of Religions: A Christian Perspective*. Washington, DC: CUA Press, 1992.

Duffy, Eamon. 'Urbi, but not Orbi … The Cardinal, the Church and the Word.' *New Blackfriars* 66 (June 1985) 272–8.

Dulles, Avery. 'From Ratzinger to Benedict.' *First Things: A Monthly Journal of Religion & Public Life* 160 (February 2006). www.firstthings.com/article/2008/08/from-ratzinger-to-benedict.

Dupré, Louis. 'The ties that bind us.' *The Tablet* (24 April 2004). www.thetablet.co.uk/article/2521.

——. *Religion and the Rise of Modern Culture*. Notre Dame, IN: University of Notre Dame Press, 2008.

Dupuis, Jacques. *Toward a Christian Theology of Religious Pluralism*. Maryknoll, NY: Orbis Books, 1997.

——. *Christianity and the Religions: From Confrontation to Dialogue.* Maryknoll, NY: Orbis, 2002.

——. 'Christianity and Religions: Complementarity and Convergence', in *Many Mansions?* Ed. Catherine Cornille. Maryknoll, NY: Orbis Books, 2002.

——. 'The Declaration *Dominus Iesus* and My Perspective on it', in *Jacques Dupuis Faces the Inquisition: Two Essays by Jacques Dupuis on* Dominus Iesus *and the Roman Investigation of His Work*, ed. William R. Burrows, 67. Eugene, OR: Pickwick Publications, 2012.

——. 'The CDF Process and Notification and My Perspectives on Them', in *Jacques Dupuis Faces the Inquisition: Two Essays by Jacques Dupuis on* Dominus Iesus *and the Roman Investigation of His Work*, ed. William R. Burrows. Eugene, OR: Pickwick, 2012.

Eagleton, Terry. *The Illusion of Postmodernism.* Oxford: Blackwell, 1996.

Echlin, Edward P. 'Unity Without Absorption'. *Journal Of Ecumenical Studies* 9 (1 December 1972) 51–73.

Eck, Diana. *A New Religious America.* New York: Harper SanFrancisco, 2001.

Eddy, Paul R. 'Paul Knitter's Theology of Religions: A Survey and Evangelical Response'. *Evangelical Quarterly* 65 (1 July 1993): 225–45.

Eilers, Franz-Josef, ed. *For All the Peoples of Asia: Federation of Asian Bishops' Conferences Documents from 1992–1996, Volume 2.* Quezon City: Claretian Publications, 1997.

——. *For All the Peoples of Asia: Federation of Asian Bishops' Conferences Documents from 1997–2001, Volume 3.* Manila: Claretian Publications, 2002.

Ellingsen, Mark. 'Joseph Ratzinger (1927–)'. *Theology Today* 62 (October 2005) 388–98.

Fahey, Michael. 'Joseph Ratzinger as Ecclesiologist and Pastor', in *Concilium*, 76–83, ed. Gregory Baum. Edinburgh: T & T Clark, 1981.

——. 'Am I my sister's keeper?' *America* (28 October 2000). www.americamagazine.org/content/article.cfm?article_id=2267.

Fernando, Basil. *Power versus Conscience.* Hong Kong: Asian Human Rights Commission and Asian Legal Resource Centre, 1997.

Flett, John G. 'In the name of the Father, the Son and the Holy Spirit: A critical reflection on the trinitarian theologies of religion of S. Mark Heim and Gavin D'Costa'. *International Journal of Systematic Theology* (2008) 10, no. 1, 73–90.

Fitzgerald, Michael. 'The Spirituality of Interreligious Dialogue'. *Origins* 28 (25 February 1999) 631–3.

——. 'Interreligious Relations Today: The Remarkable Relevance of *Nostra Aetate*'. *Pro Dialogo* 119 (2005) 182–93.

Fredericks, James L. 'Many Mansions? Multiple Religious Belonging and Christian Identity'. *Buddhist-Christian Studies.* Honolulu (2005) vol.25, 167–70.

Fridlund, Patrik. *Mobile Performances: Linguistic Undecidability as Possibility and Problem in the Theology of Religions.* Leuven: Peeters, 2011.

Gaillardetz, Richard. *Teaching with Authority: A Theology of the Magisterium in the Church.* Collegeville, MN: Liturgical Press, 1997.

Geffré, Claude. 'Double Belonging and the Originality of Christianity as a Religion', in *Many Mansions?* Ed. Catherine Cornille. Maryknoll, NY: Orbis Books, 2002.

Geffré, Claude. 'From the Theology of Religious Pluralism to an Interreligious Theology', in *In Many and Diverse Ways*, ed. Daniel Kendall and Gerald O'Collins. New York: Orbis Books, Maryknoll, 2003.

Gellner, Ernest. *Postmodernism, Reason and Religion.* London: Routledge, 1992.

George, Francis Eugene. 'Democracy and Secularism.' *Origins* 36 (19 April 2007) 709–17.

George, K. M. 'Ecumenism in Asia: Some Theological Consideration', in *Windows into Ecumenism: Essays in Honour of Ahn Jae Woong*. Hong Kong: Christian Conference of Asia, 2005.

Gibson, David. *The Rule of Benedict: Pope Benedict XVI and His Battle with the Modern World*. New York: HarperOne, 2006.

Glenn, Gary D. 'Is Secularism the End of Liberalism? Reflections on Europe's Demographic Decline Drawing on Pope Benedict, Habermas, Nietzsche and Strauss.' *Catholic Social Science Review* 13 (2008) 91–116.

Gorski, Eugene F. *Theology of Religions: A Source Book for Interreligious Study*. New York: Paulist Press, 2007.

Gort, Jerald D., et al., eds. *Dialogue and Syncretism: An Interdisciplinary Approach*. Grand Rapids, MI: William B. Eerdmans, 1989.

Gort, Jerald D. 'Syncretism and Dialogue: Christian Historical and Earlier Ecumenical Perceptions', in *Dialogue and Syncretism: An Interdisciplinary Approach*, ed. Jerald D. Gort, et al. Grand Rapids, MI: William B. Eerdmans, 1989.

Gort, Jerald D., et al., eds. *Religions View Religions*. Amsterdam: Editions Rodopi BV, 2006.

Greggs, Tom. *Theology Against Religion*. London: T & T Clark, 2011.

Griffiths, Paul J. *Problem of Religious Diversity*. Oxford: Blackwell, 2001.

Gros, Jeffrey F. S. C., et al. *Introduction to Ecumenism*. New York: Paulist Press, 1998.

Habermas, Jürgen. *Time of Transitions*. Cambridge: Polity Press, 2006.

Habermas, Jürgen and Joseph Ratzinger. *The Dialectics of Secularization*. San Francisco: Ignatius Press, 2006.

Haight, Roger. *Christian Community in History*, vol. 1. New York: Continuum, 2004.

Hall, Thor. 'Paul Knitter's presuppositions for interfaith dialogue: A critique.' *Perspectives in Religious Studies* 17, no. 1 (1 March 1990) 43–52.

Hallett, Garth. *One God of All: Probing Pluralist Identities*. New York: Continuum, 2010.

Hastings, Adrian. *A History of English Christianity 1920–1990*. London: SCM Press, 1991.

Healy, Nicholas M. *Church, World and the Christian Life*. Cambridge: Cambridge University Press, 2000.

Hedges, Paul. *Controversies in Interreligious Dialogue and the theology of Religions*. London: SCM Press, 2010.

Hedges, Paul. 'A Reflection on Typologies: Negotiating a Fast-Moving Discussion', in *Christian Approaches to Other Faiths*, ed. Alan Race and Paul M. Hedges. London: SCM Press, 2008.

Heim, S. Mark. *Salvations*. Maryknoll, NY: Orbis Books, 1995.

Hick, John. *Problems of Religious Pluralism*. London: Macmillan, 1985.

——. *Dialogues in the Philosophy of Religion*. London: Palgrave Macmillan, 1993.

——. *The Rainbow of Faiths*. London: SCM, 1995.

——. *An Interpretation of Religion*. New Haven: Yale University Press, 2004.

——. 'Ratzinger Absolutely Wrong on Relativism'. *National Catholic Reporter*. http://natcath.org/NCR_Online/archives2.

——. 'Religious Pluralism and Islam', lecture delivered to the Institute for Islamic Culture and Thought, Tehran (February 2005). www.johnhick.org.uk/article11.html.

Hick, John and Paul F. Knitter, eds. *The Myth of Christian Uniqueness*. London: SCMPress, 1987.

Hinze, Bradford E. 'A Decade of Disciplining Theologians.' *Horizons* 37 (Spring 2010) 92–126.

Horkheimer, Max and Theodor W. Adorno. *Dialectic of Enlightenment*. London: Allen Lane, 1972.

Howsare, Rodney. 'Why Begin with Love? "Eros, Agape" and the Problem of Secularism.' *Communio* 33 (Fall 2006) 423–48.

Hunt, Anne. 'No other name: A critique of religious pluralism.' *Pacifica* 3, no. 1 (1 February 1990) 45–60.

Interreligious Council of San Diego, *Bridging Our Faiths*. New York: Paulist Press, 1997.

Jakobsen, Janet R. and Ann Pellegrini, eds. *Secularisms*. Durham: Duke University Press, 2008.

Jankunas, Gediminas T. *The Dictatorship of Relativism*. New York: St Pauls, 2011.

Jeanrond, Werner G. 'Belonging or Identity?' in *Many Mansions?* ed. Catherine Cornille, Maryknoll, NY: Orbis Books, 2002.

Jeanrond, Werner G. and Andrew D. H. Mayes, eds. *Recognising the Margins: Developments in Biblical and Theological Studies*. Dublin: The Columba Press, 2006.

Jeanrond, Werner G. 'The Future of Christianity in Europe', in *Recognising the Margins: Developments in Biblical and Theological Studies*, ed. Werner G. Jeanrond and Andrew D. H. Mayes. Dublin: The Columba Press, 2006.

Jedin, Hubert, ed. *The Church in the Modern World*. New York: Crossroad, 1993.

Jenkins, Philip. 'Godless Europe?' *International Bulletin Of Missionary Research* 31 (1 July 2007) 115–18.

Jiménez Lobeira, Pablo C. 'Normative Conceptions of European Identity: A Synthetic Approach.' *Australian Journal of Professional and Applied Ethics* 12 (2010) 159–70.

Kaiser, Robert Blair. 'Dupuis Profile', in *In Many and Diverse Ways: In Honor of Jacques Dupuis*, ed. Daniel Kendall and Gerald O'Collins. Maryknoll, NY: Orbis Books, 2003.

Kärkkäinen, Veli-Matti, *Trinity and Religious Pluralism*. Aldershot: Ashgate, 2004.

Kasper, Walter. 'On the Church.' *America* (23 April 2001) 8–14. www.americamagazine.org/content/article.cfm?article_id=1569.

——. 'From the President of the Council for Promoting Christian Unity.' *America* (26 November 2001) 185.

Kasimow, Harold, et al., eds. *Beside Still Waters: Jews, Christians, and the Way of the Buddha*. Boston: Wisdom Publications, 2003.

Kaufman, Gordon D. *Systematic Theology*. New York: Charles Scribner's Sons, 1968.

Kendall, David and Gerald O'Collins, eds. *In Many and Diverse Ways: In Honor of Jacques Dupuis*. Maryknoll, NY: Orbis Books, 2003.

Kennedy, Philip. *Twentieth-century Theologians: A New Introduction to Modern Christian Thought*. London and New York: I.B. Tauris, 2010.

King, Richard. *Orientalism and Religion: Postcolonial Theory, India and the Mystic East*. London: Routledge, 1999.

Knitter, Paul F. *One Earth Many Religions*. Maryknoll, NY: Orbis Books, 1995.

——. *Jesus and the Other Names*. Maryknoll, NY: Orbis Books, 1996.

——. 'Five Theses on the Uniqueness of Jesus', in Leonard Swidler and Paul Mojzes, eds. *The Uniqueness of Jesus*. Maryknoll, NY: Orbis Books, 1997.

——. *Introducing Theologies of Religions*. Maryknoll, NY: Orbis Books, 2002.

——, ed. *The Myth of Religious Superiority: A Multifaith Exploration*. Maryknoll, NY: Orbis Books, 2005.

——. 'Mission and dialogue.' *Missiology* 33 (1 April 2005) 200–10.

Komonchak, Joseph A. 'The Church in crisis: Pope Benedict's theological vision.' *Commonweal* 132 (3 June 2005) 11–14.

König, Franz Cardinal. 'Let the Spirit Breathe', in *In Many and Diverse Ways: In Honor of Jacques Dupuis*, ed. Daniel Kendall and Gerald O'Collins. Maryknoll, NY: Orbis Books, 2003.

Köogler, Hans-Herbert. 'Beyond Dogma and Doxa: Truth and Dialogue in Rorty, Apel, and Ratzinger.' *Dialogue & Universalism* 15 (July 2005) 85–103.

Koshy, Ninan, ed. *A History of the Ecumenical Movement in Asia*, vol. II. Hong Kong: World Student Christian Federation, Asia–Pacific Region, Asia and Pacific Alliance of YMCA, Christian Conference of Asia, 2004.

Küng, Hans. *On Being A Christian*. London: Image Books, 1984.

——. *Theology for the Third Millennium*. New York: Doubleday, 1988.

——. *Global Responsibility*. London: SCM Press, 1991.

——. *Global Ethic for Global Politics and Economics*. New York: Oxford University Press, 1998.

——. *The Catholic Church*. New York: The Modern Library, 2001.

Küng, Hans and Julia Ching. *Christianity and Chinese Religions*. London: SCM Press, 1993.

Kuschel, Karl-Josef and Hermann Häring, eds. *Hans Küng: New Horizons for Faith and Thought*. London: SCM, 1993.

Lagrée, Michel. 'The Impact of Technology on Catholicism in France (1850– 1950)', in *The Decline of Christendom in Western Europe, 1750–2000*, eds Hugh McLeod and Werner Ustorf. Cambridge: Cambridge University Press, 2003.

Lai, Pan-chiu. 'Barth's theology of religion and the Asian context of religious pluralism.' *Asia Journal of Theology* 15 (1 October 2001) 247–67.

Lambert, Yves. 'New Christianity, Indifference and Diffused Spirituality', in *The Decline of Christendom in Western Europe, 1750–2000*, eds Hugh McLeod and Werner Ustorf. Cambridge: Cambridge University Press, 2003.

Lash, Nicholas. *The Beginning and the End of 'Religion'*. Cambridge: Cambridge University Press, 1996.

Lefebure, Leo D. 'Cardinal Ratzinger's Comments on Buddhism.' *Buddhist–Christian Studies* 18 (1998) 221–2. www.jstor.org/stable/1390460.

Light, Timothy. 'Orthosyncretism: An account of melding in religion.' *Method and Theory in the Study of Religion* 12 (2000) 162–86.

Lindbeck, George A. *The Nature of Doctrine*, Philadelphia: The Westminster Press, 1984.

Livingston, James C. *Modern Christian Thought*. New York: Macmillan, 1971.

Lonergan, Bernard J. F. *Method in Theology*. London: Darton, Longman & Todd, 1975.

Loughlin, Gerard. *Telling God's Story: Bible, Church and Narrative Theology*. Cambridge: Cambridge University Press, 1996.

Luntley, Michael. *Reason, Truth and Self*. London: Routledge, 1995.

Lyotard, François. *The Postmodern Condition*. Manchester: Manchester University Press, 1984.

Madsen, Richard. 'Secularism, Religious Change, and Social Conflict in Asia', in *Rethinking Secularism*, ed. Craig Calhoun, et al. Oxford: Oxford University Press, 2011.

MacIntyre, Alasdair. *Three Rival Versions of Moral Enquiry: Encyclopaedia, Genealogy, and Tradition*, Duckworth: London, 1990.

——. *Marxism & Christianity*. London: Duckworth, 1995.

McIntyre, John. *The Shape of Pneumatology: Studies in the Doctrine of the Holy Spirit*. Edinburgh: T & T Clark, 1997.

Macquarrie, John. *Christian Unity and Christian Diversity*. London: SCM Press, 1975.

Magister, Sandro. 'The Church Is Under Siege. But Habermas, the Atheist, Is Coming to its Defense.' http://chiesa.espresso.repubblica.it/articolo/20037?eng=y.

McAuliffe, Jane Dammen, et al., eds. *With Reverence for the Word: Medieval Scriptural Exegesis in Judaism, Christianity, and Islam*. Oxford: Oxford University Press, 2003.

McCarthy, Timothy G. *The Catholic Tradition*. Chicago: Loyola University Press, 1994.

McDonnell, Kilian. 'The Ratzinger/Kasper Debate: The Universal Church and Local Churches.' *Theological Studies* (June 2002) 227–50.

McKim, Robert. *On Religious Diversity*. Oxford: Oxford University Press, 2012.

McLeod, Hugh, ed. *European Religion in the Age of Great Cities, 1830–1930*. London: Routledge, 1995.

——. *Religion and the People of Western Europe*. Oxford: Oxford University Press, 1997.

——. *Secularisation in Western Europe, 1848–1914*. New York: St Martin Press, 2000.

McLeod, Hugh and Werner Ustorf, eds. *The Decline of Christendom in Western Europe, 1750–2000*. Cambridge: University of Cambridge Press, 2003.

Mannion, Gerard. *Ecclesiology and Postmodernity*. Collegeville, Minnesota: Liturgical Press, 2007.

Mickens, Robert . 'The Church's new princes.' *The Tablet* (14 January 2012) 4–6.

Melloni, Alberto. 'Passionate prophet of the conciliar Church.' *The Tablet* (8 September 2012) 6–7.

Mendoza, Ruben C. 'Regnocentrism in the theology of religions in the FABC and Paul Knitter: Discerning convergences and divergences.' *Studies in Interreligious Dialogue* 19, no. 2 (1 January 2009) 167-78.

Mettepenningen, Jürgen. 'Yves Congar and the "Monster" of Nouvelle Théologie.' *Horizons*. Vol. 27, no. 1 (Spring 2010) 52–71.

Meyendorff, John, ed. *The Primacy of Peter: Essays in Ecclesiology and the Early Church*. New York: St Vladimir's Seminary Press, 1992.

Milbank, John, *Theology and Social Theory*. Oxford: Blackwell, 1990.

Mong, Ambrose Ih-Ren. 'Approaches to Inter-Faith Dialogue: Trinitarian Theology and Multiple Religious Belonging.' *Asia Journal of Theology* 24 (October 2010) 285–311.

——. 'Hans Küng's *Humanum* and the Quest for the True Religion.' *Dialogue & Alliance* 24 (Winter 2010) 23–41.

——. 'Challenges and Opportunities for the Church in Secular Societies.' *Asia Journal of Theology* 25 (April 2011) 148–63.

——. 'Crossing the Ethical–Practical Bridge: Paul's Knitter's Regnocentrism in Asian Perspective.' *The Ecumenical Review* 63 (July 2011) 186–99.

Morali, Ilaria. 'Salvation, Religions, and Dialogue in the Roman Magisterium', in *Catholic Engagement with World Religions*, ed. Karl J. Becker and Ilaria Morali. Maryknoll, NY: Orbis Books, 2010.

Morris, Jeffrey. 'Pope Benedict XVI on faith and reason in Western Europe.' *Pro Ecclesia* 17 (1 June 2008) 326–42.

Moscovici, Claudia. *Double Dialectics*. Oxford: Rowman & Littlefield, 2002.

Murphy, David. 'The Ordinariates and Ecumenism.' http://ordinariateexpats.wordpress.com/2012/03/14/the-ordinariates-and-ecumenism/.

Murphy, Nancey. *Anglo-American Postmodernity*. Boulder, Colorado: Westview Press, 1997.

Murray, Donal. 'The Secular versus Religion?' *Origins* 37 (6 December 2007) 411–17.

Natoli, Joseph and Johannes Willem Bertens, eds. *Postmodernism: The Key Figures*. Malden, MA: Blackwell, 2002.

Nemoianu, Virgil. 'The Church and the Secular Establishment: A Philosophical Dialog between Joseph Ratzinger and Jürgen Habermas.' *Logos* 9 (Spring 2006) 17–42.

——. *Postmodern & Cultural Identities.* Washington, DC: The Catholic University of America Press, 2010.

Nichols, Aidan, OP. *The Shape of Catholic Theology.* Edinburgh: T&T Clark, 1991.

——. *Rome and the Eastern Churches.* San Francisco: Ignatius Press, 2010.

Nietzsche, Friedrich. *Twilight of Idols.* Indianapolis and Cambridge: Hackett, 1997.

Nissiotis, Nikos A. 'Secular and Christian Images of Human Person.' Theologia 33, Athens 1962, 947–89; *Theologia* 34, Athens 1963, 90–122. www.myriobiblos.gr/texts/english/nissiotis_secular_15.html.

Novak, Michael. 'Remembering the Secular Age.' *First Things* 174 (1 June 2007) 35–40.

O' Collins, SJ. *The Second Vatican Council on Other Religions.* Oxford: Oxford University Press, 2013.

——. 'Jacques Dupuis: His Person and Work', in *In Many and Diverse Ways: In Honor of Jacques Dupuis,* eds Kendall and O'Collins. Maryknoll, NY: Orbis Books, 2003.

O' Leary, Joseph Stephen. *Religious Pluralism and Christian Truth.* Edinburgh: Edinburgh University Press, 1996.

——. 'Toward a Buddhist Interpretation of Christian Truth', in *Many Mansions?* Ed. Catherine Cornille. Maryknoll, NY: Orbis Books, 2002.

Ommen, Thomas B. 'Relativism, Objectivism, and Theology.' *Horizons* 13 (1 September 1986) 291–305.

Paskewich, J. Christopher. 'Liberalism Ex Nihilo: Joseph Ratzinger on Modern Secular Politics.' *Politics* 28 (2008) 169–76.

Pelikan, Jaroslav. *The Spirit of Eastern Christendom* 600–1700. Chicago: University of Chicago Press, 1977.

——. *The Vindication of Tradition.* New Haven: Yale University Press, 1984.

——. *The Christian Tradition Volume 5: Christian Doctrine and Modern Culture since 1700.* Chicago: University of Chicago Press, 1989.

——. *Christianity and Classical Culture.* New Haven: Yale University Press, 1993.

Peterson, Michael L. and Raymond J. VanArragon, eds. *Contemporary Debates in Philosophy of Religion.* Malden, MA: Blackwell, 2004.

Phan, Peter C., ed. *Christianity and the Wider Ecumenism.* New York: Paragon House, 1990.

——. ed. 'Are there other "Saviors" for other Peoples', in *Christianity and the Wider Ecumenism.* New York: Paragon House, 1990.

——. 'The Claim of Uniqueness and Universality in Interreligious Dialogue.' *Dialogue & Alliance,* vol. 7, no. 2 (Fall/Winter 1993).

——. 'Doing Theology in the Context of Cultural and Religious Pluralism: An Asian Perspective.' *Louvain Studies* 27 (2002) 39–68.

——, ed. *The Asian Synod.* Maryknoll, NY: Orbis Books, 2002.

——. *In Our Own Tongues.* Maryknoll, NY: Orbis Books, 2003.

——. *Christianity with an Asian Face.* Maryknoll, NY: Orbis Books, 2003.

——. 'Multiple Religious Belonging: Opportunities and Challenges for Theology and Church.' *Theological Studies* 64 (1 September 2003) 495–519.

——. *Being Religious Interreligiously.* Maryknoll, NY: Orbis Books, 2004.

——. 'Praying to the Buddha: Living Amid Religious Pluralism.' *Commonweal* 84 (26 January 2007). www.commonwealmagazine.org/praying-buddha-0.

Pieris, Aloysius. *An Asian Theology of Liberation.* Edinburgh: T & T Clark, 1988.

——. *Love Meets Wisdom.* Maryknoll, NY: Orbis Books, 1990.

Plantinga, Alvin. 'On Reformed Epistemology.' *Reformed Journal* 32 (1 January 1982) 13–17.

——. *Warranted Christian Belief.* Oxford: Oxford University Press, 2000.

Plekon, Michael, ed. *Tradition Alive: On the Church and the Christian Life in Our Time/ Readings from the Eastern Church.* Lanham: Rowman & Littlefield, 2003.

Prior, John Mansford. 'Unfinished Encounter: A Note on the Voice and Tone of *Ecclesia in Asia*', in *The Asian Synod*, ed. Peter C. Phan. Maryknoll, NY: Orbis Books, 2002.

Quatra, Miguel Marcelo. *At the Sides of the Multitudes.* Quezon City: Claretian Publications, 2001.

Quinn, Philip L. and Kevin Meeker, eds. *The Philosophical Challenge of Religious Diversity.* Oxford: Oxford University Press, 2000.

Race, Alan. *Christians and Religious Pluralism.* Maryknoll, NY. Orbis Books, 1982.

Race, Alan and Paul M. Hedges, eds. *Christian Approaches to Other Faiths.* London: SCM Press, 2008.

Radford Ruether, Rosemary and Marion Grau, eds. *Interpreting the Postmodern: Responses to "Radical Orthodoxy".* London: T & T Clark, 2006.

Rahner, Karl, et al. *The Espiscopate and the Primacy.* (*Quaest. Disput.* 4) New York: Herder and Herder, 1961.

——, et al. *Revelation and Tradition* New York: Herder and Herder, 1966.

Rahner, Karl. *Foundations of Christian Faith.* New York: The Crossroad Publishing Company, 2010.

Raiser, Konrad. *Ecumenism in Transition: A Paradigm Shift in the Ecumenical Movement?* Geneva: WCC Publications, 1991.

Ramachandra, Vinoth. *Faith in Conflicts?* Downers Grove, Illinois: InterVarsity Press, 1999.

——. 'Learning from Modern European Secularism: A View from the Third World Church.' *European Journal of Theology* 12 (1 January 2003) 35–48.

Rémond, René. *Religion and Society in Modern Europe.* Oxford: Blackwell, 1999.

Reese, Thomas J. *Inside the Vatican: The Politics and Organization of the Catholic Church.* Cambridge, MA, Harvard University Press, 1996.

Rhonheimer, Martin. 'Christian Secularity, Political Ethics and the Culture of Human Rights.' *Josephinum Journal of Theology* 16 (Summer–Fall 2009) 320–38.

Roberts, Tyler T. 'Toward Secular Diaspora: Relocating Religion and Politics', in *Secularisms*, co-ed. Ann Pellegrini. Durham, NC: Duke University Press, 2008.

Robbins, Jeffrey W. 'Richard Rorty: A Philosophy Guide to Talking about Religion', in *An Ethics for Today: Finding Common Ground Between Philosophy and Religion.* New York: Columbia University Press, 2011.

Rochelle, Jay C. 'Mystery and Relationship as Keys to the Church's Response to Secularism.' *Currents in Theology and Mission* 19 (1 August 1992) 267–76.

Rorty, Richard. *An Ethics for Today: Finding Common Ground Between Philosophy and Religion.* New York: Columbia University Press, 2011.

Rosales, Gaudencio B. and C. G. Arévalo, eds. *For All Peoples of Asia.* Quezon City: Claretian Publications, 1992.

Rourke, Thomas R. *The Social and Political Thought of Benedict XVI*. Lanham, Maryland: Lexington Books, 2011.

Ruddy, Christopher. *The Local Church: Tillard and the future of Catholic Ecclesiology*. New York: Crossroad Publishing Company, 2006.

Russello, Gerald J., ed. *Christianity and European Culture: Selections from the Work of Christopher Dawson*. Washington, DC: The Catholic University of America Press, 1998.

Ryan, Thomas. 'Jacques Dupuis: Pathfinder for Our Times.' *Ecumenical Trends* (March 2005) 15–16.

Said, Edward W. *Orientalism*. London: Penguin Books, 2003.

Sanneh, Lamin O. 'Can Europe be saved? A review essay.' *International Bulletin Of Missionary Research* 31 (1 July 2007) 121–2.

Schall, James V. 'The Regensburg Lecture: Thinking Rightly about God and Man.' (15 September 2006). www.ignatiusinsight.com/features2006/schall_regensburg_sept06.asp.

——. *The Regensburg Lecture*. South Bend, IN: St Augustine Press, 2007.

Schillebeeckx, Edward. *Church: The Human Story of God*. New York: Crossroad Publishing Company, 1990.

Schmidt-Leukel, Perry. 'Pluralism: How to Appreciate Religious Diversity Theologically,' in *Christian Approaches to Other Faiths*, eds Alan Race and Paul M. Hedges. London: SCM Press, 2008.

Schmidt-Leukel, Perry. *Transformation by Integration*. London: SCM Press, 2009.

Schreiter, Robert J. 'Religious pluralism from the postmodern perspective: A response to Paul F Knitter.' *Anglican Theological Review* 74, no. 4 (1 September 1992) 443–8.

——. *The New Catholicity: Theology between the Global and the Local*. Maryknoll, NY: Orbis Books, 1997.

Schwibach, Armin. 'The "New Enlightenment": How Benedict XVI Is Attempting to Meet Its Challenge to Faith.' *Inside the Vatican* 14 (May 2006) 38–40.

Sherwin, Byron L. and Harold Kasimow, eds. *John Paul II and Interreligious Dialogue*. Maryknoll, NY: Orbis Books, 1999.

Shorter, Aylward. *Revelation and its Interpretation*. London: Geoffrey Chapman, 1983.

——. *Toward a Theology of Inculturation*. Maryknoll, NY: Orbis Books, 2010.

——. *Evangelization and Culture*. London: Geoffrey Chapman, 1994.

Smith, Barbara Herrnstein. 'Relativism, Today and Yesterday.' *Common Knowledge* 13 (Spring–Fall 2007) 227–49.

Song, C. S. *Jesus and the Reign of God*. Minneapolis: Fortress Press, 1993.

Stanley, Timothy. 'Speaking Credibly? Communicating Christian Particularism in Postmodern Context. *International Review of Mission*. Geneva: January–April 2008. Vol. 97, Iss. 384/385, 21–30.

Stetson, Brad and Joseph G. Conti. *The Truth about Tolerance*. Downers Grove, IL: InterVarsity Press, 2005.

Stout, Jeffrey. 'A House Founded on the Sea: Is Democracy a Dictatorship of Relativism?' *Common Knowledge* 13 (2007) 385–403.

Strauss, Leo. *Natural Right and History*. Chicago: University of Chicago Press, 1953.

——. *Liberalism Ancient and Modern*. Chicago: University of Chicago Press, 1995.

Sullivan, Francis. *Salvation outside the Church? Tracing the History of the Catholic Response.* New York: Paulist Press, 1992.

——. *Creative Fidelity: Weighing and Interpreting Documents of the Magisterium.* Eugene, OR: Wipf and Stock Publishers, 2003.

Swidler, Leonard, ed. *Towards a Universal Theology of Religion.* Maryknoll, NY: Orbis Books, 1988.

Swidler, Leonard. *Epilogue* in Leonard Swidler and Paul Mojzes, eds. *The Uniqueness of Jesus.* Maryknoll, NY: Orbis Books, 1997.

Swidler, Leonard and Paul Mojzes, eds. *The Uniqueness of Jesus.* Maryknoll, NY: Orbis Books, 1997.

Sugden, Chris. 'Called to Full Humanity – a perspective from Western Europe.' *Transformation,* 15 (1 January 1998) 28–30.

Tanner, Kathryn. *Theories of Cultures.* Minneapolis: Fortress Press, 1997.

Taylor, Charles. *A Secular Age.* Cambridge, MA: Belknap Press of Harvard University Press, 2007.

Tillich, Paul. *Systematic Theology,* Volume III. Chicago: University of Chicago Press, 1963.

——. *The Future of Religions.* Ed. Jerald C. Brauer. New York: Harper & Row, 1966.

Twomey, Vincent. 'When God Is Denied…' *Inside the Vatican* 17 (October 2009) 36–8.

Ustorf, Werner. 'A Missiological Postscript', in *The Decline of Christendom in Western Europe, 1750–2000,* ed. Hugh McLeod and Werner Ustorf. Cambridge: Cambridge University Press, 2003.

Van der Bent, Ans Joachim. 'Christian and Marxist Responses to the Challenge of Secularization and Secularism.' *Journal of Ecumenical Studies* 15 (1 December 1978) 152–66.

——. *Commitment to God's World: A Concise Critical Survey of Ecumenical Social Thought.* Geneva: WCC Publications 1995.

Vanhoozer, Kevin J., ed. *The Trinity in a Pluralistic Age.* Grand Rapids: William B. Eerdmans, 1997.

Vattimo, Gianni. *The Transparent Society.* Trans. David Webb. Cambridge: Polity Press, 1992.

——. *Belief.* Trans. Luca D'Isanto and David Webb. Stanford, California: Stanford University Press, 1999.

——. *After Christianity.* Trans. Luca D'Isanto. New York: Columbia, 2002.

——. 'A "Dictatorship of Relativism"? Symposium in Response to Cardinal Ratzinger's Last Homily.' *Common Knowledge* 13 (2007) 214–18.

Wessels, Anton. *Europe: Was it Ever Really Christian?* London: SCM Press, 1994.

Wilfred, Felix. 'The Federation of Asian Bishops' Conferences (FABC): orientations, challenges and impact.' *Pro Mundi Vita Studies* no. 7 (1 January 1989) 11–17.

Wilfred, Felix, ed. *Leave the Temple.* Maryknoll, NY: Orbis Books, 1992.

Windows into Ecumenism: Essays in Honour of Ahn Jae Woong. Hong Kong: Christian Conference of Asia, 2005.

Wood, William D. 'Back to Christendom: One Cardinal's Response to Secularism.' *Commonweal* 132 (12 June 2005) 8–9.

Yong, Amos. *Discerning the Spirit(s): A Pentecost–Charismatic Contribution to Christian Theology of Religions.* Sheffield: Sheffield Academic Press, 2000.

CHURCH DOCUMENTS

Dogmatic Constitution on the Church. *Lumen Gentium.* www.vatican.va/archive/hist_councils/ ii_vatican_council/documents/vat-ii_const_19641121_lumen-gentium_en.html.

Paul VI. *'Nostra Aetate*: Declaration on the Relations of the Church to Non-Christian Religion.' (28 October 1965), 2. www.vatican.va/archive/hist_councils/ii_vatican_council/ documents/vat-ii_decl_19651028_nostra-aetate_en.html.

John Paul II. *Redemptoris Missio.* www.vatican.va/holy_father/john_paul_ii/encyclicals/ documents/hf_jp-ii_enc_07121990_redemptoris-missio_en.html.

——. *Fides et Ratio.* www.vatican.va/holy_father/john_paul_ii/encyclicals/documents/hf_ jp-ii_enc_15101998_fides-et-ratio_en.html.

——. *Ecclesia in Asia.* www.vatican.va/holy_father/john_paul_ii/apost_exhortations/ documents/hf_jp-ii_exh_06111999_ecclesia-in-asia_en.html.

Congregation for the Doctrine of the Faith. *Notification to Father Leonardo Boff* (11 March 1985). www.ewtn.com/library/curia/cdfboff.htm.

——. *Notification* on the book *Toward a Christian Theology of Religious Pluralism* (Orbis Books: Maryknoll, New York 1997) by Father Jacques Dupuis, SJ. www.vatican.va/roman_curia/ congregations/cfaith/documents/rc_con_cfaith_doc_20010124_dupuis_en.html.

——. *Notification* concerning the Text *Mary and Human Liberation by Father Tissa Balasuriya, OMI* (7 January 1997). www.vatican.va/roman_curia/congregations/cfaith/documents/ rc_con_cfaith_doc_19970102_tissa-balasuriya_en.html.

Pope Benedict XVI. 'Meeting with the Representatives of Science (Regensburg Lecture).' www.vatican.va/holy_father/benedict_xvi/speeches/2006/september/documents/ hf_ben-xvi_spe_20060912_university-regensburg_en.html.

——. Declaration *Dominus Iesus* on the Unicity and Salvific Universality of Jesus Christ and the Church. www.vatican.va/roman_curia/congregations/cfaith/documents/rc_ con_cfaith_doc_20000806_dominus-iesus_en.html.

Dialogue and Proclamation. www.vatican.va/roman_curia/pontifical_councils/interelg/docu- ments/rc_pc_interelg_doc_19051991_ dialogue-and-proclamatio_en.html.

Decree on the Catholic Churches of the Eastern Rite – Orientalium Ecclesiarium. www.vati- can.va/archive/hist_councils/ii_vatican_council/documents/vat-ii_decree_19641121_ orientalium-ecclesiarum_en.html.

Decree on Ecumenism, *Unitatis Reintegratio.* www.vatican.va/archive/hist_councils/ii_vati- can_council/documents/vat-ii_decree_19641121_unitatis- redintegratio _en.html.

Joint Declaration on the Doctrine of Justification. www.vatican.va/roman_curia/pontifical_coun- cils/chrstuni/documents/rc_pc_chrstuni_doc_31101999_cath-luth-joint-declaration_ en.html.

'USCCB Doctrine Committee Faults Book by Father Peter Phan.' www.usccb.org/comm/ archives/2007/07-200.shtml.

'USCCB Doctrinal Committee Educates Peter C. Phan on the Gospel.' www.ratzingerfanclub. com/blog/2007/12/usccb-doctrinal-commitee-educates-peter.html.

Apostolic Exhortation, *Evangelii Gaudium* of The Holy Father Francis to the Bishops, Clergy, Consecrated persons and the lay faithful on the Proclamation of the Gospel in Today's Word. http://w2.vatican.va/content/francesco/en/apost_exhortations/documents/papa- francesco_esortazione-ap_20131124_evangelii-gaudium.html.

NEWSPAPERS AND MAGAZINES

AsianNews.it. www.asianews.it/news-en/Fr-Tissa-Balasuriya,-controversial-Sri-Lankan-theologian,-laid-to-rest-26925.html.

Bohlen, Celestine. 'Sri Lankan Priest Excommunicated for "Relativism".' *New York Times* (7 January 1997). www.erowid.org/spirit/traditions/ christianity/ catholicism/catholicism_media1.shtml.

'The Balasuriya File. *The Tablet* (25 January 1997). http://archive.thetablet.co.uk/article/25th-january-1997/13/the-balasuriya-file.

'The Heart of the Matter.' *The Tablet* (1 February 1997). http://archive.thetablet.co.uk/article/1st-february-1997/3/the-heart-of-the-matter.

'Curran welcomes Balasuriya to theological outcast status.' *National Catholic Reporter.* http://natcath.org/NCR_Online/archives2/1997a/020797/020797d.htm.

'The Burden on Balasuriya.' *The Tablet* (11 October 1997). http://archive.thetablet.co.uk/article/11th-october-1997/3/the-burden-on-balasuriya.

'Holy See lifts the excommunication of Tissa Balasuriya.' *The Tablet* (24 January 1998). http://archive.thetablet.co.uk/article/24th-january-1998/20/holy-see-lifts-the-excommunication-of-tissa-balasu.

Dupré, Louis. 'The ties that bind us.' *The Tablet* (24 April 2004). www.thetablet.co.uk/article/2521.

'"Aggressive secularism" threat to freedom, says Ratzinger.' *The Tablet* (27 November 2004). https://thetablet.co.uk/article/1866.

'Father Jacques Dupuis: Jesuit theologian whose experience of India underpinned his challenging views on interfaith dialogue.' *The Times* (12 January 2005). www.timesonline.co.uk/tol/comment/obituaries/article411125.ece.

'In Spain, Pope Benedict XVI lambasts "aggressive secularism".' *Christian Science Monitor.* www.csmonitor.com/World/Europe/2010/1107/In-Spain-Pope-Benedict-XVI-lambasts-aggressive-secularism.

'Healthy secularism for a peaceful coexistence.' *L' Osservatore Romano* (19 November 2008) 6.

'Pope Benedict XVI warns against "aggressive secularism" in Britain.' *Daily Telegraph* (16 September 2010). www.telegraph.co.uk/news/newstopics/religion/the-pope/8006272/Pope-Benedict-XVI-warns-against-aggressive-secularism-in-Britain.html.

Cala, Andres. 'In Spain, Pope Benedict lambasts "aggressive secularism".' *Christian Science Monitor* (7 November 2010). www.csmonitor.com/World/Europe/2010/1107/In-Spain-Pope-Benedict-XVI-lambasts-aggressive-secularism.

'Church in the World.' *The Tablet* (22 September 2012). https://thetablet.co.uk/article/1866.

'Slaying the secular dragon.' *The Tablet* (18 February 2012) 4.

'Cardinal Carlo Martini remembered.' *The Tablet* (8 September 2012) 6–9.

John Wilkins, 'Music – but jarring notes too.' *The Tablet* (23 February 2013) 8–9.

'Pope Benedict XVI warns against "aggressive secularism" in Britain.' *Daily Telegraph.* www.telegraph.co.uk/news/newstopics/religion/the-pope/8006272/Pope-Benedict-XVI-warns-against-aggressive-secularism-in-Britain.html.

'Pope Benedict XVI: Marxist ideology no longer corresponds to reality.' *Daily Telegraph.* www.telegraph.co.uk/news/religion/the-pope/9164373/Pope-Benedict-XVI-Marxist-ideology-no-longer-corresponds-to-reality.html.

Murphy, David. 'The Ordinariates and Ecumenism.' http://ordinariateexpats.wordpress.com/2012/03/14/the-ordinariates-and-ecumenism/.

Religious Tolerance.org. Ontario Consultants on Religious Tolerance. 'The diversity of meanings of the term "religious pluralism".' www.religioustolerance org/rel_plur1.htm

'Pope Benedict XVI to resign citing poor health.' *BBC News.* www.bbc.co.uk/news/world-21411304.

'Viewpoints: Successes and failures of Benedict XVI.' *BBC News.* www.bbc.co.uk/news/world-europe-21429808.

'Pope resignation: Full text.' *BBC News.* www.bbc.co.uk/news/world-europe-21412609.

'Analysis: What is the role of a modern pope?' *BBC News.* www.bbc.co.uk/religion/0/21424966.

Index

References to notes are indicated by n.

abortion   94
Abraham   6, 28, 29 188, 199, 201
Abraham, K. C.   172
absolutism   130
Acts of the Apostles   48, 49, 59, 171
Adam and Eve   170, 171
Adorno, Theodor W.   142
Africa   17, 34, 40, 77, 234
Alexandria   82
American Revolution   94
Anglicanism   73–8
Antioch   82
apostles, the   31, 38, 48, 49
Apostolic Constitution   78
Aristotle   60, 121
Arius   24
Asia   xvii–xviii, 21, 43, 223
   and Catholicism   17
   and Christianity   2, 23, 41–2
   and the church   65, 66
   and Dupuis   210
   and ecumenism   86–7, 90–1
   and interreligious dialogue   174–6,
      226–7
   and Jesus Christ   259–60
   and John Paul II   213–14
   and Mary   177
   and poverty   225–6, 256–7, 259, 260,
      261
   and relativism   133–5

   and religious pluralism   xi, xv, 228–9,
      231
   and theology   xii, xii–xiv, xvi, 34, 40,
      172–4, 234, 251, 271
   and women   166, 169
   see also Balasuriya, Tissa; Buddhism;
      China; Federation of Asian Bishops'
      Conferences; Hinduism; India
Athanasius, St   24, 325 n. 1
atheism   102, 115, 143–4
Augustine, St   7, 9, 11–15, 37, 137, 153
   and original sin   170–1
   and reforms   45
   and truth   248

Balasuriya, Tissa   xii, 116, 163–70, 171–2,
      176–81
   and Asia   172–4
   and CDF   182, 183, 184–6
   and interreligious dialogue   174–6
   and relativism   133–4
Balthasar, Hans Urs von   10
baptism   51, 170, 171, 226
Baptism, Eucharist and Ministry
      (BEM)   76–7
Bavaria   2–3
Bea, Cardinal   88
Being Religious Interreligiously (Phan)   xii,
      210, 212, 231
Benedict, St   17–18